THE LIGHT OF DARKNESS
By Nicole Moore

ALSO, BY NICOLE MOORE

SHATTERED SECRETS

A sweeping tale of love, betrayal, and redemption. It will pull you into the 18th century world of New York, Boston and the infamous pirate heaven, Nassau. Filled with danger and desires, this love story is about two souls haunted by the past who must decide if the truth is worth the risk—and if love is worth the cost.

For more information visit:
www.nicolemooreauthor.com

The Light of Darkness (Book 1 of The Darkborn Prophecies)

Copyright © 2025 Moore Publishing

This is a work of historical fantasy fiction. While it references real historical locations such as York and London, and real events like the Black Plague, the characters, plot, and supernatural elements are entirely fictional. Any resemblance to actual people, living or dead, is purely coincidental and unintentional.

Cover Design by Nicole Moore.
Edited with the support of independent editors.
For permissions, contact:
moorepublishingco@gmail.com

www.nicolemooreauthor.com

ISBN: 978-1-7638922-3-1

Content Warning: This book contains depictions of graphic violence and death, and some strong language. It also includes a chapter about a suicide attempt. Reader discretion is advised.

Table of Contents

TRIGGER WARNINGS

This book is set in a time of great spiritual upheaval, during a time of tremendous death, loss, and grief. As it is a historical dark fantasy, I have brought to life the superstitions, and mythical stories of the age. And it is ripe with graphic violence, death scenes and one attempted suicide scene. There's minimal sexually explicit scenes and some foul language. Please do not read if any of these topics will trigger or hurt your mental state of mind.

SPECIAL ACKNOWLEDGMENT

To my amazing husband. Thank you for finally hopping on the Nicole Moore Author train—even if you had no clue what station we were heading to. You've stood by me even when my writing made zero sense to your practical, logical mind (which, let's be honest, is most of the time)

You're the first man (besides my dad) who believed in me without trying to clip my wings. That's a beautiful kind of love, and I see it in everything you do. You might not understand the madness of my writing process, but you've never tried to stop it. For that— and so much more—I love you.

You are my pillar of strength and my anchor in the storm, the bringer of coffee and calm. You're the comfort that makes the chaos bearable, and the home my heart belongs to. Thank you.

PROLOGUE
December 1348, London

A deep, phlegmy cough wracked the young woman's chest, each hack scraping her raw throat.

White puffs of breath escaped her cracked lips as she stumbled through the squalid alleys of Southwark's Stews. Her boots slipped in the icy muck, the stench of rot, urine, and human despair thick in the air.

Rain clung to her fevered skin, a cold caress that only sharpened the fire raging inside her.

Clutching the tattered cloak tighter around her threadbare gown, the woman stumbled onward.

Sweat trickled down her face, stinging the raw sores mottling her neck and jaw. The plague. It was inside her, eating her alive.

The church lay ahead. Only the priest could offer salvation. Redemption.

A screech, like a dying animal, echoed through the night, cutting off her dazed thoughts like a knife.

Her breath hitched. "No," she whispered, a raw edge of terror tightening her throat.

1

She stumbled a step back, heart hammering, eyes darting across the shadows. Something was hunting her.

Then it came again—the beast's screech, closer this time, rattling the air, coming from the alley ahead.

She froze mid-step, legs trembling beneath her.

Her hood slipped off, exposing a tangled mess of black curls; they clung to her damp cheeks.

Her breaths came in sharp gasps.

She didn't dare blink, didn't dare breathe too loudly. Something was watching. Something close.

Panic rose like the bile in her throat, but the glow of the church lantern shone brightly at the end of the road. Sanctuary.

She pressed her body against the shadowed wall of a building as the rain that had been gently falling at first, turned into a deluge, drenching her as if God had determined her fate already.

She clutched her tattered cloak tighter, fabric rough and damp against her trembling fingertips.

The cold gnawed at her skin, but it was the fever that burned deepest—fire beneath flesh.

She staggered onward. The church was close now.

But she was too late.

The monster stepped out of the shadows, and she stumbled to a stop, dropping to her knees, and mumbling prayers, pleas to God... But they were ignored. Her sins too heavy.

The beast drew closer, dragging a long single claw along the ground, its elongated limbs covered in rotted loose skin of the dead. Perhaps the creature had been human once, but no longer. Its grotesque elongated limbs reached for her; its mouth opened to reveal rows of needle-sharp teeth.

The young woman couldn't move, paralyzed with fear. Silent tears streamed down her face as a wet, warm sensation spread between her legs.

The demon's arms coiled around the woman, lifting her off the ground in a grotesque imitation of a lover's embrace. She thrashed, shrieking, but it held fast.

The creature sank its fangs into her shoulder. Fire raced through her veins.

Her mind shattered under the pain, and yet she stayed conscious, forced to feel every jagged tear.

Her final scream echoed into the night, thin and broken, like glass shattering beneath the weight of despair.

The ghoul dropped her, lifted its head, and let out a soul-rending howl that pierced the night, echoing through the darkness like the wails of countless souls trapped in eternal damnation.

PART ONE

"When the breath of death curls through the streets and hides its face, the crows shall feast, and the soil shall sour. Light will falter, and the faithful shall fall—but one will carry the flame that will rise against the darkness."

The Oracle's Prophecy ~ Winter 1298

CHAPTER 1 ~ TRINITY
January 1349, Outside of London

Trinity's breath hitched as her eyes fluttered open, a shaky sob escaping her lips. Gloved fingers pressed against her eyes in a futile attempt to stifle the tears.

By the window, she sat waiting—for what, she wasn't sure. Death? Salvation? Her heart carried the weight of both.

Her fingers instinctively found the silver cross at her throat; its ruby center cool against her palm. "Lord Jesus," she whispered, the words trembling in her throat, "grant me strength. Let your will be done in me." She made the sign of the cross, then kissed the pendant and pressed it to her chest, trying to find solace in its power.

A soft knock startled her. She turned as Alfred, her uncle's steward, entered, pale and solemn. "Lady Anna is slipping away. If you wish to say goodbye, it should be now, m'lady."

Trinity swallowed hard, nodding. "Yes, Alfred. I'll be along shortly."

As the door shut behind him, she returned to the window, her reflection faint in the gathering darkness. Her golden blonde hair haphazardly breaded down her back, and dark circles under her eyes spoke of sleepless nights.

Grief squeezed her heart so tight it hurt. The weight of it settled deep in her bones.

After her aunt passed away, she'd be alone. Truly alone.

"God help me," she whispered and walked to the door. "God help us all."

At her aunt's bedchamber door, she paused.

With a deep breath, she pulled her shoulders back and pushed it open. The stench of sickness hit her—a thick, nauseating wave that made her falter. It clung to the walls, heavy and sour, the scent of sweat, fever, and death woven into the fabric of the room. The candlelight flickered against the stone wall, shadows stretching like grasping fingers.

The hearth blazed with their last scraps of wood. Heat and stench smothered the room; flames bathed the room in soft orange light.

Her aunt lay on the four-poster bed, already corpse-like. Golden hair, streaked with grey, hung limp on the pillows. Black spots marred her neck and face.

The pain had ravaged her aunt's frail body for days, leaving her delirious and coughing until, finally, she lay still. Her lips murmured faint, broken prayers, and the matching cross pendant to Trinity's rested in her limp hand.

6

"The devil's winning," her aunt said to her before sickness stole her voice. "The Lord cannot save all his flock. I've done everything I could to protect you."

Trinity's chest tightened as she stepped to the bedside, her aunt's words echoing in her mind. Her heart thundered in her ears, knowing this was her last goodbye. She reached out, trembling, and brushed her aunt's cold, wrinkled cheek. The prayers faded into silence. Her aunt's eyes closed, as she slipped into sleep.

Trinity knelt beside her, gently holding her soft, wrinkled hand. "What am I to do?" she whispered. "The estate is in ruin. The servants and field hands have abandoned us. Only Alfred stayed."

Her aunt's eyes fluttered open, sending a jolt through Trinity that made her flinch. "There's great evil among us," her aunt wheezed as she spoke. "I should have told you before. You have so much light in you, as your mother... You must fight this..."

"I don't understand," Trinity clutched her aunt's hand.

"A war... it's coming." She rasped, her grip tightening on Trinity's fingers. "Demons..." Her aunt's breath shuddered. Each word seemed torn from her, a final offering before the end. "I... I can't fight... You must..." Her aunt released a rattled cough and settled back onto her bed, gasping. "Find the others...."

"What others?" Trinity shook her head, her brows pinched. Her aunt was never one to ramble or speak of such things. "Aunty?"

But her aunt didn't answer and fell back into a deep sleep.

As the witching hour descended, silence unfurled like a shroud, heavy and absolute, pressing in on every corner of the bedchamber.

A single candle flickered near the bed, its flame stretching tall, trembling as if it too sensed what lingered in the air.

Trinity sat frozen beside the bed, her hand wrapped around her aunt's—the skin paper-thin, nearly translucent, as though time had begun to erase her. The bones beneath felt brittle, like they might splinter if she held too tightly, but letting go wasn't an option. Not now.

Her own fingers quivered despite the effort to still them.

Her Aunt's chest rose—once.

Again.

A shallow lift.

Then nothing.

A gasp so faint it barely stirred the air escaped her pale-dry lips—a ragged sigh, more exhale than breath, more release than struggle.

And that was all. The world stilled.

Trinity blinked. Waited.

But the chest remained unmoving. No flicker of breath returned. No flutter beneath the skin.

She leaned forward slightly, straining to hear—something, anything—but only the soft crackle of the fire remained. No whisper of life. No final words. Just stillness.

A sharp pressure built in Trinity's throat, thick and unrelenting, as if the air itself had turned to stone. Her lungs refused to expand as she clutched her hands to her chest.

Lady Anna was gone. Her second mother, gone.

She'd raised Trinity. Had whispered bedtime prayers and wiped away fevers with lavender oil and lullabies. Had called her beloved when no one else did.

That single truth slammed into her with such force she hunched forward, pressing her forehead against the back of the still hand, rocking once, twice.

"No," the word tore from her, raw and hoarse, catching halfway between denial and grief.

Her sob shattered the silence. It wasn't delicate or dignified—it ripped through her like something feral and wounded, sharp and full of everything she hadn't been able to say.

Now—nothing.

Another sob escaped her, broken and low. Trinity curled forward until her arms folded over the cooling chest of her aunt, clutching what warmth remained.

The scent of dried rose petals lingered faintly beneath the sterility of death; a whisper of gentler days now gone.

She didn't move as a river of tears soaked the blanket.

***

The next morning, they buried Trinity's aunt next to her husband under a giant oak tree. The rain continued through the night with no sign of relenting. Trinity and Alfred stood in the freezing rain. Her hair and clothing soaked through. Numb in more ways than just her fingers.

Rain fell on the fresh dirt, pooling in small puddles and streaking down the white wooden crosses he had built to mark the graves.

"Alfred, can you say the proper blessing, please?"

Alfred began reciting the last rites, his breath escaped in white plumes. She closed her eyes, lifting her face to the heavens, letting the rain wash away her tears.

Alfred's voice faded away as a memory of her childhood came rushing in like a river.

She stood in a small one-room cottage. Her mother on her knees in their meager dining / kitchen, sobbing, peering up at Sir Henry Ellsworth, looming in their doorway, an imposing older man, his gaze filled with pity. Her mother pleaded for more time, but he only shook his head regretfully and walked away.

Alfred touched her shoulder, the sound of her mother's voice dying away, as the splattering of rain on the ground brought Trinity back to the present.

"Would you say any words, m'lady?"

Trinity's eyes flicked open, but she didn't know what to say. Her thoughts were chaotic and voicing them now felt foolish. She loved her aunt and uncle as much as she loved her parents. After both her parents died, her aunt and uncle raised her as their own, having no children between them.

As she searched for words to express her heartache, sobs escaped instead.

The kind of sobs that came from a place deeper than grief—a sound born from a fracture in the soul, not just the heart. Her lips parted, but no words followed, only gasps, uneven and small.

She clutched her cross pendant with both hands. Her aunt had gifted it to her as a small child, making her promise never to take it off, which Trinity obeyed, happily.

The cross usually gave her comfort but not this day. Not when the one who gave it was now buried beneath her feet.

Her knuckles whitened as her fingers dug into the chain, the edges of the pendant biting into her palms.

The weight of it felt heavier now, like it carried every lost goodbye she hadn't managed to say.

Her body shook with silent sobs.

She curled slightly in on herself, as if folding her frame might somehow keep her from falling apart completely.

Rain fell over her face as she stared at the fresh mound of earth. Droplets streaked through her lashes, mingling with tears until she couldn't tell where grief ended, and sky began. Mud clung to her boots. Her hem was soaked and clung to her legs, the cold seeping up into her bones.

Her chest tightened, each breath a struggle as she whispered fragmented prayers.

"Hear me, Lord…" her voice cracked mid-sentence. "Please… please don't let her be gone. Not really. Not forever."

No answer came. Only the soft rhythm of rain tapping against the trees, and the hollow ache that pulsed where her aunt's presence had once lived.

A gust of wind stirred the leaves above her, and for a breathless moment, she imagined it was her aunt's voice, a gentle hush meant to calm her. But it passed too quickly, and Trinity remained alone in the downpour, still hoping for a miracle she knew wouldn't come.

Alfred softly touched her elbow. "Come with me inside. Your aunt and uncle gave me some things for you."

Alfred led Trinity to her aunt and uncle's bedchamber, a candle lantern lighting their way. He stopped at a large table cluttered with documents, a quill, and her uncle's signature stamp. She gently ran her fingers over the treasured items.

11

Alfred placed the lantern on the desk, took a rolled piece of parchment sealed with red wax and her uncle's family stamp, and handed it to her.

"What is it?" Trinity took it reluctantly.

"These are the deeds to everything Sir Geoffrey owned. He's named you as his sole heiress. Without a husband, however, the king will take control of the estate, and you'll become a lady-in-waiting at court until you wed."

Trinity stood speechless momentarily, then began to laugh and cry simultaneously. Tears fell as she laughed.

Alfred ignored her outburst. "I will dispatch a message to the king. You're still a young lady and must go to court until you find a husband, and it's safe to return."

"Safe to return." Trinity echoed the words, a laugh escaping her—cracked, bitter, edged with disbelief. "A husband?"

It dissolved as quickly as it came. Sobs surged in its place, and she covered her face, unable to stop the shaking. Slowly, she wiped her tears, her breath catching in her throat.

Alfred spoke again, but his words blurred. She inherited everything. The King would choose her husband; her life now led to this—a lamb at the market.

"No. York is where I will go." The idea came to her in a split second—her childhood home, where she'd been born. "I'll go there and escape this plague. You should come with me." Trinity grabbed Alfred's arm, her eyes pleading.

"I'm already dying, m'lady. It's too late for me." He pulled the collar of his tunic, exposing several small black spots.

Trinity gasped, covered her mouth and stepped back.

"But it isn't too late for you. Please. I beg you... Go to Windsor Castle. You're not safe alone."

"I can't go to court... I'm sorry, Alfred. I just can't."

Alfred shook his head; his thin lips set in a disapproving scowl he gave her. "As you wish, m'lady, but there's one other thing." He walked to the corner of the room, unlocked a large trunk with an old brass key, and opened it.

Trinity followed him, looked inside the trunk, and sucked in a sharp breath.

A woman's short sword with a hilt wrapped in black leather and a gleaming blade. At the center of the guard, a ruby—identical to the one in Trinity's cross—shimmered with an otherworldly glow framed by silver that radiated holiness. The cross-shaped guard and intricate engravings along with an infusion of what looked like black obsidian along the blade hinted at divine craftsmanship. It lay atop a small shining silver shield engraved with wings along the edge.

It was breathtaking.

"What am I to do with it?"

Alfred lifted it and handed it to her. "It was your aunts. Her legacy, but now yours. It's the sword and shield of one of a Seraphim. The sword is called Guardian's Light, and the shield is the Mirror of Truth."

"What are you speaking of?" Trinity shook her head. Each word raced through her mind, colliding in chaos. "I don't understand, Alfred. What legacy? The Seraphim are angels. Our Lord's Guardians. They do not dwell among humans." Trinity said with as much confidence as she could muster. She'd read the stories.

13

Knew this was impossible, but her assuredness flailed quickly as the shield shimmered in the light.

He reverently held it out to her.

"No." She stepped backwards, refusing to take it despite fighting the urge to touch it.

"She wished for you to have it when she died. It will keep you safe."

"Alfred, what does that mean? Why was my aunt talking about demons? Why would she have this sword?" She backed away further. "You're frightening me."

"Your aunt knew evil walked among us." He began talking faster, moving towards her as she continued to back further away. "The shield, it shows the truth. A Seraph gifted her with the sight, with the sword and shield."

She knew her aunt was extraordinarily devout, but to be blessed with sight as a saint by a Seraph wasn't an idea Trinity could accept. It was not possible. Her aunt wasn't a saint. Only the church could ordain one worthy of sainthood. What he was saying was blasphemy and sinful. Evil.

"That's impossible. How did she get this sword, Alfred? It shouldn't be here!"

Alfred laid the sword on the table next to the papers on the desk. Everything was hers now, including a potentially stolen sword and shield she would hang for if caught with it.

"It's your legacy now."

"You're mad!" Trinity walked to the door, her body trembling as she shook her head.

Alfred voice raised and it echoed around the room, "Your aunt was God's warrior, and now there's no one left."

"I don't want it!" Trinity screeched, reaching for the door to leave. To escape.

Tears stung her eyes. "Why are you doing this to me?"

Alfred flinched at her words. "Wait, please, child."

He turned from her and lifted the lid of the chest. A faint creak echoed through the room. Dust spiraled into the firelight as he reached inside with a reverence that made Trinity's heart twist.

From within, he drew out the circular shield—its surface gleamed faintly in the flickering firelight. The metal caught the flames, casting sharp, golden flashes across the walls. For a moment, the warm firelight danced across its face—then it changed.

A pulse of white shimmered along the engraved wings and runes at its edge. The flicker grew, shimmered, and then exploded into brilliance.

Trinity stumbled back, shielding her face as the light surged forward—no longer from the fire but from the object itself. A humming filled her ears, low and bone deep.

A blinding light filled the room and prickled her skin, every hair rising along her arms as if the air itself had turned electric.

The light faded, and the air thrummed with otherworldly energy. Then, a being of stunning beauty appeared before her—an angel. The light shimmered around her, casting rainbow shards all around them.

Alfred fell to his knees, prostrate, praying quietly. Trinity knew she should drop her gaze, but she could not.

"Who are you?" The words had fallen from Trinity's lips before she could stop them.

The seraph's eyes burned with a fierce yet tender flame holding her stare, and then in a human manner, she smirked. Her radiance pulsed; waves of golden light rippled through the chamber. The very air shimmered, thick with divine power, as if the space between worlds thinned. Her six wings unfurled around her, immense, white as the purest snow, with golden light dancing along the edges. The scent of a fresh rainstorm and heavenly purity filled the room.

Trinity's breath caught in her chest as she finally dropped to her knees, lowering her eyes. The sight of such beauty and terror, a manifestation of pure holiness, pierced her soul. Unbidden, tears slid over her cheeks.

"I am the Seraph, Seriella. I protect the highest levels of heaven, but I have been tasked with finding the chosen one, worthy of my sword and shield. Your aunt was that one."

Trinity trembled, her heart pounding through her veins. But then, love, so wholly profound, wrapped around her soul like a soft winter blanket, slowing her heart, and easing her tremors.

"Rise, child." That voice rippled gently through her entire body, and without conscious thought, Trinity rose to her feet but dropped her eyes to the floor. She clutched her cross in her hand so tight it dug into her palm.

"I know you're afraid." Seriella gestured towards Alfred. "Let my sword protect you, and my shield show you the truth. I choose you, child."

Like a marionette, Alfred offered Trinity the shield. His eyes filled with tears, his arms holding out the shield.

Her hand trembled as it closed around the shield. The moment her fingers met the cold metal; a tremor rippled through her body.

The room around her dimmed. Heat flashed in her chest, and her breath hitched.

Then the world vanished. It shifted.

She felt weightless, spinning through the darkness as the hiss of demons and the crackle of flames of the hearth filled her ears. Then, just as suddenly, her feet were on solid ground, and she was walking through a dark, fog-covered forest, the quarter moon hung high among bright stars blinking in the black sky.

Stepping into a clearing, she saw her younger and stronger aunt holding the shield in front of her and wielding the sword as shadows closed around her. A blue flame rippled along the blade. The angel, Seriella, stood behind her aunt, wings spread open. "You are my chosen," the angel said. "This sword will shine with my light and vanquish evil." Trinity's breath caught as she watched her aunt cut through a swarm of demons, her faith unwavering. Hordes of demons surrounding her, then Trinity.

A faint, sulphureous stench filled the air. The world seemed to expand and contract, the forest groaning as if alive. A deep voice rumbled through her mind—low, resonant, and mocking.

"You are wholly unworthy, child." The words reverberated in her skull like thunder. "Do you think a frail mortal can stand against the might of my demons?"

The ghouls before her aunt parted as a figure emerged from the shadows. A figure emerged from the shadows; demons parted. A man—if he could be called that.

Charred skin stretched over a monstrous frame, and glowing red eyes locked with hers.

Trinity's breath fled. A cold sweat broke across her skin.

This was not a nightmare. It was real.

His skin was the color of charred ash, and his eyes, glowing red, pierced her soul. His armor shimmered as though it was forged from obsidian and flame. Two curved horns jutted from his brow. A massive black shadowed sword gripped in his clawed hand hung at his side.

"Do you see now?" The demon taunted, towering over Trinity's aunt. "Your world crumbles beneath my grasp. You cannot stop what is coming."

"Be gone with you!" Trinity's aunt screamed, lifting the flaming sword higher.

The demon laughed, then stepped back into the shadows as his horrifying, grotesque army of undead shrieked and rushed towards her aunt and Trinity.

The hiss of demons surrounded her, and her hands flew to her ears, desperate to block out the sound. Then, a blinding light exploded behind her eyes, and she screamed, the sound torn from her throat as the world dissolved into chaos.

She stumbled backward, the scream still caught in her throat, flashes of bright light pulsing behind her eyelids.

Her knees hit the floor, and her vision blurred with tears. The room spun as she clutched her chest, expecting the demon's claws to pierce her—but her hand met the cold weight of her cross. The sound of the crackling firewood returned, grounding her.

"Look upon me, child."

Seriella lifted Trinity's chin with a slender finger. Trinity let out a croaked sob, the seraph's beauty so great it was painful to look upon. Golden blonde hair moved around the Seraph as if underwater, and her eyes, the color of molten gold, shone with a purity that made Trinity weep even more.

"Who was that?" Trinity's voice shook, body trembling.

"Baal. The prince of petulance."

"Baal?" Trinity whispered the name, recognizing the origin of the demon's story. A shiver ran down her spine. Stories about the demon prince her grandmother called the prince of flies, one of the most powerful demon princes raced to the forefront of her mind.

He was real. "How? I don't understand." Trinity shook her head again. "This evil… It's here?"

"Yes. Humans must fight Baal. He's trying to turn them away from our lord's light and love. Taking their souls for himself. You will all be doomed if the balance isn't restored."

"But I'm not worthy," Trinity cried out. "I'm no saint… I've sinned."

That smirk again. So human and dazzling.

"Do you believe I would choose one unworthy?"

"No. I don't know…. I…" she stammered. "But what am I to do?"

Looking down, Trinity noticed she held the shield and sword; awe filled her. Both were lighter than she imagined, with a warmth that radiated into her arms and through her entire body.

"Find the Coven of Druid ancestors in York. They will help you."

"Druids?" Trinity asked, so shocked she almost laughed. "Pagan worshipers? Why would you want me to work with pagans? They're evil and…"

"Some things are not as they seem."

Seriella reached down and placed Trinity's hand on the front of the shield, and a sharp pain ripped through her skull, causing Trinity to cry out and clutch the side of her head with her free hand.

"Watch… Listen…" The Seraph demanded, her voice vibrating into Trinity's bones as her vision turned black and her body swayed but didn't fall.

The pain subsided as she fell back into the in-between. Spinning through the darkness again until she finally stilled after what felt like forever.

Her eyes opened, and she took in her surroundings. In front of her stood a tall, man with long straight black hair hanging over his slim shoulders to his waist wearing a beige cloak with a hood pulled over his head, leaving his face in shadows. He held a long wooden staff and stood before Trinity's young aunt in the middle of a circle of megalithic stones, taller than them both. The sky swirled with grey clouds above them. The sword and shield clutched tight in her aunt's hands; the blue flame dowsed.

The man's voice boomed across the expanse between them, rattling Trinity's limbs, and making her teeth clench. "You must not go any further." He man opened his arms wide, refusing her aunt entry.

The warrior woman stepped closer, swinging the sword, pointing the tip to the druids' chest. "Who are you to stop me?"

"I am the keeper of the veil. The last tasked with guarding the veil between the mortal world and the demonic. Long before you Christians travelled to this land."

"Then why do you stand in my way, pagan?" her aunt snapped. "I come to kill the ones upending the balance - a realm you claim to protect but are not!" She stepped closer. "Perhaps you are the one encouraging the evil sweeping across the lands? Druids are the agents of the devil!" Her aunt stepped closer, digging the tip of the sword into the chest of the druid, but the man didn't flinch.

"No! We are the guardians of life. We fight the plague of demons that accursed this world." A white light emanated from

around the man, blooming all around them. The same holy power, Trinity witnessed with Seriella.

Her aunt gasped as radiant wings unfurled from the druid's back—vast and luminous, each feather edged in silver light. They rose in slow, reverent arcs, parting the air with a hush that stilled even the wind. It was divinity, cloaked in grace and woven with the breath of heaven.

"How?" Trinity's aunt whispered, her eyes wide and filling with tears.

"Not everything is what it seems child," The druid cast back his hood, and the world seemed to hold its breath. His face emerged like a statue kissed by starlight—etched in divine symmetry, as if God had sculpted him from myth and memory. Her breath caught; no mortal man had ever struck her so deeply.

He moved the sword's point away. Her aunt didn't move. "We must work together."

Agony lanced through Trinity's head, and she squeezed her eyes closed, holding her hands to the sides of her head. The sound of her aunt's voice drifted away.

The rush of gravity slammed down on her as the sword and shield crashed beside her, and her palms slammed against the cold floor. Trinity gulped air down as if she were drowning, the pain in her head easing, but her body thrashed uncontrollably like a living storm inside her bones. She clenched her jaw and ground out a moan until the tremors gradually subsided.

"Do you understand now?" Seriella asked.

Trinity panted and then bit her bottom lip as she righted herself, stumbling to her feet, determined to fight through the pain, but was unable to speak.

Seriella smiled lovingly. "When you learn to wield Guardian's Light, you will be powerful enough to stop an army of demons."

"My aunt? Was she truly…"

"Yes, my dear child, she was my chosen, as you now are. Evil is pushing through the veil again. There's an imbalance in the natural world, and humans are losing their way. A great reckoning will occur if the balance isn't corrected."

"Why did the vision hurt so much the second time?" Trinity asked, cringing, a remnant of the pain thrashing through her skull.

"Visions are gifts from our Lord, but after the first, you must pay a penance. Everyone's' is different."

"What did my aunt pay?" Trinity searched her memories of her aunty in pain but found nothing.

"She could bear no fruit." Seriella cocked her head to the side, a sad smile on her face, her golden eyes filled with such sorrow. "She loved you fiercely as her own instead."

Trinity didn't know what else to say and closed her eyes as they filled with tears. Knowing what her aunt sacrificed to be a warrior for God. To help keep them all safe. Then understanding dawned in her grief, and she stilled. It was now her responsibility.

"Trinity, open your eyes."

Trinity's eyes opened, a line of tears streaking over her cheeks. The seraph's wings softly closed as she knelt before Trinity, a knowing look in her eyes.

"From now on, keep your eyes open and look for the truth."

Trinity swallowed hard and fought back the wave of terror sweeping through her.

The Seraph stepped back, her wings unfurling, her majestic presence encompassing the entire room once more.

"I will always be with you, child." She smiled, then disappeared in a flash of blinding white light.

A log crackling and falling in the hearth snapped Trinity to attention, but the room still buzzed with angelic energy.

She picked up the shield and sword, walked to the table, and gingerly laid them down.

"I'm sorry, I didn't believe you." She whispered, looking at Alfred, standing next to the table, the firelight making his face look even more gaunt.

"I understand," he said softly.

Trinity ran her fingers over the smooth surface—it pulsed with faint warmth beneath her skin.

A deep breath filled her lungs. She closed her eyes, trying to steady the turmoil brewing inside.

The weight of the moment churned in her stomach, threatening to crush her entirely.

It's just a sword. But Druids. Demons…

"What do you wish me to do, m'lady?"

Trinity's head snapped up to Alfred.

She hesitated, unsure. "Will you help me get to York?"

"Yes, m'lady."

"How?"

Alfred walked to the door. "You'll need to see Arthur Whiting in London to get the travel documents and a chaperone and guards. You'll need a retinue and documents."

"The clerk for the Chancery? My uncle's man?"

"That would indeed be he, m'lady."

"Thank you, Alfred."

"It's been an honor, m'lady." Alfred opened the door and left.

After Alfred left, Trinity stared at the sword and shield glinting in the firelight. Outside, lightning illuminated the room, and the sword's engravings shimmered like flames. A chill ran down her spine as she traced her fingers over the hilt. She couldn't shake the feeling that someone was watching her. Trinity picked up the shield, its surface strangely warm under her fingers. The mirror-like surface shimmered; a shadow moved across it momentarily—a fair face, white hair gleaming.

She froze, her heart pounding. Blinked. Upon looking again, she found nothing but her pale, wide-eyed reflection. Trinity dropped the shield, clutching the cross pendant at her throat.

She closed her eyes and whispered a prayer under her breath. "Lord, protect me and give me strength in this darkness."

The sword on the table seemed to hum softly as if answering her plea. Thunder rumbled outside, rattling the wooden shutters. Trinity squared her shoulders and turned towards the window.

She didn't know what was waiting for her in York or beyond it. Her fate had been rewritten in a single night, her life no longer her own. The weight of the sword, the shield, the Seraph's words—each one a link in the chain now binding her to this path. But she would carry her aunt's legacy with her, no matter where the path led.

A gust of wind rattled the windows. Trinity gripped the sword tighter. Whatever was coming, she would face it.

But deep in her soul, she knew the storm had already begun.

CHAPTER 2 ~ SYBIL
The Grove & York

The icy mist that accompanied the goddess Cailleach pricked Sybil's skin. A shiver rattled through her as she huffed out a frustrated breath. White smoke floated in front of her face.

The goddess' pale-white curls tumbled past her shoulders and down her back. Her face resembled a crone, her voice a mother's, her body a maiden, and her presence that of an unforgiving, ice-tipped mountain. Dangerous and cruel, yet glorious.

Once, Sybil loved that she mirrored Cailleach in looks. Now, it only reminded her of what everyone, even the gods, expected her to become: the next oracle.

The goddess of life, storms, and seasons loomed over her. Her ethereal form shimmered as it solidified, and raw power pulsed through the air, pressing into Sybil's soul. Silver eyes locked onto hers, demanding submission.

Sybil exhaled sharply but stood her ground.

"No." Sybil's own silver eyes glared back at the goddess. Puffs of white escaped her lips, and her voice shook, not with fear, as it should have, but from the icy cold air wrapped around her.

She hated the damn cold.

She forcefully blew out her breath. "I can't do this anymore." She clenched her jaw as Cailleach strode closer. Sybil glanced behind her, nervously. "The others are waiting." Her cousins, the twins Enzo and Luca, waited nearby with her fiancé, David. They would be worried about leaving her alone for so long, but Cailleach allowed no one else at the sacred grove during Chailleach's time with Sybil.

She'd spent years resisting Cailleach's calling, but the burden remained, and in the end, she always relented.

The circle of stones surrounding Cailleach was worn down from time, wind, and weather and was barely noticeable.

Chailleach stepped from the circle, and a light flashed then dulled a moment later. "They can wait, and you will not refuse me," she said, her voice as sharp as her thin white lips.

"No one listens anymore." Sybil pressed her lips together, shaking her head. "Times are changing, mother. Our ways no longer…"

"You are the keeper of the old ways. If they do not listen, then you are failing."

Sybil clutched her hands together, her molars grinding until her cheeks ached. She knew it was true, but hearing it was like swallowing spoiled fruit.

"We are doing our best," she said between clenched teeth. "But we are hunted, killed, or forced to convert to Christianity."

Cailleach swiped her hand forward as if shooing a fly. "It's irrelevant. I am giving you a task you cannot refuse."

"Can't you choose someone else?"

"There's another, but I wait for her to be born and the threads of fate to strengthen. For now, you will become my oracle when Kendra passes."

"I don't want to be the oracle." She muttered then stopped, her head jerked up, meeting Cailleach's eye. "What do you mean when Kendra passes? Is she ill?" A spike of concern flared for her aunt Kendra, the twin's mother, and the current oracle.

Cailleach ignored her questions. "You have no choice. You are born with the spark. There is no other."

"What about Kendra? Why don't you show her?"

"This is your burden to bear, not hers. You must learn."

Sybil groaned, squeezing her eyes shut. Guilt squatted in her gut every time she rejected the gift. Anyone in her coven would have gladly devoted their life to the goddess, but she was different - There wasn't anything appealing about being the next oracle.

Raised by her grandmother, Lenora, and growing up alongside her cousins and David, she was far from obedient and often chose a conflicting path.

"Always so damn defiant," her grandmother often complained.

"No." Sybil didn't flinch. Her jaw locked tight. "I've given enough of myself. I won't let you bleed me dry."

Cailleach stepped forward, icy mist curling with every movement. "You speak as though you are a victim. You are chosen."

Sybil snorted. "No. I was forced. Without consent. You want me to carry your burden, speak your words, see horrors no one else wants to face—while the world calls me heathen."

"You are the last light of the old ways. If they do not listen, you must make them."

"I'm twenty-four," Sybil hissed. "I've seen more death in my dreams than anyone in our coven has seen in real life. I am done."

"You will become my oracle."

"I won't." Her voice cracked on the last word, but her stance didn't waver. "I have a life. People who love me. I want to marry David. I want a family. I want to grow old—slowly."

Cailleach tilted her head, expression unreadable. "You are selfish."

"I am human!" Sybil barked. "You gave me this gift without asking. You call it a blessing, but it feels more like a curse. Every vision burns me. My bones ache. I feel older. It's stealing my future."

The goddess's face flickered. Something like guilt—or ancient sorrow—passed through her eyes.

"A war is coming," Cailleach said, voice low and harder now. "Balor has sent Baal to the human realm to spread his pestilence and destroy any last druids, Christian or Viking pagans. He will poison the land and enslave humanity."

Sybil froze. Balor or as some call, the devil.

"That's not possible. The veil…"

"Was breached. There is a traitor among us."

Sybil's mouth parted, horror curling around her spine. "This can't be happening…"

"It is and now, again, as mentioned so vehemently, you have no choice. There is no one else."

She spun away. "I won't be your pawn. Find another."

"There is another," Cailleach said quietly. "But she has not come of age. Until then—it is you."

"Then you doom us all."

Her voice cracked. She hated how defeated she sounded.

"Do you think you are the only one who has lost?" the goddess snapped. "You are not the first to sacrifice everything. And you won't be the last."

Sybil pressed a trembling hand to her temple, voice breaking. "Why me?"

"Because you carry the spark. You are the daughter of prophecy."

Silence. Only the wind moved between them.

Finally, Sybil whispered, "Then show me."

She stepped closer to the goddess, holding that piercing gaze with her defiant one.

She closed her eyes as Cailleach's cold, bony fingers pressed against her forehead. A chill seeped into her skull, snaking through her body and sinking into her soul.

A shuddering breath escaped her lips as darkness swallowed the world. Weightlessness consumed her, spirit flung into the void.

Then the scene unraveling through the shadows, twisted into chaos.

Demons—clawed, twisted things with skin like burned leather—lunged from the shadows.

Her family battled against them.

A masked blood mage hurled fire, flames reflecting in Sybil's grandmother, Lenora's wide eyes.

The air reeked of scorched flesh and sulphur.

In the center of it all, a girl with golden hair raised a blue flaming blade and clutched a silver shield.

Her cousin's, Enzo and Luca stood beside her.

The girl screamed, "Baal!" The sound rippled with power, vibrating through Sybil's very bones.

Then wings burst from her back, brilliant and white, lighting up the battlefield like a rising star.

The screeches of demons and the bellows of her family dimmed and faded.

Time warped. Slowed as the edges of her vision blurred. Then the pull—cold and fierce—dragged Sybil backward into the dark.

Sybil fell to her knees, panting, her hands clutched the grass, letting the ground center her. She gasped for breath, sweat ran down her chest, as her heart pounded in her ears. The vision stuck in her mind, like damp wool left too long in the rain—heavy, clinging, and slow to fade. The sight of the golden-haired girl with the flaming sword burned in her mind.

The scent of damp earth filled her lungs. The wind howled through the trees, a reminder that she was back in the grove.

She breathed deeply, meeting her divine mother's gaze. Tears welled in the goddess's eyes, along with a compassion she never believed Cailleach could possess.

Cailleach drifted back to the stones, but glanced over her shoulder, hesitating for a moment. "You must protect the girl, help her."

The goddess mother disappeared between the weathered stones, leaving Sybil on her knees, tears streaming down her face and with more questions than before.

She stumbled to her feet as the sounds of the forest resumed around her. Cailleach's tiny snow-white owl hooted, then flew from a tree into the night sky.

Sybil's horse, Moon Pie, tied to a low branch, whinnied and stomped at the ground.

"Let's go, girl," Sybil soothed her brown mare and swiftly mounted, kicking her into a gallop. She needed to warn her grandmother.

The men were all waiting for her under a giant oak tree. Luca was playing with a white flame in his palm. He'd grown proficient with fire magic. And Enzo and David sat on their mounts, quietly speaking to each other.

"Come, we must hurry," she said, not stopping to wait for them to follow.

David caught up to her first. "Did she give you another vision?"

Sybil fought back the urge to cry. She didn't want this—none of it.

Now, more visions would come. Sybil clenched her teeth together.

Whenever Cailleach gifted her a vision, other smaller ones came, unbidden. Since she was a small girl, she'd had visions, not like the one's Cailleach gave her. Most were single images, accompanied by a sense of meaning but they were frustratingly unpredictable and hard to decipher.

"Yes, she gave me another vision." She bit her lip and shook her head.

"Alright, let's get to Lenora."

Thank the gods, he wouldn't push her to reveal the vision. She needed time to process it.

He leaned over and gave her hand a tight squeeze. "I love you."

His devotion always helped deflate the stress of the aftermath of visiting Cailleach, and she sighed as her shoulders dropped. "I love you too."

Sybil led David, Enzo, and Luca through the forest. Glancing over her shoulder, Sybil watched the men weaving through the brush behind her.

The twins rode close, a few years her senior and identical twins with straight black hair like their Italian father. Enzo preferred to wear his down around his shoulders, whereas Luca wore his in a topknot. But she could always tell them apart because Luca took nothing seriously, and Enzo did.

Enzo pulled his stallion next to Sybil. His dark brown eyes appeared almost black at night. "I thought I heard something in the forests today, but I wasn't sure what it was. It sounded unnatural." His voice shook. "I should speak with grandmother." Enzo's gift was air magic. He could summon a storm or listen to the wind that carried sounds only he could hear.

"Do you hear them now?" David asked. His blue eyes darted around them.

"I think so," Enzo said. "But I pray I'm wrong." He twisted towards her. "Do you sense anything?"

A wave of nausea coiled in Sybil's gut, sharp and sudden.

The air thickened around her, pressing in as if the world itself recoiled.

It was always the same—the way her stomach turned before demons appeared.

Cailleach had called it a gift to protect her. It felt more like a curse.

"No," she answered.

"Maybe it was something else?" Luca said hopefully as he rode up next to his brother. His brown eyes were usually mischievous but now filled with worry.

The forest was black, except for a bit of light from the half-moon that peaked through the dark clouds and softly falling rain. The brutal northern winter chilled Sybil despite many layers.

"Are you sure you don't sense anything?" Luca asked her again. "Enzo?"

"Quiet," she whispered, but just as she said the words, her stomach rolled, and bile rose in her throat. "They're close... David." Sybil clutched her belly, forcing herself to breathe and not retch on Moon Pie's side.

"I hear them," Enzo said.

"There's a lot of them." She clutched her gut and moaned quietly. "Oh gods, it hurts."

They pushed through the brush off the trail, the damp leaves slick beneath their mounts. The usual sounds of the forest—the hoot of an owl, the rustling of small creatures—all vanished. An eerie silence settled over them, thick and unnatural.

An unmistakable bone crunching sound filled the air as they pushed further into the forest—a wet, sickening sound. A hiss slithered through the air.

Luca sucked in a breath, his voice trembling. "What is that?" He knew. He just didn't want it to be real.

"It's ghouls," Enzo hissed.

David pulled his sword from its sheath, as did Enzo. "Now, Luca," David said.

Luca lifted his free palm, whispered the incantation, and a bright white flame formed that lit up the entire area. The ghouls crouched over the dead bodies of the two young teens, already ripped to pieces and being devoured.

They hissed and flew backwards, their rotted hands shielding their eyes from the light. It wouldn't kill them, but it hurt, their pupils fully dilated.

"Luca, protect Sybil!" David charged in first with Enzo at his side and carved down the creatures, one at a time, sending their corpse-like heads flying to the forest floor.

A ghoul ran into the dark trees, and Enzo raced after it, sword out.

"Enzo, no!" screamed David, but he only had a moment before the last ghoul was on him and spun, striking it down.

"Oh, gods!" Sybil said. She stared in horror in the direction Enzo had gone, and then David charged into the darkness after him. Without Luca's light, they would become prey.

Dead bodies lay scattered around the ground. After decapitation, the demons vanished, leaving the corpses silent.

"Are there anymore?" Luca asked as he stepped his horse in front of Sybil and moved his hand, holding the white flames around the dark areas surrounding them. His other hand gripped his sword.

"I'm feeling better. They're gone for now," said Sybil, clutching her stomach and trying to catch her breath.

A few moments later, David and Enzo rode back into the clearing. The dead ghoul laid over David's horse. He shoved it off, and it landed next to the others on the ground.

"We'll have to patrol this area tomorrow," David said as he dismounted. "Come on, Enzo, help me pile them together and burn the bodies."

"What about them?" Enzo asked pointing to the dismembered bodies of the young boys, the back of his other hand covering his mouth. He stood over the pieces of body parts, all that remained of the two young teens. Arms torn from sockets, torsos hollowed and gnawed.

One lifeless hand, dirt-caked and pale, still clutched a brown wool sack, timber spilling from it.

Sybil's breath caught.

She had seen battle wounds; seen elders die in their beds. But this... This was desecration. This was evil.

Her stomach twisted, a sour taste rising to her tongue.

She wanted to look away, to pretend it wasn't real.

But she forced her eyes to stay open. She had to see it. All of it.

Tears spilled freely now, tracing cold paths down her cheeks.

"If only I'd come sooner..." she whispered.

Her fists clenched, nails digging deep into her palms. A silent penance for her failure.

"We need to bring them back to town," her voice tight.

David pulled a folded blanket out from behind his saddle and threw it beside Enzo. "We return what we can and say it was wolves."

"And hopefully find out who they belong to," Sybil said.

Her heart broke as tears spilled down her face as the men went to work and she stood in silent vigil.

She should have seen this. "I'm so sorry," she whispered and wiped her face.

Maybe if she hadn't wasted so much time arguing with the Chailleach...

Maybe if she had just obeyed...

Those boys might still be alive.

The thoughts burrowed deep, relentless and cruel.

She closed her eyes, but the image of the shredded corpses lingered.

Cailleach had warned her a war was coming. And she had fought back.

Too little. Too late.

"It's not your fault, Syb." Luca tried to comfort her, but it was useless. She'd never forget the torn bodies and lifeless eyes.

***

Hand in hand, David and Sybil walked into Lenora's apothecary shop, that tucked in at the end of an alleyway in the shambles of York.

A dim light shone from the sitting room, where her grandmother waited for them to return. She knew Lenora wouldn't sleep until they were safely home.

Sybil closed the door behind them, then followed David into the warm glow of Lenora's sitting room.

Her fingers brushed her brow—still cold from the goddess's touch.

Death was no stranger to her, but this... this was war-a battle.

Lenora sat in her old chair, a blanket wrapped around her shoulders and David's mother, Evelyn sat as Ross from her. Worry lines etched deep in both the women's faces.

Evelyn's long brunette hair was braided and knotted tightly at her nape. Her blue eyes - the same as David's eyes, shimmered with worry.

Going deep into the forest to their sacred grove was always dangerous in the dark of night. Many monsters prowled those woods.

"David!" Evelyn cried, running to him. She threw her arms around her son, pulling him into a tight embrace.

She glanced up at him, withdrawing. "What happened?"

"Sybil met with Cailleach," he said, walking to sit next to Lenora, kissing her cheek first. "Hello, Lenora."

Sybil and David sat across from Lenora. Her hands still shook. "We found two boys being attacked by ghouls."

"Did they survive?" Evelyn asked.

"No, we were too late."

Sybil's voice cracked. The image of mangled limbs and hollowed eyes still haunted her.

Evelyn gasped and covered her mouth. "Oh, merciful gods..."

A long silence followed. Even the hearth seemed to flicker with hesitation.

Sybil sat rigid, trying not to break. David rested a hand gently over hers.

"How many ghouls were there?" Lenora asked, clutching her braided grey hair over her shoulder, fiddling with the end of it.

"Half a dozen," Sybil spoke, but her throat felt like it would close up on itself.

"Hmm," Lenora sniffed.

"So, they've returned," Evelyn said.

"I've sensed no demons around York or Ellsworth," Sybil said. "If there were more here, I'd know."

"Perhaps." Lenora hummed, thinking to herself.

David ran his fingers through his hair. "The twins did well, and Luca has mastered his flame."

"And Enzo?" Lenora asked, tilting her head.

"He was scared, but he didn't falter."

"Very good," Lenora nodded with a small, tight smile. She was never one to give out compliments generously. She reminded Sybil of their mother goddess, Cailleach.

"We will patrol the forest daily, and I'll let the locals know there's a wolf pack in the area and to keep their children out of the forests," David said.

Lenora turned to Sybil, lips tight, scowl sharp. "Now, tell me. What has our goddess mother shown you?"

Sybil inhaled, steadying her nerves. She rubbed her forehead, swearing it still felt cold.

David stiffened. "She's demanding too much of you."

Lenora waved a hand. "She's the next oracle. It's her fate."

Sybil cringed. If that was true, how much time did she have before David couldn't touch her, or would she forget him entirely? Every vision stole a piece of the oracle. The stronger she became, the easier the visions came. A single touch could be enough. But if Luca was right, his mother didn't even recognize her sons anymore.

"What did she show you, dear?" Evelyn asked softly.

"I saw a woman with golden hair holding a silver shield and wielding a sword with a blue flame." Sybil paused and glanced at David. "She had wings and was screaming Baal's name. She was fighting with us against the demons."

Sybil pressed her hands into her lap, fingertips twitching.

The girl in her vision—bathed in divine fire, shouting the demon's name—felt burned into her skull.

Her heartbeat thudded louder in the quiet room.

Was this girl their savior—or a warning? And what if Sybil failed to protect her?

"An angel?" David's eyes narrowed, confused.

"A human imbued with the power of a seraph," Sybil explained. "Grandmother, these demons looked like none I've ever seen. Some appeared human but with black eyes and could kill with a word. Others with the speed and strength of a demon. And there were hundreds of ghouls."

Evelyn sucked in a sharp breath and turned to Lenora. "The darkborn prophecies."

"What prophecy?" Sybil asked, looking between her grandmother and Evelyn.

"Evelyn, fetch the book for me," Lenora said, wrapping the blanket tighter around her, the lines between her brows deepening.

A few minutes later Evelyn brought in an old tomb of a book. Heavy and thick, she opened it, laying it gingerly across Lenora's lap.

Lenora's lips pressed into a firm line, and her hand trembled slightly as she turned a worn page.

"If this is true…" she murmured, voice low, "Then war isn't coming. It's already begun."

Lenora flicked through a few more pages then stopped. She cleared her throat. "When the breath of death curls through the streets and hides its face, the crows shall feast, and the soil shall sour. Light will falter, and the faithful shall fall—but one will carry the flame that will rise against the darkness."

A chill ran through Sybil. The girl with the flaming sword flashed through her mind. "What does it mean?"

Lenora's eyes were closed, and she was shaking her head slowly. She took a deep breath before explaining. "The London coven sent word last week. They've scattered. Many are dead. They spoke of a sickness. Pestilence."

"Could it be Baal?" David asked, sitting forward.

"It's possible." Lenora said.

"What can we do?" Sybil asked. Her head throbbed, still.

"I'll send a message to our coven. We need to prepare for war."

"So, war is coming again," Evelyn hissed.

Sybil rubbed her head. "Balor is pushing his demons through the veil. She said we have been betrayed." That same shiver of fear ran down her spine again, making her toes curl and her body tense.

"Who's the keeper of the veil?" Evelyn asked. "I can't remember."

"The London coven guards one and the Coven of Orkney Island the second veil," Lenora answered. "But even unguarded, the London location would be almost impossible to penetrate. The thinnest veil is in Orkney."

"We need to contact the Orkney coven and find out if any of them have turned away from the old ways," Evelyn said.

Lenora scoffed. "They are isolated so far in the north; that island is sacred."

Evelyn interrupted, "I was told, Catholics are there and converting many to their faith."

"Ripe for the picking," Lenora's scowl deepened. "I'll send a messenger."

David and Sybil stood up. "If we're finished here, I should get Sybil home."

She took his hand in hers. "Yes, I'd like that." She nodded to Evelyn, then Lenora. "Goodnight."

Her grandmother sat back in her chair, tightly pulling the blanket around her shoulders. "Goodnight, dear. Rest now, as there's much to consider and much to plan."

"Yes, there is," Evelyn said and nodded towards Lenora.

***

They rode slowly through the empty streets of the Shambles, hooves splashing through the mud. Shops were shuttered, candlelight flickering in the windows above. The breeze brought an icy chill that froze their breaths in a ghostly fog.

Sybil couldn't shake the feeling something wasn't right. That she was missing something.

"I don't feel anything here," she said quietly, trying to sense anything from the surrounding area.

"Perhaps they haven't entered the city yet," David replied.

"I don't know…" Sybil kept her eyes roaming the streets, watching for anything unusual but found nothing.

They crossed the bridge over the Ouse River, which ran through the city, towards the guards at Mickelgate. Its giant three-story archway loomed above them as they rode up to it. The Iron gate closed for the night.

"Good evening, David. Sybil," the older guard greeted them with a smile.

The guards knew them well. Sybil and David often rode between York and Ellsworth Manor, where they lived and worked. David followed his father occupation, working in the stables; Sybil worked as a scullery maid.

They had grown up alongside these men. David often filled in when the guard was shorthanded.

"Good evening," David said, shaking the older guard's hand while the other guard opened the gate for them to pass. "Keep an ear out for wolves. There's been an attack in the north forest outside the walls near the river. We'll be tracking them tomorrow."

"Should you both be riding out there at this time of night then?" the old man asked.

David patted his sword, and Sybil flashed her own. "We can handle a few unruly wolves," she said confidently. "But they got two boys on foot, so let people know to keep their young home."

"That's a shame." The older guard seemed remorseful. "Be safe then, and thanks for the warning. I'll ensure the morning shift knows and pass the word along." He put his fist to his chest, stepping back.

David nodded, then kicked his horse forward, Sybil following with the gate closing behind them.

Sybil shifted her reins as their horses clopped side by side. "David… Grandmother and your mother think we should marry sooner."

She glanced at him, watching the way his jaw tightened before he answered.

He didn't speak at first. Only stared ahead, brows drawn.

"I understand if you want to wait," she added quietly.

42

"It's not that," he finally said, pulling his horse to a stop. Rain misted around them in a hush. "I'd marry you now, this minute, but where would we go? The stable's no place for…"

"I don't care," she interrupted, smile soft and sad. "If I'm in your arms, even the hay is enough."

David chuckled, the sound warming her chest.

"I can keep my room with the other women but come at night to stay with you in yours."

"In a stable, a smelly damp stable?" He looked wretched, his eyes sad, his shoulders slumped not just because he was tired. He wanted more for her, for them.

"It has a cozy little hearth." Sybil smiled and he harrumphed. "It's not what you want for us, but I don't care where we are if I'm in your arms every night. I've waited all my life to marry you, David. I told you so."

"Yes, you did. You were five and announced to my parents you would be my wife." He laughed.

"It makes no difference to me if we live in a stable, under a bridge, or in a cottage." Sybil took his hand in hers. "Let's do it on the next full moon."

"Anything for you," David said and kissed her hand.

They kicked the horses into a slow trot down the dirt road, leaving the lights of York fading behind them.

CHAPTER 3 ~ MICHAEL
Windsor Castle

Michael's footsteps echoed through the stone corridor like drumbeats at a funeral. The usual courtesans absent. The chatter and excitement of the day gone.

The great gallery loomed around him—pillars stretching toward vaulted ceilings, gilded tapestries rustling in a stale breeze. Candlelight shimmered off the polished floors, but the warmth it promised didn't reach him.

He passed a window. Beyond the arched glass, a funeral procession wound through the outer courtyard. Mourners in black shuffled behind a cart laden with two sheet-covered bodies.

Another. The sixth funeral this week.

A faint metallic scent lingered in the air—lye and blood. Somewhere in the shadows, a servant coughed—a wet, phlegmy sound that made Michael flinch.

The palace still dazzled with its splendor, but rot had set in beneath the gold. Not obvious. Most ignored what was happening in London. All around them.

And he'd been summoned to the king with no reason.

Servants hurried through the corridors with their heads bowed, their hushed whispers swallowed by the thick stone walls.

Near an arched window, a nobleman stood rigid, hands clenched behind his back as he stared into the courtyard below. His fine velvet doublet creased, and a faint shadow of sweat darkened his collar. A companion whispered fervently to the lord. Hushed whispers laced with urgency. The lord caught Michael watching them and lifted a hand to stop his companion from talking.

Michael quickly walked away, trying to ignore the sense of dread lingering behind him.

He stopped momentarily before a sizable, gilded mirror and checked his appearance, adjusting the deep green folds of his cape. His hands trembled.

Perfect. Always perfect.

He clenched his jaw, straightened the collar, and adjusted the pin with the Ellsworth crest—a lion rearing over a broken spear.

To the world, he was everything Lord Ellsworth had raised him to be.

Stoic. Flawless. Dutiful.

Inside, his ribs felt caged. Pressure coiled beneath his skin like a fist tightening in his chest.

How many times had he heard his father's voice?

Control your expression.

Straighten your back.

You are my son. You must always be better.

He forced his shoulders back. The sooner this audience ended, the sooner he could breathe again.

45

"Relax, it's most likely nothing of consequence," he muttered, taking a deep breath and adjusting his family cape draped over his shoulder.

His tunic and boots were spotless; his dark hair tied back with a leather strap.

But why did the king summon him? He searched his memory for something he'd done wrong but found nothing. However, that didn't mean there wasn't something.

Rumors moved through court like wildfire. Perhaps someone whispered falsehoods against him? Had he said something to offend the crown? Or was there something else entirely?

Michael smoothed out his cape and squared his shoulders. He was the image of obedience and perfection—exactly what his father expected and demanded. H was the flawless son, the future lord of Ellsworth.

He turned away from the mirror and made his way to the king.

Two guards stood rigid at the throne room doors. A nobleman opened one door and motioned him inside.

"Sir Michael, his majesty is expecting you."

Michael stepped through.

Gold-trimmed pillars lined the hall, and tapestries and paintings covered the walls. While crystal chandeliers cast rainbows of light. The ceiling, painted like a perfect sky, gleamed with gold along the edges. The sheer artistry left him breathless.

A harp played softly as groups of courtesans and nobles mingled.

At the far end, King Edward III sat on a dais, listening to a group of noblemen.

As Michael waited at the edge of the great hall, a nobleman stepped forward to speak.

"The plague spreads further north, Your Grace. But cases in London are declining."

The king rubbed his chin. "Where up north is it spreading?"

"To villages along the coast mostly. Bristol is said to be suffering but... Your Majesty," the man said, voice trembling slightly, "a village west of Eton—Tarnwick—is gone. Not a soul left. Every man, woman, and child dead."

A murmur spread through the court. Several courtiers paled.

The king leaned forward; his face grim. "And what of burial?"

"There were none left to bury the dead, sire. The village burns now. By priest's order."

A heavy silence followed, broken only by the crackle of a torch. The harpist's hands stilled for a beat then resumed.

Michael's best friend, Shaun spoke with him a few nights before about the disturbing rumor of the plague.

The disease swept through London, but it hadn't reached the court. The thought chilled him.

He forced his attention back to the king.

"I understand, Your Majesty, but the people can't afford more taxes. Their sons are dying fighting this war, and they don't want to pay more on top of their children dying in battle."

"Are you saying they are refusing?" asked the King.

The second noble jumped in, shaking his head. "No, Your Grace, they love you, adore you, but the talk..." He hesitated, as though weighing his words carefully.

Michael's palms itched. He resisted the urge to rub them against his tunic. Sweat gathered beneath his collar.

The noblemen's words about unrest, plague, and faltering faith mirrored the unrest inside him.

Michael shifted on his feet. This was dangerous ground. Few men dared to suggest the people had lost faith in the war—fewer still would risk speaking it before the king himself.

"What talk?" the king pressed.

"The talk, Your Grace, is that many are losing faith in the war, not you. It's gone on for so long, costing them greatly."

The king clutched the armrests of his throne. "It's cost my now empty coffers, too."

"Yes, but your majesty, the common folk of your land are already pressed hard, and more taxes will cripple them."

Michael turned away, his gaze sweeping across the hall. Nobles clustered in small groups, whispering or listening to the music. No one here felt the weight of taxation or illness.

He watched a servant enter the room carrying another arm full of flowers.

The harpist began another song, and Michael winced as the song brought with it the memory of the previous night's ball. Now scorched through his mind.

A misstep, the lady's startled yelp, the crowds' gasps. Then his friend Shaun swept in with a charming smile and lifted her to her feet.

He'd never live it down. As soon as they returned home, Shaun would tell Enzo and Luca, close friends in York, and they'd tease him relentlessly. More material for the Lord's son.

He shut his eyes, forcing the thoughts away and his mother's voice echoed: You need grace on the dance floor to woo a lovely lady.

Another image surfaced—golden hair, bright laughter, a sunlit wheat field.

"Trinity," he whispered. He shook his head. It had been years since he thought of his childhood friend. A friend he'd loved above all others, even his best friend, Shaun.

"Sir Michael, come!" The king's voice cut through his thoughts. The two noblemen strode past without a glance.

His knees felt tight, stiff from standing too long. As he stepped forward, he wasn't sure if the cold sweat on his back came from the court's tension—or his own rising dread.

King Edward III sat on the dais, waiting. Michael had always admired the King. As a boy, he watched the man command his court with nothing more than a glance and a word, his very presence a banner of unshakable strength.

But today, the king looked… different.

The golden crown sat firm on his head, but the weight of it seemed heavier than before. His once-sharp hazel eyes, lined with quiet cunning, were rimmed red. He still held himself with the air of an unshakable ruler, but there was a tightness to his jaw, a rigidity to his knuckles where they gripped the throne's armrests.

A strand of silver ran through his russet beard, neatly groomed but now speckled with white. That hadn't been there the last time Michael had seen him.

The war in France had taken its toll. Or was it something more? Michael felt the question settle in his chest like a stone.

Hazel's eyes, warm with fondness, settled on Michael.

"Your Majesty." He bowed.

"I got word that your father is ill. They've asked for you to return home, believing you will improve his health. Your father is dear to me, so I expect you to

49

The Light of Darkness

leave with haste, and I want reports of his wellbeing immediately."

Michael's stomach churned, a cold sweat prickling the back of his neck.

He should have expected it—his father's age, the worsening state of the country. And yet, hearing it from the king's lips sent ice down his spine.

Lord Ellsworth had always been unyielding, immovable—a man who wielded discipline like a sword and expected his son to follow the same path. Michael had spent his life trying to meet those expectations, trying to be the flawless heir his father demanded. And now, that man lay sick in bed.

"Your majesty, have they said what this illness is?" He asked. "Or how severe is it?"

"Only he has taken to his bedchambers and insisted on seeing his son. I'm sure if he's demanding anything, I dare wager it's not too severe." The king smirked, giving Michael some comfort. "Your father is a man of strength, yet I expect you to depart at once."

"Of course, Your Majesty. Might I humbly request my companion Shaun join me?"

"Is that the red-headed man pursuing half the ladies of my court?"

Michael coughed and cleared his throat. He was sure his face was red, embarrassed by his friend. "I assure you, Your Majesty, he is a gentleman."

The king didn't look convinced. "Indeed, it may be wise for him to accompany you. You have my consent."

"Thank you, your majesty."

Michael turned to take his leave when the king's voice dropped. "Stay a moment."

The king leaned forward, his golden crown catching the light. The great hall felt colder suddenly, the flickering torches casting long, wavering shadows across the dais.

Edward's hazel eyes bore into him, not with command, but with something Michael had never seen in them before.

Unease.

"Do not trust every man who calls himself friend." The king's voice was barely above a whisper. "There are forces moving in the dark." The king exhaled, rubbing his temple as if suddenly weary. "Take care on the road to Ellsworth."

Michael hesitated, then bowed low. "Yes, Your Majesty."

But as he stepped back from the throne, the king's words echoed louder than the court's harp.

"Do not trust every man who calls himself friend…"

Michael's mouth had gone dry. His hands curled into fists at his sides.

It wasn't just plague and war. It was something darker…

He left the throne, but the weight of the crown's shadow followed him out.

***

Michael's and Shaun's bedchamber were modest. The room contained two single beds, a small table with chairs, and two large wooden chests. Plush carpets softened the floor, and a grand fireplace kept them warm. An adjacent bathing chamber—an uncommon luxury was a privilege granted by the king.

Michael finished tidying his side and completed his packing. Shaun sat on the edge of his bed, nudging a boot with his foot. He raked a hand through his shaggy red hair and stared at the floor.

"And remind me," he muttered, "why exactly do I need to go with you?"

"Because I need you to," Michael said.

"I'd rather stay here." Shaun slumped forward, elbows on his knees, hands covering his face.

Michael huffed. "You wouldn't even be here if not for me. You're unbelievable."

Shaun let out a sharp breath. "You're an ass." His voice dropped to a hiss. "She's different from any woman I've ever met. You don't understand."

Michael didn't. The lady in question wasn't staying at court long, and Shaun wasn't a suitable match for her. At best, he might steal a kiss before she left.

The time away would keep him from disgrace or, worse, the king's wrath.

"I beg you, Shaun, do not vex me. I told you what the king said. He's heard of you strutting around like a cock and is not impressed." Michael picked up a jacket on the floor and threw it at Shaun. "Can you please clean up your mess?"

Shaun caught it quickly, gave a loud, exaggerated sigh, and laid back on his messy bed. "By God, you are infuriating! I don't know why I tolerate such a lout as a friend."

"The King insisted you join me, so I dare say you are the lout. It will only be until father recovers." Michael walked to Shaun. "What about your mother? Do you not wish to see her? I'm sure she misses you, greatly."

"Enzo and Luca are helping her… Ugh. Are you seriously doing this to me?" Shaun covered his head with his jacket.

"Yes, my friend. I am." Michael laughed, pulling the jacket off Shaun's. "Start packing!"

There was a quick, sharp knock, and Shaun lifted his brows. "Maybe I am saved?"

Michael chuckled, opening the door. Stephen, one of the king's messengers, stood stiff-backed, holding out a silver tray with a folded note.

"Hello, Stephen," Michael said, taking the missive.

"A message from your mother, I believe, sir."

Stephen nodded, then stepped back.

"Thank you, Stephen."

"It's my pleasure, sir."

Michael closed the door and opened the letter.

"My pleasure, sir," Shaun mimicked Stephen, "you know he's besotted with you."

Michael barely heard the jest as he scanned the short message and let out a loud, "Ugh!"

"What is it?" Shaun asked.

"Mother insists that I give the prospect of an engagement to Fleur Devonshire serious regard."

"Still?" Shaun asked, aghast and amused, a smile spreading over his face. His blue eyes sparkled with mirth. "I thought you declined the offer." He laughed again.

"I did." Michael sighed, folding the letter tightly before tucking it into his coat.

The pressure in his chest hadn't lifted—it only grew heavier.

As he reached for his gloves, his eyes swept over the room one last time.

The fire crackled softly. Shaun's chest rose and fell on the bed across from him, boots still scattered on the rug.

York already felt a world away, but he couldn't get there fast enough.

He tugged his cloak tight around him. "Come on. We should leave."

***

They stepped out into the morning light; the sky painted in iron grey.

53

Shaun still grumbled to himself about going, but the wind had teeth, and he sucked in a breath as it bit his cheeks.

A raven cried overhead, the sound sharp and strange in the quiet.

"Something feels off today," Michael murmured.

"Everything feels off," Shaun replied then leaned back, arms open to the sky. "Why, God, have you cursed me with such an awful friend?"

Michael ignored him, pulling his cloak tighter.

Shaun did the same. "I hate winter."

"I've listened to your grumblings the entire time we packed. I'm growing tired of it." Michael adjusted the travel bag over his shoulder.

"You're forcing me to leave!" Shaun glared at him, and Michael laughed.

"You need to see your mother, Shaun. It's not easy for her to manage the shop without you."

"I know, but for the first time, I feel… I'm happy here. I don't understand why you loath it so much."

"I guess I'm just a country boy." Michael slapped him on the shoulder. "We'll be back in no time."

Shaun huffed.

The stable boy walked their horses into the yard, saddled and ready to go. "Good morning, Sir Michael, Master Shaun."

"Good morning lad," Shaun said cheerfully.

"Thank you, George," Michael said and mounted up, ignoring Shaun.

Six young men rode in, their mounts' heads hung low to the ground, frothing at their muzzles.

The men nodded at Michael and Shaun.

"How goes your journey?" Michael asked.

The stables smelled of damp hay and fresh leather. Frost bit at the air, swirling around the horses' breath like smoke.

Six riders emerged from the road; their mounts lathered with sweat despite the cold. One horse stumbled as it entered the yard, ribs heaving like bellows.

Mud clung to the riders' boots and cloaks. Their eyes were sunken, faces tense from hard riding.

"Word of warning, sir," one said, voice hoarse, "sickness has taken London. Entire streets sealed. Fires burn night and day. And still, the bodies pile."

"I've heard that London is recovering." Michael's gut twisted.

"No, it has not."

Michael's brows pinched. Why would a noble give the king conflicting information?

"How far has it spread?" he asked.

"Too far," the rider whispered. "A village near here was wiped out in days. Not a soul left. They say it isn't natural. They say demons walk with it."

"Yes, I've heard of this village," Michael murmured. "It's horrific, but demons? Truly, they think such things.

"Aye, they do," another lad spoke, as he dismounted.

The stable yard quieted. Even the horses seemed to still.

Michael's stomach twisted. His spine stiffened. A drop of cold sweat slipped down his back.

If his father was already sick…

He clenched his fists, trying to stop the dread from taking root.

Michael shook the man's hand. "Thank you for sharing this news. I'm sure the king would need to know this immediately, so I'll bid you good day."

The young men nodded respectfully and led their horses inside the stables.

Shaun looked more pale than usual. "Demons? Are they kidding?"

Michael glanced at Shaun. "I don't know, but I need to see my father. If it's the same sickness, I may be too late.

CHAPTER 4 ~ JULIAN
London

The cave beneath the manor's dungeon breathed darkness—damp stone walls exhaled a cold that clung to skin.

A sweet, metallic scent lingered in the air, sinking into the bedrock itself. Blood.

Once, this had been a sacred place. A gateway guarded by the druids—ancient protectors of the veil.

But that time was over.

Now, the veil belonged to Baal.

A single wall sconce flickered near the only visible door, casting a dim orange glow that trembled across the carnage. Once a sacred place, the room was now soaked in the blood of the witches who once protected it. Stone walls, veined with moss and shadow, bore silent witness to the massacre.

Julian stood with 12 other men dressed in the same black cloaks. But they weren't men anymore; they were legionnaires. The most powerful demons ever created and able to walk the mortal realm. And with the veil in their control, Baal could create an army.

He glanced around the room. At the other's faces, set in stoic obedience. Their skin, chiseled like stone, was clear of blemishes—untouched by time, as he once was.

Julian was one of the few remaining ancient ones.

However, his reflection no longer mirrored theirs. His skin, once radiant, had dulled to a sickly grey, the veins beneath it dark and swollen. His cheekbones jutted too sharply, his hazel eyes sunken, rimmed with the shadow of something festering inside him. His once thick red locks dulled. A side effect of the blood oath to Baal and staying alive far longer than the Prince of Pestilence intended.

They quietly watched as Baal brought two initiates into the cavern, guiding them by their elbows to the center of the room; twin women with straight black hair that hung to their waists. They were from another continent, a gift to become part of his elite warriors, his legionnaires, born and bred to be devoted to Satan or as some called him Balor.

Baal stood before them in front of a stone altar with a carved bowl of the same stone. He was tall, built like the Roman gladiators of old, his long-sleeved black tunic taut against his muscled arms. A fur-lined cloak attached to his shoulders flowed around him. Long wavy black hair framed his chiseled alabaster face.

Julian knew it wasn't his true form. Julian had been one of the few who saw the demon prince in full glory—something of nightmares: Black leather wings, thick spiraling horns, with cloven hoofs. Half man, half beast.

58

Baal took the girls' wrists one at a time, pulling the tunic dress sleeve to their elbows, exposing the soft, smooth inner flesh. He held it over the stone bowl on the altar.

Eyes as black as coal locked to Julian.

Now, Julian. The command rang through his mind—Baal's voice like stone grinding against steel.

Julian stepped forward and brandished a long slender knife with a bone handle, white and polished. He handed the knife hilt first to Baal and stepped back among the others.

"It's time," Baal looked at both girls, his heavy Italian accent vibrated through the room.

Their deep brown eyes stared into Baal's without flinching. Their thin lips curled upward, excited, anticipating the power they knew they'd receive.

Baal began speaking, an old incantation that would open the door of the veil to the demon world, their home. The language was ancient, but Julian had memorized it over the years, watching Baal perform the ritual many times. Thick black fog flowed all around them, caressing their legs and wrapping around the stone altar.

Baal sliced the woman's vein that ran down the inside of her elbow to her wrist. She didn't move-not even a twitch as blood instantly began to spill.

Julian breathed in the coppery scent of her blood and could smell the power inside of it.

Baal reached for the other woman and did the same. Again, not a single flinch. They would be unique as twins always were.

Julian closed his eyes and sucked in the scent again, sending shivers through his body. The smell awakened the wraith inside of him. It begged for more, coiling in

59

his chest, whispering in a language older than man, a relentless hunger clawing at his insides.

"With the power of the wraith, you will have the strength of ten men along with immortality."

A thick, unnatural silence fell over the room. Wraiths stirred, shifting within the black mist. Julian's pulse quickened as he watched them twist and coil, their forms indistinct, searching. Waiting. Then— The wailing began.

Baal held the knife out for Julian. He stepped forward, took the knife, and stepped back again.

"You will be bound together." Baal took the girls' arms, held them over the bowl, and began the chant again. After several minutes the black fog filled the entire chamber. The wailing inside the black mist grew louder.

"Come, my wraiths of hell, join with them." Baal held up the girl's wrists, blood continuing to spill forth. "Do you swear fidelity to your master, our true lord?"

Both girls answered together. "Yes."

"Say the words."

The girls spoke together in the same ancient language, but their voices sounded like a beautiful dark, violent song of death and fidelity.

The power rushed through Julian as the girl's blood emptied. Every legionnaire was affected by the ritual, a few hissed but all remained still. It was intoxicating.

The girls' bodies began to sway from losing so much blood, and as they came closer to death, the black fog began to move more frantically around them. The wailing grew louder as the girls recited the blood oath, their voices growing fainter until they spoke the last word. Then silence.

The black fog formed into a corporal shape. The wraiths were hungry to be among the living.

Baal held the girls' arms tight and steadied them as the wraiths brushed against everyone. Demons were greedy and would try to take over any host they could find.

The open wounds and blood in the bowl drew the wraiths' attention, and with a shrill cry, two black abstract forms pulled away from the black mist. They flowed like black tar into the bowl of blood, and when they emerged, they were more distinguishable. Their black eyes large and open, with no noses and sharpened teeth, akin to a beast. They screamed and then disappeared into the girls' open wounds.

Both girls closed their eyes, and their bodies shuddered.

Their wounds shimmered with unnatural light, veins knitting together as if time reversed itself.

Their skin paled, their muscles grew leaner, sharper. Still, they stood, heads bowed, lips parted—silent. Then, slowly, their eyes opened.

Black. Endless. Inhuman.

Baal released his grip on the girls, and they stood still.

Baal sealed the veil in the same language he used to call the wraiths forth, and the fog withdrew.

After the fog disappeared completely, the cavern was silent. The girls breathed slowly, but Julian could still hear their heartbeats. The wraiths settled in; the twins would survive, while some did not.

The host would die if they weren't strong enough or if the wraiths waited too long to join to them. It was a risk every initiate understood.

The girls opened their eyes, and their eyes were dilated, solid black. Their skin began to lose its tanned color immediately, turning pale, and their bodies became more muscular.

"Who do you serve?" Baal asked.

"The dark lord," they said together, in a monotonous voice that sounded inhuman, deeper than a woman's voice would sound. "We are bound for eternity and in death, our souls return to him."

"You will be bound to each other in life and silence. Only if one dies will the other be able to speak, but the other shall perish soon after. Do you accept this sacrifice?"

"Yes," they both replied at the same time.

"You are each other's keepers. It is done."

***

Julien led the legionnaires through a narrow corridor, the air thick with the scent of old stone and burned herbs.

They entered a wide, circular chamber carved entirely from bedrock—the Landon coven's war room. Once a place of strategy and protection, now claimed by shadows.

At the center stood Baal, hunched over a large stone table where a crude map of England lay unfurled.

He'd placed a few stones where the city of London was, a few to the northwest of London where the king held his court at Windsor Castle, a larger stone on Bristol and a group of stones placed north at York.

The two women stood beside each other, straight-backed; their pale faces and dark eyes watched their master. Their eyes had returned to their usual dark brown, the wraiths inside well controlled. The girls were indeed powerful.

"We have much to do," Baal began. "But first, I want to know..." He put both hands on the table before him and dropped his head.

Baal's fingers curled over the edge of the table, his knuckles pale.

"What happened in London?"

The words slithered out like a blade. Silence followed. Tense. Heavy.

Then his gaze locked on one man.

"Johnathan." He glared at a man with bright reddish-orange hair.

Johnathan stepped forward. "We have most of London secured, the remaining witches have scattered, and the death toll rises daily, my lord."

"I needed them all dead, not scattered!" Baal thundered as he slowly made his way next to Johnathan. "They are the only ones who can complicate my plans. This cursed island is mine, and I will rule it!" He paused and walked around the table facing Johnathan. "I can't do that with them... Scattered around. Can I?"

"I'm sorry, my lord," his voice cracked.

In a blur, Baal's hand snapped out and closed around Johnathan's throat.

The sound of vertebrae cracking echoed through the chamber, louder than it should have been.

Johnathan didn't even gasp—his eyes widened once before his neck twisted unnaturally to the side.

The body hit the stone floor with a thud, then began to disintegrate, the flesh turning to ash.

A soft, haunting wail slipped from the dust as if something inside him was torn free.

Julien clenched his jaw and lowered his gaze.

"Yes." Baal swiveled around, going back to the head of the table. "They will all die, and I will not tolerate any more failure."

"Now, now, Baal. There's no reason to kill our creations just because one has disappointed you," Baal's blood mage, strode into the room, dressed in her usual black gown and cape, a shining black mask covering her upper face leaving her full blood red lips exposed, with a wide black hood covering her entire head. No one knew who she was. Only that she was a powerful necromancer and Baal's right hand, as Julien was his left.

"Where have you been?" Baal demanded.

She walked around the table, pausing near Julien and sniffing the air close to him.

You stink, Julien. You know I can't stand your stench. Only Julien heard her, of course, and before he could answer, she turned towards their prince with a sweet smile.

"My great lord, I see you have conducted the rite without me," she flicked her gaze at the twins.

"I do not have time for your games. If you cannot abide by me, I will allow Julien to perform the rite next time, and perhaps you won't be needed any longer."

Her head snapped towards Julian, and he didn't dare move or breathe.

The woman slowly turned back to Baal and lowered her head in a show of submission. "But I have a gift for you. My devotion will always be to you, my lord."

A hip slid against the edge of the table, the motion deliberately, seductive. One finger trailed slowly down the curve of her neck.

"What is this gift?" Baal asked, his voice low with interest.

"My daughter. She has come of age and is ready."

"Yes, very good," he murmured. "You've trained her well. I've heard she already shows promise—skill with manipulating the mind, even without the aid of my wraiths."

"She has grown into a powerful blood mage."

Baal turned towards Julien. "Julien, tomorrow you will go north and take the twins. I want York and that coven of Druid-kin in my hands when I arrive. I want the location of every pagan witch in that city and nearby villages. I want the locations of every church. Every bishop, priest and the archbishop watched. Spread your poison my son and let the pagans and the Catholics tear each other apart."

"My lord, shouldn't we finish off the coven in London, find them first?"

"I'm sending the rest of you after the London coven and take the ghouls with you to hunt them down."

Julien nodded, then stepped back.

Baal's blood mage stepped forward. "What shall I do for you, my lord?"

"You will join Julian, and he will help you initiate your daughter. I want all my legionnaires possessing the people's minds and spreading my pestilence throughout the land."

"I thought I am needed here," she said. "I had planned on joining you and doing the rite with you, my Lord. It is expected that you…."

"Very well," Baal growled.

Julien exhaled slowly through his nose, careful not to let it seem like relief.

He'd endured the woman's presence before—her magic clung to the air like rot, and her words twisted even the strongest minds.

65

Traveling with her again would be a disaster.

The sorceress leaned closer to Baal, whispering in his ear.

"Julian, this family, the Ellsworth, I want you to find out the names of their entire staff but do not make yourself known."

"Take note of any pagans that might work for them. They will be problematic," Baal's blood mage said, standing beside Baal like his queen. Maybe she was, with her golden eyes and porcelain skin-the perfect demon queen.

"Do not engage with the York coven. They are powerful and you will not win against them alone. Break them down, weaken them and wait for us to arrive." Baal paused, putting a finger to his chin in thought. "Take some ghouls with you and let them loose in the forests around the villages and York and create more once you get there."

"Yes, my lord," Julien said, trying not to let his disappointment show or his thoughts left open. He hated ghouls. Unlike Legionnaires, they were minor demons that inhabited the bodies of the dead. He'd seen many packs go wild at the smell of blood and turn on their masters.

"You have a problem with that?" Baal asked.

Julien immediately checked his mental barrier, but it held. "No, my lord."

Baal stood up. "Kill any pagan filth you find along the way, destroy the towns you travel through, and bring the fury of our lord and the chaos of hell with you."

"Yes, my lord." He nodded.

CHAPTER 5 ~ TRINITY
London

Trinity rode through London, glancing up at the sun that dipped behind thick black clouds. A gloom settled over the city, thick and suffocating, as if the heavens themselves had recoiled from the despair below.

It had taken her too long to get there. She pulled her fur-lined cloak tighter, her breath escaping in white plumes.

"Thank god it stopped raining," she whispered, peering around at the abandoned city.

The silence was unnatural. No merchants calling out their wares, no children's laughter, not even the clatter of carts on the cobblestones. Only the distant creak of a swinging shop sign and the soft rustle of the wind through empty streets. Something wasn't right, and a ripple fear shivered down her spine.

"Please, lord, protect me."

The city's lanterns remained unlit, leaving only the dim orange haze of fading daylight. Ahead, pitch torches flared near the graveyard, their rancid smoke curling through the air.

Her mare's hooves clattered on cobblestones as she turned onto the main road. She needed to find Arthur Whiting—obtain travel documents, money, and a chaperone. Preferably before nightfall. But as she scanned the streets, unease settled in. The city appeared deserted.

The plague's grip was clear. Shuttered windows. Barred doors. White crosses mark the doomed.

"Dear lord, what's happened here?" she breathed, afraid her voice would rouse the dead. Something sinister echoed in her bones, deep into her soul. A knowingness. A wrongness.

Trinity instinctually reached down and touched the sword, which was now wrapped and secured on the side of her horse. A warmth spread through her hand, up her arm and into her chest, bolstering her courage.

"How am I to fight this?"

The fog thickened as Trinity neared the church. Coughing, she pressed a gloved hand to her mouth. Ahead, a man dragged a wooden cart through the haze. To her left, torchlight flickered over a gaping pit—a mass grave. Bodies lay twisted and lifeless, dumped like refuse.

Bile burned her throat. Her mare reared, nearly throwing her. She fought for control as the horse danced sideways.

Suddenly, an old man, the cart-puller stood in front of her—filthy, his cart overflowing with the dead. His head lifted slowly, revealing hollow eyes, skin stretched too tight over his skull. He blinked, once, twice, as if seeing her for the first time.

Nicole Moore

Her scream ripped through the night. The man flinched, dropping the poles. The cart tilted, bodies tumbling to the ground in a grotesque cascade. A woman's pale hand flopped onto the cobblestones.

Trinity yanked the reins, kicked hard, and the mare bolted. The man's curses were lost in the wind.

The mare rode hard through the maze of streets and tightly packed houses. Trinity held on for dear life, eyes clenched tight, tears falling down her cheeks.

"No…No…No.." she murmured again and again.

The mare finally slowed, and Trinity dared to open her eyes. Fog swallowed the unlit streets, and every door bore a white cross. She was riding through a tomb.

An owl shrieked. A jolt shot through her as she clutched the reins, her body tightening.

"It's just an owl. It's not a demon," she whispered, but Seriella's vision echoed in her mind.

"This can't be happening to me," she whispered, and her mare whinnied as if telling her, "You have no choice."

They turned onto a main road, hooves echoing in the silence. Trinity exhaled, relieved. The houses loomed two or three stories high, and every window shuttered tight. The River Thames was to her left. She knew where she was.

A massive square opened before her, a fountain at its center, and stale water pooled in its stone bowls.

Trinity sighed, shaking her head. Once a bustling landmark, now abandoned.

"Not far now." She kicked the mare forward, turning down a street towards Arthur's small cottage wedged between two towering buildings.

69

Slipping from the saddle, her legs felt like lead as they hit the ground. She groaned as pins and needles ran up her legs. Her ears rang.

She gripped the documents taken from her uncle's chamber and glanced at the shield and sword, securely wrapped and strapped to her horse alongside her pack.

She quickly scanned the area. There wasn't a soul in sight. "It should be safe enough to leave them."

She patted her mare. "I'll be right back."

No cross marked the door and light glowed behind the wooden shutters. Her breath came out in white plumes as relief washed over her.

She knocked. Moments later, the door opened.

Arthur Whiting stood, wrapped in a fine wool cloak. He slid his tiny wooden-framed spectacles up his bulbous, red nose and frowned.

"Good god, girl! What in heaven's name do you think you're doing in the streets alone at this hour?" He squinted at her, trying to see who she was. "What is it you want?" He asked, obviously still not sure who she was.

"My name is Trinity Ackerman, and I'm the niece of Sir Geoffrey Denton."

"Yes, yes. I remember you. Come in."

Arthur moved back and allowed Trinity to enter. It was a modest home with little furniture, no paintings or rugs, and scented rushes covering the floor. The room smelled of lavender and a slight touch of dried hay.

He walked to a table covered with papers. A candle lantern centered on the table, softly illuminating the space.

It was as cold inside as outside, with no fire burning in the fireplace against the far wall, and Trinity pulled her cloak tighter around her.

"May I offer you some tea?" He asked politely.

"No, thank you, sir." Trinity wanted to leave as soon as possible, but now she wasn't sure she'd find any inn or boarding rooms available.

Arthur studied her closely, waiting for her to tell him why she was there.

She nervously laid the scroll on the table and unrolled it, smoothing it out under the lamp's light.

"I need you to look after my uncle's affairs. My aunt and uncle have died from the illness spreading here." Trinity paused, awaiting a response, but Arthur stood silent, waiting for her to continue.

"They've left me as their sole heiress. And I intend to travel north to York, where I was born, so I will need a chaperone and travel documents, oh, and money." She tapped the documents. "It's all there." She tried to sound as confident as she could.

He read the papers, ignoring her declaration.

"Did you hear me?" She asked again, irritated by his silence.

Arthur looked up at her. His condescending look made her want to scream.

"I'm sorry for the loss of your uncle and aunt. Your uncle was a close and dear friend, and I'll miss him."

"Thank you," Trinity answered, her composure softening slightly, but her eagerness increased. "How can I obtain a travel document to get lodging and meals on my way to York?" she asked.

Arthur contemplated her request. "I have no desire to argue with you under the current circumstances, but what you're asking is extremely brave or unwise." He grew silent again, looking over the papers one more time. "Unwise, I reckon," he murmured under his breath.

Trinity ignored his insult, but she was growing tired and, to make matters worse, nauseous. She clutched her stomach, experiencing a cramp, realizing the paltry amount of food and wine that had barely sustained her for so many days. Her legs shook, and her head ached.

Arthur immediately offered her a chair, and she instantly collapsed into it.

"Are you ill, Milady?" Arthur asked, concerned, then whispered a quick prayer. "Please, Lord, don't let it be the plague."

"My head..." Trinity said as she rubbed her temples, the ringing in her ears growing even louder.

"Would you prefer to lie down?" Arthur asked, his voice suddenly muffled and distant.

Trinity tried to stand up, but the room lurched sideways, the walls bending, stretching, wrapping around her. A dull ringing filled her ears, drowning out Arthur's concerned words.

The floor heaved beneath her feet like the deck of a storm-tossed ship. She reached for the table—missed.

Heat flushed through her veins, then ice, her body at war with itself. She heard a whisper—not Arthur's voice, something softer, slithering in the edges of her mind. The scent of lavender twisted into something sharp, metallic.

Bile filled her mouth. Her knees buckled.

The world tilted. Then darkness swallowed her whole.

***

Trinity awoke but could barely distinguish the figures above her as she drifted in and out of a dream state she could not escape, so she closed her eyes and fell back to sleep.

She walked through the blackness. Or was she floating? Her feet didn't touch the ground, yet the fog curled around her legs, cold and slick, like the fingers of something unseen.

A light flickered ahead, dim, beckoning. It pulsed with unnatural energy, its glow not golden, but a deep, bloodied crimson.

She reached out.

An instant later, she stood in a dark cavern. The air was thick, stagnant, pressing into her lungs. Before her, two beautiful women, twins with long, silky black hair, stood together, their eyes closed.

But something was wrong. Something inside the black fog cried out in a high-pitched wail. It caressed her legs and pricked her hand, which hung loosely at her side like a needle. She snapped her hand to her chest.

The women's gazes swung to Trinity. Black as a night with no moon. Trinity screamed.

She woke up and jolted upright. Her body convulsed, and her teeth rattled together as she tried desperately to stop shaking. A dried bead of blood clung to her palm.

What's happening to me?

She scanned the room, heart pounding. A dim light seeped through a small opaque window, casting shadows over the tiny bedchamber. A wool blanket covered her.

She gasped for air. A vice gripped her lungs—each breath sharp, shallow, unbearable.

The door creaked open, and Arthur carried porridge and a steaming drink.

"Dear God!" He placed them on the table next to the bed and clasped her arms. "Are you alright, child?"

"I. I. I had... bad dream... never happened... before." She could barely get the words between chattering teeth.

Her shaking subsided after she felt his hands on her arms. She tried to take another breath but immediately felt dizzy.

Arthur let go; she pushed herself upright and pulled the blanket to her neck.

After several deep breaths, her body relaxed, and the shaking subsided.

"I apologize," Trinity spoke first, embarrassed. "I shall be out of your way as soon as possible. I promise." She still felt shaken by the nightmare but didn't want to give him a reason to deny her request to travel to York, so she pulled herself together as best as she could. Ignoring her throbbing head and burning lungs.

"It is truly no inconvenience. Are you sure you are well?"

"I feel much better, thank you."

"The healer examined you last night, and I brought your belongings inside." He nodded to her things on the floor next to the door. The sword and shield remained wrapped. "I tried to tie up that beast of yours, but she bit me, so I'm afraid she spent the night in the rain."

"Oh?" She was suddenly highly relieved it was a healer and not him who removed her clothing and worried her mare would be in a dreadful state. "Thank you so much. She was my aunt's horse and always very temperamental. I'm sorry she bit you."

74

"It's no bother. Not the first time I've been nipped." Arthur cleared his throat. "The healer said you're exhausted and malnourished, and you must eat and rest."

That was a relief. At least she wouldn't die.

"Please." Arthur gestured to the bowl of porridge and cup sitting next to her.

Trinity lifted the cup. She sipped the hot liquid, and it tasted like cherries. "Thank you. What is it?"

"It's my own mulled cherry wine. When was the last time you ate anything?" He asked.

"I honestly can't remember."

She shut her eyes, cringing as a painful throb clanged through her head. The image of the twin girls flashed behind her lids. She opened them immediately.

"Are you alright?" Arthur asked, taking the cup from her.

She wouldn't let him know how badly her head hurt. He wouldn't let her leave then. "Yes, I'm really sorry."

"Have your breakfast, and when you're strong enough, get dressed and join me in the living area to discuss your plans."

"I will and thank you again for caring for me."

***

Arthur sat at his table, reading over her uncle's paperwork. She could tell he wasn't happy about letting her go.

"When you arrived last night, I was packing and had planned to leave today for court. The king has requested my presence."

Trinity took the seat next to him. "I do apologize, sir."

Arthur interrupted her, "You have given me a serious dilemma." Arthur tapped the pages in front of him. "It would be best if you departed with me to court, where I could at least plead your case."

"But…" she interrupted, but he stopped her.

"Listen to me, child. The king will keep the lands you inherited until you're married, but you'd be safe. Cared for. I'm afraid the inheritance doesn't belong to you until you marry."

She opened her mouth to argue, but he held up a finger, stopping her from interrupting again. "And if you don't return to court after I file the papers, you'll be stripped of your inheritance. Young ladies may not go traipsing off alone. It's inappropriate and, frankly, quite dangerous. I already explained this to you last night, but I wanted to give you another chance to reconsider."

Arthur's words stung, but she wouldn't let him detain her.

"I need to go to York. It's where I was born, and it's something I must do. I have friends there."

"Who are these friends?"

"The Ellsworth. My father used to work for them, and I am positive they'd remember me."

Arthur sighed heavily and took his glasses off to clean them. "It is by my rights and the king's law to take you to court."

"I don't want to go. I'm not ready." Trinity interrupted.

"It doesn't matter what you want."

Tears sprang to her eyes, and she pushed her palms into them to stop them from falling.

Arthur walked to her side and took her hand. "I was your uncle's friend, and I understand your fears of court, but they are unfounded and reckless. You are forfeiting your rights to your inheritance unless the king forgives you, and you'd be lucky to be pardoned for such reckless and un-ladylike behavior." Arthur let out a long sigh, closed his eyes, and shook his head.

"And what if they can't find me?" she asked.

"If you're not found within a reasonable span, the inheritance shall by law become the rightful possession of the king. All claims shall be forfeited, and the court shall deem you as one departed from this life. You'll be left with naught."

Tears rolled down her face; she stopped fighting them, looked at Arthur, and pleaded. "Please, I'll only go for a short time and then return to court, I promise. You can hold my uncle's documents. You don't need to report anything straight away."

Trinity sat silently, watching Arthur contemplate her request. His breath heaved several times as he paced the small room in circles, his brows knitted together, and his mouth pinched.

Arthur ran his hand through his thinning grey hair. "I must leave post haste. I'll take your uncle's documents and not report them until end of spring," he conceded. "But you will travel with me as far as Windsor Castle. I'll find you a proper retinue for your journey. It will be easier from there."

"And money? Lodgings?"

He clicked his tongue and bent over the table, pulling out a piece of paper that was part of her uncle's papers. Arthur read over it, then grabbed another blank sheet of paper and his quill. "I'll write introductions to secure lodgings ahead of you, to the Abby's and at noble estates along the way.

He scribbled the names of several Abby and estates in cities she'd never heard of, folded it and handed it to her. "You'll stay in these places. They'll be expecting you."

"Thank you."

"Don't thank me yet. If I can't find a suitable retinue at Windsor to accompany you, I will not allow you this journey."

"I understand." Trinity tried to hide her disappointment and desperately hoped he'd find someone.

"I'll supply you a purse of silver for smaller purchases and a few gold coins for larger ones, but your uncle has already organized a writ of credit in your name, giving you access to funds in York." He scribbled onto another blank page, the sound of the metal quill scraping across the paper as he held his spectacles on his nose. "This is a letter of passage. Permitting you to travel."

"Thank you, Arthur. I promise to return to court by end of spring." Trinity clasped her hands together, relieved. "Thank you."

CHAPTER 6 ~ SYBIL
Feb 1349 - Ellsworth Manor

People imagined witches as haggard old crones—child-snatchers who cursed villagers over petty slights. Fairytales and nonsense.

Sybil cringed as Prudence, the new scullery maid, prattled on to Mrs. Bartlett. Another ridiculous tale about a so-called witch. She barely heard the words, but the smug certainty in Prudence's voice prickled her skin. If anyone resembled a witch, it was Prudence.

That word—witch—made Sybil's blood burn. Keeper of the Old Ways. Druid-kin. Elemental mage. Anything was better than, Witch.

"I'm telling you, she had wild black hair, and... skin as green as a goblin!" Prudence flapped a dishcloth like a battle flag. "And her eyes!" Prudence spun around to face Sybil; her brown eyes wide. "I swear, they were black as night!"

Sybil scoffed.

"It's true!" the girl insisted, then thankfully turned back to Mrs. Bartlett.

Sybil's fingers skimmed over her pale, milk-white arm. Her silver-blue eyes narrowed, locking onto Prudence with a sharp glare. Every word from the girl's mouth grated on her nerves.

Heat rose up her neck. She gritted her teeth, forcing herself to breathe.

Think of something else. Anything. Sybil winced. *At least it's warm.*

She hated the cold. The manor's kitchen was the only refuge from the brutal winter.

Mrs. Bartlett, hands on her wide hips, shook her head. "I doubt it was green, dear." She tucked a stray red curl back into her braided coil.

Sybil wished she was shapely like Mrs. Bartlett. People often commented that Sybil resembled a boy. But perhaps her actions contributed.

She shook off the negative thoughts as she stirred the pot hanging over the fire. None of it mattered. She had David. And she could forgive anything when she thought of him.

A smile tugged at her lips. The chatter faded into the crackle of flames. All she wanted was to curl into David's arms and feel the warmth of his muscular frame.

"David," she murmured under her breath, like his name was her salvation. She loved him beyond measure.

Her eyes fluttered shut, remembering the night before—how he pulled her back against his chest in his little room behind the stables, his breath hot against her neck, his lips brushing her cheek, her ear…

"That herring won't prepare itself!" She jumped as Mrs. Bartlett barked at her, sending a shock through Sybil's body.

"Yes, ma'am." She walked back to the table where the cold fish lay.

"Prudence, make up the dining room," Mrs. Bartlett ordered, uncovering a large loaf of rye bread.

"Yes, ma'am."

Sybil sighed in relief after Prudence disappeared.

Mrs. Bartlett chuckled. "You'll need to try harder, dear."

Sybil huffed out a laugh. "Sorry, am I so obvious?"

"Yes." Mrs. Bartlett chuckled and went back to cutting the loaf of bread. "She's only trying to be accepted."

"I'll try harder, I promise. It's just… The things she says are ridiculous!"

Sybil continued to scale the herring, blowing loose, curly hairs out of her face.

"She's young. They're only stories. Witches don't truly exist."

Sybil closed her eyes and took a breath. She wouldn't talk about this with Mrs. Bartlett. "Yes," she answered instead.

At Ellsworth Manor, everyone was Catholic and believed that women with visions or who used magic were evil witches—just like Prudence said. But Sybil wasn't evil, and she'd never harmed anyone.

She grimaced at the herring she scaled, trying to focus on the task.

"Have you always been a cook?" Sybil asked.

Mrs. Bartlett continued to slice the bread. "Since Sir Henry and Lady Susana arrived about seventeen years ago, I believe. Why do you ask?"

81

"Just curious."

"I was a scullery maid before I came here. Your grandmother, Lenora, got me an interview with Lady Susana, and I was hired on the spot."

"Same as me."

"Yes, Lady Susana respects Lenora a great deal."

"Grandmother has been close to the family for years, even when they lived at court. Did you know she delivered Michael there too?"

"I did, and the Queen's children too," Mrs. Bartlett said. "Your grandmother's a strange woman, but the best healer and midwife in the whole of England, I'd wager."

Sybil smiled at the compliment.

Footsteps echoed down the hall. The kitchen's massive wooden doors remained open. Lady Susana Ellsworth walked into the kitchen. She wore a stunning blue cotehardie with silver stitching and embroidery tied tightly under the bust. The neckline was square under her collarbone, and the long sleeves hung low. She clutched her thick fox fur-lined cloak at her neck. Her chestnut-colored hair coiled, pinned up in buns at both sides of her head, and covered by caul and a sheer white veil held in place by a small golden tiara. Despite the lack of guests, she appeared regal. Straight back, chin up, deep blue eyes forward.

But now, furrowed lines etched her forehead, and her usually full lips that smiled so often pinched tight.

"His lordship needs another tonic." Lady Susana stopped at the large table in the middle of the room and surveyed the supper preparations.

"I'll make one right away," Sybil said. Her herbal skills nearly matched her grandmother's.

She put the herring aside, quickly wiped her hands on the brown apron tied around her beige tunic dress and went to the cupboard where Mrs. Bartlett neatly stacked the jars of dried, and fresh herbs. She had purchased most of them from her grandmother's apothecary shop for Lady Susana and some more expensive imported roots from a merchant who visited York once a year.

"How is our lordship?" Mrs. Bartlett asked.

"He's improved, but the cough is still wet." Concern laced into her words.

Sybil took the cast-iron pot from the fire and poured the warmed mulled wine into a smaller pewter kettle, where she mixed mint, horehound, and a pinch of another ground powder she wasn't sure what it was. Her grandmother put it in everything. She placed the small kettle and a mug on a wooden tray.

"Thank you, Sybil. You're a godsend to us," Lady Susana said, glancing at the table, then to Mrs. Bartlett. "I'll dine with my husband. Elizabeth and the twins will dine in their rooms, so there is no need for a fuss."

"As you wish, m'lady." Mrs. Bartlett curtseyed.

Sybil felt sorry for Elizabeth. Their 22-year-old daughter, older than her brother Michael, was still unmarried.

Once, Sybil saw a vision of Elizabeth with a damp grey shawl hanging around her shoulders, looking down at her hands lovingly, which held a single pretty red rose with sharp thorns.

It made no sense to Sybil, leaving her frustrated. Thankfully, these visions impacted her less than the ones the Goddess Cailleach gave her.

Michael stayed at court since he'd been knighted. It was almost a year since his last visit.

The Ellsworth's youngest children were twin girls, Ruby and Rose, ran wild through the manor all day. Barely ten, loud, and untamed. Sybil overheard Sir Henry grumbling, "they'll never be fit for court."

And as if the girls knew Sybil had been thinking of them, a shriek and laughter echoed outside the kitchen, and Rose flew into the room, almost barreling into her mother, chased by her identical twin sister, Ruby. Rose, hysterically laughing, dodged her sister around the table in the middle of the room. Both girls wore matching green cotehardie dresses similarly styled to their mothers with dark wool fur-lined cloaks, but they were barefoot, and the bottoms of the dresses stained and dirty. The girls' chestnut brown hair was loose and wild down their backs.

"Ruby! Rose!" Lady Susana shouted. "Stop this instant!"

They skidded to a halt, and Ruby snatched the doll from Rose's outstretched hand and stuck her tongue out at her sister.

"Sorry, mama, we were just playing," Rose said. The girls cleverly feigned remorse.

"Where are your slippers?" Lady Susana shook her head, then touched a delicate hand on her neck. "Your feet will freeze!" She let out an exasperated breath.

Ruby and Rose both mumbled, "Um...."

"Go put them on immediately! I need to tend to your father; can you please stay out of mischief for the rest of the day?"

Both girls nodded, their faces colored with guilt.

"Sybil, carry the tray for me."

Sybil picked it up and followed her out of the kitchen. This was usually Olivia's job. Lady Susana's Lady's Maid.

"Is Olivia feeling alright, m'lady?" Sybil asked.

"She's gone into York. To see your grandmother. How is your grandmother?"

"She's well."

"That's good to hear. I'd like her to come to see Henry again. I've sent a message with Olivia."

They walked through the grand hall. The floor tiled with oak wooden floorboards, covered in chamomile scented rushes. Large wool tapestries hung on the walls, depicting different war scenes and landscapes. Six long, thin glass windows lined the wall behind the dais, where two cushioned armchairs sat empty upon a dark blue wool rug. The far wall's fireplace burned brightly; however, a chill lingered.

Two large chandeliers hung from the ceiling, burning candles scented with lavender. An extra expense Lady Susana insisted on having. She once told Sybil, "If I have to live in the country, at least my home doesn't have to smell like a paddock."

The torches lining the screen passage between the great hall and the entryway created an orange glow, and shadows moved along the walls as they passed.

"Did you know that Sir Henry was a childhood friend of the king?" Lady Susana often spoke of court, passing on sporadic bits of information here and there. Sybil could tell her ladyship missed it.

"I didn't, m'lady." She had but wouldn't let her think she was a gossip.

Lady Susana opened the screen passage door to the entryway, allowing the sun to shine through the high ceiling and long windows beside the great double oak doors. Stain glassed. Another gift from the king and breathtaking.

They made their way up the spiraling stairs to the residence.

"We've been here so long now…" Lady Susana said sadly. "I don't know what I'd do if anything happened to him." Lady Susana said, speaking of her husband.

She stopped outside their bedchambers. Her hands folded neatly in front of her; her eyes closed as if saying a prayer.

"It wasn't always easy when we first arrived," she continued softly. "I cried and begged him to return me to court, but he insisted I would eventually come to love it and would see what a wonderful home it could be."

"And it was, it is, m'lady." Sybil quirked her lips.

Lady Susana looked over her shoulder and smiled politely, tears in her eyes. "Yes, it is, but now we must help our lord recover because I don't want any of it without him."

"I understand."

Lady Susana pressed her fingers to her eyes, took a slow breath, and stepped into the bedchamber. Sybil followed.

Sir Henry was already sitting up, glaring. His mouth pinched as if he'd bitten into a sour plum, and his blue eyes were sharp with accusation. Loose waves of dark brown hair framed his shoulders, and his neatly trimmed chestnut beard added to the severity of his expression.

Beside him, old Joseph, the manor's steward, sat straight-backed with the accounts book on his lap. He managed everything—staff, garrison, land, taxes. Like Mrs. Bartlett, he had served the Ellsworth since they inherited the manor. Despite his age, nothing escaped him. As they entered, his sharp gaze lifted to them.

"Do not scowl at me, husband," Lady Susana said. "You too Joseph."

She pointed to the table beside his bed so Sybil could place the tray. "Thank you, Sybil. Please pour the tonic."

"Yes, m'lady."

Joseph closed the book and stood up to leave. "M'lady."

Lady Susana placed a hand on the large ledger. "Joseph, leave it. I want to look over it." She smirked. "How's my new system working out?"

His mouth tightened before he answered politely. "Adequate, m'lady." He laid the book down, giving Sir Henry a curt nod and then left them alone.

Lady Susana gave a small triumphant smile, walked to Sybil, and took the cup of tea from her.

She handed it to Sir Henry. "You must drink it to recover."

"I feel better already. I don't need to drink this concoction and stay in bed like an invalid!" Sir Henry's hand gestured around in front of him.

"You will stay in bed as long as I say." Lady Susana held the cup in front of him. "Take it."

Sir Henry took it and downed it quickly. His face crunched up. "It's horrible!" He handed it back. "So, I must be poisoned as well?"

"Henry, no one smokes this fifth here. I understand…" She took a deep breath before continuing, trying to calm her nerves, speaking in a controlled tone. "I understand that some cultures partake in such rituals, but we do not."

"I like it," he said, flatly.

"We are nobles. We do not… Smoke."

Henry scowled, waiving a hand.

"Lenora told it's blocking your lungs. It's making you sick and these herbs will fix it and hopefully ease the cough."

As soon as she mentioned his pipe, he looked for it at his bedside table, but it was gone. Lady Susana ordered Olivia to discard it which resulted in Sir Henry bellowing that had the servants scattering like mice.

His brows creased even further. "She's an old woman. What would she know?"

"More than you, old man!" Lady Susana clicked her tongue and glanced apologetically toward Sybil. "I have sent for Michael to return to help while you recover." Lady Susana sat beside her husband on the chair Joseph had been sitting in.

"No! You send another rider immediately and tell them I have recovered. He's only been knighted, and the king needs him there. What are you thinking?" He looked at her furious. "You can't do this!"

"I can, and I did! You have not recovered and cannot do your duties in your bed chambers. Michael can help and the king absolutely does not need him. Don't be ridiculous."

"I will not burden my son."

"He's old enough to take on these duties," she argued. "It's time, Henry!"

"I'm not in a damn grave, woman."

Lady Susana poured more tea, picked it up and handed it to him. "Then drink up, my love, or you may well be."

Sir Henry grabbed the mug, quickly gulped it down, and thrust it back at her. "Bah! No more!"

Lady Susana didn't bother hiding her smirk.

Sybil stood by the table, silent, waiting for dismissal. Then, the vision struck.

The edges of her sight blurred. Lady Susana and Sir Henry faded into a muted haze, the world around them greying like a gathering storm. A black mist coiled around Sir Henry, his face pale, a sickle resting against his shoulder.

Lady Susana's face twisted—haggard, red, and bloated. Tears streaked her cheeks. Her eyes bulged wide with terror.

It lasted only a moment. Then her vision cleared, and the room returned to normal.

"Sybil, pour another mug; then you may leave us."

Sybil tried to steady her hands as Lady Susana handed her the mug. It wasn't easy to look away from Sir Henry, the vision apparent. Death. After she handed Lady Susana another cup, she curtsied and excused herself.

They were good, kind people who treated her fairly. Knowing they would die brought tears to her eyes and made her chest tighten.

Instinctively exiting the room, she swept her hand downward. A gush of wind shut the door behind her, and she jumped, not realizing what she had done.

She needed to be more careful.

Although she knew the family cared for her, they'd throw her out and report her to the church as a witch if they ever found out what she was.

Sybil walked into the kitchen, shaken. Mrs. Bartlett fussed over supper, humming a pretty tune. Prudence was blessedly gone.

She returned to the herring on the table amongst the carrots and leeks.

"So, how is our lordship fairing?" Mrs. Bartlett turned her back to Sybil, chopping vegetables.

"He seems better. Upset, he's forced to stay in bed."

89

"If he's complaining, he must be recovering." There was a chuckle, then humming.

"I'm not so sure. He still looks sickly, and I think we should encourage Lady Susana to make him rest more, and perhaps Lady Susana should take a tonic as a precaution for herself, too," said Sybil.

"Lady Susana? I thought what Sir Henry wasn't catching. Has your grandmother said something?" Mrs. Bartlett turned worried eyes to Sybil.

"She hasn't, but they shouldn't take any chances."

Sir Henry and Lady Susana's deaths were inevitable, although she didn't know when. The thought ached. She just hoped Michael would return soon.

CHAPTER 7 ~ MICHAEL
Ellsworth

Michael slowed his horse, siding it next to Shaun's. "Thank god it's not raining or snowing." His breath curled into the air, faint and white in the cold.

Shaun refused to speak with him the entire way. Punishing Michael for forcing him to leave court.

"Yet! And it's still bloody freezing," Shaun grumbled, pulling his wool cloak tighter at his neck.

They followed the main dirt road to Ellsworth Village. A couple of miles from Ellsworth manor, his home.

As they entered the village, Michael and Shaun dismounted and an older woman hobbled towards them, using a cane to balance herself.

"It's wonderful you are home, m'lord," she said, taking his hands into her soft, wrinkled ones. "You've grown so much." She let go of him and patted Shaun's cheek. "You too, you little devil." Shaun beamed at the endearment.

91

"It's lovely to see you, Daphne. How are Joshua and Alex?" Michael asked about her husband and son.

Michael knew every tenant and their children by name-a lesson learnt from his father.

"My husband is cantankerous as ever. Still thinks you stole those apples, and Alex and his new wife, Angela, are in London visiting her family."

"Alex is married?" That shocked Michael. "Wait. The apples? Still? That was years ago, and I swear I wasn't the culprit." Michael laughed. It was Shaun who'd stolen the fruit as a dare. "I heard someone returned them the next day?"

Daphne chuckled and patted his hand. "The entire village celebrated your knighthood, m'lord. We are all very proud of you."

Shaun snorted then covered it with a cough, turning away to hide his smirk.

"Thank you, Daphne," Michael said softly.

"See you later, Daphne," Shaun called as he crossed the street with his mount to greet a few friends.

The old woman let out a soft huff, smiling. "That boy." She shook her head. "Anyhow, it's a comfort to us and your parents, that you've returned."

"That's very kind."

Daphne hobbled away and Michael turned back to the road. His horses pulling the reins up and down. She was tired and needed a feed.

"We're almost home, girl."

Midway through the village, the blacksmith, Johnathan Stonewell, approached Michael. His usual scowl set even deeper in his tanned, weathered face.

"Good day, m'lord. Welcome back," he said. His voice sounded rough as sandpaper, with a strong Scottish accent.

Michael shook his hand, a bone-breaking grip. "It is a good day to be home." He winced.

"I'm sorry then to give bad tidings, but I was hoping you'd speak with your father about a matter."

"What is this matter about?" Michael asked.

Shaun strolled up beside Michael. "Good day Johnathan."

"Good day Shaun," he said and shook his hand. "My cousin Jonah, from Scotland, went missing a few nights ago. He'd gone to York for drinks but never returned. Do you remember the lad? He's your age."

"Yes, I know him," Shaun said.

Michael frowned and put a hand on the older man's muscled shoulder. "I'll speak to father immediately," he said sincerely, praying it wasn't serious.

"Thank you, m'lord."

"I'll also ask around," Shaun added.

Michael nodded as the blacksmith turned and walked back to his shop.

After a few more greetings, they rode out, leaving the village behind.

***

As they arrived before the thick portcullis gate of Ellsworth Manor, two guards dipped their chins, hello. Michael's entire body relaxed.

An impressive defensive curtain wall surrounded the estate. Two gate guards manned the gate, and a dozen other guards walked the walls and guard towers. Two servants remained at the front doors of the manor, their eyes forward and pretending not to be watching them. It always unnerved him.

The three-story, multi-winged manor, initially white limestone, aged to light grey; ivy and lichen now cloaked the kitchen side walls, and large torrents were erected on either side of the front doors.

The grand estate had once belonged to the King's uncle, who'd passed away with no heirs and the king gifted it to Michael's father soon afterwards.

It was a large manor, but now it appeared smaller as he looked at it. After spending time at court, anything else looked dwarfed.

Ellsworth's master–of–horse, David, walked from the large stables to his right, greeting them with a smile. Michael enjoyed David's company far more than David's father, who was the previous master–of–horse. A grumpy, serious man. He'd passed away several years before.

Michael noticed David's light brown hair had grown out, and he'd put on some weight. Muscle, too.

"So much changed in a year." Michael dismounted and handed his horse's reins to David.

"Not that much," grumbled Shaun.

"Welcome home, m'lord," David said.

Shaun vaulted himself off his horse, legs sideways like a ten-year-old boy.

Michael just shook his head. "Thank you, David. How are things? You look well."

"I am. I'll be marrying Sybil soon."

"That's wonderful! I always thought you had something going with her," Michael teased.

"Thank you. Yes. We've been friends all our lives." David blushed, which surprised Michael.

"So, what other news?" Shaun asked.

David scowled, looking from Shaun to Michael. "There have been some problems with wolves. They attacked a couple of boys north of York, and a cousin of the blacksmith here in Ellsworth has gone missing."

Michael let out a breath. "I saw Johnathan on our way here, and he asked me to speak to father." He paused. "Wolves? We haven't had any incidents in years."

"I know. I've volunteered to help track them."

"If anyone can find them, it's you," Shaun said as he handed his reins to David.

Michael began to untie his travel bag from the saddle.

David walked around the horse. "Leave it. I'll have one of the grooms bring your belongings to your rooms.

"Not mine," Shaun said. "I'll be heading home shortly, so don't bother to unsaddle the old woman," Shaun said and patted the mare affectionately. "Just some water and oats."

"As you wish." David untied Michael's travel pack and set it on the floor. "So, how court life?" David asked as he began unbuckling the saddle.

"Well enough, better since I've been knighted. Squiring isn't for the faint of heart. Even for a lord's son," Michael said.

Shaun clasped Michael on the shoulder affectionately. "Yes. I've become a well-educated gentleman, and Michael a knight!" He said sarcastically, then walked away before Michael could retort. "Good to see you, David," Shaun called as he strode away.

David smirked, shaking his head.

"He's upset I forced him to come home." Michael put his hands up, shrugging, and cringing.

He jogged after Shaun into the main yard and glanced around to the left and laughed at the wild garden his mother tended herself with the help of their gardener, old man Dreyfus.

"Seems more plants have been added to the jungle," Shaun chided.

It was a mosh pit of herbs and vegetables interspersed with beautiful native flowers and fruit trees. Michael's mother even planted olive trees in the back and several varied species of vines for wine making. It looked more like a wild wonderland than a formal garden of nobility.

It was good to be home.

"Michael!" Ruby came running at full speed from the side of the manor.

A moment before impact, she threw herself at him so he could catch her, nearly knocking him over. He swung her around, laughing as her fur-lined cloak streamed behind her. He glanced at her blue cotehardie dress, covered in dirt and her boots in mud. Her chestnut brown wavy hair was uncombed, a wild mess as it flew in the air.

He closed his eyes, a broad smile on his face.

"I'm so happy your home!" she shrieked.

Rose wasn't far behind, dragging an overflowing wicker basket full of flowers from the garden on her arm. She looked as filthy as her sister, but at least she pulled her hair back in a rough plait.

Michael sat Ruby down, lifted the basket from Rose, and wrapped his other arm around her waist, lifting her into a tight squeeze. She let out an ear-shattering shriek.

"Put me down, you brute!" Rose smacked his arm, laughing.

"Does mama and papa know your home?"

"Not yet. I only just arrived." Michael gently set her on her feet.

Shaun sauntered up next to Michael. "Where're my hugs?"

Both girls wrapped their arms around Shaun, giggling.

"I see your mother hasn't been able to tame you monsters." Shaun teased them as Michael handed the basket to Rose.

"She tries." Rose frowned.

"Well, you should try to ease her moods while I'm here, please," Michael said in his big brother's voice.

The girls laughed. "Moods?" They said together.

Michael sighed, and Shaun chuckled.

"Come on then. I want to see father," Michael said, a little nervous.

Both girls sobered. "He's in his parlor. He gave us a fright, you know," said Ruby.

"But mama says he's on the mend," Rose finished.

They walked up the manor's steps, and the servants silently opened both doors to allow them to enter. The enormous double wooden doors closed behind them loudly, echoing through the foyer.

It was a wide hall with lofty ceilings, chandeliers hanging with lit candles, and beautiful tapestries on every wall.

Two maids curtsied as he passed, then ran up the spiraling staircase to his right.

He sighed and watched them disappear into the resident's section of the manor; desperately wanting to retire to his bedchambers, but he had to see his father first.

Double wooden doors, flanking the right of the entry, opened into his mother's parlor. A guest waiting room occupied the left.

From the manor's distant kitchen, the aroma of baking bread reached him, and he groaned. Hunger gnawing at his stomach.

"Are mother and father expecting guests?" he pushed open the doors to the screen passage and let the girls enter first. Shaun at his side.

Rose and Ruby giggled at the same time, and it made Michael grin stupidly. He loved their laughter. "Papa would never... Mama knew you'd arrive today." Ruby explained.

"She told us this morning," Rose added. "Oh, and Fleur Devonshire is staying with us. Mama is tutoring her while her mother and father attend court in France.

"I see," Michael said, thinking about the last time his mother and father argued about having a guest.

His father's words burned in his mind, making Michael chuckle. "I've had a belly full of court life and have no more appetite for it any longer."

Certain aspects remained constant; however, managing a ward was new. It didn't take much to figure out why. She wanted him to marry Fleur.

"The same Fleur your mother and father desperately want you to wed?" Shaun said, not trying to hide his amusement.

"Yes," Michael said, preferring to drop the subject. Spending time together always ended poorly for them. Her beauty was undisputed; however, she was humorless and frigid. She called him childish and unintelligent.

"When did she arrive?" Shaun asked.

"Only a few days ago," Ruby said.

"How long is she staying?" Shaun elbowed Michael in the side and wiggled his eyebrows.

"A couple months, I think. She doesn't really like it here."

That made Michael pause before entering the great hall. "Why wouldn't she be happy here?" he asked, silently offended by Fleur already.

"She says it's too cold and has no, um..." Rose paused, thinking of the word.

"No culture," Ruby said and lifted her chin, her eyes narrowed.

"What's culture?" Rose asked, her brows pinched in confusion.

"I have not a clue, but obviously we lack it," Ruby huffed.

Shaun laughed, and Michael chuckled but bristled inside. "Is Mrs. Bartlett well?" Michael asked, quickly changing the subject and ignoring Shaun's huff.

"Yes. She made us small cakes," Rose answered him.

"Why isn't father in his bedchambers?" Michael asked.

"You know, papa." The girls chorused together, rolling their eyes. "He's stubborn as a mule! Mama says so." They both pushed the heavy doors to the great hall open.

Michael chuckled and followed them inside.

His father being up indicated improvement. That was promising.

An empty, oversized chair with a smaller chair next to it, sat at the end of the great hall; fur lined and with pillows. A sizeable fireplace on one wall warmed the manor's largest room. His family crest hung on a tapestry behind the chairs, and on both sides of the crests, long narrow stained-glass windows shone lightly from outside.

Large trestle tables were being assembled for supper, and Michael could smell something rich and decadent wafting through the air, making his stomach grumble with anticipation. It had been too long since he had a good home cooked meal.

Joseph exited a side door of the parlor, carrying a heavy book and papers.

"Michael. You've returned. How wonderful! Your father will be pleased." He smiled at Michael.

"Hi, Joseph!" both the girls sang out together.

"Hello, m'ladies," he bowed respectfully. "Good day to you, Shaun." He stood and gave Shaun a slight nod.

"It's a pleasure to see you, Joseph," Shaun said.

Michael loved Joseph; he'd been like a grandfather to him. He was a strict man but genuinely cared about the family, and Michael trusted him completely.

"Father still has you working like a dog?" Michael nodded towards the pile of records and the large tomb in Joseph's arms.

"Oh, it's nothing, truly."

"Thank you, Joseph," Michael said, and Joseph walked away, lugging the book and papers with him.

His father's parlor offered refuge from daily burdens. Michael spent many hours there, discussing his future, duties, and responsibilities. He missed it more than he realized.

Inside, Michael wasn't surprised to see his sister, Elizabeth, arguing with his father. She abruptly closed her mouth when she saw them come in. His father lay reclined on a daybed that someone had brought in. Elizabeth stood beside him, glowering down at him, with her hands fisted on her hips.

His mother and Fleur sat quietly to his father's other side, with their needlepoint in hand, calmly ignoring the two as usual.

Sybil politely nodded and excused herself.

100

He'd only met her briefly. Several times, Michael spotted her in the stables flirting with David, and he always thought they were up to mischief. He was right, after all. He smirked as he watched her close the door.

His mother was on her feet. A smile lit up her face, and tears springing into her soft blue eyes while Fleur stayed seated and briefly looked up to scowl at him. Her golden blonde hair coiled under a transparent white lace veil. Her porcelain skin and her expression reminded him of an ice princess. Fitting as it was the color of her eyes.

"Michael! You're home!" His mother walked to him gracefully, taking his hands and kissing both cheeks. "How we've missed you so."

Michael couldn't believe how much she'd aged. Her beauty remained exceptional, yet grey streaks now appeared within her chestnut hair, and wrinkles formed near her eyes. Immaculately groomed, his mother still maintained the current fashion of the courts, even though they lived in the country.

"Are you well, mother?" He asked. She looked tired.

She tsked at him, "Is that how you greet me? Do I look so wretched?"

As usual, Shaun saved the day. "Lady Susana, you look as radiant as a glorious sunrise."

His mother let out a soft, heartfelt laugh. "You flatterer! Oh, it's so good to see you too, Shaun." She took his hands into her own and squeezed them affectionately.

While they greeted his mother, Michael noticed his sister had gone quiet. She and their father waited politely. He walked to them, his mother retaking her seat next to Fleur.

"Elizabeth, it's always good to see you." He kissed her cheek and glanced at Fleur. "Fleur, nice to see you again." Then faced his father, not waiting for a reply from her. "Father, you look well. I was worried you fared worse. I'm relieved."

"I told your mother not to send for you. I am perfectly able to manage things." His father said as he rose slowly. Too slowly.

He stood a head taller than Michael, a formidable man even for his age. His father trimmed his chestnut-colored beard just above his chest and tied his wavy dark locks back away from his face.

Michael noticed more grey than brown in his father's hair and it had receded since the last time they saw each other. Some things indeed had changed.

His father wrapped his arms around Michael with more strength than Michael imagined he would be able to.

"It is a great day; my son has returned to us though; I have missed you."

Michael pulled back. "I've missed you all as well. Truly, are you better, father?"

Mother cut in. "He's far too ornery to allow anything to keep him in his bedchambers for long." She huffed but looked at his father affectionately. "Thank God for his stubbornness."

His father released Michael, turning his attention to Shaun. "Shaun, by god, son, it's impossible that you've grown even taller!" he boomed and shook Shaun's hand. "They must be feeding you well at court, hey?"

"Indeed, they do, m'lord," Shaun said, smiling, and nodded hello at Elizabeth and Fleur. His gaze lingering on Fleur. "It's nice to see you again Elizabeth and what a wonderful surprise, Fleur."

Elizabeth stood straight-backed and swiped a hand across her light blue dress. "Thank you, Shaun," she said.

"It's a pleasure to see you as well, Shaun Donaldson." Fleur replied.

Michael noticed the two held each other's gazes a moment longer than he thought appropriate. Fleur didn't smile at Shaun, but she seemed far more amicable towards Shaun than him.

"Was I interrupting something important?" Michael noticed his sister's mouth was still pinched as she fidgeted with her hands.

Elizabeth sighed, and Michael thought she had given up whatever fight she was waging with their parents. Only for a moment, though.

"Mother and Father refuse to allow me and Fleur to attend a soirée in York unless properly chaperoned, and mother doesn't want to leave father, and you were due home, so they insisted on Joseph, smelly old Joseph, chaperone!" She crossed her arms and narrowed her blue eyes at their father like he was the enemy.

Michael laughed, picturing Joseph's face as if he'd been there, and glanced at Fleur who hadn't looked up from her needlepoint.

"It's truly not amusing, Michael!" Elizabeth said.

"Then I have the perfect solution. I shall be your chaperone." Michael bowed towards his sister. Looking up, he gave her a wink. "Is this acceptable?"

"Better than old Joseph! Thank you, brother." Elizabeth uncrossed her arms, kissed him on his cheek, and then walked to the door. "Be ready after supper, and dress in something a little nicer."

He smiled; his sister's criticism gave him comfort. "Of course, dear sister."

She just lifted her shoulder. "Come Fleur," she said without even looking at the girl. Fleur sat her needlepoint down and stood. "Excuse me, m'lady, m'lord," she said demurely, then scurried after Elizabeth without a single glance in Michael's direction.

The twins had quietly disappeared, unbeknown to anyone.

Michael sat opposite his father; in the chair Elizabeth had recently occupied.

"Father, I was worried. There were rumors of sickness in London, taking many lives. I rode as fast as I could, afraid it could be the same."

Shaun turned to Michael and put his hand on his shoulder. "I should take my leave to see mother."

Michael's father turned to Shaun. "I give you my thanks for accompanying my son home. It is always good to see you, but you need to know Isabella has been ill of late as well."

Shaun paled. "I didn't know, m'lord."

"You didn't receive word?" mother asked.

"No, m'lady."

Henry smiled at Susana, then at Shaun. "My wife has told me Isabella is recovering, but she's been lamenting about her loneliness."

Susana reassured Shaun, "I visit her as often as I can. You are her only child, and managing the shop has been a struggle, but she is so proud of you. Your return will surely strengthen her."

"Thank you, I'll take my leave now, knowing you are both in good health." Shaun stood and left them, walking as fast as he could without bolting from the room.

Both his parents looked at Michael.

"What is this talk of sickness in London?" his father asked.

"Young men rode from London to court; they informed us of it," Michael said. "Has there been any strange sickness here or in York?"

"No, there's been nothing here or in York. Only the normal afflictions during winter. Coughs, colds..." Henry said then scoffed. "I had a cold in my chest, and Lenora convinced your mother the cause was my pipe. It's ridiculous! It's been a freezing winter, but as you can see, I've recovered."

"I'm not so convinced she is wrong, husband," Susana said, narrowing her eyes at Henry over her needlework.

"Father, Johnathan Stonewell, from the village, stopped us on our way through the village. He claimed that his cousin, Jonah visiting from Scotland, disappeared a few nights ago, and they searched for him but haven't found his whereabouts."

"Yes, David informed me, and I told the sheriff, but he's found nothing." He paused, then shook his head. "I'm afraid it looks like he ran off, although I don't know why." His father scratched his beard and narrowed his eyes. "It's bad business, that is. Not the thing to do to one's family. They're worried sick."

"Yes, indeed," Michael said. "I also heard about the two young boys from the north."

"Wolves are hunting in the forests, so I've put a curfew in effect for our villagers. No one out after dark."

Michael couldn't shake the cold chill creeping up his spine.

"I hope they find the pack soon."

"Me too, son."

Michael cleared his throat, trying to think of a delicate way to address his next issue. "Why is Fleur here?"

His mother sat straight-backed and looked pointedly at his father. "Did you receive my message?"

"Yes, mother, right before we departed." Michael cringed.

"I've spoken to her mother, and we've decided the two of you have wasted enough time dancing around each other, and it's time to get to know one another, properly."

"She cannot stand me and truthfully, I find her extremely disagreeable."

"Michael, that is unkind," his mother said.

"Mother, I mean no disrespect but…"

His father smacked the wooden arm of the daybed. "The matter is settled. I expect you to spend time with the girl. Get to know her." Henry glanced at Susana. "Perhaps dance with her tonight."

"Father, please. I agreed to chaperone, but I do not agree to this."

"I'm not asking, Michael. Be chivalrous." His father pursed his mouth tight and gave Michael the look he always did right before Michael would argue about something his father asked him to do.

"Yes, Father."

CHAPTER 8 ~ MICHAEL
York

The soirée took place at one of York's largest estates. Michael wasn't well acquainted with the family. They were from London. A large family of four girls and two boys. The eldest son a few years older than himself. However, his court duties prevented him from spending much time with any of them.

Carriages lined the circular driveway, unloading elegantly dressed guests. Dozens of candle lamps illuminated the manor's facade, and the front garden, trimmed to perfection, put his mother's garden to shame.

As they pulled forward, Michael watched men and women ascend the stairs to the open doors. A flicker of anxiety surfaced. At court, Shaun's presence eased the pressure. Tonight, he was alone.

The carriage halted. The door swung open. He stepped out, then helped his sister and Fleur. They walked in silence, but he caught the tremor in his sister's breath.

"Are you nervous, sister?"

"Don't be ridiculous," she said and hurried ahead of him.

She dressed elegantly in a beautiful deep blue gown with gold embroidery from the bust to the bottom, like flowers fluttering in the wind. Her dark brunette hair was curled and pinned up, covered with a gold caul. Quite pretty.

Fleur walked straight back and confidently next to Elizabeth, wearing a similar gown but far less filigree embroidered on her dress and her hair braided and coiled at her nape covered with a caul. She didn't spare Michael the slightest glance.

He stepped beside Elizabeth. "Are you sure everything is alright, sister?" He whispered. "We don't have to go."

"It's fine. Stop worrying." She replied, pulling her shoulders back, lifting her chin higher, and smiling. "These things can be difficult sometimes, but I promise you I do not want to leave."

He patted her hand where it rested on his arm.

Introductions complete, they moved to the room's edge. He scanned the crowd for familiar faces but recognized no one. It was still early—more guests would arrive. Hopefully, the night would prove exciting but without Shaun, it would be tough. His sister had the right of it. These events could be most difficult. Even for him.

Elizabeth glanced around anxiously as the music swelled. The vast hall shimmered under golden chandeliers, hundreds of candles casting a soft glow, scented with roses. Furniture lined the walls, a massive extravagant rug covering the floor for dancing. People mingled, though most lingered near the edges.

Nicole Moore

"Shall I get us a drink?" he asked.

"Yes, please," Elizabeth said, eyes fixed on the front door. Fleur gave a small nod.

Michael frowned at his sister's odd behavior but left without comment.

When he returned, a red-haired man, about Elizabeth's height and build, stood beside her. He wore a dazzling frock jacket; his hair tied back with a golden ribbon. They whispered, and Elizabeth laughed at something he said. Fleur remained nearby, looking utterly bored.

"Hello," Michael said, handing his sister, then Fleur, a glass of wine.

"Brother, I'd like to introduce Theodore Canmore," she said, a smile lighting up her face. "Theo, this is my brother, Michael.

"From the Canmore clan up north?" Michael asked. Theo's father, Robert, was Scottish; his mother, Amelia, was English.

A long-standing, unspoken feud divided Theodore's father and Michael's father. They hated each other. This would be a disaster.

"That's correct."

Theo gestured towards his mother, speaking with a circle of older women. "Mother was gracious enough to attend tonight."

She had long strawberry blonde hair, fair skin—pretty, but severe. Her gaze flicked to them; eyes narrowed. Not too pleased, either.

"How long have you two known each other?" Michael asked.

Theo and Elizabeth exchanged a look so sickeningly love-struck that Michael fought the urge to groan.

Oh God.

They responded together, erupting in laughter. Michael rolled his eyes. Fleur, beside him, looked equally unimpressed, narrowing her eyes at them.

"Please, you go ahead," Elizabeth said, blushing so hard her face nearly matched the roses in the vases next to them.

"We met last year at another ball and started writing to each other," Theo said. "We've often bumped into each other at the market and a few other parties."

Michael barely had time to process that before Elizabeth cut in. "Michael, Theo has made his intentions clear. He wants to marry me."

Straight to the point. So very like her.

Michael's mouth dropped open. "This is… unexpected," he said, biting back a laugh.

He turned to Theo. "Do your parents approve?"

Theo glanced at his mother, who was watching them closely now. "Mother said that if your father agreed, she could get my father to agree." Theo instinctively took Elizabeth's hand in his own. "I love your sister with all my heart and can provide for her a good life. I would never hurt her or leave her wanting."

He seemed so incredibly sincere and naïve that it surprised Michael even more. "How do you feel about this, Elizabeth?" He asked.

"I've loved Theo for as long as I can remember, and I'd give anything to marry him. Please, Michael, you must help me convince Father." She looked at Michael pleading. "Fleur promised to try to sway Mother."

Michael lifted an eyebrow at Fleur. "You knew about this?"

She lifted her chin a touch higher. "Yes, I did, and I believe it is a fine match."

"How would you know?" His words escaped him before he thought better of it.

"Michael, don't be rude!" Elizabeth scolded him. "I have told her everything."

Michael let out a deep sigh. "Alright." He turned back to Theo. "Do you collaborate with your father in the family business?" Michael asked Theo.

"Yes, but I've been training with the bailiff here, learning about taxes and numbers. I will take over the business eventually, as I am the oldest, but initially, we would live in the estate, in town. It's more modest than our family manor but would give us privacy and a place to start our own family."

So, the boy was clever and totally in love with Elizabeth.

Michael knew he wasn't getting out of this trap and had to convince his father. It indeed did seem a good match and a way to end the feud. "I'll help you with Father." He agreed. "But Theo, you must also do your share of convincing. Father will want to meet with you."

Elizabeth handed her glass to her soon to be betrothed, Michael almost groaning at the thought, and she hugged her brother, smiling. He'd never seen her look so happy. He noted a slight smile on Theo's mother's lips, too. At least he wouldn't be on his own in this battle.

"Shall we dance then?" Theo asked, holding his hand out to Elizabeth.

"Yes, please."

They disappeared into the growing crowd of people on the dance floor, leaving him with Fleur. He thought of his father, telling him to dance with Fleur, but he couldn't bring himself to do it. He hated dancing and especially didn't want to with her.

They stood next to each other, sipping their wine silently. After several moments of uncomfortable silence, Michael drained the rest of his sister's drink, set it on a table nearby, and extended his hand to Fleur.

"Shall we?"

"I'm not interested," she said sharply.

"To dance with me, or to dance in general?"

Fleur huffed.

"Why do you despise me so?" he asked.

"As you loathe me?" She rolled her eyes and sipped her wine, letting her gaze follow the flow of dancing couples.

Moments passed, and Michael caught Fleur's foot tapping. He could see she wanted to partake, and a pang of guilt sat in his stomach. Perhaps he did behave disagreeably, but the woman didn't strike him as sensitive—quite the contrary.

"You told me I was ignorant and boring," he blurted out.

"You are."

"Why would you agree to come back then, knowing our parent's intentions for us to marry, if you found the prospect so repugnant?"

Fleur exhaled twice before responding. "I had no choice. Just as you have none, either."

This was true. His father would insist and make the marriage contract whether he agreed or not.

"I do not desire you, nor do I see myself ever loving you," Fleur said.

"Is there someone else you love?" Michael saw a slight twitch in her jaw and knew he nailed it. Her affection belonged elsewhere, and her parents disapproved. "That is why you are here," he said, putting it together.

"Lord Henry sent a message to my father first, giving my father an excuse to send me away."

"I'm sorry, Fleur."

"I do not need your pity or want it," she hissed. "It doesn't matter. None of it."

A part of Michael thawed towards her, knowing she was there as much against her will as his. Neither of them wanted the marriage.

"And you called me an ice queen with no soul, if I remember correctly," she murmured.

"I'd like to apologize for my insensitive remarks, but you are quite indifferent, m'lady."

"Perhaps because I do not fancy you, and you're used to the ladies throwing themselves at your feet."

Michael laughed loudly. "I am unsure where you got that notion."

They stood in silence for several moments before Fleur gave in and lifted her hand. "I suppose we should appease your father's wishes."

"You will dance with me?" Michael startled.

"Quickly, before I change my mind."

Michael took her hand and felt something akin to nausea settle in his stomach. She wasn't repulsive. In fact, she was quite beautiful, but she made his insides curdle.

"This doesn't mean I like you," she said as they approached the dance floor.

"That's alright with me, as I feel the same about you, Fleur."

CHAPTER 9 ~ SYBIL
York

Sybil settled onto the cushioned bench beside Lenora, fingers curling around the edge of the wood table. To her left sat David, posture relaxed but eyes alert, and next to him, his mother Evelyn—ever elegant, her pale gown stiff with embroidery and shoulders held high as if bracing for battle rather than discussion.

Directly across, Lenora's younger sister, Leigha, kept her head down, hands busy with a needlepoint. Wild strands of raven-black hair spilled in thick, unruly waves past her waist, catching flashes of firelight. A pair of silver rings glinted on her slender fingers. Despite the calm task, there was something restless in the way she worked, like a spell woven into each loop and stitch.

At the far end of the table, Duncan stood in silence, not seated, his figure half-swathed in shadow near the window. Broad-shouldered and lean, with golden hair pulled back in a leather tie, he remained still as a statue, watchful. His hazel eyes lingered on Sybil until their gazes met. She held his stare for a moment, searching for a reason behind his presence. Duncan never attended coven meetings. Without a word, he turned his attention elsewhere, his expression unreadable, his jaw tight.

A quiet murmur came from further down the bench. Lucas leaned toward Enzo, whispering something with a crooked grin. Enzo's face twisted into a scowl, eyes dark and piercing under a heavy brow. Unlike Lucas, whose every gesture radiated mischief, Enzo carried tension in his shoulders—always the brooding one, serious and sharp-edged. The twins mirrored each other only in bone structure. Everything else diverged.

Three women sat to Enzo's left—Fey, Wanda, and Leanne—cousins of Sybil's grandmother and as tall as legends. Each wore deep green cloaks clasped with matching obsidian brooches. Faces weathered yet striking. Braids of dark-brunette hair hung like ropes down their backs, some streaked with silver, others still untouched by time. Silent, dignified, they resembled ancient statues come to life.

Next to Fey sat someone unfamiliar. A stranger, yet not. His presence struck like a bell in Sybil's memory. Late twenties, perhaps, with broad shoulders and calm composure that didn't match the tension in the room. Thick waves of black hair framed a sculpted face. Skin the color of pale ash. Then the eyes—silver-blue, like mirrors in moonlight. The same as hers.

Nicholas.

The name stirred something sharp and buried. Fey's only son, exiled long ago, sent to live among his father's kin in Ireland after the council had deemed his shadow magic too volatile. His magic had frightened them. Even now, a subtle weight clung to the air around him.

He sat perfectly still, watching no one, yet aware of everything.

He wasn't supposed to return.

And yet—there he was.

"So, after all these years, the demons return," Fey scoffed.

"We believe so," Lenora said, nodding toward Sybil. "And our goddess mother, Cailleach, has given a vision to Sybil."

Nicholas tilted his head, studying her. "You're the one with visions, like the oracle?" His voice was deep, rough—feral. The sound made the hairs on her neck rise.

She swallowed. "I have visions, but they're more like symbols. Not like the oracles, unless Cailleach touches me."

Lenora clapped her hands, cutting her off. Sybil shut her mouth, face burning as Nicholas smirked.

"Tell them what our mother goddess has shown you, Lenora said and Sybil cheeks flush for the second time.

She wasn't used to having so much attention on her or discussing her gifts openly.

"I had a vision of a woman gifted with the strength of a seraph. She had wings and wielded a shield and a blue flaming sword. She screamed a name. Baal. With him were blood mages, and a horde of demons I've never seen before. Sybil swallowed hard; her mouth suddenly dry. "Our mother Goddess Chailleach said we have been betrayed."

"An angel?" Nicholas smirked. "You mean Fae?"

Wanda cleared her throat throwing her son a disapproving look, "Betrayed?"

"Yes." Sybil tried to press on, but everyone started speaking at once. Arguing about who could have betrayed them, who the girl was, the darkborn prophecies were thrown around the table.

The voices grew so loud Sybil couldn't follow one thread, and her heart began to race.

Lenora slammed her fist on the table several times, rattling it, but it quieted everyone down.

"Let my granddaughter finish!"

Sybil coughed, "Excuse me." She swallowed again. "I believe the girl is crucial to the coming war and we must find and help her."

"You believe or you have a vision?" Fey asked, lifting an eyebrow.

Heat spread up Sybil's neck and over her cheeks. This was the difficult part of her visions, even the one's she received from Chailleach. Interpreting the flow of thoughts and feelings that accompanied each one.

"It's a knowingness," she said quietly. "And with the rising number of ghouls—more than we've ever seen— suggests a powerful necromancer is here."

Fey tsked. "A necromancer doesn't always create those monsters. You should know that, but Baal, is another matter. He's the strongest of all the demon princes. And who would dare betray us?"

Sybil glanced at Lenora, who answered for her. "One or two ghouls rising alone is normal. But dozens at once? That requires control. And it's anyone's guess who has betrayed us, but if Baal is creating an army, we can all ascertain that it is one of the keepers of the veil."

Arguments broke out around the table. Outrage and disbelief. A keeper of the veil was one of their most holy men.

It was impossible.

Lenora pulled the book of prophecies out and set it on the table with a thud.

Her voice boomed around the room, "Remember the oracle's prophecy: When the breath of death curls through the streets and hides its face, the crows shall feast, and the soil shall sour. Light will falter, and the faithful shall fall—but one will carry the flame that will rise against the darkness."

She leaned back; hands folded in her lap. Everyone chewing it over.

"The prince of pestilence is Baal," Evelyn said.

"And the girl in Sybil's vision, the one who will carry the flame." Fey said, eyes narrowed.

"And he's leading this army of...?" Wanda asked, eyebrows lifted high, her mouth pinched.

"We do not know." Lenora unwrapped the cloth-covered bundle in front of her, carefully unfolding it. She lifted a thick slab of black obsidian. "I need it cut into weapons with steel—blades, arrowheads, and spears, then warded."

She passed it to Evelyn, who then handed it to David and the others.

"How much do you have?" Nicholas asked.

"Enough for our army." Lenora folded her hands and watched as Nicholas inspected the stone.

Wanda gestured for Nicholas to give her the obsidian and turned it over in her hand, inspecting it closer, then handed it over the table to Duncan.

Duncan checked the obsidian's weight.

"Duncan has the oracle given any more information, at all?" Wanda asked.

"No."

"No?" she parroted.

Duncan raised one eyebrow, ignoring her as he continued to inspect the stone.

Silence settled as Duncan passed the obsidian to the twins and then Sybil. She ran her fingers over the cold, smooth surface—magic tingled through her fingertips, snaking down her arms.

She handed it back to her grandmother.

Lenora wrapped it and sighed. "There's more."

Sybil anticipated the announcement, cringing. She still had a tough time believing it.

"The London coven is gone. They've been killed or scattered, but no one has heard anything in weeks since my last letter from them. A plague has hit London and all the cities in the south."

"That's impossible!" Fey said as the table erupted with concerned arguments.

"You must be mistaken!" Wanda said.

"I'm not," Lenora said, her voice booming across the room once more. Everyone fell silent again. "Someone I trust, sent me a letter saying that their god has forsaken them, and the devil rules those lands now."

"That's preposterous!" Fey said. Her eyes narrowed as she shook her head no. "They are the strongest coven in the whole of England!"

"Not anymore," Evelyn said in a hushed voice.

She was usually the quiet, reserved one, but the news had hit her hard when Lenora had told them a couple weeks before. Her departed husband, David's father, was from the London coven until he left to join Evelyn in York many years before. The London coven never forgave him. Or her.

"There's also the issue of Johnathon Stonewell's cousin, Jonah, who's gone missing in York," David said. "The guards talk to me, and there have been several other disappearances in York recently."

"It's true. I've heard the same," Enzo added. "Young men don't just run away."

Lenora held her cousins' eyes. "With the oracle's prophecy and Sybil's vision, along with the plague hitting London, we need to prepare for war. Train everyone how to fight and create the warded weapons. I seek the agreement of this coven to summon the other covens to aid us."

"We don't even know what demons we'll be facing," Nicholas pointed out, and he was right. They didn't. Besides the ghouls, and if a necromancer was in York, creating them, then a blood mage was here, controlling them. And Baal would be here soon.

"If they wiped out the London coven, they will be powerful," Evelyn said, sadness tinging her voice. "Ghouls could not do this."

Fey huffed an irritated breath. "Again, it doesn't help. That narrows it down to what? Hundreds of different demons! Maybe all of them?"

"I can consult the oracle and see if she will give me any more information," Duncan offered.

But Sybil knew it was a slim chance. The oracle gave cryptic prophecies, rarely elaborating; destiny, it seemed, was governed by personal choice.

"Do I have your agreement?" Lenora asked.

Everyone said yes. Even Fey, who was irritated beyond measure, agreed.

"Nicholas will stay and train the others. There's been too many years of complacency! These young ones have no idea what's in store for them." Fey said sharply, then stood up to leave. "Come, we have much to do."

120

She gestured for her sisters to exit, then paused at the doorway. "Lenora, any sense of when?"

"No, but if they already attacked London, and with Sybil's vision, I could only guess it will not be long before it finds its way here. I will send the summons to all the covens immediately."

"It'll take weeks to organize everyone," Nicolas said. "And to train the others who have never fought in battle before."

"We can only do what we can, boy," Lenora said"

Fey huffed out a breath, then followed her sisters out.

"Nicholas, you'll stay here with me. I have plenty of spare room," Lenora said.

"Thank you."

"David, you will work with Nicholas. Organize training schedules. I know you're busy at Ellsworth, but I'm sure they can make do without a stable boy a few days a week."

"Grandmother, he's no longer the…" Sybil tried to correct her grandmother, but David cut her off.

"I'll come on my day off and at night," David said, clutching Sybil's hand under the table and giving it a gentle squeeze.

"Enzo, Luca, you both are the most trained, but not for what's coming." Lenora sighed deeply and shook her head. "I want you training every day with Nicholas."

"What can I do, grandmother?" Sybil asked.

"Start making the protective amulets I taught you to make when you were younger. Make one for everyone at Ellsworth, then as many as you can for others. We can sell them at the market."

Sybil's mouth fell open. "But it takes weeks, even months, to get them right, and they must be bathed in the light of the full moon to have full strength."

"As I said before, child, we can only do what we can."

Duncan stood up to leave but looked hesitantly around the table. "The oracle has asked me to relay another message, specifically to you, Lenora, but I was told to wait until the other ladies departed."

"Let's hear it then," Lenora snapped.

"Seek the one blessed with the strength of the God, Tiw. Eyes of new grass and verdant gold. Hair black as obsidian. He will find darkness in the young moon's light in the forest that bleeds. The fates have woven the threads together."

"I think that's tonight," Luca said. "Might be wrong, though. Clouds are dense."

"It is tonight," Lenora said. "And it's the forest with all the Alder trees."

Everyone rose except Lenora. "Enzo, Luca, Nicholas, go with David and Sybil."

***

Luca nudged his horse forward into the forest, leaving the open trail behind them. Sybil moved next to him. David and Enzo behind them, with Nicholas at the rear.

Luca glanced back over his shoulder then leaned closer to Sybil. "Mother said that a man with the strength of Tiw." He paused; forehead crumpled in thought. "The God of War." He huffed a small laugh. "I wonder who this man is that's so strong?"

"I don't know, but it would be helpful if we could see the moon." Sybil rechecked the sky, but the clouds moved above them like a thick blanket. The cold caught their breaths, turning it to a pale mist around them.

Luca looked up at the cloud-covered sky. "Mother is almost always right with her predictions, and I'm pretty certain it's a young moon tonight."

"Maybe it's tomorrow night?" She spoke. She hadn't felt any sign of demons—no stomach pains.

"Perhaps."

They rode further into the forest for another hour, and Sybil thanked the Gods it wasn't raining. But it was freezing, and every time they spoke, plumes of smoke accompanied their words.

"I think we should turn back," said Luca blowing heat into his cupped hands.

"Shh, quiet for a minute," Enzo said as he tilted his head. "I hear something."

"I don't hear anything," Luca whispered.

Then Sybil felt it. Nausea swept through her, her stomach cramped up, and this time, she couldn't hold it in and leaned over and vomited. "Oh gods," she moaned.

The men drew their swords as Luca's palm ignited with white flame, casting flickering light around them. Something barreled toward them—fast.

It came from David's left crashing through the trees and underbrush.

"Hold!" David commanded, halting them.

Sybil breathed in deeply, her hands shaking, acid burning her throat.

The sound of breaking branches drew closer, until a tall, dark-haired man jumped from the brush, giant axe drawn, bow and quiver at his back. He stumbled to a stop, nearly colliding with David's flank. His horse reared, skirting sideways.

"Whoa!" David yanked the reins, steadying the animal.

"Run, you fools!" the man shouted, trying to push past them.

Then came low, guttural moaning, closing in. Sybil unsheathed her sword. "Stand behind us!"

He hesitated, eyes flicking to their weapons. Instead of fleeing, he turned to face the thicket he'd just escaped, gripping his axe with both hands.

Brave. She had to admit.

"Cut their heads off," David said, repositioning beside him.

"There's too many," the man panted.

"Stay calm." David glanced at Sybil. She knew that look. I love you.

The ghouls crashed through the underbrush—fast and chaotic. Clawed hands reached forward. Three of them. Once women, their gowns, elegant in life, now draped over decayed bodies. Their skin was stretched and grey. Freshly buried.

A ghoul lunged for the man, but he swung his axe into its shoulder. Decomposing red hair tangled in the axe as the creature shrieked. David finished it with a single blow, severing its head.

The other two charged Sybil. Luca and Enzo cut them off. One shrieked and lashed out, claws slashing Luca's horse. The horse collapsed, throwing Lucas. His flame snuffed out. Darkness swallowed them.

Sybil's horse reared as the last ghoul lunged.

"David!" she screamed.

Luca sprang to his feet, flame bursting to life— brilliant white. In the sudden light, the ghoul only inches away from her, recoiled, decayed arms shielding its eyes, howling.

Nicholas struck, blade flashing. Head rolling to the ground.

Silence fell.

Nicholas urged his horse forward, sword glinting in the firelight, dripping with black blood. "Are you hurt?" he asked her.

"Oh gods," Sybil breathed, feeling lightheaded, like she would pass out. "No."

The man they were chasing collapsed to his knees. David dismounted and checked the corpses. "Enzo, you know what to do."

"What are they?" the man whispered.

"Why are you out here?" David asked him, giving him a hand up.

The man took his hand, rose, and sheathed his axe on his belt. "I was hunting the wolves... They killed my sister's boys."

"You're the uncle," Sybil said.

"What's your name, sir?" David asked.

"Jacob."

"I'm David."

Pale, wide-eyed, the man stared, his gaze shifting between the corpses and Luca's light.

"Enzo, get him back to town. Bring him directly to Lenora," David said, nodding towards the white flame that danced in Luca's palm. "He knows what Luca can do."

Sybil knew they'd have to explain it somehow, but for some reason, the oracle deemed him necessary enough to save. "Go, we'll deal with this," she said.

Enzo offered a hand to Jacob and pulled him up behind him.

Just as they disappeared into the trees, the clouds moved, and the moon's dim light shone above them, a waxing crescent moon, the young moon indeed.

CHAPTER 10 ~ TRINITY
Ellsworth March 1349

Tiny brown birds fluttered along the dirt road, startled into the trees by the steady clatter Trinity's chestnut mare's hooves as they strolled down the path; its coat covered with dust from the long journey.

After repeated assurances that Ellsworth Manor lay only a few hours away, Trinity's escort agreed to allow her to travel alone the rest of the way.

She would stop there first before arranging lodging in York.

She wore a plain white wool cotehardie beneath a heavy cloak cinched at her throat, but the hem of her gown was as filthy as her horse.

Trinity breathed in the air. The familiar scent of freshly turned earth and damp hay filled her with childhood memories.

She loved spring, often helping her father in the fields, preparing them for sowing. Her father called it "breaking the ground."

Trinity smiled at the memory as she meandered through the narrow path through a small patch of woodland nestled among rolling green hills south of her childhood home in Yorkshire.

The sun finally broke through the heavy clouds. The storms had doubled her journey time, draining her purse with more inn stays than she'd planned. And fraying her nerves. Too many hours stuck inside small rooms, waiting out the storms gave her too much time to ponder. But finally, her luck turned.

So many questions filled her mind, daily. Never ending and never answered.

Who truly was her aunt?

How was she to find the druids?

The seraph Seriella told her to find them in York. But where? Who? How?

If she found them, would they kill her or help her?

Trinity clenched her eyes, jaw tight and shook her head.

"This is impossible. What am I to do?" The weight of responsibility was crushing. The notion that demons actually existed, terrified her. "How am I to fight them?" she whispered to the wind. Not that she'd get an answer. Since the night the seraph came to her, she hadn't seen or heard from her since.

She tried again, each time, praying to receive an answer but receiving nothing.

"I've never even lifted a sword before. How on god's earth am I expected to kill demons?"

Nothing.

She huffed. "Unbelievable," she grumbled, then breathed in the crisp air.

Gravel crunched behind her. Someone was behind her, and a jolt shot through her chest.

Was I speaking too loudly?

"A farm girl with a horse like this? Is it truly yours?"

The voice was sharp, authoritative. Trinity tensed. No one had questioned her before, but she'd had an escort. She should have worn a proper gown and ridden sidesaddle.

She turned.

Surprise stole her breath. Then she laughed.

Michael Ellsworth. She'd recognize that face anywhere.

Michael stepped closer to her, his thick, wavy dark hair framing his sharp features, piercing blue eyes watching her with confidence. A fine beaver hat cast a shadow over his face.

"You find my question amusing?" He adjusted the black fur-lined cloak draped over his broad shoulders, fastened with an ornate brooch. A bow and quiver rested at his back, a dead red grouse dangling from his other hand.

"No, my lord." She shook her head, releasing a quiet breath.

"State your business on my father's land then," he demanded, calm and authoritative.

Trinity slid from the saddle as gracefully as her travel-weary legs would allow, steadying herself before stepping forward, reins gripped firmly. Michael towered over her, forcing her to tilt her chin to meet his gaze.

"Michael is it not?" she asked lightly, one hand shading her eyes from the sun. "I had hoped you'd recognize me, though I suppose it has been quite a long time."

Recognition then flickered on his face. A slow, boyish grin spread across his lips.

"Trinity?" His voice softened. "Is it really you?" His brows creased together. "What are you doing here?"

Her heart dipped. That wasn't the welcome she had envisioned. It must have shown.

"Oh—no, I didn't mean—" He exhaled. "It's been so long. I didn't expect—" A chuckle broke through his words, as his smile widened.

He took her hand, as he had when they were children, his fingers warm and firm. His eyes held hers.

Trinity searched for traces of the boy she once knew. He was there buried beneath the sharp edges of manhood.

A burst of laughter shattered the bubble Trinity felt they stepped into.

Two young girls tumbled from the underbrush, shoving at each other playfully. Their dresses were smeared with dirt, their fur-lined cloaks half slipping from their shoulders. They seemed oblivious to the chill in the air.

Twins. Michael's mother had given birth to them before Trinity's mother took her away.

"Michael, we got another one!" They screamed in delight as they stretched a dead bird between them.

They stopped short.

Michael let go of Trinity's hand, and drew back from Trinity as the girls approached, but he didn't break his eyes from hers.

His sisters waited for some explanation, and Trinity became slightly embarrassed after Rose coughed.

"Oh, yes, sorry." He cleared his voice. "Girls, this is Trinity. You wouldn't remember her because you were just babies when she left, but she used to live here a long time ago with her family." Michael smiled sweetly at Trinity. "We were best friends."

That made Trinity chuckle as she remembered the mischief and shenanigans they got up to as children.

The girls relaxed and curtseyed, looking at one another, their eyes wide with silly grins.

"Nice meeting you, Trinity." The girls said in unison as they sprinted off, leaving Trinity and Michael alone again.

A long silence followed as they stood and watched the girls dash away. A moment later the girls laughed hysterically.

"And those two are Ruby and Rose. I apologize for their rude behavior. They are young and incorrigible."

"A little like you were, I presume," she said jokingly.

Michael smiled. "Yes, they do remind me of us when we were younger."

"And your friend with the red hair and freckles. What was his name? I can't remember," Trinity asked, "Where is he now?"

"Shaun. He lives in town. His father passed away a few years ago, and now runs a shop with his mother, but he's been at court with me for the last two years studying."

"It would be wonderful to see him," Trinity said, "What are you studying?"

"Mathematics, Latin, but father insisted that we study law, and I became a squire of course."

"Have you already been knighted? Will you join the army, then?"

"Yes, only just recently, and I will join If I must, but I'm needed here for now."

A silence fell between them; words failing her. Michael took her mount's reins with his free hand.

"So, are you accustomed to dragging young girls through the fields, killing wild game, and ruining their beautiful dresses?" Trinity smiled.

Michael laughed. "Those girls are better hunters than most men I know."

"Your father must be pleased."

"No, he is not." He shook his head, smiling again. "How long are you here for?"

"I haven't decided yet. I was only stopping by on my way to York. I'll be finding lodging there."

Michael didn't respond.

"How are your parents?" She asked.

"My father was ill, but he's recovering."

"I'm sorry. Is it the plague?"

"God, no. Mother says he smokes too much." Michael sounded frustrated and surprised by her question.

After another moment, Michael cocked his head and beamed at her. "You must stay with us," he said. "We have another young woman staying with us as my mother's ward. I'm sure you'd get along, and Mother would love a visit from an old friend."

"That would be lovely. I'd like that very much—as long as it's no trouble."

"You could never be trouble." Michael cleared his throat, his cheeks turning a shade of red. "How have things been for you over the years?"

Trinity hesitated. She didn't want to talk about London, her aunt, or her uncle. The loss was too raw, the grief too close, and she wouldn't cry in front of him. Taking a steadying breath, she pushed the pain away.

"I've been well," she said carefully. "I studied under my aunt, learned what I could about running a manor, being a lady, but…" The words caught in her throat, refusing to come.

Michael slowed beside her. "What's wrong?"

She stopped walking, eyes squeezing shut as she fought the wave of emotion.

"My aunt and uncle passed recently," she whispered, forcing the words out before they could choke her. Her chest tightened, and she took a deep breath, exhaling slowly. "I'm sorry. It's just… still hard to talk about."

"I'm sorry for your loss. What about your mother?"

"She passed many more years ago. I'm alone now."

"You most certainly are not." Michael gave her an encouraging smile. "You will always have a home here… You are not alone."

Trinity felt the sting of tears but held them back. No matter what he said, she couldn't stay forever. By the end of spring, she would return to court. Hopefully, by then, she would have more answers—she just needed time. She had to find the Druids.

"Michael, we're no longer children. As your sisters made clear, rules between men and women matter." She tried to sound firm, though the thought of keeping her distance saddened her. "I should only stay briefly, then be on my way.

"I'll speak to my father. You'll see—there will be no issue. You are welcome here, I promise."

"I appreciate the offer, truly, but I didn't return to be a burden."

"That's nonsense." Michale huffed, smirking. "I intend to spend much time catching up with you. We have had too many years between your departure and now."

"We can't run about like foolish children, Michael. I won't dishonor your family."

Michael chuckled and kicked at the ground. The mare startled, rearing back, but he steadied her with ease.

"I am not without honor, dear girl. I would never disgrace my family. I'll get my father's approval—we will have time together."

Trinity laughed. "Have you not observed? I'm no longer a girl."

She plucked a pretty blue flower from the side of the road, then tucked it behind his ear. Just as she had when they were young.

He huffed a quiet laugh.

"What?" she smiled up at him.

"You haven't changed so much."

A prolonged gaze passed between them; she smiled and looked away. "Oh, I have, in many ways, m'lord."

What was she thinking? Flirting with him!

It left him speechless, and she laughed nervously at her boldness.

"Come on then," he said.

She hadn't noticed they'd already arrived, and she sucked in a surprised gasp as he led her through the gates of Ellsworth.

A stable man came into the yard to meet them and take her mare.

"Thank you, David. Please have one of the boys bring Lady Trinity's belongings inside."

"No, please leave them for now." Trinity patted the neck of the mare and checked the sword and shield were still wrapped and well hidden under her travel bag. "I prefer to speak with Sir Henry first."

"Very well, m'lady," David said and took her horse and belongings to the stables.

"Let's not be presumptuous, Michael," Trinity said as her lips twitched up.

"Of course not," he said, gesturing towards the front doors of the manor.

Two perfectly dressed, stoic manservants opened the wide double doors. The foyer was twice as big as her aunt and uncles, and the tapestries were stunning.

"Oh, Michael, it's as beautiful as I remember."

An elderly gentleman exited a nearby room.

"Good day, m'lord."

"Hi, Joseph," Michael greeted the older man and handed him the bird.

"I'll bring this to the kitchen with the one your sisters brought in." He held it by its feet with an expression of disgust.

"Thanks. Joseph, this is Trinity. Trinity, this is Joseph, father's steward. She'll be staying with us for a while."

Trinity gave him a sideways look. He was quite assuming.

"May I take your cloak, m'lady?" Joseph asked.

"No, that's alright." She pulled the cloak tighter around her. She preferred to keep it on for her audience with his lordship.

Joseph only nodded. "Your father is with Miss Elizabeth in the kitchen. I'll inform him that you've arrived."

"No need. We're going there to see him now."

"As you wish," Joseph said, carrying the bird away.

"Joseph?" Michael called him back.

The gentleman turned around, holding the bird far away from his clothing. "Yes, m'lord?"

"Have you seen Fleur? I'd like to introduce her to Trinity."

135

"She's in the garden with your mother."

"Thank you."

Joseph nodded and then turned back toward the end of the hall.

Michael placed Trinity's hand on his arm as they walked in the same direction, but Joseph had disappeared ahead of them.

Several maids and manservants bowed and curtsied as they passed through the great hall. Michael smiled politely but didn't stop.

When they reached the double doors to the kitchen, they could hear a woman's high-pitched screaming. Michael cringed and looked at Trinity.

A kitchen maid and young serving girl pushed out of the room, their eyes wide and their hands to their mouths.

"Sorry, m'lord." The first one curtsied, and they hurried away.

He took Trinity's hand, leading her to a bench seat across the hall. "Sorry about this. Would you mind giving me a moment to inform my father of your arrival?"

"Of course," she said, "I'll wait here."

CHAPTER 11 ~ MICHAEL
Ellsworth Manor

Michael walked into the kitchen, caught Sybil's raised brows eye, and then she glanced at his sister in silent warning. He gave her a quick wink and a knowing, apologetic smile.

Elizabeth stood in front of their father, hands fisted at her hips, and tears streaking down her face.

Michael's father sat in his wooden armchair beside the kitchen fire and ran a hand through his thinning hair; his eyes momentarily closed as he took a deep breath.

The stand-off didn't last long as Elizabeth let out a high-pitched whine. "WHY? It's not fair!"

By God, she can scream. Michael cringed and pinched his brows together.

"You don't understand! I love him!" Elizabeth turned her back on their father to face Michael. "Michael, tell father! You've met Theo! You know he's a good man!"

"May I speak, father?" Michael stood poised and straight.

His sister's face looked ripe to explode, huffing quick breaths, and it was clear their father was close to losing his patience. Michael thanked God that he showed up when he did.

Henry roughly set his pipe on the table with a thud, coughed loudly, and cleared his throat. "My daughter has such a loud voice these days. By all means, speak your mind as well."

"Father, is it so unspeakable that Elizabeth should fall in love with this man? Unlike his father, he's a good man and holds no issues with us. I've spoken to him myself at the ball that I accompanied Elizabeth. He's an educated, well-sorted young man with the financial capacity to provide for Elizabeth.

Michael looked at his sister. "Father, we're all tired of this feud, and it would finally unite our families. Theodore proclaims his undying love and devotion to Elizabeth. In my opinion, they should be allowed to wed." He paused, glanced at Elizabeth with a sad smile and whispered. "She's beyond the appropriate marrying age, father. It's time."

Elizabeth looked at her father with tear-filled eyes, and new hope. Her fingers interlocked in front of her mouth as if praying.

"Please, father," she breathed, ignoring Michael's final comment. Knowing it was true. She confided in him; no suitor had called in over a year.

Henry picked up his pipe and took a long drag, then exhaled. He seemed to soften a bit, and when he spoke, it was kinder.

"Are you sure this boy adores you as much as you proclaim?"

"Oh yes, father, he does. He loves me and no other. I will die without him, Father, please!"

"Fine! Bring him to me. I'll hear him out." Henry pinched the bridge of his nose and waved her away.

Elizabeth wiped her tears away and smiled again.

"Thank you, Father!"

"Now be gone with you. I can't stand any more of your carrying on."

Elizabeth kissed him affectionately on the cheek and ran from the room.

His mother and Fleur walked into the kitchen from the back garden.

Fleur's blonde hair was braided and coiled at the back of her head. She locked eyes with Michael, and he swore she narrowed them even more.

He truly wished they could at least be friends, and she would forgive him for being so direct. He didn't mean to hurt her when he told her he did not want to marry her. It surprised him, it had.

"Is it safe to come in?" His mother called as Fleur carried a wicker basket filled with flowers beside her.

"Yes, mother," Michael laughed. "Hello Fleur."

"Hello, Michael." She turned to his mother. "I'll bring these to the hall."

"Thank you, Fleur, that's a fine idea."

Fleur gave Henry a rare smile and a small curtsey before she left.

Michael sighed and wished again he could fix things with her. He thought maybe Trinity could help smooth things over.

Susana moved toward the table to take Henry's pipe, but he seized it first.

"Lenora says no more smoking, Henry!"

"Leave it be woman!" Henry snapped. "I don't believe a word that old hag says anymore."

"Henry!" Susana looked at Sybil, who was tending to the fire behind his father. She gave her an apologetic look and silently mouthed, "Sorry." Michael almost laughed, but held it in.

Sybil just shook her head and smiled. It wasn't the first time his father complained about old Lenora.

"What?" Henry looked genuinely confused and then coughed, but he kept going despite the mortification on Susana's face. "What God-fearing woman won't pray over the sick?"

Lenora refused to offer prayer with Michael's mother, which infuriated his father.

Michael knew his father tolerated Lenora out of love for his wife because she adored Lenora. The older woman birthed him and his siblings.

He always saw her as a grandmother figure. She nursed him back to health during childhood illnesses and injuries. He trusted her completely.

If Lenora said her father was smoking too much, which was why he had gotten sick, Michael believed it.

His mother let out a groan. "Fine! It's getting dark. Michael, Sybil, help light the candles, please." His mother gave his father a disapproving look.

"Mother, father, do you remember the girl that Shaun and I used to play with as children? Her father tended the north fields for you."

Michael tried not to be so obvious about his joy over her arrival, but he couldn't believe she was in his home again and barely kept the grin off his face.

At the wooden table, his mother sat, tilting her head to the right, a slight smile making her appear younger.

His mother sighed deeply. "Yes…" She patted his father's arm. "Dear, I'm sure you remember. Her name is Trinity—Eric and Beatrice Ackerman's daughter. Sweet girl. After her father passed, we sent them to London to stay with her mother's sister. Oh, what was her sister's name?"

Michael felt his face heat up as his mother spoke about Trinity. He lit the candles on the table then turned back to his parents.

"Her mother died years ago, and her aunt and uncle recently perished, leaving her alone. She was travelling to York to find lodging when I met her on our road. It would be most charitable to allow her to stay with us for a time, and I thought Fleur and mother would also appreciate the company."

Henry took a puff on his pipe and exhaled. "Bring her in then," Henry said, then coughed hard into a handkerchief.

Susana grabbed the pipe before he could argue any further. "This will be the death of you, husband. No more."

Michael smiled at his mother and then disappeared out the door, where Trinity waited for him. She didn't notice him at first, and he stopped, momentarily breathless as he watched her.

She was turned towards the hall, watching the servants setting up the trestle tables for supper. She fidgeted, covering her soiled gown with her cloak—a smudge of dirt on her left cheek.

He smiled. She was beautiful.

He wanted to run through the fields laughing as they did when they were children. Free. The freedom only childhood gives, the one he lost after she left.

Memories of the last day sped through his mind.

Trinity's mother held her hand as she looked over her shoulder at him, tears falling down her face. His mother held him as he cried, and then another sharp memory of Michael yelling furiously at his father.

Michael always adored her, and when she left, it gave him a taste of his first heartbreak. It changed him. That day marked the end of his childhood.

As he sucked in a deep breath, Michael knew one thing for sure. He still loved her and swore never to let her go again.

His heart pounded as these thoughts swept through him, swinging back and forth from the past to the present. He couldn't believe she was there; it felt like a dream.

He walked to her, and she stood up, straightening her cloak and holding it closed.

He gently wiped the smudge of dirt from her cheek, and she sucked in a sharp breath.

"Michael."

"You had a smudge of dirt…"

"Oh. Thank you." She laughed nervously. "I saw Elizabeth, your sister, correct?"

"Yes, she's in quite the state."

"She ran past without a word."

"It's fine. You'll see her at dinner; I'm sure she will be more herself. Hopefully." He laughed.

"And a young woman carrying a wicker basket full of flowers, muttering something about a half-brained, ignorant man. It was truly the oddest thing."

"That was Fleur, my mother's ward. She's upset with me. Long story, but I'm certain you will get on with her fine."

"I'm sure." Trinity laughed.

Michael put his arm out for her. "Come. Mother and father are waiting for us.

They walked in together, and Trinity stood poised next to Michael. His mother smiled warmly. Mrs. Bartlett and Sybil discreetly busied themselves with food preparations, but he didn't miss Sybil' raised brows.

"Father, Trinity Ackerman. Trinity, my father, Sir Henry Ellsworth and my mother, Lady Susana Ellsworth." Michael bowed slightly and grinned at Trinity as she curtseyed.

"Do come closer, my dear girl. I'm old, and I'm having a hard time believing these tired eyes of mine." Michael's father said.

His mother sighed, smiling with a sheen of tears in her eyes. "Is it really you? I remember you as a tiny little girl, quiet as a mouse."

"Yes, m'lord, m'lady, it has been a long time," Trinity said respectfully.

"My son tells me you've travelled quite a distance." Michael's father reached for his pipe, but Susana smacked it away.

"From London."

"Unaccompanied?" Michael's father asked, his eyes narrowed.

It was highly unusual for a lady to ride alone. Michael had been so overwhelmed, he forgot to ask her about it.

"No, m'lord, I had a chaperone from court until this morning. I assured him I could ride a few hours on my own and left him at the village south of here."

"It's not safe to journey unaccompanied these days. Some wolf-related problems have occurred recently, resulting in attacks; consequently, I implemented a curfew. No ones to travel after dark, and I'd recommend not travelling alone during the day either, my dear girl."

"That's frightening. Thank you for telling me."

"Michael has also informed us that you've lost your uncle and aunt, Sir Geoffrey Denton and Lady Anna; I believe that was their names?" He glanced at his wife. "To illness, I presume?"

"Yes, almost two months ago."

"I am grieved to hear this and sorry for your loss. Life seems to have been unkind to you, so perhaps we can offer some solace here in our humble home."

"Thank you, m'lord, but I possess means and was going to York to obtain proper lodgings. I don't want to be a bother."

"It isn't frequent that we receive guests. We'd happily accommodate you for as long as you like."

"Trinity? Did your aunt teach you needlepoint?" His mother asked.

"Yes, she did, m'lady, and poetry, and some music. I read a little Latin too. My aunt was very devout and insisted I learn so I could read the Bible at church and at home."

"That's delightful. I love poetry, but I'm sorry to say no one in this house has an ear for music." Lady Susana stood up. "Come, let's get you settled in. Do you possess belongings we can bring up?"

"I travelled as light as possible, m'lady, so I only have a small travel bag."

"Then I suppose we should do some shopping in York tomorrow."

"That would be quite agreeable." Trinity turned back to Michael's father. "Thank you, m'lord, for your generosity, but first, I need to tell you some news, if I may."

"Of course," said Henry.

Trinity paused. "I'm sorry I must be the bearer of unwelcome news, but a plague has ravaged London and killed many people, including my aunt and uncle. All their livestock, as well as the servants, were lost." She blinked a couple of times as tears glistened in her eyes, but she didn't let them fall. "I possess notes granting me credit and travel documents..."

"Thank you, child. It is grave and sad news." Father nodded politely, then placed a hand over mothers protectively. "We've also heard these tales."

"I assure you, m'lord. They are not tales but truth. London is practically abandoned. More people perish every day or leave."

"My men are looking into these issues, but I thank you again and welcome you to Ellsworth Manor." Henry gave her a stiff nod.

Trinity curtseyed.

Susana took Trinity's arm and walked from the room, with Michael following them.

CHAPTER 12 ~ SYBIL
Ellsworth Manor & York

The next day brought a relentless downpour of rain and biting winds. Like a raging beast, the wind slammed against the stable's wooden doors, rattling them without mercy.

Sybil stepped out of the manor doors and hunched her shoulders against the onslaught; her face turned into the driving gusts. Though her cloak and mittens were lined with sheepskin to keep out the chill, the damp cold still wormed into her bones.

"Gods, it's supposed to be spring," she muttered, glancing about to ensure no guards patrolled the front wall.

She thrust a hand forward, palm out. Energy crackled through her veins, sending a tingling heat to her fingertips. As the power surged, she released it, forcing the wind to bend around her. Without hesitation, she sprinted toward the stables.

Magic took its toll though, leaving her drained, but it was a small price to pay. By the time she reached the doors, her limbs felt leaden.

Better exhausted than frozen.

One last glance confirmed the guards remained inside, seeking warmth of their own.

She yanked open the stable door, slipped inside, and let her power fade as she shut the door behind her. The rush of warmth eased her tension, and she drew a deep breath, relief settling over her.

"We saw him holding her hand," Ruby was telling David.

"He was looking at her all strange, like this," Rose made an exaggerated lovesick face.

What on earth are they doing here so early?

"I think she's pretty," Ruby said.

"Do you think she is pretty?" Sybil asked David, smiling.

The three looked up at her. David's cheeks turned pink, but he smiled in return.

"Not as pretty as you," he said.

"Ew!" Rose covered her face.

"It's disgusting," Ruby added to her sister's moaning.

Sybil loved the twins and marveled at how they finished each other's thoughts or continue them as if they were one person. Even Enzo and Luca, as much as they looked alike, had opposite characters. These twins were extraordinary.

"What brings you, girls, here so early?" Sybil asked. It was unusual for them to be awake at this time.

David answered for them. "They were trying to sneak out with horses, and I caught them."

"In this weather!" Sybil said, shocked.

The twins peered at their boots and tried to hide further into their grey fur-lined cloaks. They resembled a couple of young boys with their hoods on.

"Listen to me. It's not safe to wander in the forests and fields alone. There's a wolf pack in the area. Your father told you this," David reminded them as gently but firmly as possible.

"They don't hunt during the day, though. I heard Papa tell Michael," Ruby said, looking up at him and then back at the ground. "Will you tell papa?"

"No, but you must swear not to wander alone outside these walls."

"We promise," they both said as one.

"Good, now go to the manor before anyone notices you're gone." David patted them both on their shoulders.

"I made some fresh bread this morning. It's nice and warm." Sybil said, hoping it would tempt them to return instead of breaking their promise and sneaking out, anyway. "Mrs. Bartlett will be up any minute, though, so you best hurry. You remember where to find the honey." Sybil lifted a brow. It was hidden, but she suspected they had an inkling of where to find it.

The girls linked hands and then left. Sybil sucked in a breath as two black lines appeared like thin snakes circling their hands. Something clenched inside her stomach as the snakes wrapped around their necks.

Sybil looked away shaking her head. Whatever the vision meant, it was not good.

The door closed, banging loudly, and Sybil winced.

What's that supposed to mean?

"We need to talk." Sybil laced her fingers through David's as he leaned down to kiss her gently on her lips—a feather-soft kiss.

He wrapped his hands around her hips and pulled her close to him. She fell into his embrace as her eyes fluttered closed, breathing in his earthy scent of hay and cloves. She wanted nothing more than to disappear in his arms and kisses for the rest of the day, but she needed to see her grandmother immediately.

"I have to go to town," she murmured against his chest.

David groaned quietly against her hair as Sybil tried to pull away. "No, stay."

She smiled and pushed away gently, reluctantly.

"What's so urgent?" David asked.

"So, you met the new girl that Michael brought home yesterday? Her name's Trinity."

David smiled. "The pretty blonde-haired girl?" he teased.

Sybil laughed. "Yes, the one."

"Only briefly, my love."

David tried to pull her closer again, but she stopped him and slapped him away from her. He looked at her thoughtfully, eyes narrowed. "You met her, and I assume it's not good?"

"I'm not sure. I had a vision yesterday in the kitchen when Trinity walked in with Michael. She was gripping a flaming sword and wearing a winged helmet."

"She wore a winged helmet?"

"Yes."

"Could she be the girl in the vision Cailleach gave you?"

Sybil sighed. "I'm not entirely confident of this. She could be. Cailleach's vision didn't give a clear view of the girl's face. It was dark." She closed her eyes, trying to remember every detail. "Wings coming from her back. Not a helmet."

149

"But your visions are not the same, love. They're more symbolic."

"Yes." That was true, but to have the girl of Cailleach's vision suddenly appear?

David pulled her into his arms again, and she went willingly. She had to leave, but he was so warm.

"Joshua told me a tale about an archangel who banished Adam and Eve from Paradise."

Sybil scoffed.

"Listen. Perhaps there's something here. I understand you doubt the existence of angels, but the story fits.

Sybil moaned. "Fine."

He pulled her to him. "This angel guarded this holy place with a flaming sword. She was the archangel, Jophiel. Some would refer to her as a seraph. Angels of the highest order."

Sybil interrupted him. "You're saying I had a vision of an angel?" she scoffed again. "They don't exist, David. You're spending too much time with that Christian man."

"Joshua is a kind man and very knowledgeable. I love his stories; they share a common thread with many of our own, Sybil." His tone softened. "We've discussed this, my love."

"This story sounds shockingly similar to our keeper of the veils." Sybil gave an unbelieving sniff and rolled her eyes.

He shrugged and gave her a thoughtful look. "I'm not sure that angels aren't fey. And maybe you're right, too, and they're druids. The keeper of the veils."

David was obsessed with the various goddesses and gods of other cultures: the Irish Celtics, Pecs, Vikings, the Jews, Romans, Greeks and, more recently, the

Catholics. During the summer solstice, he'd spend evenings in ale, listening to any story he could. He argued that they were not separate gods but were called by different names by each society.

Sybil disagreed with him vehemently and maintained that Brigantia was a goddess in her own right, and their mother goddess, Cailleach, was the creator of life.

It was an old argument for which she was not in the mood.

She changed the subject. "Anyway, Trinity's aura is one of kindness, but of great sadness. Sadness so heavy most women would never leave their beds. She hides her pain well."

"That's awful. The poor girl."

"The vision shows she's blessed by the gods," Sybil said definitively. "But I had a sudden spike of nausea when she entered."

"Are you saying Trinity's a demon?"

"No, but… There's something."

"Did you see anything else around her attached to her?" David took her hands in his large, calloused ones and kissed the top of her knuckles.

"No, but… I think a powerful demon was close by, following her, maybe."

David gently rubbed Sybil's arms up and down. "The demons of Balor roaming our lands. We know this."

He pulled her into his arms—her safe spot. Fear seeped through her soul so strongly that she shivered.

"Yes. I need to speak to my grandmother. "I think evil has arrived."

"Albeit on the wings of an angel," David whispered.

She laid her head back on his chest and sighed.

151

"I'm scared. It wasn't a ghoul but I'm not sure what it was." She breathed a sigh into his chest. "It was close, too."

"I promise you. I will not allow harm to come to you."

Sybil didn't want to let go. She grasped what was coming and wished there was a way to stop it before it claimed too many victims or people she loved.

"Did Michael introduce Trinity to Fleur?" David asked.

Sybil pulled back and rubbed the small space between her eyes. "They met at dinner, but Fleur is so cold. She didn't speak to anyone and acts if she hates it here. They are so different, Trinity and Fleur."

"That's a pity. Perhaps she needs more time to warm up to people." David kissed Sybil on the forehead. "Not everyone is as kind or loving as you."

"Oh, hush."

"The parents are hoping Fleur and Michael will marry, and that is the main reason she's here?" David said.

"No!" Sybil hissed. "She repulses him. His feelings for Trinity are far more loving and open."

"I'm afraid Sir Henry isn't considering his son's desires. He wants his son married, and Fleur is a suitable match. Her father and Sir Henry were in the same regiment and have been close friends for years."

"Michael won't marry Fleur. If he marries anyone, it will be Trinity."

David pulled her into his arms tight and laughed. "Is that a premonition?"

"No, my love, it's obvious."

***

Sybil didn't take the shortcut through the forest; the main road was safer. It took longer, but she kept her head down and pushed Moon Pie faster.

Moon Pie been her horse since she was old enough to ride. A creamy beige mare that was braver than any horse she'd ever ridden.

She forced the air ahead of them away so the rain and wind wouldn't slow them down.

Halfway there, her stomach clenched up, and bile rose into her throat. Her heart quickened as she glanced in every direction but couldn't see anything. No ghouls, no demons. But it was close enough to make her unwell, which made no sense.

She let her concentration falter, and a cold breeze whipped around her, bringing with it a stench of sulphur. Ghouls smelled of rot, but this demon was much more powerful.

She became dizzy as her energy weaned and kicked Moon Pie, faster.

She came to Micklegate just as the gates opened and only slowed her mount after they crossed into the city. Her vision cleared as her heart calmed.

Only a few people went to the market square in the heavy rain. Grey-hooded cloaks tied tightly around their shoulders; heads bowed.

She brought Moon Pie to a gentle trot, mindful to stay clear of anyone, her stomach still rolling.

The horse's hooves clipped on the new cobblestone street. York had expanded a great deal in the previous years during the war.

Many found safety within its walls, with external malevolence increasingly rumored to still be happening. The church put the fear of God into the people of York, and those who didn't believe their gospel were forced to hide, like her and her coven of Druid descendants.

She turned through several narrow, muddy streets, going through the Shambles.

The road she followed led to a dead-end at the edge of Marketshire with an old double-story cottage tucked inconspicuously at the end—her home, where she grew up most of her life.

"Home sweet home," she murmured.

The local apothecary sign hung from above the door. A wooden plank with an image of a pestle and mortar burned into it. Herbs sprouted wildly along the window seat beside the old wooden door.

Moon Pie nudged her shoulder as she tied the reins to the post, waiting for her treat, the one she could scent in Sybil's pocket. Sybil laughed and pulled out half of a plump carrot, patting her neck affectionately.

"Thank you, my friend, for getting me here so fast."

She pushed the door open and almost ran into Nicholas as he went to leave.

He jumped back, surprised, then laughed. "You gave me a fright!"

"Sorry," she said, sliding past him. She hadn't seen him since the last meeting. "How's the training coming along?"

He paused. "It's progressing, but most of them have never even held a blade, much less killed anyone with one. They're scared."

"Is there anything I can do to help?"

"No, they require more practice, only then will they'll gain more confidence."

"Are Enzo and Luca helping?"

"Yes. They're impressive. They need some polishing, but they're natural. David and Evelyn have done well training them."

"Can I ask you a question?" She said, hoping it wouldn't be too direct, but he was family after all, and her curiosity needed quenching.

"Depends," he said as his eyes darted towards the street. "Of course, go on."

"Where have you been all these years? And how'd you learn to fight?"

"My father took me to Ireland, his homeland. His tribe are warriors, and they trained me." He glanced at the open door, obviously uninterested in saying anything further. "I should go. I'm late already."

"Yes, of course, and welcome home," she said, and he nodded, then ran out and down the street.

That was odd. She thought to herself. Why would he be so nervous about speaking about his father's "tribe"? His Tribe. That's strange...

Inside the apothecary, rows of bottles filled with liquids and dried herbs lined the counter and packed the towering shelves. A careless thief could easily poison themselves—none of the containers bore labels. Only Lenora knew what each one contained.

The room remained dim, lit only by a large candle flickering on the table beside the door leading to her home's inner sanctuary.

A hallway stretched ahead, with two rooms branching off on either side—one used for consultations, the other as her sitting room. Further along lay the kitchen and dining area, while her grandmother's chambers occupied the upper floor.

Sybil ascended the stairs, carrying the candle to light her way. Even before she reached the top, she could hear her grandmother muttering curses under her breath.

When she entered the living room, she found the older woman crouched under a table, trying to coax out a tiny creature—not quite a cat, not quite a rat, but something in between.

"Sybil, be a dear and grab that wicker box beside you. Quickly now!"

Her grandmother, though older than anyone Sybil knew, remained sprightly. Short and stocky, with thick grey hair braided down her back, she moved with surprising agility as she cornered the critter.

"What is that?" Sybil asked, picking up the wicker box.

"Slowly, dear. It's a ferret. Clever as a fox but with a nasty spray when frightened." Her grandmother shot her a wary look. "And sharp little teeth, too. Now, quickly, hand me the box."

In a swift motion, she trapped the ferret beneath it and plopped down on top, exhaling a long breath. "Going to be the death of me, flaming ferret!"

"Where did it come from?" Sybil chuckled, always amused by her eccentric grandmother.

Lenora sighed and rubbed her temple. "Payment. I thought it would make a nice pet. The demon gets into everything, sprays his rancid stench over my herbs, and bites. It's a nightmare!"

She stood up and slipped a piece of wood under the basket. "Help me, dear."

Sybil helped her flip the box over, capturing the little guy inside. Lenora laid a large cast-iron pot over the lid to keep it closed.

"So, what brings you here so early?" Lenora asked.

She took the candle Sybil had carried in earlier and began descending back down the stairs to her shop, and Sybil followed behind.

"There's a girl, a guest of the Ellsworth. An old friend of Michael's. Her parents used to work for them years ago. She's returned." Sybil paused. "Her name is Trinity Ackerman."

Lenora clicked her tongue and sat in a large armchair in front of the fireplace that was still lit. "Beatrice's daughter has come home."

"You know her?"

"I knew her mother. Trinity's arrival brings evil tidings and darkness on her heels?" Lenora guessed correctly.

"I think so, grandmother."

"What did you see, child?"

Sybil closed her eyes and told her about the vision of the sword, Trinity's bond with Michael and the girl's inner light, and the sadness she carried on her shoulders like an old shawl.

"Interesting," Lenora said after she finished. "Perhaps she is the one?"

"She is pious and will deny it, deny us."

"Perhaps. Anything else?" Lenora asked, knowing there always was. Sybil had symbolic visions, but her intuition was unparalleled. "Dig deep, child."

"Evil will seek to destroy her." She paused, breathed again, and looked at her grandmother. "We must help her."

Sybil was still learning to decipher her visions. Most of the time, it did nothing but confuse her.

"Darkness is coming, my dear. We must do our best to protect our loved ones and be ready to fight."

A heaviness fell upon Sybil's shoulders. She closed her eyes and tried to steady her breath. "I understand, but no one will listen or accept, grandmother. Trinity will not believe."

Sybil sat next to Lenora and clasped her hands. They were warm, soft, and wrinkled, but they gave her a familiar comfort.

Lenora's brow furrowed. "You must help the girl awaken the spark inside of her."

"How, if she won't even listen?"

"Be a friend to her. Protect and guide her. If she is a part of the destruction you see, perhaps you can stop it. And get her an amulet immediately."

"What if she dies?"

"Many shall die, dear. It's the way. Light and darkness are always at war. The balance teeters in one direction, then another. We'll do our best."

"What if I'm wrong about her? I'm not sure, grandmother."

"There's more to the girl than you realize, but time will tell."

"And what of Sir Henry and Lady Susana?" Sybil was close to tears as she said their names. Her visions always came true. She'd told her grandmother about the vision.

"I shall speak with the oracle about this myself. Perhaps we can do something to change this fate." She went to a shelf, poured some ground herbs into another bottle, and corked it, handing it to Sybil. "Keep making him drink his tonic and add this to it from now on."

The door opened, and Shaun walked into the shop.

"Good morning, Lenora, Sybil."

"Good morning, Shaun," Sybil said.

"What brings you to York?" he asked.

158

Nicole Moore

"I'm visiting my dear grandmother."

"What do you want, boy?" Her grandmother interrupted briskly.

Sybil chuckled as she watched Shaun handle her grandmother's sharp tone with ease. He was well accustomed to Lenora's blunt manner—after all, he had grown up next door. His mother, Isabella, had been her closest friend for years.

With a polite smile, he said, "Mother needs something for her the aches in her knees and she also asked if you had any more of your... um... 'special biscuits.'"

Lenora snorted. "Of course she does. Sybil, in the kitchen, there's a plate of biscuits—wrap a few in a cloth for her highness." Lenora pointed to a few bottles corked on the shelf across from her. "Give him the one rust colored tonic."

Sybil grabbed the tonic off the shelf and handed it to Shaun.

"Thanks, Syb," Shaun said.

She slipped into the kitchen and found the greenish-hued biscuits. She lifted one to her nose and inhaled the earthy blend of herbs and honey.

"Can I have one?" she called out.

"No! They're not for you!" Lenora's voice rang back.

With a grin, Sybil wrapped a few in a linen cloth and returned to the sitting room, setting the basket in front of her grandmother.

Lenora plucked one from the pile, about to bite, then paused, eyeing Shaun. "So, have you heard the news?"

"What news?" he asked.

159

She studied him for a moment. "Remember that little whelp you were so smitten with as a boy?"

A faint blush crept over Shaun's cheeks. "There were a few, I'll admit."

"Ha! Always the scamp," Lenora cackled. "The blonde girl—you and Michael used to play with her. Trinity."

Shaun blinked, momentarily thrown.

"Well? Do you remember her or not?" Lenora pressed.

"Of course... yes. It's just been a long time."

Sybil giggled, sensing his energy shift. It wasn't as strong as Michael's, but she was certain Shaun had once loved the girl, too.

Sybil's grandmother cleared her throat. "Did you hear me, boy?"

"Sorry, what?" he asked, clearly distracted.

"She's back."

"When?"

"Not sure. She's staying with the Ellsworth as a guest."

"That's kind of them."

"I imagine Susana still carries some guilt over the girl. She never truly wanted to let her go. So, I suppose you'll be riding off to see her?"

"Not today, but tomorrow, most definitely. Thanks for the news, Lenora."

"Thanks, Sybil!" he added before practically bolting out the door.

CHAPTER 13 ~ TRINITY
Ellsworth

The afternoon air was crisp, and the sun battled the thick clouds for dominance. But thankfully, no rain yet. Trinity glanced at the darkening sky.

Susana had insisted she and Fleur join her in the garden, claiming herb-picking soothed the soul. Trinity doubted it helped Fleur, who held a wicker basket beside them. Straight back, lips tight and barely speaking. Downright miserable.

"Trinity?"

She looked up to a red-haired man walking beside Michael. His broad smile reaching striking blue eyes.

"Yes?" She smiled at Michael as she rose, handing Susana the basket of herbs. Brushing dirt from her green cotehardie, she tucked a blonde strand behind her ear.

Her gaze lingered on Michael for a second too long. *He's so handsome.*

The few days they spent together were unlike anything she'd ever experienced. Michael brought her

161

flowers every day and insisted on helping her with everything until Lady Susana would run him off. He gave a different excuse several times a day just to be near her, and she loved it.

The red-haired man stopped in front of her, cheeks-tinged pink. He grinned, as his eyes gleamed.

She stepped back. "Yes?"

Shaun let out a nervous chuckle. "You don't recognize me?"

She tilted her head.

Could this man be, Shaun?

The boy she remembered was gone—no wild red curls, no mess of freckles. The man before her stood tall, strikingly handsome, his russet hair neatly tamed, his freckles faded. His smile brimmed with confidence and mischief.

Could it be him? He's far more handsome than I ever imagined he'd become.

"Shaun?" she asked as he stepped forward, sweeping her into a sudden, breath-stealing embrace.

"Oh, what a joy to have you back!" He laughed, spinning her.

"Put me down! Right now!" she yelped.

"Shaun! Your manners!" Susana scolded.

Her dark fur-lined cloak billowed as she strode toward them, shaking loose the dirt from her light blue gown. Eyes narrowed; she sighed at Shaun's antics. Fleur hovered behind her, arms crossed, lips pressed into a thin line.

"Sorry, m'lady." Shaun set Trinity down with exaggerated care and bowed, but his grin remained intact. The tension broke, and they all burst into laughter.

"You're a right boar!" Michael clapped Shaun on the back, then turned his attention to Trinity. His glorious, affectionate smile sent warmth fluttering through her.

Despite Shaun's transformation, her heart belonged to Michael. She couldn't deny it.

An awkward silence stretched between them as she blushed.

Susana smoothed the moment over. "I'm finished here. Go now, have the rest of the day together."

Trinity hesitated. "Are you sure? I wouldn't want to leave you if I'm needed." She hoped it was the correct thing to say but prayed she could spend the rest of the day with Michael and Shaun.

Susana waved her off. "I've nothing to do but my needlepoint. Go enjoy yourselves but be back before dark."

Michael kissed his mother's cheek. Shaun tucked Trinity's hand over his arm.

Trinity glanced at Fleur. "Would you like to join us?" She hated excluding her, even if the girl barely acknowledged her.

"No, thank you," Fleur replied coolly. "If Lady Susana allows, I'd prefer a ride through the fields."

Susana gave her hand a gentle squeeze. "Of course."

"I love riding," Trinity said. "Perhaps we can go together another time?"

Fleur's polite smile barely reached her eyes. "Yes, that would be nice."

"I'll have Henry accompany you," Susana added. "He won't want you riding alone, and the fresh air will do him good."

Fleur's eyes lit up, if only slightly. "Yes, that would be nice."

***

Beyond the gates, the three walked hand-in-hand, Trinity in the middle—just like old times.

They stopped by the small stream, once a raging river, in her childhood eyes. Now, it barely reached her ankles.

They drank from it, and as she stood up from the stream, she was taken aback at the ease she felt with them. As if she had never left, but at the same time, she was looking at two strangers who weren't strangers.

She stood, brushing water from her hands, watching the boys toss rocks into the stream, laughing. Still the boys she remembered and then Michael caught her eye and smiled, making her breath hitch.

"I can't believe everything looks the same but feels so different," she murmured.

"Some things are the same," Michael said, holding her eyes.

Shaun turned to her, eyes twinkling. "Except you have grown up to be beautiful." His cheeks colored, but he held her gaze.

"So have you," Trinity said before she could think better of it. Heat rose to her face. She quickly added, "What happened to all your freckles? They were charming."

Michael stepped closer, subtly placing himself between them.

"They disappeared the moment I became a man," Shaun quipped.

Michael snorted. "As soon as they were gone, every girl in town chased him." He clapped Shaun on the back. "Or was it you who was chasing them?"

"A bit of both," Shaun admitted with a wink.

Trinity laughed, then grew serious. "What's wrong with Fleur? She seems… unhappy."

Michael cringed, then shrugged. "Her parents travel a lot. I think she's homesick."

"But why does she dislike you so much? What did you do?"

Shaun barked a laugh, and Michael's brows furrowed. "Michael doesn't know how to talk to women."

Michael groaned, rubbing his eyes and shaking his head. "Our parents wanted us to marry. Thought if we spent time together…" He trailed off, glancing at Trinity.

She stiffened. "You're to marry her?"

"No!" Michael practically shouted. "I told her I wasn't interested. She got mad. I suppose our parents still hope something changes."

Relief flooded her, but so did sympathy for Fleur. He hadn't let her down gently. "Does she want to marry you?"

"God, no! She said she'd never consider me either. Stormed right out of the room."

Trinity sighed. "I think she does. You hurt her feelings."

Michael scoffed, stepping backwards. "How can I hurt someone who doesn't have any?" His boot splashed into the stream. "God!" He cursed, hopping back.

Shaun doubled over, laughing. "See? Hopeless with women."

Trinity covered her mouth, trying not to laugh but failing.

They continued walking, trading stories of childhood mischief. The boys regaled her with tales of their wild adventures. She listened, smiling, though they never noticed how little she spoke of her past.

Her childhood had been different. Friends closely supervised, always girls. There were no boys. No freedom.

The heartbreaking part: the girls she'd grown close to died from the plague.

Some things were better left unsaid.

"Shaun thinks he is the king of York, and every girl swoons for him," Michael laughed. "Even at court, keeping up with his newest conquests is exhausting."

"Ha, you're jealous, my friend, because I have more luck than you."

"You see, Trinity. He hasn't changed one bit. Once a rascal, always a rascal."

"Michael has higher obligations," Shaun said mockingly in a deep voice, trying to sound like Henry. "He doesn't have the luxury of dalliances. He is to become a lord!"

"That's enough, Shaun," Michael said, rolling his eyes.

They left the small forest into a field of wild wheat. It looked much smaller and far more overgrown, but she was sure she'd been there before and then… She stopped walking.

Off a short distance was a small shack almost entirely overgrown and sagging into the earth, abandoned.

"Trinity? Are you alright? You look like you've seen a ghost," Shaun said as he strode up beside her.

Michael's voice softened. "Your home."

A sharp ache tightened her chest. She had avoided this moment, but now it was here. Trinity touched her lips with her fingers and fought the ache in her chest.

"I haven't seen it yet."

After a deep breath, she stepped forward. Heart hammering.

Inside, dust choked the air. A rusted iron pot lay toppled near the hearth, and the wooden table beside it overturned. A single grimy window barely let in the light.

The small room where her mother once hung a delicate curtain now stood bare: a collapsed bed frame and rotted fabric—nothing left but ghosts.

Memories slammed into her.

Her mother is cooking by the fire. Her father sweeping five-year-old Trinity into his arms, squeezing her until she giggled—her parent's quiet, unwavering love.

Tears burned her eyes.

Then, in the haze of memory, an image flashed.

An angel with white wings outstretched—a sword and shield. Silver and obsidian blade, runes etched along its length. It glowed with a blue flame.

She gasped, staggering back—And crashed into Michael's chest. She let out a small gasp and turned into him. His arms wrapped around her, steadying her as her breath shuddered. Leaning into him, she gripped his waist like a lifeline.

I don't want this responsibility… I can't do this… She couldn't say it out loud, but it rippled through her. Fear, uncertainty, and unworthiness.

But even as she thought it, she knew she didn't have a choice. To be given a task from a seraph was a holy mission she couldn't refuse.

But how was she to tell Michael? Could she? Would he believe her?

Michael held her tighter. "I'm so sorry, Trinity. For everything."

167

She stepped back and wiped her tears, heart hammering.

Embarrassed. Confused. Scared.

"I'm fine," she lied.

She couldn't tell him or anyone but how was she supposed to find the druids that the angel told her to search for?

Michael gently took her forearms in his hands, looking at her with such kindness it took her breath away.

"I remember your mother. She was the sweetest woman I'd ever met." He huffed a small laugh and smiled. "Always hugging me."

"She wanted a son for my father, but she couldn't have any more babies." Trinity laughed, sobbed and added, "I think it was a miracle they even had me." She swiped at the tears falling over her cheeks.

"I was told you went to live with your aunt in London. But other than that, I knew nothing about what had happened to you."

Michael fixed a flyaway strand of her blonde hair and tucked it back into her braided coil and adjusted her caul.

Trinity looked up at him, tears still in her eyes as she tried not to think of it. "I miss them all so much." She closed her eyes and pushed her palms into them, stopping the flow.

Michael let out a deep breath and hugged her against him again. She curled into him and breathed him in. Lavender and Sandalwood.

Michael nodded. "Come on," he said softly. "Tonight, we celebrate."

She wasn't sure she had anything left to celebrate. But she let him lead her away just the same.

168

***

After dinner, Susana, Henry, Fleur, and Michael's sisters retired early, leaving Trinity alone in the great hall with Michael, Shaun and a couple dozen staff and guards still enjoying their meals.

She tried once more to include Fleur, but the girl stiffened, mumbled a polite decline, and practically fled the room. Michael sighed as his mother shot him a pointed look before leaving.

The trio drank and laughed, recounting childhood mischief—pranks, punishments, and the unforgettable trouble they'd stirred.

The clatter and laughter of others filled the great hall. It did indeed feel like a celebration.

Trinity had never consumed so much wine in her life. Everything wobbled. If she stood up, she'd fall flat on her backside. Yet somehow, Michael and Shaun remained upright, as if years of practice had hardened them against its effects.

Shaun slung an arm around Michael's shoulders, his grin lopsided.

Trinity started to laugh but suddenly swayed, the room spinning. Time for bed. She rose—too fast—knocking over her chair.

"Oh, Lord. I think I've had too much wine."

Shaun barked a laugh as she clapped a hand over her mouth, giggling.

Michael was at her side in an instant, steadying her. "Easy," he murmured, looping her arm over his neck and supporting her waist.

"I don't drink often," she slurred, mortified.

"It's alright. I shouldn't have given you so much." He guided her towards his father's parlor then up the staircase to the residence.

169

"I'm so embarrassed," she whispered.

Michael chuckled. "You have nothing to be embarrassed about."

"Just... don't tell your mother."

That earned another laugh. "I wouldn't dare. She'd flog me and say it was my fault."

In her bedroom, Michael set her down on the bed.

She sat at the edge, feet dangling, head still spinning.

Michael sat beside her, his hand resting lightly on her back, sending a shiver down her spine.

"I'll have Sybil bring you something in the morning," he said softly. "You'll need it."

He stood to leave, but panic flickered in her chest.

"Don't go yet."

He hesitated. "I should."

She wobbled to her feet, facing him. "Why?"

"You know why, Trinity."

She did. Of course she did. But the wine loosened her tongue and her morals.

"No, I don't," she lied, then sighed when he grimaced. "I know... I can't be alone with you."

Michael exhaled, raking a hand through his hair. "You're too drunk, my love. We both are. You'll regret it in the morning."

My love?

He turned for the door, but she caught his arm.

His eyes darkened. The way he looked at her stole her breath. A pulse of panic flared, but she ignored it and kissed him—too hard, too eager, clumsy with drink.

The moment she pulled away; she knew. That wasn't how their first kiss was supposed to go.

Michael stared at her, stunned, his lips parted in surprise. Then she started giggling.

He blinked, then chuckled, his face flushing.

"That was awful, wasn't it?" she admitted. "I've never—"

Michael silenced her with a second kiss—slower, deliberate. This time, her body melted into his, hands tangling in his hair, his fingers pressing firmly into the small of her back. Heat flared low in her stomach, spreading like wildfire.

When she finally pulled back, breathless, he whispered against her lips, "I don't want to marry anyone but you."

Her heart stilled.

"I know you just returned," he continued, "but I feel like I've known you forever."

He leaned his forehead against hers, exhaling.

"What about Fleur?" she asked.

"My father wants me to marry a lady with land and title. Fleur has both. He's friends with her father." He sighed. "But I don't want her. I want you."

His words struck like a blow to the chest.

She wanted him, too. She had from the moment she saw him again. And yet…

She swayed, suddenly unsteady. Michael caught her, easing her back onto the bed.

"I'm required to marry a lady with land and title," he said again, almost to himself. A bitter truth. Yet he never asked if she had those things. He assumed she didn't.

Trinity swallowed hard.

"Michael, I think I need to lie down. You're right—we've had too much."

He studied her, then nodded, stepping back.

"You're not angry, are you?" he asked.

"No. How could I be?"

171

"We'll talk tomorrow."

Michael kissed her forehead, then turned, closing the door softly behind him.

CHAPTER 14 ~ SYBIL
Ellsworth Manor & York

Before dawn, Sybil woke in David's arms. They couldn't risk being caught together before marriage by anyone at Ellsworth. Catholics believed fornication before marriage was a sin.

Sybil huffed. *Ridiculous.*

But breaking free from her lover's embrace was the last thing she wanted to do. His arms tightened around her tiny waist, pulling her against him, his breath warm on her neck. Gods, she wanted to stay—wrapped in his warmth, safe, and loved.

She carefully lifted his arm, but he held her tighter. "No, don't go." His voice was husky with sleep.

She grinned as he stirred behind her.

"I must," she whispered. "I need to be in the kitchen before anyone wakes."

"I can't wait until you never have to leave my bed again."

She slipped from under the covers and pulled her dress over her head. "That's impossible. I'll always have work."

David pushed himself upright, the blanket pooling at his waist. Soft brown curls dusted his chest, and she fought the urge to run her fingers through them.

"Kiss me before you go," he murmured, eyes dark with longing.

"You didn't get enough last night?" She smirked as she tied her apron. Climbing onto the bed, she leaned in, pressing her lips to his.

He pulled her closer, deepening it with a low moan. Her breath hitched as his tongue slipped between her lips, and her hands instinctively found his chest. He groaned, his body reacting to her touch.

"I have to go," she murmured, pressing one last kiss to his lips before pulling away. Her heart raced. She had never known anything as consuming as this love, this connection—their magic flowed together effortlessly, like two streams from the same river.

She sat to tug on her boots, her body still tingling. "Michael and Trinity will be unwell today."

David raised an eyebrow. "A vision?"

Sybil laughed, standing as she ran her fingers through her white-blonde curls, then braiding them. "No, just common sense. They drank too much wine last night. The poor girl could barely walk, and Michael had to carry her back to her chambers. I'm sure all the staff will be gossiping about it today." She sighed.

David's brows lifted. "Did he stay in her room?"

"I followed them," she admitted. "Nothing happened as far as I could tell. He left soon after she was inside."

"So, she's more proper than my daring fiancée?" he teased.

"I hope so. Sir Henry would have a fit." She rolled her eyes. "It's different for them. Their rules are stricter, my love."

She sighed again as she tied on her caul. "I really must go now."

David caught her hand, tugging her back for one last kiss. "I can never get enough of those," he whispered. "I love you."

Sybil closed her eyes, warmth blooming in her chest. "I love you too," she breathed.

He reached for her again as she stepped away, but laughed, dodging out of his grasp.

"Come see me at supper," she said, slipping through the door before temptation pulled her back.

Sybil moved swiftly across the yard, glancing up at the guards patrolling the wall. The sky had shifted to a wash of grey-blue and orange. The sun began to stretch over the horizon. She pulled her black cloak tighter around her shoulders. If they saw her now, they'd be the first to report her whereabouts.

She halted inside the kitchen. A figure sat at the table in near darkness, illuminated only by a sputtering candle lantern.

"Michael?" she asked, startled.

He glanced up, his hair tousled, last night's clothes clinging to him.

"M'lord, you frightened me."

"Sorry, Sybil. I couldn't sleep."

She hesitated. He appeared exhausted, shadows under his eyes, his usual composure fraying at the edges.

"Are you unwell?"

"No." He sighed. "But I'm afraid Trinity will be. Could you tend to her discreetly? I'd rather my parents not know. I shouldn't have given her so much wine. I was a fool."

"Of course. I'll prepare something right away."

"Thank you."

Sybil hesitated. "Would you like anything to eat or drink?" She wasn't sure what else to do. He barely ever spoken to her in all the years she'd worked here.

"No, I'm not hungry…" His voice trailed off. He rubbed his hands over his face, and whispered, "Is it alright if I sit here? Am I making you uncomfortable?"

"No. Your father spends much of his time here. We're all used to it."

Michael huffed softly, running a hand through his hair before dropping his head into his palms.

***

Sybil carefully balanced the tray and kettle as she climbed the stairs. When she reached the hallway, she froze.

Fleur slipped from Shaun's chambers, wrapping a cloak around her nightclothes. She darted down the corridor toward her bedchambers.

Sybil bit her lip, wincing. *This will end badly.*

Pushing the thought aside, she continued to Trinity's chambers and knocked before entering. Trinity remained asleep, tangled in the blankets, so Sybil set the tray on the table and drew back the thick blinds. Sunlight poured in, golden and soft.

A rainless day, thank the Gods.

"Good morning," she called.

Trinity groaned, rolling onto her side and draping an arm over her eyes. "My head. Oh, Lord, my head," she moaned.

Sybil smiled knowingly. She remembered her own experience with too much wine—her grandmother, Lenora, refused to ease the headache at first, insisting she deserved the suffering. In the end, though, her grandmother relented, as Sybil would now.

She poured a cup of mulled wine infused with peppermint and brought it to the bedside. "This should help."

Trinity pushed herself upright, eyes wide in horror, as she glanced down at her gown. She hadn't changed since the night before. "Oh, my Lord." She pulled the blanket higher. "Please, I hope you don't think less of me."

Sybil chuckled, handing her the cup. "Drink. It will help. I've been drunk once, so I understand how you feel. I don't judge you."

"Thank you." Trinity took a cautious sip, blinking at the taste. "The peppermint is strong."

She looked up from her cup. "I've seen you around. What's your name?"

"Sybil."

"You're a scullery maid, but your duty isn't to serve me. And you seem close to Lady Susana."

Sybil was surprised by Trinity's sharp observations.

"Michael asked me to help you this morning, m'lady. He knows I can be discreet. I've known the family for years—my grandmother is the local healer and midwife. She delivered all of Lady Susana's children."

"I see." Trinity cringed as she closed her eyes, pressing her fingers to her temple. "You were in the dining hall last night, too?"

"Yes. Lady Susana asked me to stay in case you needed anything."

"Was that the only reason you were there?"

Sybil met Trinity's gaze. She was an intelligent woman. She knew exactly what she was asking.

"For your protection, as well as his, m'lady."

Trinity exhaled slowly. "I see. Thank you." She closed her eyes again, brows furrowing. "My head…"

Sybil plucked a few peppermint leaves from the kettle, rolling them between her fingers before handing them over. "Crush these and inhale. It will help."

Trinity mimicked her movements and took a deep breath.

Sybil dipped a cloth into the cool water from the tray and handed it to her. "Press this to your forehead."

Trinity sighed. "Thank you for your kindness, though I hardly deserve it. I was foolish. I've never drunk so much before."

Sybil hesitated. "May I speak freely?"

"Yes, please." Trinity took another sip, pressing the cloth against her forehead.

Sybil smiled. "It's clear you and Michael are quite taken with each other—perhaps even in love?"

Trinity's expression tightened. "Was it that obvious after watching us dine together once?"

"It was." Sybil nodded. "Love has a way of making people oblivious to everything but each other. And when it's overwhelming, it can blur a woman's judgment. Be careful, m'lady. You understand the risk of being alone with him."

"I appreciate your honesty, but I'm well aware of our positions." Trinity handed back the empty cup and leaned against the pillows.

The sadness in her eyes struck Sybil deeply. She carries great weight—loss and uncertainty.

"I love him," Trinity admitted softly, "but it's so…"

"Overwhelming?" Sybil finished.

Trinity nodded. "Please keep that between us. Maybe he's caught up in nostalgia—what we had as children. It's all happening so fast."

"You're wise to consider that," Sybil said gently.

"I feel something, but… Perhaps I'm just not ready yet."

"That's fair enough, m'lady."

"Call me Trinity." She smiled, the first genuine one since Sybil arrived. "Perhaps we could be friends?"

"I'd like that." Sybil smiled back. "But now I must return to the kitchen before Mrs. Bartlett wonders where I've gone."

"Thank you, Sybil."

"It's my pleasure."

Trinity hesitated. "Do you think Michael's father would force him to marry Fleur?"

"Oh." The question took Sybil off guard. She straightened.

"Sorry, I shouldn't have asked. It's only, you've been here for so long. You know them."

"No, it's alright." Sybil perched on the edge of the bed, hands folding in her lap. "I think he would. But if they knew you were a potential match, Sir Henry wouldn't insist on Michael marrying Fleur. He loves his son and is a bit of a romantic himself."

Trinity leaned back, closing her eyes as if absorbing the weight of that truth.

"How long is she staying?" she asked.

"Not much longer. Her father returns from France in a few months to collect her. He expects an engagement to be settled by then."

Trinity's eyes snapped open. "Does Michael know?"

"I'm sure he does."

Trinity exhaled heavily. "So, there's not much time."

"I'm sorry," Sybil said softly. She couldn't imagine being forced into a life-altering decision so quickly. Then again, her situation had been different—she had always known she would marry David.

"If you love him, tell him," Sybil urged. "Tell him if the thought of him with Fleur makes you ache. Be brave."

Trinity swallowed hard and said in a whisper, "Thank you, Sybil."

***

Sybil entered the kitchen and sighed when she saw Michael still seated at the table still, clearly waiting for her. The moment he noticed her, he stood.

Thank the Gods, they were alone. Mrs. Bartlett must have been in the garden, and Prudence hadn't woken yet.

"Is she awake?" he asked.

"Yes, m'lord, but she needs time to recover."

Michael hesitated. "Did she say anything to you about…?"

"No, m'lord. She has a terrible headache." She wouldn't betray Trinity's trust—not even for him.

His jaw tightened. "I should go to her. This is my fault…."

Sybil stepped forward. "Wait. Lady Trinity won't appreciate your presence right now."

He stopped, brows knitting together. "You're in love with David, aren't you?"

"Yes, m'lord, but I don't see—"

"You know what it's like. To be in love."

She hesitated, then nodded. "I suppose I do."

Sybil walked to the counter; she uncovered a basket of warm biscuits. "Here, take one. You should eat something."

Michael accepted it, staring at it as if searching for answers. Then, in a voice so quiet she almost didn't catch it, he asked, "Can you describe it to me?"

Sybil blinked. "That's a very personal question, m'lord."

He exhaled, shaking his head. "You're right. I shouldn't have asked. I just…" He trailed off, rubbing his temples before sitting back down.

Sybil placed a small bowl of freshly creamed butter beside him with a knife. He murmured a thank-you, taking a bite of the biscuit.

She studied him. He was struggling, torn over Trinity, searching for clarity. She huffed and sat across from him.

"I don't know if this will help," she said, "but when I fell in love with David, it was like an avalanche—love cascading through me, impossible to contain. A thousand times stronger than anything I'd ever experienced before. I knew, without a doubt, that I'd spend my life with him." A small smile touched her lips. "I was… certain."

Michael's shoulders relaxed. "Yes. It does feel like that." He let out a breath, chuckling softly. "I think I'm in love with Lady Trinity. But father will never allow… He wants me to marry Fleur. Her father is coming soon." His gaze drifted toward the door. "I need to speak with her."

Sybil stood, returning to the stove before Prudence arrived. "M'lord, if I may suggest—don't rush things. You still have time."

Michael pushed back his chair, running a hand through his hair. "Thank you, Sybil. I truly wish you and David all the happiness in marriage. I envy you both."

She dipped her head. "Thank you, m'lord."

As he walked out, his head hung low, shoulders slumped.

Sybil hoped her words had helped.

CHAPTER 15 ~ MICHAEL
Ellsworth Manor

"There you are!"

Trinity jumped, a hand flying to her heart, the other to the wall of the stairway. "Michael! You scared me half to death!"

"Are you alright?" He took both of her hands in his, searching her face.

Despite looking pale and tired, she was breathtaking in a rose-colored cotehardie. Her hair, braided and pulled away, framing her striking hazel-green eyes.

"You look beautiful," he murmured.

She pulled free, slipping past him down the stairwell. "You shouldn't be here, Michael. Please, I feel awful from last night."

He caught up, stopping her midway. "I'm not marrying Fleur. I'll speak to my father—make him understand."

Trinity spun to face him, placing a hand on his chest. Whether she meant to push him away or simply needed to touch him, it didn't matter—his pulse raced, heat rushing through him.

She looked up, wide-eyed. "Michael, you don't need to do this. Your father has already made agreements with Fleur's father."

"I don't care."

He had to make her see—nothing would stop him from being with her.

She exhaled sharply. "You've hardly spent time with me, yet you claim certainty about marriage with me. You haven't even told me how you feel. I don't know your heart, Michael, and right now, my head hurts too much to think."

His jaw clenched. "How can you say that?" Frustration crept into his voice. If he didn't love her, why would he fight for her? But truthfully, he hadn't been sure himself until speaking with Sybil.

"We were both very drunk last night." Trinity smiled weakly, and his heart dropped. "I won't take your declaration seriously under those circumstances."

Michael grasped her forearms, firmly. "I don't want anyone else. You must see this."

"Michael, you're hurting me." Her voice was soft, but her eyes held fear.

Shame hit him instantly. "I'm sorry." His voice was hoarse. "I just—I can't stand this distance between us."

"What's going on?" Shaun's voice cut through the tension. He stood a few steps away, watching closely. "Let her go."

Michael placed himself between Trinity and Shaun, his frustration twisting into fury. "Mind your own damn business, Shaun."

Shaun's glare sharpened. "Trinity is my business."

"Shaun, it's alright." Trinity touched Michael's shoulder, and warmth spread through him, calming him for the briefest moment—until she pulled away and stepped past him toward Shaun. "He's upset, but not with me."

"What do you have to be upset about?" Shaun asked Michael directly.

Trinity turned back to Michael. "Talk to him. Tell him what you told me. Let him help you understand."

She left them to sort it out.

Michael watched her retreat down the stairs. He'd respect her wish for space—but he wasn't giving up. He wouldn't marry Fleur even if Trinity hadn't returned.

His head pounded, his stomach twisted with frustration, clawing at his insides.

"I need a drink," he muttered, running a hand through his hair as he descended the stairs.

Shaun followed close behind looking fresh and energized despite the night of drinking.

"How dare you put your hands on her, Michael?"

Michael ignored him, unwilling to have this conversation in the stairwell where anyone could overhear.

"What the hell has gotten into you?" Shaun pressed.

Back in the foyer, Michael led them into his mother's parlor. Shaun shut the door behind him as Michael poured wine for both of them.

Shaun crossed his arms. "A little early for that, don't you think?"

Michael downed his drink and poured another. "I need to tell you something. But you must swear never to repeat it."

Shaun exhaled, took the glass, and eyed him warily. "Sounds ominous, even for you."

Michael poured another. "I told Trinity I want to marry her."

Shaun nearly choked on his drink. "What?" Shaun's eyes widened. "Are you in love with her?"

"I am."

Shaun groaned, rubbing his face. "Are you light in the head? You can't marry her."

"Why not?"

Shaun exhaled sharply. "Your father has all but signed the marriage documents accompanying Fleur!"

"I care not."

Shaun groaned louder, raking his fingers through his neatly combed red hair. "Oh, God."

Michael scowled. "Why are you so upset?"

Shaun slammed down his cup. "Has she accepted your proposal?" He shook his head as Michael cringed, not answering. "You're a damn imbecile."

Michael's stomach twisted. "I ruined everything. What do I do?"

Shaun grabbed Michael's shoulder and squeezed it firmly. "It's not me you need to talk to. It's Trinity and your father. But before you do anything, for the love of God, find out if she even wants to marry you." Shaun cocked his head to the side. "When did you speak to Trinity about this?"

"Last night."

Shaun groaned. "Oh, God. Tell me you didn't go into her room."

Michael clenched his jaw. "I did. That's when I told her I wanted to marry her."

Shaun paled. "And?"

"I kissed her."

Shaun inhaled deeply, then exhaled in a slow, measured breath. "Did she reciprocate?"

"Yes."

"Did she tell you she loves you?"

Michael's silence was answer enough.

Shaun dragged a hand down his face. "Go. Go and speak with your father. Not me."

***

Michael left Shaun in the parlor with the rest of the wine. His best friend murmuring insults at Michael. Ones he probably deserved but he'd make things right.

He found Trinity first in the garden. He'd speak with his father afterwards.

"Trinity?"

She looked up from where she knelt in the garden, picking flowers with Sybil, who gave Michael a knowing smile before returning to her task.

Guilt gripped him.

Trinity shielded her eyes from the sun and stood. "Michael, this isn't a good time."

"Can we walk together?"

"Your mother asked me to join her in her parlor." She crossed her arms, leaned in and sniffed him. "And drinking more won't help anything. Thank you very much. You smell as if you've drowned in a cask of wine."

Chagrined, Michael stood speechless. She was right of course.

Sybil stood, keeping her gaze fixed on the basket but he didn't miss the smirk, she quickly hid.

Trinity walked to the kitchen with Sybil on her heels.

Michael stepped forward. "Why are you acting this way? I know you feel something to…"

Trinity left Sybil at the kitchen door and marched back to him, holding the wicker basket like a shield.

"Because we have only begun to become reacquainted after so many years apart. You don't know me." Her voice was soft but resolute. "You're already promised whether you like it or not. I will not bring shame or dishonor to your family."

His frustration boiled over. "I do know you! And I will never marry Fleur!"

She turned away. "I must go. I'm sorry, Michael."

Michael caught her arm—gently this time. "Please don't go."

Tears filled her eyes. "Michael, don't do this."

He cupped her cheek, wiping away a tear with his fingers. "I love you, Trinity. I will not lose you again."

Her breath hitched. She closed her eyes and shook her head side to side as if trying to rid her mind of an unwelcome reality.

His heart clenched. She doesn't love me.

She finally opened her eyes and peered into his, before whispering, "I love you too. I think I always have. But…"

His forehead rested against hers. "As do I… Please… We will make this work."

She exhaled shakily.

Michael pulled away, his eyes dropping to her pink lips, then leaned in and kissed her—slowly, reverently. She dropped the wicker basket as he folded her into his arms and pulled her close. Deepening the kiss. His entire body thrummed with overwhelming need. Everything disappeared.

"I'll speak to my father."

***

188

Nicole Moore

Michael took the stairs two at a time. He needed to find Shaun.

His parents had given Shaun his own chambers years ago, a second home for his closest friend.

Michael didn't bother knocking. He burst inside to find Shaun slumped on his bed, the empty wine decanter beside him, a glass abandoned on the floor. Thoroughly drunk.

The room was modest, with tapestries covering the walls to keep out the cold. A small fireplace flickered, its glow barely reaching the reading table and chair in the corner. The private washroom door hung slightly ajar.

Shaun lifted his head, eyes unfocused. "So, tell me— did your father approve of you marrying her?"

The words stung. Michael's chest tightened. "I haven't spoken with father yet."

He picked up the pitcher, sniffed the remnants of wine, and then set it back down. "Did you drink the entire thing?"

Shaun smirked. "Why do you care?"

Michael huffed out a breath, sitting on the edge of the bed beside Shaun. "Because I do. Tell me what's wrong."

Silence stretched between them. A shiver crawled up Michael's spine. Something was off.

Shaun lifted his hands, palms up, in a dramatic flourish, his body swaying. "So, you're here to gloat, then?"

Michael exhaled, confused by Shaun's bizarre behavior. "You're drunk. We'll talk later."

He stood to leave, but Shaun's voice cut through to the bone. "Did she say she loves you?"

The raw pain in his tone made Michael freeze. The realization hit like a hammer—Shaun was in love with Trinity, too.

Michael swallowed hard. "I told her I love her. She said she loves me." The words came with difficulty, knowing what they would do to his friend.

Shaun let out a bitter laugh. "Well, aren't you always the lucky one?"

Michael's fists clenched. "What is that supposed to mean?"

"You never loved her."

"Of course I did! I still do."

Shaun's face twisted. "I always loved her. But you must take everything."

Michael's pulse hammered. "You never told me!"

Shaun shot to his feet, voice breaking. "You bloody knew!"

The force of the accusation sent Michael a step back. He turned and stormed out, slamming the door behind him.

Shaun's voice echoed down the corridor. "You knew!"

Michael barely registered the sound of his name until a figure stepped into his path. He skidded to a stop.

Fleur stood against the wall, arms crossed, face flushed. "You nearly ran me over! What is wrong with you?"

He let out a breath, forcing himself to focus. "I apologize if I hurt you."

He reached for her hands, but she jerked away as if burned.

"I'm sorry, Fleur. For everything. For how I handled our situation—"

She cut him off with a sharp laugh. "There's nothing to apologize for, m'lord."

The title again. He hated it when she used it.

His patience frayed. "Then why do you despise me still?"

Her chin lifted. "You think too highly of yourself. I don't think of you at all."

The words struck harder than he expected. He stepped back. "Why are you here?"

"Checking on Shaun. He was a wreck in the sitting room before I found him." Her tone turned mocking. "Seems there's trouble in paradise. Your dear Trinity is causing quite the stir."

Michael stiffened. "This has nothing to do with Trinity." A lie.

Fleur huffed. "Perhaps I should speak with your father, after all. He's fond of me, and I'm sure he'd love to hear about his son's… indiscretions."

Michael's temper snapped. "You will not." He stepped closer, his voice low, dangerous. "You will not speak a word about Trinity or Shaun. This is none of your concern."

Fleur tilted her head. "Isn't it?"

Michael exhaled sharply. "Why do you even care?"

A slow smile curled her lips as she touched his chest, stepping closer. Heat surged between them, unexpected and overwhelming. His stomach clenched, the force of it choking him.

"We are to be betrothed, Michael. Whether we desire it or not. Our parents do."

His entire body recoiled. "Even if Trinity never arrived, I'd never marry you."

"Your father won't give you a choice."

The certainty in her voice sent ice through his veins.

191

Michael backed away, turning on his heel. "He would never force me."

Fleur laughed softly. "You think so?"

She pivoted toward Shaun's door, glancing over her shoulder. "I'll check on Shaun. I'm sure he's devastated." Her voice dripped with mock sympathy. "You have always been so selfish."

Bile rose in Michael's throat. "Leave him alone, Fleur."

She didn't stop. "Why would I listen to you?"

Michael clenched his jaw, watching her disappear down the hall. His hands curled into fists.

His father wouldn't force him.

Would he?

***

Michael's father sat in his fur-lined oak chair at the end of the great hall, flanked by stone columns and ancient tapestries. Michael stood beside him, back straight, expression unreadable. But his jaw clicked. Shaun's words rattled around in his mind as he tried to focus. An almost impossible task.

His father had insisted he attend this meeting—watch, listen, learn. One day, this would be his duty. There was no time to speak to his father about Trinity before they were inundated by demands.

Michael's attire reflected his station: fine leather hunting boots, a rich brown cotehardie—a gift from a friend in the Far East. His hair, freshly cut to his shoulders, framed a sharp, noble face. A beaver hat sat neatly atop his head, completing the look. He was every bit his father's son.

But today, his mind was elsewhere. He had to fix things between him and Shaun and speak with father about Trinity. Make him understand there would be no marriage to Fleur. His heart belonged to Trinity, and nothing would change that. Shaun would come to understand and accept this truth. He had to.

The hall was tense. The Herald stood before Michael's father, eyes fixed on the stone floor, sweat glistening on his brow despite the chill in the air. He was a man of average build, but his nervous energy put Michael on edge.

To Henry's other side stood Friar Brook and Joseph. The friar, ever composed, clasped his hands at his mid-section, his brown robes pristine. The Sheriff, Lord Usher, loomed beside the Herald, his presence as insufferable as always. Michael had never liked him—arrogant, smug, the kind of man who believed himself above everyone else.

The Sheriff stepped forward. "There have been more attacks in the forest, m'lord."

Henry's brow furrowed. "More?"

"Yes. Three more villagers killed on the game trail to York."

Henry's fingers tightened around the armrest. "Why haven't these beasts been dealt with?"

The Sheriff hesitated. "They vanish. No trace left behind."

"Isn't it your job to explain these things, handle them?" Henry demanded.

The Sheriff dipped his head. "I've done everything I can, but no one will track them at night anymore. Strange sounds, unnatural occurrences—fear has gripped the people."

"Unacceptable. Find brave men and deal with it immediately. I want those beasts dead, and their pelts hung in my hall." His gaze shifted to the friar. "And you—remind your flock of their duty. Tell them to trust in our Lord, not childish superstition."

The friar bowed slightly. "Yes, m'lord."

Henry turned back to the Sheriff. "Leave Joseph the names and times of the funerals. We will attend."

"As you wish."

As the Sheriff stepped back, Henry sighed and pinched the bridge of his nose. "And what of London?"

"London is in peril. The plague has taken many. Those who survive flee. Even the churches stand empty and abandoned by all but a few who tend to the dying."

Henry's face darkened. "London? The church? Everything in ruin?"

The Sheriff, ever eager to insert himself, stepped forward again. "M'lord, there is no cause for alarm. We are far from London. The plague won't reach us."

"I hope you're right, but I've heard similar reports."

A chill crept over Michael's skin. Trinity had mentioned her aunt and uncle dying from the plague, but she'd said little about the state of the city. Perhaps she didn't know the full extent.

The friar cleared his throat. "We must pray, m'lord. I recommend an extra mass on Wednesday. Let the people confess their sins, seek forgiveness, and cleanse our land."

"More prayers won't hurt." Henry's gaze returned to the Herald. "You're certain the clergy has fled or died?"

The Herald's face was grim. "Yes. Many believe God has turned His back on us." He hesitated. "They say the north will not be spared."

Michael's stomach twisted.

The Sheriff scoffed. "These are mere rumors."

The Herald squared his shoulders. "I apologize, m'lord, but I do not exaggerate. I saw London. The churches were abandoned, and the dead buried in pits outside the walls."

A ripple of unease moved through the room. Father Brook whispered a prayer and crossed himself. The Sheriff smirked but said nothing.

Michael's father inhaled deeply. "I want you to go to town and find Archbishop Zouche. Tell him we must meet immediately."

The Herald bowed. "Yes, m'lord."

Henry's expression darkened. "And what of Trinity Ackerman?"

Michael tensed.

The Herald cleared his throat and pulled out a letter. "Arthur Whiting has written, knowing her family once served you. He hoped you'd watch over her. Lady Trinity is expected to return to court by the end of spring."

Henry sat back, processing the news. "Are you certain?"

"I spoke to Arthur myself. She insisted on returning to York first. Her uncle left her everything and she has his titles, and lands but if she doesn't return to court soon, she will be disinherited."

Henry drummed his fingers on the armrest, deep in thought. "Why would she do that?"

Not waiting for an answer, he dismissed the men. "That will be all."

The hall emptied, leaving only Michael and his father.

Henry exhaled heavily. "What am I to do with this girl?"

Before Michael could respond, Ruby and Rose entered, their arms linked.

Henry waved them off. "Go fetch your mother."

"Yes, Papa!" they chorused and darted out, their long, wild hair bouncing behind them.

Michael smirked but felt a knot forming in his chest. "They'll never be tamed."

His father nodded. "Probably not."

Then his father's expression sobered. "I want to speak with you about Trinity."

"What is it, Father?"

Henry waved a hand. "Relax, son. You're not on trial." His eyes narrowed. "I know you're close to her. I allowed it because of my fondness for the girl… and perhaps my guilt for sending her away all those years ago."

Michael's throat tightened. "Yes, Father, we are close. She is…" He trailed off.

Henry smirked. "Intoxicating? Beautiful? Clever?" He laughed. "Your mother sings her praises every night before bed."

Michael smiled as pride filled him.

Henry studied him. "You love her."

Michael met his father's gaze. "I do."

His father nodded. "Then let's discuss what that means. The King expects her to return so he can match her with a husband."

Michael clenched his fists. "Does she have to return?"

Henry exhaled. "Have you even asked her if she'll marry you?"

Michael straightened. "She knows how I feel. But I would never make such a decision without speaking to you first."

"Has she told you, her feelings?"

"Yes."

His father nodded, seemingly satisfied. "I will send an appeal to the King. Until then, could you find Trinity? Both of you will meet me before supper."

Michael swallowed hard. "Yes, Father." He hesitated. "And Fleur?"

Henry scoffed. "Jeffrey will not be pleased. His wife has been pushing for an arranged marriage since the two of you were born."

"You do know she hates me, father?"

His father laughed, a booming sound that echoed through the room. "Son, I must agree with your mother. You know nothing about women."

Michael's lips pinched as his father's words rolled over him. He'd been told that a lot recently.

His father continued, "We have been patient with you, but you've been at court for four years with not a single acquaintance or interest. You're a knight for Christ's sake and almost 22 and it's time to find a wife and start a family."

"I understand, father, but I wanted to love my wife. Like you love mother."

"Then you are fortunate Trinity has returned."

Michael walked back towards his father. "Would you have truly forced me to marry Fleur?"

Henry didn't answer at first and gave Michael a piercing look. "I would have, for your own good."

Michael let out a huff.

His father clicked his tongue. "Fleur is a fine young lady, and if you'd have taken the time to break that cold exterior, you would have found a gentle soul underneath."

"I think she has blinded you, father, tricked you into believing she has a heart."

"Michael. Be kind to her." Henry narrowed his eyes. "She has a heart, dear boy."

"I promise to be kind until she leaves." Michael gave his father a half bow and then turned to leave. He had to find Trinity.

CHAPTER 16 ~ TRINITY
Ellsworth

A horse whinnied and hoofbeats stopped outside. Trinity stopped tidying up her old home. She tried her best to bring it back to its former state. From what she could remember.

Her childhood home mainly held happy memories. Her parents had loved each other profoundly and adored her, despite her mother's many moods and episodes. But during the worst spells, Trinity's father took her to work with him, assuring her that mother would be fine. She always was—until the last time.

Michael stood in the doorway, holding a food basket. The scent of bacon and fresh bread accompanying him.

"Hello, Michael."

"I was looking for you."

"It appears you've found me." She smiled.

He handed her the basket and spread a blanket over the table. Silently, she unpacked the food. Her stomach rumbled, but Michael said nothing.

199

He picked up a chair without broken legs, set it next to the table, and lifted the long bench beside it.

Trinity smiled. "Thank you."

"Please take the chair."

She sat, and he settled beside her on the bench.

"Sometimes I'm scared I'll turn out as my mother and go mad," Trinity admitted. "She wasn't well even before father died. I understand that now."

"You're not her. If you were, it would have shown by now," Michael said.

"Unless it wasn't an illness but something that just broke inside her mind." Trinity picked at her food. Her mother's words, manic ramblings, echoed in her head, and she shivered.

"I don't want to go mad."

Michael sipped his mead, watching her. "You won't, you're different. Even as a child, I remember her as fragile. You're not."

Trinity finished her bacon and washed it down with watered down mead. It was still too sweet, but it helped her relax.

He took her hand.

She stiffened. "Why have the fields been left unattended? I thought your father needed us to leave so someone else could work them." Her brows pinched. "I don't understand why he made us leave if he wasn't going to tend the land."

"I think he always carried some guilt for sending you away. But it was never about that. This land isn't worth much for yielding crops, so we use it for sheep grazing."

"I still don't understand."

Michael frowned, appearing unsure how to answer. "All I know is that my father gave your mother time to

200

sort out her affairs and offered her work in the manor, but she was in a bad state. One day, father found you half-starved, crying. Mother, Isabella, and Lenora tried to care for her, but she wasn't coming out of the state she was in. Do you remember staying with us for almost a month before father sent you to London?"

Trinity searched her mind. The memory was vague, but she recalled meals with Michael and Elizabeth, Susana caring for her. She had often visited the manor, even spent nights there. But she hadn't remembered that.

"I think so, but I never realized..." She reached for his hand. "How do you know this?" She barely remembered those last days. How could he?

"Mother talked about you over the years."

"Why would your father send us away, knowing my mother couldn't care for herself or me?"

"He hired someone to escort you both to London. He carried a letter to your aunt and enough money to see you safely there." Michael hesitated. "Did he not?"

"No, Michael, he did not. He took the money and abandoned us on the road." Trinity wiped her tears. "We made it—barely. My aunt didn't even recognize us when we arrived. We were covered in filth and fleas. She thought us beggars at first."

She stood, gathering the cups and leftover bread. She needed to do something.

Michael wrapped his arms around her, his mouth at the side of her head. "I'm so sorry."

He lifted her chin upwards so that he could see her face. "Trinity, I was so upset when you left... More than upset. I lost my best friend that day." He hesitated. "Mother told me after you left that she never wanted to let you go either."

"Me too." She gently palmed his stubbly jaw. "I found peace eventually. But after everyone died and left me again, the only place I wanted to be was here with you."

Michael smiled and pulled her tighter.

"Trinity, a message was delivered to my father today. You inherited all your uncle's land, estate, and title and are expected to return to court to be appointed a husband."

She stiffened as her breath caught. *How is that possible? Arthur promised.*

She stepped away, her arms hanging at her sides. Tears fell before she could stop them.

"Did you know?" Michael's voice was calm but urgent. "Please, tell me."

She wanted to be the one to tell him and prayed she wouldn't lose him. The King would send for her and marry her off to some stranger.

She lowered her gaze. "Yes. I knew."

"Please look at me."

"I was going to speak with you about it today." She met his eyes, praying he would understand.

"But why, Trinity? Why would you keep this from me?"

She saw the hurt in his eyes.

Her chest tightened. Now, Henry would send her away for sure. She let out an anguished sob and covered her face.

"Please, don't cry. I didn't mean to upset you." Michael pulled her into his arms, holding her gently.

She laid her head against his chest, her body trembling. "I don't want to leave. I kept it a secret because I needed to be sure you truly loved me, and I didn't want to bring dishonor to you or your family.

202

You are practically engaged to Fleur. Her father and yours have made an accord."

Michael looked down at her, but she wouldn't meet his gaze.

"Trinity?" His voice was barely a whisper.

She wiped her tears. "I never meant to deceive you. I was only trying to protect you and your family. You all mean so much to me." She had to make him believe her. She couldn't handle losing him again. Being alone again.

"I know." He cupped her face. "I understand your fears more than you realize. I've never met a woman who truly loved me and not my title."

Michael brushed away her tears.

He kissed her cheek, then her lips, a feather-light touch. Overwhelming longing pulsed through her, heat rising like a sleeping dragon. Her breath shivered.

He kissed her again, deeper this time. Her lips parted, sharing each other's breath, letting their tongues slide against each other. Their arms wrapped around one another as if letting go would drown them.

"I will never let you go," Michael whispered.

"You promise?"

"I swear to you. Never."

"What about Fleur? Your father?"

"It will be rectified."

She pulled away. "I need to show you something then... Before..."

Michael watched as she disappeared into the alcove that had been her bedroom. In the darkness, she picked up the sword her aunt had left for her. She'd hidden the sword and shield here to keep it safe from being discovered.

She said a silent prayer that he would understand and that he wouldn't think she was mad.

As she picked up the sword, warmth spread through her hands. A ripple of light snaked down the blade.

Trinity froze.

Taking a deep breath, she turned and carried it into the room. Leaving the shield in the corner. *One thing at a time.*

Michael's eyes narrowed as they flicked from the sword to her face. "Why do you have a sword?"

"My aunt gave it to me."

"A sword?" His brow furrowed. "I don't remember you with a sword."

"I wrapped it under my travel bag. It looked like part of my sleeping mat."

"Why would your aunt give you this?"

"It's called Guardian's Light, and it comes with a shield called the Shield of Truth."

"I don't understand."

Trinity hesitated. "My aunt told me demons walk among us. That I was to find others and fight them, she was sick. Delusional. But..."

Michael watched her. "What do you believe now?"

She paused for a moment, took a deep breath and told him about the encounter with the Seraph, called Seriella.

By the end, she'd retrieved the shield, but it didn't tell any truths or show anything other than Michael's handsome reflection.

He studied the sword thoughtfully, not once interrupting her. But a crease grew deeper between his eyes as she described the vision of the demons and her aunt fighting them, especially as she told him that she was ordered to find the druids.

In the end, Michael blew out a breath. "I'm not overly religious, Trinity. So, I can't say I have great knowledge of what you speak of, but it sounds dangerous…" He cringed and shook his head slightly as if trying to shake off the thoughts. "I don't think we should say anything about this until we understand it better."

"I agree," Trinity said softly. She didn't want anyone to know but understood that Seriella wouldn't allow her to shirk the responsibility. Somehow, she needed to find the "others" and fast.

But how?

"Maybe the shield will show us how to find the others?" She lifted the shield back onto the table.

"Are you sure this is a good idea?" Michael shifted nervously beside her. "It didn't work when I touched it before. It just looks like an ordinary shield."

"Perhaps…" she paused thinking. Seriella told her it would show her the truth, but it hadn't shown anything since that first night.

She took Michael's hand and placed it on the shield's surface, then put hers on top of his.

She held his gaze, waiting. Nothing happened.

"Close your eyes," she said.

Michael did as she said and a moment later his body stiffened, and his eyelids clenched tightly. A crease formed between his brows and a light sheen of sweat formed at his brow and upper lip.

She froze. Watching. Waiting.

A few moments later, Michael ripped his hand away and clutched the sides of his head, stumbling backwards off the bench. The bench crashed to the ground. His frantic gaze found hers and his eyes widened.

"Trinity, the demons. I saw you with the shield and sword, fighting the demons!"

Trinity shivered, clutching her hands to her chest. "Seriella said I would fight them."

He moved back to her, palming her cheek in his hand, his expression filled with a mix of awe and pity.

"Did you see who the others are that we must find?" she asked.

"No."

Her heart plummeted. Hope sputtered out. "I don't know what to do."

"We mustn't speak of this to anyone," Michael said, helping her stand.

"I know but you believe me, right?"

"I do."

"Are you sure, you still want to marry me?"

Michael folded her into his embrace. "More than anything I've ever desired." He kissed the top of her head. "We'll figure this out and I promise to protect you."

**

They entered the audience hall where Michael's father, Sir Henry, waited.

"Father," Michael announced.

"M'lord," Trinity said, curtseying. She forced herself to meet Henry's gaze.

"Trinity, has Michael informed you of the news brought to us this morning?" Henry asked, getting straight to the point.

"Yes." She lowered her eyes. "I'm sorry I kept it from you." Heat crept up her neck. She should have told them sooner.

"So, you knew of your position and inheritance?"

"Yes."

"Do you realize you must report to court?"

That surprised her. "I thought I had until the end of spring. I was planning to leave then."

"Well, that would have been a pity." Henry stroked his beard, considering. "Has Michael made his intentions clear?"

Trinity's eyes snapped to Henry's, relieved to see him smiling. "Yes, m'lord."

"And you accepted?"

"Yes," she said, suddenly self-conscious.

"Wonderful! Then we shall celebrate tonight!" Henry's voice boomed.

Trinity stared at him, open-mouthed and blinking several times.

"Oh, for such a clever girl, have we left you speechless?" He laughed. "I am pleased with this match. You have nothing to fear. I'll do everything I can to keep you here. We will prepare for the wedding as soon as we hear from the King. We have much to celebrate."

"Thank you, Father," Michael said, taking Trinity's hand.

"Michael, ensure your mother moves Trinity from the guest wing to a proper room near Elizabeth. Inform her at once."

Henry stood, walked to Trinity, and took her hands. "I thought of you often over the years, young lady. I am delighted you've returned. Welcome to our family, though you always felt like family." He kissed the top of her hands.

Trinity smiled. "Thank you, m'lord."

"Call me Henry from now on."

CHAPTER 17 ~ SYBIL
The Grove

Sybil planted her feet; sword raised as Nicholas swung at her. She blocked, lunged—he jumped backwards just in time.

"Good!" he said, resetting his stance. "Again!"

His dark hair was pulled back, sharpening his high cheekbones and striking silver-blue eyes. He moved as a predator. His magic rolling off him in black ribbons of mist. He was a master of shadows. Typically seen as black magic but he'd been born with it. It was the main reason the coven sent him and his father away. To hide him from persecution from their own coven.

Sweat dripped down Sybil's body; her muscles burned, but she pushed through. Nicholas moved like a spirit—there one second, gone the next. She wanted to learn that. His black ribbons whipped around her sword, pulling it from her grip.

"That's not fair!" she complained, retrieving it.

He pulled them back into the palms of his hands, grinning. "The demons won't fight fair either, Syb."

She huffed and lifted her sword again. "Fine!"

"Come on, Sybil, finish him off!" Luca called from the sidelines, taking a break from sparring.

She glanced at him and grinned.

Nicholas struck with the broad side of his sword.

"Hey! I wasn't ready!" She arched away, rubbing her backside. "Gods, that hurt!"

"Never get distracted. Number one rule." Nicholas smirked, resuming his stance.

Sybil lifted her sword, arms screaming. "I thought balance was the number one rule?"

She feinted, then kicked his feet out from under him. Nicholas's backside hit the ground with a thud.

Laughter erupted from the boys. Some clapped, others whistled. Sybil lowered her sword and offered a hand.

"Well done." He let her pull him up and brushed himself off.

"My arms are dead." She shrugged.

"You have good instincts."

Luca and Enzo approached, a few younger boys trailing behind. Luca slung an arm around her. "Our tough girl."

"Ha! I feel like death." She shoved his arm off. "Thanks, Nicholas. What you're doing for us is invaluable."

Nicholas nodded. "It's my pleasure. I was born for this."

"What? Fighting young girls?" Luca teased.

Nicholas shook his head, grinning as he walked away.

They trained at the grove many miles north of York, behind an old monastery. The coven owned the land and held celebrations and ceremonies there. A thick forest surrounded the property. The stone building had a bell tower—though the bell was long gone. Inside, they stored their weapons, including the newly warded obsidian swords, arrows, and spears.

"If you ever want to train with an axe, let me know." Jacob strode toward them, axe slung over his shoulder, black hair flowing down his back. He pulled her into a crushing hug.

She laughed. "I'm not ready for that."

"Well, are you ready to get married?" His gaze flicked behind her.

David walked toward them. Her David. Her soon-to-be husband. Butterflies stirred.

"Yes. Most definitely, yes." She passed her sword to Luca and met David halfway. Throwing herself into his arms.

He lifted her off her feet. "Is Jacob trying to steal you from me again?" he whispered.

She kissed him. "He's old enough to be my father. Possibly my grandfather."

David kissed her again.

The boys hollered comments, laughing and smacking each other's backs.

"Can't you wait until you're married?"

"Shameful!"

Sybil laughed against his lips, rolling her eyes. "I can't wait to marry you."

David tensed.

She stepped back. "Hey, what's going on? You still want to get married, right?"

"Of course." He kissed her and then stepped back. "It's just… Are you sure about a chapel wedding? It feels wrong."

"Sir Henry and Lady Ellsworth insisted. It's a huge honor. Refusing would insult them and appear suspicious."

He took her hands. Behind her, the sound of sparring continued.

"I understand, but I always thought we'd marry under the trees here, like our parents."

"The Ellsworth can't come here."

"I know." He sighed and pulled her into another hug.

The wind picked up, carrying the scent of earth and spring.

An idea struck her.

"Let's marry here. Under the full moon tonight. Then tomorrow, we'll marry in the chapel for the Ellsworth."

David yanked her close, his blue eyes gleaming. "Truly!"

"Yes!"

He turned, grinning. "Jacob! You're giving Sybil away tonight! We're getting married here!"

Sybil laughed as the boys whooped and cheered.

"I'll get Lenora and Evelyn," Enzo called.

"I'll get the wine!" Luca bolted for his horse.

Jacob strode up, leaving his axe behind. He clasped David's arm. "It would be an honor."

He had become a father figure to them both. He had no magic and wasn't part of the coven, but after fighting ghouls together, he was family. He had taken an oath of secrecy and no harm.

"What am I going to wear?" Sybil asked.

David smirked. "Nothing?"

"David, no."

"My parents did it."

Jacob doubled over, laughing. "Son, I don't think your bride wants that. And I, for one, don't want to see it."

Sybil planted a hand on her hip. "Are you saying there's something wrong with how I look?"

David and Jacob both burst into laughter.

"No, my dear," Jacob said. "But you're like a daughter to me, so…"

She grinned and David kissed her cheek.

"Fine," she said. "But I still need a dress. And a bath."

***

Sybil stood before the long mirror, tears streaming down her face. Speechless.

Her grandmother had brought the dress—more beautiful than she'd ever imagined.

White lace covered a cream gown, clinging to her bust before flowing to the ground—lace sleeves draped past her elbows. A white belt embroidered with gold runes hung loose on her hips and trailed down the front.

She looked like a goddess.

She cupped her hands to her mouth and sobbed.

"Come now, child, it can't be that bad," Lenora teased, entering with a wildflower wreath, delicate purple blooms lacing the edges of green ivy.

Evelyn bumped the door open with her hip and arms full of flowers. "Got the flowers!" She kicked the door shut before anyone could peek inside.

Lenora placed the wreath on Sybil's head, adjusting the braid beneath it.

"What's wrong?" Lenora asked.

Evelyn dropped the bouquets on the counter and turned, concerned.

Sybil shook her head. "I'm just so happy. I never thought I'd have a dress like this."

She didn't tell them she wished her parents were alive, how much she ached for them in that moment.

Evelyn saw through the excuse. She hugged Sybil from behind. "Your mother and father would be so proud of you."

"You think?" Sybil sobbed again.

Evelyn handed her a white-linen cloth.

Sybil wiped her eyes, then tried to return it.

"No, keep it. Your wedding handkerchief—for luck."

"Thank you." Sybil dabbed her tears again and laughed. "Do all brides cry like this?"

Lenora cackled.

Evelyn shot her a warning look. "Don't you dare."

Lenora ignored her. "Evelyn cried so hard her eyes puffed up. She could barely see."

Sybil burst out laughing. "I can imagine." She studied her reflection—her silver-blue eyes glossy and swollen. "I wish Trinity could be here."

"Hm, you're becoming friends?" Lenora asked.

Evelyn busied herself arranging the bouquet, tying on a small iron horseshoe. Lenora fussed with Sybil's train.

"Yes. She's kind and intelligent."

"Any signs of magic?" Lenora asked.

"No, not that I've seen. She hasn't said anything, but she and Michael are engaged now."

"Really?" Evelyn glanced up. "Interesting. I always thought she'd marry Shaun."

Lenora cackled again. "He may still want to."

"Oh dear," Evelyn murmured, wisely dropping the subject.

Sybil adjusted the flowers in her wreath. "He was supposed to marry Fleur but fell for Trinity instead."

"It was fate," Lenora said. "Just like you and David."

Evelyn handed Sybil the bouquet. "Are you ready, dear?"

Was she? She'd waited her whole life for this. Still, her stomach flipped.

"Yes."

"Did you give Trinity the amulet?" Lenora asked.

"Yes. A light green one to match her eyes. But she already had one."

"Of course," Lenora muttered.

"She added mine to her bracelet. The pendant on her cross is old—the magic is fading, but it still works. Mine will amplify it."

"And the Ellsworth?" Evelyn tied a ribbon around the bouquet.

"I gave one to Prudence, and some maids. I'm almost finished with Mrs. Bartlett's. She doesn't wear anything in the kitchen, so it must be given to her as a gift somehow… Without raising any suspicion."

"What about Lady Susana?" Evelyn asked, stepping back.

"Lady Susana won't wear it but keeps it in her pocket."

"The twins? Michael? Henry?" Lenora listed them off.

"The twins keep losing theirs. Henry refused—it's 'improper' to take a gift from a servant. I tried saying it was a thank-you for letting us marry in the chapel." Sybil huffed. "Michael said the only ring he'll wear is

214

his wedding band. I might spell it before they marry, but I'm unsure how to get it."

"Perhaps a small brooch? Something discreet?" Evelyn suggested. Clever, but not foolproof.

"I'll try."

Lenora squeezed Sybil's arms and kissed her cheek. "You're doing an excellent job, dear. I'm proud of you."

"Thank you, Grandmother." Sybil took a deep breath. But she wished she could do more.

***

The night was clear, with a few wispy clouds drifting across the sky. The moon shone brightly, illuminating the grove in its magical rays of light.

Sybil walked into the grove; her arm entwined with Jacob's.

"You look beautiful, young lady," he said softly. "Nervous?"

"My nerves are on fire."

"That's normal. You're taking a big step. It's natural to be on edge."

"Thank you, Jacob. For everything."

"Anytime. I've always wanted a daughter." He squeezed her hand affectionately.

They stepped between two towering oaks into the clearing, where family and the entire coven waited. David stood in the center beside the Fili, a singer who had travelled from Ireland.

Silence fell as Sybil entered. The Fili began to sing in an ancient Celtic tongue she didn't recognize. David had explained it was a traditional wedding song.

She smiled at her cousins and friends, then met David's gaze.

He appeared impossibly handsome in the moonlight. His dark hair, tied back, almost black. His blue eyes sparkled. Dressed in a long white tunic with green embroidery and runes, he looked like he belonged to another world.

She ached to kiss him.

Jacob led her to David, placed her hand in his, and stepped backwards.

David guided her towards the Fili. The elder, with silver-grey hair tied back, wore a simple tunic and black leather belt. As the last haunting note of his song faded, he began the ceremony.

He wrapped the cord around their hands, securing it with a wedding knot.

It was the moment she had dreamed of. And it was perfect.

***

After the ceremony, they danced, sang, and drank until they could barely stand. Lenora and Evelyn departed early, having prepared the only available room in the old monastery. They made a bed and left wine on the table and flowers scattered across the floor.

Their first night as husband and wife.

David walked her into the room, his arm firm around her waist. For the first time, she was nervous. Silly, considering they had made love before, but this... She had no words.

David frowned when she hesitated at the door. "Are you unwell?"

She laughed, stepping inside, running a hand over the bed. "Do you feel different?"

David embraced her from behind, his chest warm against her back, arms circling her belly. "Yes and no.

216

But I can't wait another moment to take this dress off you," he whispered, fingers already working the ribbons.

The fabric loosened, slipping from her shoulders, pooling at her feet. She turned to face him.

David inhaled sharply.

He lifted her as if she weighed nothing, laying her on the bed before pulling his tunic over his head in one smooth motion.

"I promise to worship you for the rest of our lives," he murmured, untying his pants and letting them fall.

And he did—all night.

CHAPTER 18 ~ TRINITY
April 1349 - York & Ellsworth

Trinity drifted through York's market as if walking on clouds. Tomorrow, she was marrying Michael.

The King had approved of their marriage. The manor buzzed with excitement.

She'd hoped for a small wedding like Elizabeth's and Sybil's, a few weeks before but Susana insisted it had to be grand. Michael would be Lord of Ellsworth one day. They had to play the part.

Trinity suspected Susana simply wanted an excuse for a grand celebration.

They'd come to the market for last-minute wedding supplies.

"Lady Trinity Ellsworth," she whispered, her heart bursting. She hadn't thought about anything but the wedding. Not even the angel Seriella. Demons. Finding the Druid-kin. Nothing else mattered but her and Michael. Neither brought it up again.

The market bustled with jugglers, mimes, and merchants. A juggler fumbled, a young boy snatched a ball, and the chase was on.

Trinity laughed as the juggler stumbled after him.

Sybil and Fleur flanked her, wicker baskets in hand. They all but ignored one another.

Trinity hung back as Fleur and Sybil joined Susana, who was browsing trinkets at her favorite stall. Fleur wore a striking red gown, Sybil's usual white tunic, and a brown apron.

Trinity observed them, smiling to herself. I have a family, friends, and true love. Life is perfect.

Sybil remained at the maid's quarters; David's room too small for them both. But she lay in his arms every night, exactly where she belonged. Trinity couldn't be happier for them.

Sybil was obnoxiously happy—openly, shamelessly in love. Around Trinity and Fleur, she and David were overly affectionate. Trinity wasn't used to it. Her aunt and uncle had loved each other, but never so indiscreetly. It wasn't proper. But she'd never scold Sybil. She understood.

Fleur, though—Trinity worried about her. Not because of Michael. God, no. The two could barely stand to be in the same room. But sadness clung to Fleur like an old shawl draped over her even on the brightest days. Trinity saw it in the way she lingered behind, looking into the distance as if searching for something she'd lost.

Susana approached with two baskets full of tiny plants for her garden. "Hold this, dear." She handed her one.

Trinity accepted it happily as Susana rejoined Fleur and Sybil, who admired a deep blue fabric at another stall.

Susana's light blue cotehardie swished as she walked, the same shade as her eyes. Trinity watched her with quiet admiration. Lady Susana was everything she hoped to become—the mother she desperately needed.

Trinity, lost in thought, was suddenly lifted off the ground. She yelped as someone spun her.

Shaun grinned down at her.

"You're a fool, Shaun Donaldson!" she scolded.

They hadn't seen each other since that morning in the corridor. Michael had tried to mend things, but Shaun refused. He even skipped their engagement celebration. No one knew why they had fallen out, and Michael wouldn't speak of it.

Susana had told Trinity that Shaun's mother, Isabella, had been ill. He'd likely been caring for her.

"You look like a princess," Shaun said, kissing her hand before taking the basket.

"I heard a horrific rumor." He leaned in mischievously. "That you're a titled lady with lands and are marrying someone we both know is a complete ass."

Trinity studied his face. He was still angry with Michael, but she didn't understand why he had avoided her.

"I've missed you. Why don't you visit?" she asked bluntly.

"I was upset with Michael... I don't know what to say."

"'I'm sorry' would be a start."

Silence stretched as they continued to walk.

"I'm sorry," Shaun said sheepishly.

220

"Apology accepted." She grinned. "But now you must come home and speak with Michael. If you miss the wedding, he'll be devastated. I'll be devastated." She caught his hesitation and added, "There will be games, drinks, and many young ladies. You'll have a grand time."

His lips twitched. "Now you're talking." He wrapped her arm through his. "I was planning to see him, Trinity."

As they reached the others, Susana spread her arms. "Shaun! You devil, why have I not seen you for so long?"

He kissed the back of her hand. "I do apologize for my absence, m'lady."

Fleur, standing beside Susana, smiled.

Trinity's mouth fell open. Fleur—who barely smirked—smiled at Shaun.

Shaun fumbled, mumbled an awkward hello, and kissed Fleur's hand.

Sybil snorted. Shaun's face burned red.

Trinity coughed. "Shaun is coming home with us." She beamed.

"Lovely! It's always a pleasure," Susana said warmly. "And Isabella? Is she well? I meant to stop by today."

"She's much better. She'd love to see you."

"Then let's collect her, too. Some country air will do her good. And ogling all the young men won't hurt, either." Susana laughed, taking Shaun's arm as they walked.

Trinity, Fleur, and Sybil followed.

***

It was the happiest time in Trinity's life. As she rode in the carriage, surrounded by the people she loved, she gazed out the window, feeling like the luckiest girl alive.

"I always thought you two would end up married." Isabella pointed at Trinity and Shaun.

Trinity and Shaun laughed, caught off guard.

"Mother, please," Shaun muttered, sneaking a glance at Fleur. "Trinity, I deeply apologize. My mother's been ill—I believe it's addled her mind."

Isabella, draped in a wool shawl, her red-streaked-grey hair neatly braided, scoffed.

"I may be old, but I'm not blind." She leaned forward, patting Trinity's hand. "Fate simply put you somewhere else."

Shaun's face burned even redder.

Trinity smiled warmly. "Any woman would be lucky to marry you, Shaun." She meant it. Had she not fallen for Michael, perhaps... But it wasn't meant to be.

Shaun chuckled. "I'm not so sure about that. I am a scoundrel. Or so I'm told." He winked at Fleur.

The women laughed.

"That you are," Susana teased, "but a beloved scoundrel."

Trinity caught the glances between Shaun and Fleur but said nothing.

Perhaps, if they all found love, it would be a blessing.

But she knew Fleur's father would never allow it. Shaun was wealthy, but not noble.

As the manor came into view, cheers and laughter rang out. Henry had insisted on jousting tournaments and three days of celebration. Over two dozen guests—family from across England and Scotland—had arrived.

Two of Susana's younger sisters were among them, whom Trinity had quickly befriended. Like Susana, they were petite, with chestnut-brown hair and bright blue eyes.

They spent hours in the garden, whispering about married life, laughing over secrets only young wives shared.

Trinity had been unsure about her wedding night. One of the sisters had eagerly explained—in detail. It had frightened her to death. She had run to Susana in tears. Susana, ever patient, held her and reassured her everything would be fine.

Trinity had never felt so foolish. But she'd never even kissed another man before Michael, and he only kissed her a few times.

The carriage halted. The driver opened the door and helped them down.

The courtyard was packed, alive with celebration. It resembled the market, filled with laughter, music, and merriment.

Sybil carried the baskets inside, nodding and smiling. The rest of them moved through the crowd gathered in the front yard.

Guards stood at every entrance. Each nodded to Susana as they passed.

The great hall, where Henry usually held court, was empty—everyone outside, riveted by the jousting.

"I told that stubborn man not to spend too much time outside," Susana grumbled, speaking of her husband.

Henry's health had worsened, and Trinity was worried. The tonics no longer seemed to help.

Elizabeth entered, humming softly. She wore a light blue cotehardie with a silver chain around her thick waist. Her hair was coiled tight under a matching blue caul.

"Mother! Trinity! You're back." She smiled at Fleur, then frowned at Shaun. "Shaun."

"Where's your father?" Susana asked.

Elizabeth sighed. "Being an absolute brute to my husband. You must tell him to be nicer."

Susana smiled. Trinity understood now—this was Henry's way of bonding. Soon enough, they'd be thick as thieves.

"He's outside," Elizabeth said before disappearing through the back door she'd just come through.

They followed her to the field, where guests of high rank gathered around the jousting pit. The tournament had been running since sunrise. The air was thick with dust, ale, and the clatter of armor.

A horse galloped past, sweat glistening on its flank. The rider, in full armor, aimed his lance.

Two knights charged.

A clash of wood and metal. Both hit their mark and tumbled to the ground.

The knight in white scrambled to his feet and yanked off his helmet—laughing, breathless, gripping his side.

Trinity gasped.

Michael.

He could have been killed.

He caught her stare. After the applause, he strode toward her, took her hands in his gloved ones, and kissed them gently.

"My love," he whispered, still catching his breath.

He pecked his mother's cheek.

"Father is itching to compete," he said to his mother. "I told him I wouldn't make it to my wedding if I let him."

"Ha! Good boy," Susana laughed.

She spotted Henry sitting in the family section and excused herself to join him.

Michael turned to Shaun. Silence stretched between them.

"I wanted to say congratulations," Shaun said stiffly. As if speaking to a stranger.

"They didn't drag you here kicking and screaming?" Michael teased, then laughed.

Shaun smirked. The two men embraced, clasping each other's hands.

"I'm relieved—and happy—you're here, my friend," Michael said. "I've missed you."

Trinity exhaled. She couldn't imagine getting married without Shaun there.

"I wouldn't miss it," Shaun assured them. Then, grinning, "But honestly, I was expecting more ale. And more young women!"

He laughed, and for the first time in days, Trinity felt everything was as it should be.

***

That night, the great hall overflowed with guests— eating, drinking, singing. Jugglers performed, musicians played, and storytellers recited rhymes. Chandeliers blazed with candlelight, and a roaring fire filled the hearth.

Henry banged his cup against the table, demanding attention. He stood, raising his drink, and the room quieted as everyone followed suit.

225

"A toast to my son Michael and his enchanting bride-to-be, Trinity. To their future happiness! May all your dreams come true, and may you be blessed with many children."

He sat back down—too heavily—then laughed.

"Here, here!" The hall erupted in unison, and then conversation resumed.

Trinity placed a hand over Henry's. "Thank you."

A heaviness clung to him. There was so much to celebrate, yet concern lurked in his eyes.

"Are you alright, m'lord?" she asked.

Michael studied his father. "Is something wrong?"

Henry hesitated, then exhaled and coughed into his hand.

"I don't want to trouble you before your wedding. I'm sure it's nothing."

"Father, please. I can see it's weighing on you." Michael leaned forward. "Have there been more attacks? We haven't found the wolves.

"No. Since the curfew, no others have been harmed." Henry took a long drink of ale. "I have news from the South."

"From London?" Michael asked.

"No. Closer. A day's ride from here." Henry's voice dropped. "The plague has wiped out an entire village. Not one soul left." He glanced at Trinity. "My scouts found no one alive." His face paled as he spoke.

Michael stiffened. "Are you certain?"

"I am. But your mother must hear none of this. I won't have her worrying more than she already does."

Michael fell silent, his grip tightening on Trinity's hand.

Trinity's mind reeled. How had it spread so fast?

Michael spoke first. "What does this mean for us?"

Trinity answered before Henry could. "It takes the young, the old—everyone. It has no mercy." Her eyes filled with tears. "None of us are safe."

Michael took her hands and kissed them softly. "Enough, my love. I promised you'd be safe here."

She knew better. No one was safe.

Henry's voice was gentle but firm. "No tears at this table. You'll have a glorious wedding, and I assure you—everyone will be safe." But he sounded like he was trying to convince himself more than her.

Susana slid into the seat beside him, glancing between them.

"What's going on?" She studied Trinity's face.

"Nothing, mother." Michael forced a smile. "Father is just being sentimental again."

Susana scoffed. "Well done, Henry! You're supposed to make her happy, not sad." She laughed lightly, but her eyes lingered on her husband as if sensing something wasn't right.

CHAPTER 19 ~ TRINITY
Ellsworth & York

Sybil shook Trinity awake. She cracked an eye open. The sun hadn't fully risen, shadows still stretching across the room.

Trinity groaned, rolling to her side and yanking the blanket over her head. "What are you doing? It's too early."

"I wanted to give you a wedding present before you left," Sybil said. "I won't see you for the rest of the day."

She pushed herself up, moaning and squinting. "You didn't have to, Syb."

"I know." Sybil pulled a small white cloth from her pocket and unfolded two embroidered handkerchiefs. Green initials stitched in intricate scripts into the corners—T.E. on one, M.E. on the other. Strange but beautiful, intricate filigree framed the edges.

Trinity took them reverently. "These are beautiful!"

"One for you, one for Michael. A gentleman should always have a handkerchief, and I promise you will need one too."

"Thank you so much." Trinity hugged her tightly.

"It's a tradition in our family," Sybil explained. "When a couple marries, they carry a handkerchief for good fortune."

Trinity smiled, dabbing at the tears already pooling. "Then it's perfect because I think you're right, I'll definitely need it today." She laughed, hugging Sybil again—then a sob shook her.

Sybil pulled back. "What's wrong? Why are you crying?"

"I'm scared." Trinity wiped her eyes, pressing her fingertips against them to stop the deluge.

"Oh, you have nothing to fear. Being married to the man you love is wonderful! You'll see."

"It's not that." Trinity took a shuddering breath. "I know Michael will always love me." Her voice faltered. "The plague is here, Sybil. Henry told us last night. After what I saw in London…" She swallowed hard, her chest tightening. "None of us will be safe."

What if everyone dies? What if I'm left alone again?

Sybil squeezed her arm gently. "My grandmother will help as many as she can. She's a great healer."

Trinity exhaled, meeting her friend's eyes.

Be strong.

"We'll need to pray more. I'll see the priest for confession before the ceremony."

"That's a good idea."

"Will you pray with me now?" Trinity had never seen Sybil at Sunday mass, which struck her as odd.

"Of course." Sybil took Trinity's hand in hers.

They closed their eyes, clasped hands, and Trinity whispered prayers, adding one more—for protection from the plague.

***

After Sybil departed, Trinity clutched the handkerchief, wishing her parents, aunt, and uncle were here.

Morning light streamed through the windows, casting a golden glow.

Her room, once meant for one of the twins, had remained empty for years—their refusal to be separated had left it unused. Susana had joyfully given the room to Trinity, insisting it would remain her private chamber even after the wedding. Every woman needed her own space.

A soft knock at the door startled her.

Susana entered, carrying a long white silk and lace gown. Olivia followed, a wooden form in her arms. She set it beside the window, and Susana carefully draped the gown over it.

Trinity's wedding dress.

"Good morning," Susana sang, adjusting the fabric.

Trinity stretched, yawning. "Good morning."

"Olivia, fetch the mirror from Elizabeth's room."

"Yes, m'lady." Olivia curtsied and slipped out.

Trinity wrapped herself in a white robe and approached the gown. It was as if she were dreaming. She ran her fingers over the delicate silk. "Thank you, Susana. It's breathtaking."

Tears welled up—again. They seemed endless these past few days.

"Darling, no tears," Susana soothed, rubbing her back.

"I'm sorry." Trinity wiped at them, laughing weakly. "It's like the rain in winter."

Susana studied her. "Are you sure you're well? Or is something else troubling you?"

Trinity hesitated.

I shouldn't lie—but Henry had asked me not to speak of it.

She shook her head. "Nothing anyone can fix. I just wish my mother and aunt were here."

That was true. And thankfully, Susana didn't push.

"They are," Susana said gently. "Watching over you, proud of you." She smiled, hugging Trinity before kissing her cheek. "You know, I always desired another child. The Lord didn't see fit to bless me again, but you…" She stepped back, exhaling softly. "You've become like a daughter to me."

Trinity's throat tightened.

Susana hesitated before continuing, voice softer. "I never wanted you to leave when you were little. We thought you'd be happier with your mother, that your aunt could care for you both." She touched Trinity's cheek. "But I never forgot about you. And I'm so happy to be here for you now."

Trinity swallowed back the lump in her throat. "Thank you."

Susana smiled, crossing her hands in front of her chest. "Now, no more tears. Olivia will help you dress and do your hair."

"Is Heather sick?" The lady's maid usually helped Trinity.

"She's fine. But today, you must shine. Olivia is the best."

With that, Susana left, shutting the door behind her.

Trinity turned back to the gown—a labor of love.

She felt safe, cherished, and happy. But something gnawed at her.

She crossed the room to the large newly carved chest at the end of her bed, a wedding gift from Susana. Trinity lifted the lid. The sword and shield now lay wrapped in thin cotton. Carefully, she unwrapped them, holding the blade into the light. The runes shimmered along the silver edge. The hilt was smooth and cold—no heat, no pull—not this time.

She sighed, the words haunting her.

"There's great evil among us… You must fight this evil… Find the others…"

But who were the others? And how was she supposed to find them? It had been months, and she wasn't closer to solving that riddle.

She laid the sword in the chest.

Fingers traced the blade, and a tingle shot through her skin. She yanked her hand back, pressing her fingertips to her lips.

This belongs in a church, locked away safely—not hidden in her chambers.

"You must fight the demons… Find the others…"

Trinity whispered, "Who are the others?"

A knock.

Heart hammering, she slammed the lid closed. "One moment!"

She straightened her robe, smoothed her hair, and opened the door—expecting Olivia. It wasn't.

Michael stood in the doorway.

She gasped. "You're not supposed to be here!"

He stepped inside, closing the door behind him.

"I had to see you." His eyes scanned her face. "Why do you look so pale? Like you've seen a ghost."

She didn't answer; she leaned into him as he pulled her closer, holding her tightly.

"I'm scared," she admitted, her cheek pressed against his chest.

His arms tightened. "I promise I'll be a good husband."

She stepped back, laughing softly. "Don't be ridiculous. I know you will." Her fingers curled into his tunic. "It's not that…" She sighed heavily. "It's the sickness. It's coming."

Michael cupped her face, making her meet his gaze. "Everything will be fine, darling." He kissed her gently.

She wished she could believe him.

"You must go. Olivia's arriving any moment."

He sighed but obeyed, pressing one last kiss to her lips before slipping out the door.

Trinity exhaled and collapsed onto the bed, eyes drifting shut, willing herself to think only of his kiss.

Not of the sword and shield.

Not of the seraph, Seriella.

Not of the fear clawing at the edge of her mind.

***

The chapel overflowed with friends, family, and noble guests, but the moment Trinity stepped through the doors, a hush fell.

Henry stood beside her, his hand gently covering hers. She clung to his forearm like a lifeline. She wasn't scared—at least, that's what she told herself. But marriage was a step into the unknown. Would she be a good wife?

Henry coughed into a cloth, his body shuddering.

She gripped his arm tighter. "Are you sure you're alright?"

"I'm perfectly well, my dear." He patted her hand.

Trinity searched his face, unconvinced, but nodded. He looked wretched. His skin was pallid grey, and he had dark circles under his eyes.

At the end of the aisle, Michael waited, smiling at her. He was impossibly handsome in a wine-red cotehardie and matching satin hood. He winked, and warmth flooded her chest.

Friar Brook stood before him, murmuring prayers over the Lord's Book, held open in his hands.

Trinity glanced at the crowd—Susana and Fleur rose together, their arms linked. Susana wiped away a tear while Fleur dipped her chin in silent encouragement. It was the most she would give, and Trinity wouldn't expect anything more.

Shaun and Isabella were on Susana's other side. Shaun looked pale. But the moment he caught her watching, he plastered on his infamous grin and shook his head.

The ceremony stretched on. Latin prayers. Sacred vows.

Her heart pounded so hard she could barely speak, not from nerves but from love so overwhelming it took her breath away.

When the Friar finally pronounced them husband and wife, Michael didn't hesitate. He kissed her, sealing their fate.

The room erupted in cheers.

Trinity felt like she had stepped into heaven.

Hand in hand, they walked back down the aisle as husband and wife.

Trinity barely noticed the guests, the music, the laughter—only the warmth of Michael's touch as he led her through the chapel into his mother's adjacent parlor.

Inside, he helped remove her long robe. She barely registered the guards opening doors or the servants curtsying and offering blessings. Her head spun.

Michael pressed a glass of red wine into her hands. She took a grateful sip, the incredible sweetness easing the dryness in her throat.

Michael stood at the table, pouring himself one. He turned, met her gaze, and froze. His breath hitched.

So did hers.

Their wine was forgotten the next second as they crashed into each other. His lips claimed hers, urgent, hungry. She gasped but melted against him, grasping his tunic and pulling him closer.

His hands slid down her spine, gripping her waist, pressing her against him. Heat pooled in her belly as his fingers traced the delicate skin at the nape of her neck.

"Michael," she breathed.

He moaned against her throat, his lips trailing under her ear. "Oh, my love, I want you so badly." He kissed her again, deeper, hands roaming, tugging her closer. "Must we wait until tonight?"

Trinity's entire body burned. She would have given herself to him at that moment—

But a knock broke the spell.

They pulled apart, breathless, desperate. A wave of longing crashed through her.

Michael turned swiftly, retrieving his wine just as the door opened.

A maidservant entered with a fruit, cheese, and bread platter.

"M'lord. M'lady." She curtsied and set the tray on the table. "I'll take your robe, m'lady, and redo your hair."

Michael barely glanced at her. "Thank you, Heather, but give us a few more moments."

Heather's cheeks flushed. "Of course, m'lord." She curtsied again and left.

Michael turned back to Trinity, brushing his fingers over her cheek. "Are you happy, my love?"

She hesitated. She wanted to say yes, but the shadow of the plague loomed over her.

Michael watched her closely. "Trinity?"

She met his gaze, swallowed the fear, and smiled. "Yes, husband." The word tasted foreign but sweet.

He grinned. "I love the sound of that."

"As do I."

He kissed her again, softer this time. "Come sit. Heather will be back soon."

Grateful, she sank into a plush armchair. Her feet throbbed, her legs wobbly from exhaustion and perhaps too much wine before the ceremony.

Michael handed her another sip of wine, then prepared a small plate of fruit and cheese.

A soft knock made Michael chuckle. "Mother wouldn't allow us any more time, I'm sure."

Heather was waiting at the door.

"My apologies, m'lord, but your mother says everyone is ready to receive you."

Trinity sighed, setting her wine down.

"Yes, of course." Michael lifted his eyebrows at Trinity, making her laugh.

Heather quickly fixed her hair, then left again.

But before they left to receive their congratulations, Michael tugged her back into his arms, kissing her fiercely.

She melted against him, pushing closer until the world around them disappeared.

His hands roamed down her body, then lower—gripping, caressing.

A growl rumbled from his chest as he pulled her hips against his. His noticeable hardness pressing into her sent a fiery ache through her core.

She gasped, her body arching instinctively.

Michael's mouth traced her throat. "I need you," he murmured against her cheek. "You're so beautiful."

His hand slid up her thigh, tracing along the edge of her stocking before slipping under her gown. He moaned as his fingers reached her bare skin.

Boisterous singing erupted from the hall.

Michael cursed under his breath, pressing his forehead to hers.

Trinity groaned. "What is that?" She readjusted her dress.

"You'll see." Michael grinned, opening the door.

Shaun and a group of men stood in the foyer, singing at the top of their lungs.

Trinity burst out laughing.

Flowers decorated the great hall, children ran about in their finest, and Henry and Susana stood at the dais, beaming.

Michael placed Trinity's hand on his arm. Together, they walked forward as husband and wife to receive the family's welcome.

Trinity felt blessed. Happier than she'd ever been in her life.

Then Henry started coughing—a violent, hacking fit. Blood spewed from his mouth as he collapsed to his knees, clutching his chest.

Michael ran to him.

Trinity froze as screams echoed throughout the hall. Her heart stopped.

CHAPTER 20 ~ MICHAEL

"Trinity, please wake up." Michael held her in his arms. He'd been so worried about her.

She'd tossed and turned for hours and then started crying and screaming in her sleep, frightening him to death. He wasn't sure what else to do except attempt to rouse her.

She opened her eyes, searching for his, and after a soft intake of breath, she cried even harder. He held her tightly against his chest until she relaxed and stopped crying.

"Shh, I'm here, and it'll be alright." Michael tried to reassure her, but in his heart, he knew the truth: the plague had reached his home, and death was taking his father first.

"No, Michael, your father," Trinity cried.

"He's resting in his bedchambers. Lenora and the priest are with him," Michael said, trying to sound brave. It was all he could do to save himself from the panic that settled in his gut.

After his father collapsed, everything was complete chaos. Guests screamed, some cried, and all fled.

The day, which was supposed to be the happiest in his life, had turned into a nightmare.

The priest from York arrived, and he and Lenora confirmed his worst fear: the plague.

Trinity ran to 'her' bedchambers, not 'theirs', and by the time he found her, she was curled up under the blankets, sleeping, with tear stains on her face and the pillow still wet. She lay asleep in her wedding gown. He'd gently removed it, leaving only her thin tunic.

His arms weighted down as he undressed, his body sluggish as he climbed into bed with her and held her close until, exhausted, he fell asleep.

Until she woke him screaming.

She pulled her arms tighter around him, sniffling.

"Shh… my love," he whispered against her head.

"Michael, I'm so sorry," her voice cracked as she turned to face him, her bare legs entwined with his.

He swept her hair away from her face and kissed the tears on her cheeks.

She curled in closer to him as he tightly wrapped his arms around her. He breathed in the lavender scent lingering around her.

"I love you so much. I will never let anything happen to you," he promised, kissing her neck.

She sighed as his lips softly speckled her neck to her shoulder. His entire body shuttered as she pressed herself against him. Their desire, their love, unquenched. He gently kissed her.

"Please… Make me forget…" she moaned against his lips.

He rolled on top of her. Her fingers clutched his back.

He wanted to take his time; he had many plans to make their first time special. But now, all he could think about was being inside her, drowning their fears with passion. He ached for her in a way that he could never describe. No other woman made him burn so strongly.

He pulled her thin tunic over her head and kneeled between her thighs, her nakedness making his breath abate. She was mesmerizing. Her small round breasts were firm, her nipples pink. He bent and took one in his mouth, not wanting to wait a moment more to taste her.

Trinity moaned and shivered as goosebumps rose on her body and her back arched.

He paused, then kissed her soft navel, the inside of her thighs, and when she was moaning again, pleading for him, he wrapped his mouth around her center. Her whole body trembled as she cried out in pleasure. He lapped and sucked until he sensed she was close to releasing; her body shaking, her ass clenching, and then he stopped and kissed her stomach.

She let out a disappointed moan, and he smiled as he tried to contain his own desire and passion, but it was almost beyond his control. He raised himself gently above her and kissed her swollen lips, which she'd been biting down on.

He lined himself up to her core but paused. "It may hurt briefly, but it will pass quickly, my love."

"Yes, yes," she said impatiently, and he couldn't hold back another moment.

He held her close to his chest, her breath hard against his neck. Slowly, he arched himself into her, so slowly it was agonizing, but he was terrified of hurting her too much. He ached to be buried completely.

When she cried out momentarily, he froze until she relaxed and began to push her hips into him. His heart thrummed through his body. Moaning, he moved inside her slowly until her hands pulled him against her and her hips thrust into his.

He trembled violently as he tried desperately to hold back, to let her reach her pleasure first. She arched her hips harder against him, frantic, needy, until her body quaked with release.

"Michael!" she called his name, almost in surprise. Her entire body trembled as she arched her back and let out a low moan of satisfaction.

He was only a moment behind her as he released himself, exploding in complete and utter rapture.

He rolled to his side so he wouldn't hurt her, pulling her along so he could stay inside of her. They lay face to face, breathing each other's air, their arms and legs still entwined. He kissed her lips, tugging her tighter.

"I will always, always love you. My beautiful wife."

"Michael, that was…." She sobbed against his neck.

"Did I hurt you?" He asked and withdrew, concerned she was upset and that he'd done something wrong.

Tears ran down her face. "I never understood it could be so wonderful. I've never experienced anything like what you did to me."

He kissed her deeply. A moment later, she pleaded with him to pleasure her once more.

Afterwards, she laughed as they collapsed, wholly exhausted and spent. "I could get used to this."

He pulled her into his chest, holding her from behind, kissing her neck. "Any time, my love."

***

Michael couldn't fall asleep, so he lay there, quietly stroking Trinity's back as she slept, her head resting on his chest. Something inside of him knew it would be their last peaceful moment for a while. So, he savored it. Savored her.

A quiet knock on the door, and his mother walked in.

"Good morning," she greeted both as if all was normal and nothing was amiss. She had a smile on her face as if the day or night before hadn't happened at all.

"Mother?" Michael said, concerned about her overly cheerfulness. "Is everything alright?"

Trinity sat up, pulled the blanket up, and rubbed the sleep from her eyes.

He put a protective arm around her.

"Everything is fine," his mother chirped as she pulled open the curtains, letting in a bright ray of morning sunlight. "I'll have breakfast brought up; stay here with Trinity. I'll tend to your father."

"That's not necessary; we'll come down," Trinity said, rubbing her eyes.

His mother paused before the window, looking out into the yard.

"Mother?"

"No one will be in the dining hall. Most departed, but a few are waiting for more carriages to return; they're in the sitting room and don't want to see any of us." She sighed, frustrated, then said, "So incredibly rude."

"What was that, mother?" Michael asked.

Trinity had moved off him, and he was about to rise when his mother turned around, tears streamed down her face. She lifted a hand before he could jump out of bed, and his heart plummeted to his stomach.

"No, stay with your wife, Michael. Please."

She swiped her tears and walked to the door. "Your father is still alive, and I refuse to lose hope; our lord will spare him."

Susana smiled and left the room.

Trinity looked into his gaze, then softly touched his face with her fingers. Tears fell in streams down her cheeks, her green eyes glossy and red.

"I'm so sorry," she whispered.

He needed to have her closer and didn't want to think about his father dying only a few rooms away. He wanted to savor the bliss of lying with his new wife, not the unbearable fear making his heart pound in his ears.

"Michael, your father's sick; you should be with him," Trinity said softly.

"You heard my mother. She wants me to stay here with you. She's with father, so you're stuck with me." He wiped her damp cheeks with his finger. "You're my wife now, and as my wife, I'd like you to sleep in my bedchambers next to me where I can hold you in my arms every night." He paused, watching her. "I've already taken the liberty of moving your belongings there."

Trinity smiled and then kissed his mouth, sending a shock of that fire through his body. "Of course."

He didn't want her to leave his side for a moment, and relief made his shoulders drop as his arms wrapped around her, pulling her against him.

"I noticed none of my possessions were here last night." She chuckled, then sniffed.

"Good. Then I will arrange for us to have breakfast there.

"Perfect," she sighed, and he kissed her again.

***

244

His mother hadn't permitted him to see his father all day; only Trinity had been allowed to help care for his father.

Trinity told him that his mother had said, "Evil spirits possessed her husband." And she'd violently shoved a servant out of the room. It was bizarre behavior that he'd never witnessed before.

He needed to see his father, even if his mother was adamant that he didn't. So, Michael walked to his father's bedchambers. Determined.

He waited until he was sure his mother wasn't there and entered quickly, closing the door gently behind him.

"Father?" He called.

A silver candelabra lit the room, and the fire was ablaze, making it stifling hot.

He spotted Fleur first, sitting by his father's side; she stood up, blocking his view of his father.

"Michael, you shouldn't be here, your mother...."

"She has no right banning me when you, of all people, are allowed," he snapped, walking closer.

She stepped back but closed her mouth, her eyes throwing a hateful glare at him. He couldn't understand why she loathed him so much, but he didn't care at that moment.

His father lay still in bed. He wasn't sure if his mother's ravings held any truth, and logically, he didn't believe it, but as he approached the bed, Michael's entire body trembled in fear and revulsion.

"Father?" It was a shock, and he stumbled backwards, his hand over his mouth, stifling a scream.

Puss oozed from giant black lumps on his neck onto the pillow, and his face was bloated; Michael barely recognized him.

He stumbled to the door, fumbling clumsily with the door, trying to escape the horror. The horror that had become his father.

"Michael, wait!" Fleur said, but he had to get out.

He slammed the door behind him as his mother came down the hall.

"What did I tell you?" she shouted. She'd never yelled at him before. "I told you to stay out!" She screamed again, tears in her eyes. "Stay out!"

He stumbled to the side as she swung open the door, glaring at him. "He wouldn't want you to see him like this!"

He stood frozen, his breath coming in heavy gulps.

Was mother, right? Had father been possessed?

He hurried down the hallway shaking, tears flowing unburdened. He didn't know where he was going; only he needed to get outside.

He pushed through the front doors, startling the manservants.

"M'lord?" One man said and nodded.

Michael ignored him and ran down the stone steps, then into his mother's garden, where he collapsed onto a stone bench—the spring day carried a cool breeze and the scent of his mother's lavender bushes. He took a deep breath and put his hands over his face, leaning on his knees and sobbing, his body heaving.

"Why is this happening?" He asked no one in particular. "Please, God, please do not take my father. I promise to serve you and live a pious life... I will devote my life to your service. Please, my lord, don't take him from us."

Michael opened his eyes and looked at the sky. The clouds moved gently in a cerulean spring sky.

Silence.

Another voice echoed in his mind.

There's no god. No god would be so cruel.

"There has to be, please god, help me, save my father," he whispered, then sobbed.

CHAPTER 21 ~ SYBIL

Within days, the manor fell eerily silent. Most of the servants became ill or slipped away without a word, too afraid to stay under the same roof as their ailing lord— or Lady Susana, whose erratic behavior unsettled even the most loyal among them. Even Olivia.

"They say she's possessed," one of the younger maids whispered to Sybil in the corridor. "That the devil's got hold of her."

Another girl nodded; eyes wide. "She's gone mad. Won't leave his side, not even to sleep."

No matter how many tonics Lenora administered or how many prayers Susana murmured by Henry's bedside, his condition only worsened.

Sybil carried a tray with three soup bowls, stepping carefully into the sickroom. The door had been left open. The stench inside—rotting flesh mingled with the sharp scent of incense—hit her like a blow. She tightened her jaw, forcing down the bile rising in her throat.

Henry lay still, his face bloated, neck riddled with oozing boils.

Fleur reached for the tray as soon as Sybil stepped inside. "Thank you, Sybil. I'll take it." She moved to the small round table, setting the tray down with practiced care.

Sybil watched her. Fleur rarely left Susana's side now, offering quiet prayers and silent support. Susana trusted her and relied on her. Yet there was something else—an unbearable weight in Fleur's gaze, a regret Sybil couldn't quite name.

Susana didn't acknowledge Sybil's presence. She knelt at Henry's bedside, clutching his limp hand, eyes closed in fervent prayer. Her gown was crumpled and stained, her hair tangled and loose over her shoulders— a far cry from the composed lady she had once been.

Sybil gathered the soiled linens used to clean Henry's wounds, stacking them neatly by the door before lifting the basin of murky water.

"I'll bring fresh water, m'lady," she said, glancing at the pile of linen. "And I'll see to the washing once I return."

Fleur moved from the table, a bowl of soup in her hands. "Thank you, Sybil. I'm not sure how we'd manage without you."

"If you need a break, let me know," Sybil offered. "I can help."

Fleur hesitated before shaking her head. "Lady Susana has asked me to stay. But thank you."

Sybil shifted toward the door, then paused. A thought struck her—she hadn't made a protective amulet for Fleur.

She glanced back, studying the young woman carefully. If she didn't already have one, she'd need one immediately.

In the firelight, something glinted on Fleur's hand. A ruby ring, rich and deep, caught Sybil's eye before vanishing as Fleur moved. Magic shimmered faintly around it.

Relief flooded Sybil. She must have bought it at the market, or perhaps it was an heirloom. Either way, it would offer some protection.

"Is anything wrong?" Fleur asked, catching Sybil studying her.

"No, m'lady," Sybil said quickly. "I'll return shortly."

***

The following day, Sybil woke more exhausted than when she'd collapsed into bed. Her body ached, her limbs sluggish and sore from doing the work of a dozen servants, tending to a dying man, and finishing the protective amulets before sleep finally claimed her.

She dressed slowly, the quiet of the manor pressing in on her. The bedroom she once shared with another girl was vacant. All the staff quarters were empty—except for her and Mrs. Bartlett. Old man Dreyfus and Joseph. She'd barely seen either of the men.

Sybil grabbed the bracelet she'd made for Mrs. Bartlett from the small table beside her bed. Two more amulets lay outside in the moonlight, meant for the twins. They'd lost their previous ones—again. These would be the third set.

In the kitchen, she searched for Mrs. Bartlett. Not finding her, she opened the pantry door to the basement and called out.

250

"I'll be right up, dear," came the reply.

Sybil sat on the bench and exhaled slowly, touching her belly. Nausea churned, thick and rolling, and bile rose in her throat. The faint but unmistakable scent of sulphur lingered in the air. A demon was close, hiding skillfully.

A moan escaped as she clutched her arms around her abdomen, scanning the corners of the kitchen. The sickness built, her breath coming in shallow pants. Clenching her eyes shut, she whispered the incantation to ease the nausea. A moment later, the cramping subsided, and she could breathe again.

The fact that she couldn't see the demon unnerved her. She always saw them. Her eyes darting around the room, searching the shadows.

Where are you?

Mrs. Bartlett stepped into the kitchen, a freshly plucked chicken in her hands. She eyed Sybil with concern as she set it on the counter. "What's wrong?"

"I'm just tired," Sybil said, forcing herself upright. "I was up late helping Lady Susana and Fleur." She reached into her pocket and pulled out the bracelet, holding it out for Mrs. Bartlett to see—a tiny clear crystal dangled from the chain.

"I made this for you."

Mrs. Bartlett smiled. "It's lovely, but it's not my birthday."

"It's custom in my family to give gifts to friends and family during Easter," Sybil lied. She needed an excuse—anything to make her take it.

Mrs. Bartlett's expression softened. "That's kind of you. Thank you."

"Here, let me put it on." Sybil clasped the bracelet around her wrist.

251

Mrs. Bartlett admired it, turning her hand in the firelight. "It's pretty."

"I need to fetch something from David's room," Sybil said. "I'll be right back."

"Do be quick. We'll have to cook and serve on our own now. The rest of the kitchen help and servants left last night, including Prudence. The poor girl was out of her mind with fright."

"I noticed." Sybil sighed. "I'll be right back."

She had no doubt Prudence believed the devil had taken up residence in the manor. And for once, Sybil feared she wasn't far from the truth.

She stepped into the foyer just as Michael and Trinity descended the stairs, arm in arm. Michael looked like he hadn't slept in days, dark circles shadowing his eyes. Trinity wasn't much better; her hair was in a thick single braid down her back.

"Sybil, is breakfast ready?" Trinity asked, her voice soft, weary.

"Yes, it's in the dining room, but there's no one serving," Sybil said. "Prudence and the others left last night."

"I don't blame them," Michael muttered.

"That's alright," Trinity reassured her. "We'll manage."

"I'll be back to help," Sybil promised and hurried outside.

The yard was empty save for a few guards lingering at the gates. None patrolled the walls. They'd deserted their posts—forsaken the family.

She ran to the stables, breathing hard. Her chest was tight as fear clawed at her insides.

The twins needed new amulets. They had lost theirs again. She had given one to Lady Susana, but she refused to wear it, tucking it into her pocket instead. Trinity wore hers, but Sybil had yet to see Michael's handkerchief. She'd embroidered protective ruins into it, and she prayed he had it.

Inside the stables, David was saddling his horse.

"Where are you going?" she asked.

"The twins have fallen ill," he said, tightening the straps. "Lady Susana sent me to fetch Lenora."

Sybil froze.

No.

The weight of it crushed her, knocking the air from her lungs. She sank to the ground, tears spilling from her eyes.

"No, not them," she choked out, staring at David in disbelief.

He crossed the space in two strides, scooping her into his arms. She barely recalled him carrying her to his room at the back of the stables, setting her gently on the bed.

"You did everything you could," he said. "No one could have known it would happen so fast."

"I should have been better prepared." She sat up, legs dangling over the edge of the bed.

David crouched in front of her, meeting her gaze. "Sybil, listen to me. This isn't your fault."

She swallowed hard, nodding, but the guilt pressed down on her.

"I have to go," he said. "I'll bring Lenora as soon as I can."

"Go. I'll see what I can do until then."

David lifted her chin, pressing a soft kiss to her lips. "It will be alright."

She stood to follow him out, but he caught her arms. "Look at me, Syb."

She met his eyes, deep and steady.

"I love you," he said, voice firm. "We'll defeat this evil together."

She shook her head. "David, I can't fight a demon, I can't see."

He didn't answer, just held her closer.

"I've tried the incantation," she whispered. "It didn't work. What kind of demon can hide itself like this from me?"

He led his horse into the yard, glancing up at the sky, heavy with dark clouds. "I'll ask Lenora. Perhaps she'll know."

"She must."

David lay his forehead against hers, eyes closed.

Sybil's breath hitched as a warm flow of his magic ran through hers, easing her tight muscles. "Ride fast," she said. "And watch the forests."

"Always." He swung into the saddle. "I love you, Syb."

He disappeared through the gates, a knot tightening in Sybil's stomach.

A sulphureous stench wafted towards her. She whirled around, searching.

Nothing.

"Show yourself, you coward," she hissed under her breath, wary of the guards. "I know you're here."

Her stomach twisted again, but the sickness was weaker this time.

"Yes," she murmured. "Scurry away like the rat you are."

Pushing open the main doors, she strode inside, her footsteps echoing in the empty foyer.

Michael and Trinity sat alone in the dining hall at the massive table, picking at their breakfast. Trinity tapped on her soft-boiled egg, staring at it as if wishing it would take her elsewhere. Michael toyed with a pastry, lost in thought.

Sybil cleared her throat, stepping beside him.

"Excuse me, m'lord."

Michael turned. "Yes, Sybil?"

She hesitated. "I was told…"

Trinity stood; eyes wide. "What is it, Syb? Tell us."

Michael had risen too, gripping Trinity's hand. "Is it Father? Has he—?"

"No," she whispered. "Not your father. Your sisters have fallen ill."

Michael sucked in a sharp breath, his whole body going rigid. "No. Not the girls."

"Are you sure?" Trinity clutched a hand to her chest.

"Yes. David has gone to fetch Lenora."

Trinity inhaled shakily. Michael bolted from the room. Trinity remained frozen for a moment, then turned, following him.

Sybil stood alone, the weight of everything pressing down on her.

She had to stop this.

***

Lenora tended to the twins all day and checked on Henry and Susana. Sybil stayed by her side, helping where she could.

It was heartbreaking. The girls hadn't developed black spots and boils like Henry, but their coughing was far worse. Their bodies were failing, lungs giving out as if something was rotting them from the inside.

The herbs and tonics did nothing.

Even when Lenora secretly poured her magic into them, the healing energy was rejected instantly. The rot had set in too deep.

They couldn't do anything but try to make them comfortable.

As Sybil returned to the kitchen, Lenora carried a bowl of fouled water behind her. Sybil held a bundle of linen stained with blood and pus.

"I don't understand," Lenora muttered, her frustration barely contained. "No common demon could do this. My magic is useless."

Sybil clenched her jaw. "I know there's a demon here. I can sense it, but I can't see it. The incantation doesn't work either. It must be behind this. But how? The house is warded. How did it get in?"

They fell silent as they stepped into the kitchen. The flames burned low, casting flickering shadows, and Mrs. Bartlett had already gone to bed. Sybil dropped the soiled linen by the back door and added one more log to the fire. It would be another long night, and they needed boiled water.

Lenora sank into Henry's chair at the table. She rubbed her temples, eyes closed. "The wards need checking. We should have done it sooner." She sighed, squeezing the bridge of her nose. "Sybil, bring my grimoire."

Lenora had taken over Sybil's small room behind the kitchen.

A few minutes later, Sybil returned and placed the heavy book before her grandmother.

Lenora flipped it open. The old, yellowed pages filled with handwritten text and sketches. The collection had been passed down through generations. Sybil hadn't seen it in years.

Lenora turned each page carefully, murmuring under her breath. After a long moment, she exhaled and tapped a passage. "Here it is."

Sybil sat beside her, peering over her shoulder.

Lenora turned the page, revealing a crude sketch of a monstrous figure—grotesquely elongated limbs, clawed fingers, a head like a deep-sea creature, its gaping mouth stretched wide—looming over a child's cradle.

Sybil sucked in a breath, her chest tightening. "What is that?"

"A devil that feeds on souls while you sleep," Lenora said grimly. "It drains the life from infants and children, but adults have more energy, more life force. They survive longer. It's said that the demon Lilith controls them. They're the baby snatchers."

Sybil swallowed. "What about ghouls?"

"Another breed. They can endure daylight, but only in shadows. Direct sun burns them—their eyes are too dilated. They're more beast than man. They hunt in packs, feeding on flesh. Minor demons are not very bright, but dangerous when controlled by a stronger master. Usually a blood mage."

Lenora pointed to a different illustration—an emaciated figure with hollow black eyes and elongated limbs.

"Ghouls," Sybil murmured, remembering the screeching creatures she had once fought. "They move fast. Their screams sound like dying animals."

"The dead were brought back through blood magic," Lenora confirmed. "There are many types. Some retain intelligence. Some don't."

She flipped through the book and stopped on a page filled with dense small script. "The most dangerous demons are the legionnaires."

Sybil frowned. "Weren't legionnaires Roman soldiers?"

"These are not." Lenora's voice dropped. "They were named after them—created in their likeness. Some say actual Roman soldiers were the first to be created. They are the dead who walk by day, stronger than any other demon." She pointed to the text, reading aloud, "They appear human because they are turned at the moment before death and possessed by wraiths. Filled with rage, hunger, and bloodlust, their eyes turn black when they attack. The strongest of them can control minds—even bodies. They can heal almost instantly, and some rare ones can heal others."

Lenora hesitated, then met Sybil's gaze. "They can twist a person's thoughts. Make them believe the ideas are their own. They've driven men to murder their own wives."

Sybil's stomach knotted. "But Henry—the twins— they didn't do this to themselves."

"No. But a powerful legionnaire—or a blood mage—could."

Lenora turned to the last page of the section. A full-page sketch depicted a tall, noble-looking, dark-haired man with sharp features and piercing eyes. He looked utterly human besides the thick curved horns growing out of his forehead.

Sybil stared. "That's a demon prince?"

"Yes."

Lenora thumbed through more pages until she reached a section titled The Darkborn Prophecies. She traced her fingers over several passages to a date scrawled beneath one: 1298.

She read aloud, "When the breath of death curls through the streets and hides its face, the crows shall feast, and the soil shall sour. Light will falter, and the faithful shall fall—but one will carry the flame that will rise against the darkness."

She shut the volume with a thud. Sybil flinched.

"You wrote that?" Sybil whispered.

"Yes. From the last oracle." Lenora's fingers tapped the book. "If Baal is in York, creating legionnaires... We, the hunters, will become the hunted."

Silence stretched between them.

"That must be what I've been sensing," Sybil murmured.

Lenora turned to another passage dated 1301 and read it out loud. "When the shadow swallows the moon, the earth will weep with ash and blood. Darkness comes with a hunger that will devour the light."

"An eclipse?" Sybil asked.

"Yes."

"Is there going to be an eclipse soon?" Sybil knew the answer before her grandmother said the words.

"Seven Moons." Lenora flipped to another section, not elaborating on the answer. "Wards that repel legionnaires." She ran her finger along the script. "No human weapon can kill them without the proper wards carved into the blade. Anything else will only slow them."

"The black obsidian," Sybil muttered.

Lenora nodded. "Check the wards on every building. If even one is damaged, it won't hold. David must redo them all. And he needs to inspect the village, too.

"I'll tell him immediately."

"I'll summon the covens." Lenora's grip on Sybil's hand tightened. "It's time to prepare and fight. The eclipse is in seven moons. We have time."

Before Sybil could respond, the kitchen door slammed open.

David stumbled inside, blood covering his tunic.

She gasped. "David!"

He gripped the table, breathing hard. "Not all mine."

Lenora's eyes sharpened. "What happened?"

Sybil grabbed a cloth, wetting it quickly before pressing it to the long gash along his scalp. "Who did this?"

"Not human," David panted. "But she looked like it. A blood mage, maybe…" He clenched his trembling hands. "She was powerful. Almost killed me."

Lenora straightened. "Describe her."

"Dark hair. Black eyes. She fought like a demon, wielding magic to shield herself."

Sybil handed him a cup of Henry's hidden wine. He drank it in one gulp.

"Where were you?" she asked.

"I had dinner with Lucas's family. Enzo left at the same time, but we split ways. I was close to the Ouse when she dragged me off my horse." He shook his head. "She was fast. I barely got away."

"Was she alone?"

"I thought so. But for a moment, I swore there were two."

Lenora's expression darkened. "How did you escape?"

"I shielded myself and fled. I didn't have time to draw my sword. When I crossed the river, she vanished. The guards at Mickelgate caught my horse."

Sybil traced her fingers over his hand, feeling the tremors. "How did you get covered in so much blood then?"

"A pack of ghouls ambushed me halfway home. I killed most. A few escaped."

Lenora's voice was grim. "There's a blood mage here controlling the ghouls, but that woman wasn't a blood mage. She's a legionnaire."

Sybil swallowed hard. "There are female legionnaires?"

"Yes."

David frowned. "What's a legionnaire?"

Lenora handed the tome toward him.

He scanned the page. "That's just what we need. Blood mages and ghouls weren't enough?"

Lenora shut the book. "We need the proper wards on every weapon. David, collect all the blades from the coven. Tomorrow."

David exhaled, shaking his head. "And what if we can't see them?"

Sybil squeezed his hands. "We'll be ready."

CHAPTER 22 ~ MICHAEL

Michael hadn't left the girls' side for days, but they worsened despite his mother's prayers or Lenora's administration.

At dawn, he finally ventured outside for air.

The sky shifted from a dull grey blue to a soft orange-pink glow. Once, he would have called it beautiful. The wind rustled the leaves of the trees, and a crow cawed. He searched the branches but couldn't see it.

Crows are bad luck. He recalled a story about a crow being the Harold of death and the grim reapers companion.

"Leave!" he screamed.

The crow cawed again, mocking him but it didn't show itself.

"Coward!" He let out a breath, turned, and returned indoors. As he neared the girls' bedchambers, his mother's sobs echoed down the hall.

His chest tightened as he entered, gagging at the overwhelming stench of sickness.

"Mother?" he whispered.

Susana and the priest hovered over his sisters. Their tiny bodies curled toward each other in the large four-poster bed, hands clasped. Their breathing was ragged, lips tinged blue.

They were dying.

Michael froze, mouth open, tears burning his eyes.

"Please save them. Please." His mother clutched the priest's robe, her voice raw. "Please, please, please."

"Mother?" Michael knelt next to her, his voice catching.

She turned and collapsed into his arms, sobbing hysterically.

He held her, the tremors rocking through her body as she beat against his chest in helpless fury.

"No, no, no. Not my babies," she howled.

Tears streaked his face.

A gentle hand rested on his shoulder.

"Michael," Trinity whispered. "Take your mother to her bedchamber. I'll have Sybil bring her something to calm her."

"NO!" Susana shrieked, shoving him away, stumbling backward. "Don't. Touch. Me."

She fell to her knees again, sobs shaking her frail frame. "Why... Why... Why?"

Michael stood, stunned, his breath caught in his throat as his mother sobbed, moaning in despair.

One of the girls coughed violently, and Susana's head snapped up, her eyes wild. She scrambled to her feet, gripping the bedpost for support.

"Mama's here, my doves," she cooed, her voice breaking.

Rose's tiny body convulsed as she coughed, each spasm wracking her fragile frame.

"Mama," she managed to say between coughing fits. Michael was amazed it didn't shatter her bones.

Susana threw herself onto the bed, pulling Rose into her arms.

The coughing did not stop. Blood spewed from her lips, splattering across her mother's gown.

Ruby didn't stir.

Susana rocked Rose, whispering desperately into her hair. But the coughing stopped suddenly, as did his sister's breathing.

Michael stepped forward. "Mother…"

Tears poured down Susana's face, her grip tightening around Rose's limp body.

A broken wail tore from Susana's throat.

Michael crouched beside her, resting a trembling hand on her shoulder. "Mother, you need to let her go."

She wouldn't release her daughter's limp body.

The priest moved in, and together, they peeled Rose from her, placing her beside Ruby.

Susana fought them, her cries turning to gasping, frantic breaths.

Michael lifted her into his arms. She buried her face in his chest, sobbing so hard he thought she might choke.

"Shh, everything will be alright," he whispered, but she only wept harder, his eyes glued to his sister's still forms. "I promise, Mother. It will be all right."

"We've been forsaken," she gasped between sobs. "We've been forsaken."

Michael swallowed, but her words sent a spike of dread through his heart.

They were good people—his parents were faithful, loyal, and devoted. Why would God turn his back on them?

He carried his mother to her bedchambers, where Trinity waited with a wooden tray, a kettle, and a cup.

"I've brought some tea," Trinity said, pouring a measure into the cup. "Lenora's. It should help."

"No! No!" Susana shrieked, trying to sit up.

Michael held her down gently. "Please, Mother," he begged, tears still wet on his face.

Trinity handed him the drink, and he pressed it to Susana's lips. "Drink, Mother."

Her eyes opened, but they were empty. Vacant. Dead.

Michael sucked in a shaky breath. The walls closed in on him. His sisters were gone, and he was powerless.

His mother drank without resistance. Laid back, staring at the ceiling. "We're forsaken," she whispered repeatedly until her voice faded to nothing, and she finally fell asleep.

Michael stood over her, numb, his chest so tight he could barely breathe.

"Michael?" Trinity called softly.

He ignored her.

He turned and walked out.

The word haunted him. *Forsaken.*

He wandered into the gardens, past the lavender bushes and olive trees. Wild roses tangled among the brush, and the blackberries were ripe for harvest. The small prickles snagged his clothes and cut his hands. He didn't care.

Rage simmered in his veins.

He was a newlywed. He should have been happy. Instead, everything was crumbling apart.

What kind of benevolent God would do this?

His feet carried him aimlessly through the winding paths. He barely noticed when he entered the open field beyond the manor.

All he saw was his father's face—bloated and covered in boils.

His sisters—pale, lifeless bodies.

His mother—lost in grief and despair.

The world had gone silent. The birds, the crickets… nothing reached him.

Only the sound of his mother's voice. *We're forsaken.*

His knees hit the ground.

He tilted his head back and screamed to the heavens.

"Why have you forsaken us?"

His fists slammed into the earth.

There is no God.

He didn't know how long he sat there, but by the time he lifted his head, the sky had darkened with heavy clouds with promise of rain.

"Why?" he whispered.

No answer.

Only silence.

Because there was no God.

He pushed to his feet, unsteady, and turned toward the manor. He needed a drink.

As he rounded a corner, he nearly collided with a young man bent over, pulling weeds beneath a red rose bush.

The man jumped, startled.

"Sorry, m'lord," he said, his Irish accent thick.

Michael blinked at the stranger.

Old Dreyfus must have hired him.

"No, it's my fault. I didn't see you there," Michael said, studying him. "Have we met?"

The redhead wiped his hands on his trousers. "Just started a few weeks ago, m'lord. Name's Julian."

Michael took in the dirt-streaked face and the calm demeanor. "I'm surprised you haven't run like the others."

"I've nowhere to go, m'lord," Julian said. "And there's no escape from what's happening."

Michael considered that. "A fair point. But are you not afraid? Do you not believe we've been forsaken?"

"If there is a God, he's cruel," Julian said, snipping dead leaves from the bush. "But I don't leave my fate in his hands alone."

Michael frowned. "That's an unusual belief."

"Perhaps." Julian's lips quirked.

Something lifted in Michael's chest—just slightly. "I suppose it's comforting to be in control of your destiny."

"It is."

Michael exhaled. "Thank you for tending my mother's garden."

"It's a delight. And if I might say, if you ever need an ear, I'm here."

Michael hesitated, then nodded. "Perhaps I'll take you up on that."

"Anytime."

Michael shook Julian's hand. "It was a pleasure meeting you, Julian."

Julian returned the handshake with a firm nod. "Likewise."

***

Michael strode into his mother's parlor, heading straight for the decanter of wine. Lifting it, he sniffed. Sitting there for days, it had begun to sour, but it would do what he needed. He poured himself a full glass and took a long drink.

Nearly vinegar. He didn't care.

He turned at the sound of footsteps.

Fleur walked in, carrying a fresh bottle in one hand and a clean glass in the other.

"What are you doing here?" she hissed, stopping in the doorway.

Michael took another sip. "What does it look like?"

She frowned. "May I suggest you retire to your father's parlor?"

He set his glass down. "Are you serious?"

"Very." She stepped forward, setting her glass and bottle on the table.

"No."

"No?"

"This is my home. Not yours."

Her eyes narrowed. "You are rude and childish."

Michael held her gaze. "Yes, you've mentioned this before. Repeatedly. And yet I never tire of hearing it."

She ignored him, uncorked her bottle, and poured herself some wine. Swirling it, she inhaled the aroma and let out a satisfied sigh.

Michael pressed his lips together. There was no way he was asking her for some.

Does she not realize my sisters had just passed?

"Shouldn't you be with your mother? Or are you too much of a coward?" She sipped her wine, watching him. "Perhaps you can't stomach it. Will you flee from her as you fled from your father?"

Her words sliced through him. He opened his mouth, but nothing came out. Because she was right, he had run from his father's bedside. He was a coward. But he would never admit it—not to her or anyone.

268

Anger surged up, hot and uncontrollable. He turned and hurled his drink past her head. It shattered against the wall.

"You are a wretched woman! Get out of my house!"

Fleur didn't flinch. She gripped her wine glass so tightly he thought it might crack in her hands.

"What. Is. Wrong. With. You?" she hissed.

"You are what's wrong! Since you arrived, you've vexed and snubbed me at every turn."

"Perhaps, m'lord, you deserved it." She took another deliberate sip of wine.

"Get out of my house! I want you gone by tomorrow."

"You can't throw me out!" She slammed her glass onto the table, spilling her drink across the polished wood and onto the floor. Her breathing quickened, and her hands balled at her hips.

"What's going on in here?"

Trinity's voice cut through the tension.

He turned, his chest heaving. He trembled. He wanted to strangle Fleur.

"Michael?" Trinity's brow furrowed. "I heard glass breaking—screaming."

She stepped closer, studying his face as if trying to recognize the man she married beneath the fury.

She took his hands in hers. "What happened?"

Michael exhaled sharply. "I believe it's time Fleur returned to her own home."

Trinity's expression twisted in disbelief. "She is helping your mother so much. We need her here—now more than ever. How could you send her away?"

"Because your husband loathes me," Fleur muttered, pouring herself another drink. Her hands shook slightly.

269

Trinity sighed. "Why can't you two get along? Even after everything, Fleur has been nothing but kind to me. Your parents love her. She's like family."

Michael bristled, closed his eyes, and dropped his head.

Trinity was right. Removing her would devastate his mother.

He let out a slow breath.

"Fine. She stays." He held his wife's eyes, unflinching. "But she stays away from me."

Trinity didn't even try to hide her disappointment. How she looked at him—as if he were fragile, weak— infuriated him.

A failure of a son. A failure of a husband.

He could not run his father's estate or employ the servants or guards. They had abandoned him. Everyone had.

"Lenora needs us all in your father's bedchambers. Now," Trinity said, breaking through his thoughts.

His eyes snapped to hers. "Why?"

"She's certain he won't last the night. I'm sorry, Michael."

"I can't..."

"Of course you can't," Fleur said as she pushed past them out of the room.

He ignored her, his stomach clenching, bile rising. "The girls... Father..."

"I know, my love." Trinity wrapped her arms around him. "Breathe..."

He couldn't take a breath in. Every attempt, his lungs cramped and sent agonizing pain into his chest.

"Come, they're waiting," she tried again.

He stepped back, clutching his chest. Eyes clenched tight as the tears spilled over his face. Trinity's fingers softly brushed them away.

"I'll be right here, beside you."

They walked down the dark corridor toward his father's chambers. The closer he got, the harder his heart pounded.

He muttered, sniffing back tears. "I'm so angry."

"I understand… We will pray for him and the girls," she said gently.

He pulled away from her. "How can you say that?"

She hesitated. "Say what?"

They stopped in front of his parent's bedchambers.

"Don't lose faith, my love." Trinity reached for his hand again, but he ignored her and pushed open the door.

He didn't want her to touch him. How would prayers help? His mother had prayed—pleaded with God. And for what? His father was dying. His sisters were dead.

Lenora passed them on her way out, eyes wet with tears. "I'm so sorry, Michael."

He nodded stiffly. "You did what you could. Thank you."

Inside, Elizabeth knelt beside their father, murmuring a prayer.

Michael clenched his jaw.

She was pregnant. Her husband demanded that she return home at once, but she refused.

She finished praying, stood, smoothed her dress, and wiped her tears.

"Hello, brother. Trinity."

Michael barely registered her. His anger boiled over.

"I don't know why you bother," he said, low, bitter. "It's useless, praying to a God who has turned his back on us."

Trinity gasped, pressing her hand to her lips. "Michael! The devil has infiltrated the Lord's lands. He is wreaking havoc on his flock—we do not blame God. How can you say that?"

Elizabeth hissed, "You'll go to hell speaking like that, brother. Those are the words of the devil."

Michael let out a harsh laugh. "I know of no hell but the one we live in now. Look around you."

His voice rose to a shout as he swept his arm toward his father's motionless body.

"This is blasphemy," Elizabeth cried. "Stop it at once!"

"You pray to a God who has abandoned you! Abandoned all of us!" Michael's fury spilled out. "I have prayed. Trinity has prayed. Mother has prayed! And look what good it has done!" His voice cracked as he pointed at their father. "He lies here, dying! And the twins are…! And yet you still kneel!"

Elizabeth squared her shoulders. "You are wrong, brother. The devil has stricken us—he has taken the innocent."

"If there were a God, he would never allow this." Michael's voice was thunder. "It is a lie. And I will not have it in my home any longer."

Trinity flinched, stepping back. Elizabeth stood firm.

"This is not your home yet," she spat. "And you are wrong. You will pay for your blasphemy—I promise you." Her voice trembled, but she didn't waver. Then she turned away and began to weep.

He clenched his fists.

Trinity placed a gentle hand on his arm, urging him to stop. "Please, Michael. Enough."

"Yes! Precisely!" He whirled on her, his voice sharp as a blade. "It is enough!"

Trinity recoiled, knocking into a small table.

Then a weak, rasping voice cut through the tension. "Stop this…"

All turned to Henry.

His eyes fluttered open. His chest shuddered with a ragged cough. He tried to speak again, but no words came. He shut his eyelids once more.

Elizabeth rushed to his side, fell to her knees, and took his frail hand. "I'm sorry, Father," she sobbed. "Please forgive me."

Trinity left Michael in the doorway and moved to Elizabeth, coaxing her up.

"Come, Elizabeth. You must rest. It's not good for the baby. Please, come with me."

Elizabeth let Trinity lead her toward the door.

As they passed Michael, Elizabeth whispered, "I forgive you, dear brother. But I can only pray the Lord will as well."

Michael didn't move. He stared at his father's still body.

He should have gone to him and said something, but there was nothing left to say. Nothing he could do.

He turned and walked out.

Outside, he moved automatically, heading for the stables. The barn was empty, so he grabbed a saddle and threw it over his horse.

"Going somewhere?"

Michael turned.

Julian stood near the back wall, setting a shovel among the other tools.

"I'm going to York," Michael muttered, adjusting the bridle. "I need to get away from here."

Julian grabbed another horse. "Want company? I was heading home myself."

Michael hesitated. "I was told its poor form to drink alone." He forced a weak smile. "I'd appreciate the company."

Julian smirked as he saddled another mare. "Hard times for everyone, my friend."

Michael studied him. The man was smaller in frame, but stronger than he should have been.

"Have you always been a gardener?"

Julian chuckled. "No. I was a farmer."

They mounted up and rode from the horrors Michael couldn't face.

Away from the father and sisters, he was unable to save.

Their horses' hooves thundered against the dirt, carrying them from Ellsworth.

Only when Mickelgate's cobbled streets rang beneath them did Michael rein his horse to a slower pace.

The guards greeted him as he passed, but he barely heard them.

His mind drifted.

To his mother's voice.

To the weight of his father's stillness.

To his sisters, the rot in their lungs.

There is no God. We are forsaken. The words repeated like a chant.

And as he rode deeper into the city, he welcomed them.

***

"You're all fools! Fools!" Michael bellowed; his words slurred.

He wasn't sure how many ales he'd had but certain he'd finished a pitcher of wine.

"There is NO GOD!" he bellowed, pushing himself to his feet, swaying slightly.

His unkempt hair hung wildly around his face. His tunic stained—ale, food, maybe even blood. He wiped at the smears absentmindedly.

"You need to shut your filthy mouth," one of the men at the table hissed.

Another stood, hand resting on the pommel of his sword.

They had all started as friends. But when Michael spoke his mind, they turned on him. Julian had warned him it would happen.

Julian was the only one who agreed with him.

Michael let out a slow, mocking laugh.

"What? You're going to cut me down?" he slurred, throwing his head back laughing.

Some patrons rushed to the door. Others stayed eager to watch.

Michael cast a glance toward the far corner. Julian sat there, sipping his ale, his expression unreadable. Michael winked at him, grabbed the table's edge, and flipped it over. The crash of wood and shattering mugs flew across the floor.

"Then come on!" he roared. "Do us all a favor!"

The second man jumped to his feet, yanking his sword free.

They were both strong men—farmhands or blacksmiths, judging by the thick cords of muscle in their arms.

"I've heard enough of your blasphemous ramblings, boy!" one bellowed. "You need to go home to your mommy!"

Michael smirked. "It's not blasphemy if there's no God." He spat at their feet. "Weak. Pathetic. That's what you all are." He sniffed, sneering. "No one can stop what's coming."

"What did you just call me?" The first man growled.

Then he punched Michael so hard his head snapped back. Blackness swallowed his vision for several seconds as he stumbled back but didn't fall.

Blood dripped from his split lip. He wiped it with the back of his hand and smirked. "That's all you've got?"

"Gentlemen."

Michael knew that voice. He turned.

Shaun stepped inside; hands raised in front of him. "Let's not get carried away."

One of the men sneered. "Is this a friend of yours?"

Michael narrowed his eyes. "No friend of mine! He's in love with my wife!"

The words landed like a blade to Shaun's chest. Color drained from his face. Michael saw the flicker of pain in his eyes. He didn't care.

"Look at him," Michael spat. "Always with a new lady—and now he wants my wife too."

Shaun inhaled slowly. "That's enough, Michael. We both loved her for years. But I've respected your vows. You're my brother."

Michael raised his fists ready for a fight. "Really, Shaun?"

Shaun shook his head. "I'm not fighting you."

"Come on!" Michael's voice taunted, slurring his words and lifting his fists higher. "You know you want

276

to beat the hell out of me…" he gestured wildly and bellowed an obnoxiously, "…For stealing the only woman you've ever loved. For having more than you ever did!"

Shaun's jaw tightened.

Michael swayed on his feet; fists still raised. "You've always been jealous!"

Shaun exhaled through his nose. "Really, Michael."

"You admit it, then." Michael scoffed. "You loved her."

Shaun met his gaze, unwavering. "Yes. But she chose you. And I respected her decision."

Michael's anger surged.

"I hate you!"

"That's not true."

"Don't tell me what I know." His voice shook. "Who do you think you are?"

"I'm your brother. And I'm here to take you home."

Michael laughed coldly. "Home?"

"To your wife. Your mother. They need you."

Michael's laughter died. His fists lowered. "They need me to kneel at my father's bedside and watch him die." His voice cracked. "They need me to hold their hands while they bury my sisters." His shoulders slumped his lips morphing into a cruel sneer. "They can all go to hell."

Shaun's face didn't change. "They need your support—just as you need theirs."

Michael turned his back. "No."

The familiar weight of shame settled in his chest. It crawled under his skin and threatened to drown him. "Leave me be, Shaun." His voice dropped. "Go."

"I will always be here for you," Shaun murmured. "I will not go. I will not leave my brother in torment."

Michael closed his eyes.

"You're making it worse." His voice barely carried over the hum of the tavern. "I don't want you here."

Shaun was quiet for a long moment. "I will never abandon you." He walked to the bar, where he sat, silently watching Michael.

Michael's gaze landed on Julian sitting in the corner, lifting an eyebrow.

CHAPTER 23 ~ TRINITY

Trinity paused at the kitchen doors that were wide open. The fire from inside warmed her chilled skin. She'd just finished cleaning the twins' bedchambers and just needed a moment to catch her breath.

Sybil and David sat at the table in the kitchen, sipping something warm in mugs. Looking as exhausted as she was. Sybil hadn't slept barely at all. None of them had.

"I want to go to sleep," Sybil said softly, closing her eyes, making Trinity huff.

David held her hand in his, squeezing it.

Trinity entered the kitchen balancing the wooden tray stacked with cups, empty bowls, and spoons. "Good evening," she said softly.

Exhaustion seeped through her bones as she deposited the items on the kitchen counter. Her shoulders slumped forward as she hung her head low; eyes closed as she breathed out.

"Good evening, m'lady," David said.

"How are you?" Sybil asked.

279

Trinity lifted her gaze as Mrs. Bartlett emerged from the basement carrying a pitcher of milk.

"M'lady," she said softly.

Sybil and David, now stood before her. Sorrow and pity in their eyes.

But before Trinity could answer, Susana's screams tore through the manor. A wail so raw, so full of grief, it was as if her soul were being ripped from her. It echoed through every corridor and chamber. There was no escape from it.

Henry was gone. The twins were gone. Michael had vanished. Only Elizabeth and Fleur stayed by her side.

Trinity clutched her eyes closed and shook her head, clutching the counter to help hold her up.

She just wanted it to all stop! Just stop!

"Oh God," she tried to take a breath, but it stuck in her throat. "I can't," she sobbed.

"It will be alright. Lenora's with her. Elizabeth and Fleur are too." Sybil took away the tray in front of her. "I'll clean this up."

Trinity barely registered them. Her mind was foggy with scattered thoughts, as if she walked through a dream. Or a nightmare.

"I needed to ask you…" *What was I going to ask Sybil?* There was something important she needed to speak with her about.

Everything was crumbling around her—everyone she loved slipping away. She blinked and forced herself to focus.

"What is it?" Sybil asked, bringing Trinity back.

"Sorry—yes." She nodded toward their cups. "Is that mulled wine?"

"Yes, m'lady. Would you like some?" David asked.

"I'd love some. Thank you."

Another scream rang out. Ripping through Trinity's nerves, her muscles tensed as she cringed, holding the sides of her head. "Oh God."

Trinity closed her eyes, inhaling deeply. Her own grief clawed at her insides, but Susana's was something else entirely.

"She suffers so much," Trinity whispered, sinking into Henry's chair at the head of the table.

Mrs. Bartlett sat across from Sybil and David, rubbing her temples. Strands of red hair had fallen loose from its usual coil, and deep worry lines framed her red puffy eyes.

"Where is Michael?" she asked.

David took a long sip of his wine. "He rode out the other day and hasn't returned. Shaun's keeping an eye on him in town."

"Thank God for that boy," Mrs. Bartlett muttered.

Joseph entered, his arms piled high with linen and blankets from Henry's chambers. He'd taken it upon himself to strip the room, though grief had etched itself into every line of his face.

He discarded the bundle by the back door and wiped his hands together.

"Joseph, join us for a cup of mulled wine," Trinity offered, hoping he'd sit even for a moment.

He hesitated, glancing toward the door as if debating leaving. But then, with a heavy breath, he pulled out a chair beside Sybil. David poured him a drink.

Susana's wailing did not stop. It was relentless.

It was only the five of them and Dreyfus left.

"Has anyone seen Dreyfus?" Trinity asked. It had been days since she last saw him.

Everyone murmured the same answer, "No."

"He has family up north. He's probably with them," Joseph said," his voice tight and professional. "It's just us now."

Trinity exhaled—just us.

"Lady Trinity, you must manage the affairs," Joseph continued. "Lady Susana won't be able to for some time."

"I understand," she murmured. "But I've never done it before. I have no idea where to begin."

"I'll help you. Henry's account books are in his sitting room. We should review them tomorrow—especially with so many having left, including the guards."

"The guards?" Sybil asked, shocked. "All of them?"

"Yes, child. All of them. We must keep the gates and manor doors always locked."

Mrs. Bartlett stood abruptly. "I'm going to sleep. Tomorrow, we have a funeral to prepare."

"Goodnight, Mrs. Bartlett," Trinity said softly.

The older woman paused beside Trinity, gently touching her shoulder. "We are here for you. We won't abandon you, dear."

"Thank you so much," Trinity released a breath she didn't realize she was holding.

She drank the last of her mulled wine, feeling the warmth spread through her limbs. Sybil had added something to help them relax, but the herb's name eluded her.

"David, Joseph—may I speak with Sybil alone?"

Both men rose together.

"Of course. Good night, m'lady," David said.

"Good evening, m'lady. Sybil," Joseph added before following David out.

Trinity waited, listening to their retreating footsteps. Doubt clouded her mind despite Sybil's unwavering friendship. But she needed to tell someone.

She poured herself another cup of wine and took a sip.

Sybil waited quietly; hands clasped in her lap.

Trinity studied her.

Sybil was pretty. Her fair-blond hair was nearly the color of snow, and when she blushed, her cheeks bloomed pink against her pale skin. But her eyes—those were something else. Light silver-blue, ringed in black, almond-shaped. Almost feline. Otherworldly.

Trinity realized she was staring. "Sorry," she muttered, rubbing her temple. "I feel... adrift."

"It's been a difficult few days," Sybil said, sipping her wine.

Trinity hesitated. "I know you and your grandmother understand herbs and healing…"

"My grandmother is the healer. I've only learned a little."

"Perhaps you could help me." She took a deep breath. It was dangerous to admit her affliction of tremors. Especially now. But she needed help. The tremors had worsened, along with the nightmares.

"I've been having nightmares." Trinity admitted, hesitantly.

"That's understandable," Sybil said.

"Yes... of course." Trinity huffed a dry laugh; her hands tightened around her cup. "But when I wake, my body shakes so violently I can't stop it. It hurts. In my bones. My head pounds—like it will split apart."

"Has this happened before?" Sybil leaned in.

"Yes. It started after my aunt and uncle died and has happened several more times... especially recently."

"It could be your body's way of reacting to distress. I could make you a sleep tonic. Lenora uses it sometimes—it's perfectly safe."

Trinity exhaled. "Yes, that would be nice. Thank you. Do you have some now?"

"I do." Sybil stood, gathering herbs from the cupboard. She rekindled the fire, warming the rest of the wine.

"May I ask what your dreams are about?"

Trinity hesitated. "Not long ago I dreamt of a man with black hair running through the forest, screaming. Monsters chasing him beneath a waning moon. I couldn't see his face, but I thought it was Michael at first."

She took a sip of wine, her hands trembling slightly.

Sybil almost dropped the clay pot and turned; eyes wide.

"What's the matter?" Trinity asked.

"What about your other dreams? Do you always wake up shaking?" Sybil asked urgently.

Trinity swallowed. "Once, I dreamed of twin women with long black hair and dark eyes. One cut her arm over a stone, blood dripping into it. Something in the fog bit my palm. I woke up, and it was bleeding, but I thought it was from my nails—I'd been shaking so badly."

Sybil didn't move. Her face paled even more than usual.

Trinity sighed. "You think I'm mad. My mother was mad. I suppose I am, too." She almost wished she was going mad. The reality of the seraph Seriella's demands practically drowned her.

I wish I could tell Sybil.

284

Nicole Moore

"No," Sybil said firmly. She sat beside Trinity. "You are not."

Trinity clenched her eyes tight, trying to stop the tears from welling, then met Sybil's gaze. She desperately wanted to tell her the truth of it all.

"Trinity," Sybil said gently, "in Christianity, pious women are called to fight with angels against the demons of hell. Have you heard the stories?"

"Yes, of course. We all have," Trinity whispered. "My aunt told me about them often. She loved the saints. But what does that have to do with my nightmares?"

"I think you're a traveler," Sybil whispered. "A seer of sorts."

Trinity blinked. "Excuse me?" But the word triggered something inside of her.

Alfred's voice echoed in her mind. Your aunt knew evil walked among us. She could see them.

"Trinity?" Sybil squeezed her hands.

Trinity struggled to breathe. "What's a traveler, a… what did you call it, a seer?"

"A woman who can see demons," Sybil said. "Or the future, maybe the present."

Trinity shook her head. "No. No, they're just nightmares. Stress. Fear."

Sybil breathed out, reaching for Trinity's hand. "I won't tell anyone. I promise."

Trinity's chest tightened but her resolution to confide in Sybil strengthened. Then, quietly, she said, "I need to show you something."

She led Sybil up to her bedchamber, both sipping their warm wine. Trinity's hands trembling in fear. She prayed that Sybil wouldn't condemn her or run to the church.

285

Susana must have fallen asleep as the wailing had ceased, and the manor grew quiet as a tomb.

Trinity closed her bedroom door behind Sybil and placed her wine on the table.

"Please don't fret. And please, I beg of you to try and stay open minded. Trinity cringed as she tentatively opened the carved chest at the end of her bed.

Sybil stepped closer. "You can share anything, Trinity. I'm here for you."

Trinity huffed an incredulous laugh, shaking her head. "You might feel differently after…" She unwrapped the sword and shield.

Sybil stood behind her and gasped, putting a hand over her mouth. "Where did you get that?"

Trinity stiffened.

"These are powerful, Trinity. They're not made for mortals. How did you come by it?"

"How do you know what these are?" She didn't move her eyes from Sybil's.

How could Sybil know these things?

"They're what the church would call angelic," Sybil explained softly, almost reverently, as she touched the obsidian hilt. "Lenora would love to see it."

A tear ran down Trinity's right cheek. "They belong to a seraph called Seriella. She named the sword Guardian of Light, and the shield is the Shield of Truth."

"Similar to the sword of Jophiel." Sybil laughed softly. "Oh, David would love this."

"Yes, I suppose it is. I hadn't thought of that." Trinity placed the shield and sword on the bed and paced the room like a caged animal.

"There are even older stories," Sybil continued. "The flaming sword of King Rhydderch Hael." She sighed. "Oh, David definitely will love this."

Trinity stopped. "How do you know all this, Sybil?" She studied her friend, confusion flickering in her eyes.

Sybil held her gaze. "Search your heart, Trinity. What do you feel? What do you hear?"

Trinity suddenly felt exhausted, but she needed answers and needed someone to listen to her.

So, she told Sybil everything—her aunt's dying words, what Alfred had said about her aunt seeing demons about the encounter with Seriella.

When she finished, she placed the sword and shield back into the chest and closed it. They sat on the bed, sipping their mulled wine.

There was one more thing Trinity had to confess. She sucked in a deep breath of courage, spearing Sybil with her gaze, unblinking. "Seriella told me to find the druids. I suppose Druid-kin, as I can't imagine any are still alive."

Sybil looked stunned. Her mouth opened and closed like a fish gasping for air. Finally, she spoke, and her sent a shiver down her spine. "You've found them already."

"What? Where?" Trinity shook her head, her brows pinched in confusion. "Who?"

Sybil took Trinity's hand in hers. "My family are descendants of the clan of the goddess Cailleach. Trinity, we are Druid-kin, and my grandmother, Lenora is a druidess."

Trinity snorted, her head shaking side to side. "That's impossible. You've prayed with me. You married David in our chapel, blessed by our priest."

287

"Yes. To keep appearances, we must do things that…"

"Oh God." Trinity stood up, backing away from Sybil, her fingers pressed against her temples. She'd confided in Sybil. Became a friend to a pagan.

All her catholic teachings slammed into her, along with the prejudice and fear. "Druids were pagans who worship the devil," she said softly. "Oh Lord, help me." She clutched her cross pendant.

Sybil didn't move or acknowledge Trinity's ramblings. "You could be a traveler or a seer, like your aunt," she whispered. "Why else would she and the angel give you the sword and shield? And the seraph told you to find us. What did she say?"

Trinity shook her head. "That not everything, was, as it seemed. Oh, God." Trinity swayed, shaking her head in disbelief. "She showed me a vision of my aunt fighting a Druid, who called himself the Keeper of the Veil. The Druid pleaded with my aunt to work together to hold back the demons. But I don't understand. The church teaches…" she trailed off, the implication dawning. The hurt and confusion palpable.

Sybil stepped closer to her. "It's alright, Trinity. We can help."

Trinity covered her face with her hands. "I showed Michael the sword and shield. We were going to bring it to Henry, but too many things distracted us. And now it's too late."

"It's not too late." Sybil's voice was steady. "But I encourage you to seek counsel with my grandmother."

"No, Sybil. You promised not to tell anyone." She couldn't reconcile her lifelong teachings and beliefs to what the seraph, Seriella told her to do. It was impossible. The church wouldn't lie. The Bible was written…

"I did promise." Sybil hesitated. "But she knows more about this than anyone." She stood but didn't leave. "I promise not to say anything unless your life is in danger," she said. "But you must promise to tell me when you have these nightmares and seizures. Let me help you."

Trinity looked up at her friend, a pagan Druid-Kin, then nodded.

"I promise."

CHAPTER 24 ~ SYBIL

The coven was called together, in York.

Sybil rubbed her forehead as she stood in the window at her grandmother's, overlooking the alleyway. Rain poured down in a relentless blanket. Lightning lit up the sky.

"One, two, three," Sybil counted until a boom of thunder accompanied it.

A pounding headache caused her to clutch her jaw. She warred within herself to tell her grandmother about Trinity or not, but in the end, she'd promised not to. So, she didn't. She needed Trinity's trust.

She closed the wooden shutters and blinds over the window—the sun was setting. Someone had lit the candles on the large oval wooden table.

Sybil huffed an irritated breath and settled beside Lenora, with David on Sybil's left side. Lenora's younger sister, Leigha, sat at Lenora's other side.

Men and women from different covens around the England, Whales and Scotland squeezed around Lenora's giant table.

Lenora and Leigha's three cousins shuffled into the room. Fey was leading them, her chin up and shoulders back.

Sybil could sense the animosity flowing off her whenever the older woman looked towards Lenora. Based on rumors, Sybil understood that Fey wanted the mantle of the coven's leader and openly complained about Lenora being too old.

"Lenora," Fey said, nodding hello and sitting across the table as her sisters, Wanda and Leanne, silently took their seats next to her.

Sybil noted Fey hadn't even glanced in her direction.

Nicholas pushed through the door carrying an arm full of wrapped weapons fashioned from Lenora's stash of obsidian and steel, dumping them unceremoniously on the table and sitting next to his mother, Fey.

"Thank you, Nicholas," Lenora said.

"The rest are almost finished," he said, nodding hello to Sybil and David. "David, Sybil."

"Very good," Lenora said.

Sybil scanned the people gathered around the table.

She had never met the covens from London and was surprised when an older man and woman—apparently siblings—arrived. Josephine and Roberto. They had the same long, straight, jet-black hair and nearly identical deep brown eyes.

Lenora shared with Sybil; the London coven suffered heavy losses. However, several family members escaped.

Next to them sat three blonde women, all tall and broad-shouldered. Their sturdy frames spoke of strength, their presence unwavering. The eldest, Agnes, led the Bristol coven. Beside her were her sister Deloris and her daughter Angelina. They wore simple white cotton gowns, like nuns. Sybil knew nothing of their coven's fate; months had passed without any contact.

Across from Lenora, two massive men sat, draped in fur capes and kilts. Malcolm and Lachlan, the coven leaders from North Scotland. Brothers.

Their long, thick beards and reddish-blond hair framed faces that looked carved from stone. Their fierce hazel eyes promised death. Energy coiled around them, thick and wild, whispering of violence and mayhem. Even seated, they were terrifying.

Evelyn sat at David's side, somber and calm, avoiding the stares of the London coven.

The last woman sat quietly beside Evelyn, her presence almost ghostly in its stillness.

Her hair—pale-blond, similar to Sybil's—cascaded down her back in long straight waves, half braided and secured at her crown in a bun. But it was her eyes that unsettled Sybil. When they locked gazes, it was as if looking into a mirror and she sucked in a sharp breath.

Sybil sensed familiarity yet couldn't explain it and tried to push aside her unease.

She—and many others her age—were still considered apprentices. Normally, she would never be allowed into the inner circle, and being here was a great honor. So, it wasn't a surprise to hear a few of them grumbling about her presence.

Lenora cleared her throat. The low murmur of conversation ended as all eyes turned to her.

"It's taken too long for everyone to travel here," Lenora began, her voice firm. "And we have many issues to discuss tonight. But I would like to begin with the most urgent."

"I have studied the Darkborn Prophecies, and I believe two are coming to pass." She paused, waiting for everyone's full attention. "In 1298 the oracle predicted: When the breath of death curls through the streets and hides its face, the crows shall feast, and the soil shall sour. Light will falter, and the faithful shall fall—but one will carry the flame that will rise against the darkness. And another in 1301, a few years later: When the shadow swallows the moon, the earth will weep with ash and blood. Darkness comes with a hunger that will devour the light."

"What does one have to do with the other?" The man from Scotland demanded in a gruff deep voice.

"This prophecy makes no sense," the leader of the Bristol coven said, shaking her head.

The others all murmured agreements.

"There's an eclipse in just over six moons from now," Lenora said raising her voice.

Arguing and muttering broke out across the group until Lenora banged on the table.

"Let my granddaughter speak and it will become clear." She turned to Sybil. "You all know Sybil."

There were murmured affirmations and nods of recognition.

Sybil swallowed hard, trying to loosen the knot in her throat. Her voice was steady, but her hands were clenched in her lap shaking.

She revealed her vision from Chailleach and everything she had seen at Ellsworth, including the growing number of ghouls in the forests.

She hesitated before mentioning Michael. Before speaking of Susana. But the coven needed to understand. However, as she spoke, a weight settled over her. Guilt.

Henry. Susana. The twins. Michael. They felt like family. And now, here she was, exposing them. Betraying their privacy.

"Also," Sybil cleared her throat again, "When a demon is near me, I become ill. Terribly ill." Her voice was steady, but the weight of her words filled the room. "I sense it. Usually, I can see them too, even without magic, but I can't see this one. It's different. It has a strong sulfuric smell and disappears into the shadows."

She let the silence settle before continuing. "We have ascertained they are legionnaires. And that Baal is creating an elite army of them, but this demon— whoever or whatever it is—must be extraordinarily powerful. To hide from me so easily and to cause disease in a human that withstands our healing magic is rare. Only the strongest demons or blood mages have such abilities."

"Could it be Baal himself, here, you sense?" Nicholas asked.

She held his piercing gaze. "No. We will all know when he comes." Pausing to gather her thoughts, she looked at the woman who resembled her so much, and the woman smiled encouragingly. "But it's an exceptionally rare and deadly demon, none the less."

She met each one's gaze, pausing briefly as she searched for signs of doubt.

Her ability to detect and see demons was a unique and coveted gift. She needed them to believe her.

"Can you find it?" a woman asked.

"No," Sybil admitted.

There were murmurs of surprise, but most sat quietly, waiting.

She took a deep breath. "This evil is coming for all of us. It has already wrapped its arms around York, but we are its thorn." Sybil glanced around at each person. "Since I'm the only one who can sense them, I will begin searching the city and surrounding villages to track and find their hive."

She had already planned everything with David, Lenora, and Evelyn, including weekly scouting missions around York. Her absence from Ellsworth would be noticed but she had no choice.

"If we don't find them soon, in six moons the legionnaire army may be too large to defeat," Lenora said as Sybil reclined in her seat, letting go of the air trapped in her lungs. "David, Nicholas, Enzo, and Luca will accompany Sybil." Lenora continued. "Enzo can hear whispers in the wind—he may be able to help locate them."

Nicholas nodded at Sybil, leaning back, arms crossed over his chest.

The murmuring resumed. Sybil noticed the strange blonde lady watching her again, this time with a smirk, as if amused.

The older woman from London, Josephine, finally spoke. Her long black hair framed her sharp, lined face. "If an army of legionnaires exists, why have they not shown themselves?"

Her brother interrupted, "The demons in London came with tremendous speed and strength. We were unprepared. They didn't hide in the shadows—they struck before we knew what they were."

"Baal has learned from his mistakes," Lenora said. "I believe he's building an even bigger army."

She picked up a bundle of sage and herbs in one hand and a short spear in the other. The spear was an ancient weapon passed down through the senior coven leaders. The metal gleamed with delicate script carved along its blade and handle.

"Then we have no hope," Josephine said, her voice clipped.

Lenora's gaze sharpened. "We have been preparing, as they have." She lifted the spear slightly. "We now have warded weapons that can kill a legionnaire. You did not."

Josephine held her glare but said nothing.

"We have ways to defend against them this time," Lenora continued. "Sybil shall lead this group. I've performed a protection incantation to mask her magic. I'll do the same for the men who accompany her. Every mage who fights alongside us will receive a warded weapon."

Several people started talking at once. Arguments broke out.

Sybil sighed, catching David's eye. They knew this wouldn't be easy. The covens had too many different opinions and ideas about how to fight.

Lenora stood and took Sybil's hand. "Come."

She called for a break, leading Sybil and David out of the room.

As they left, Sybil glanced back. The blonde woman—the one who looked so much like her—met her eyes.

Outside, Lenora stopped. "Have you finished the wards?"

David nodded. "Almost. The rain slows it down."

Lenora placed her wrinkled hand on his arm. "That's not good enough." Her tone was firm. "Both of you need to practice every night. Defensive and offensive magic. Some energies can be manipulated with sound—to cause demon's pain. The twins use it."

She turned, walking toward a cupboard. "David, you'll be interested in this one." She pulled out a small handwritten book. A small manual of sorts. "It's a summary of my original grimoire, but it'll give you enough to start with. Study and practice and David use the sound spell."

"Thank you, grandmother." Sybil kissed Lenora's cheek.

"Go, now. Be safe."

***

Sybil and David rode through the city, the streets eerily empty. Most people stayed inside at night, especially when it rained.

The wind picked up, pushing against them. The rain fell harder, soaking them even though they had thick hooded cloaks.

"I hate this weather," she grumbled, and Moon Pie shook her head and blew out air between her lips. Obviously agreeing. David smirked and kicked his mare ahead. Sybil patted Moon Pie's neck. "I know. You hate it too. I promise extra sweets when we get home."

Sybil followed behind David for a few blocks before the river Ouse when her stomach lurched.

Nausea struck fast. She barely had time to stop Moon Pie before she leaned over and emptied her stomach onto the street.

She wiped her mouth, glancing at David.

He had little time to react before his eyes widened.

"Ride!" he yelled, smacking the rear of her horse.

A group of ghouls charged toward them, screeching, their ragged clothing soaked from the rain. More ghouls poured in from another street, cutting off their escape.

Sybil kicked Moon Pie forward, turning sharply down an alley.

David rode hard beside her, but a second pack of ghouls pushed through a broken fence, blocking them again.

They were surrounded.

David circled her, sword drawn, his energy shifting as he pulled the magic into himself. Sybil tried to steady her breathing and focus. She needed to join him, but—

Her hand instinctively went to her belly. She hadn't told David yet. A shock of fear swept through her. Too much power could hurt the babies.

She pulled her sword free.

The stench of sulphur thickened, clawing at her throat and burning her eyes. The presence was here— the demon she could never see.

The ghouls hissed and screeched but did not attack. Two tall women emerged from the darkness, stepping through the horde.

Long black hair. Black eyes.

Sybil's grip tightened on her sword.

David cursed under his breath. "It's her. The same woman who attacked me before."

One of the women threw open her cloak, lifted her fists, and twisted them in the air.

There was a sickening crack.

Sybil spun as David's sword fell from his hand, clattering onto the cobblestones.

His body slid sideways off his horse. Limp. Lifeless. Dead.

Sybil screamed, but she didn't hear it. Everything slowed. Another scream tore from her throat as the ground rumbled, everything shaking around her. A flood of magic drew into her faster than she'd ever pulled it in before, and as she let out another earth-shattering scream, white light exploded outward. The white light, bright as a star.

She didn't have a moment to sort out what she did or even how. It never happened before.

The ghouls flew back, crashing against buildings and scattering like dry leaves in a storm.

She threw herself from her horse, stumbling toward David.

His beautiful blue eyes stared up at her—empty.

She dropped to her knees, pulling him into her lap. "No…" Her voice broke. The light faded.

She cradled his head, fingers tangling in his damp hair. "Don't leave me," she sobbed, rocking him. "Please don't go."

His skin felt cold, his face drained of color, and his head slumped sideways, doll-like.

The ground beneath her trembled again. A moment later, it violently ripped apart. Cracks splintered through the street, splitting the earth wide open in front of them.

And yet—A warmth spread over her. A feeling of love and peace wrapping around her like a cocoon.

She dared to look up.

The twin women were gone. Instead, a different woman stood before her. Straight, white-blond hair. Silver-blue eyes—her eyes.

Sybil barely registered the others behind the woman—several from Lenora's meeting. Hands joined, chanting, forming a circle around her and David.

The woman so much like her stepped closer, kneeling at David's side. She placed her hands on his chest. A bright light bloomed between them. It pulsed, sinking into David's body.

Sybil let out a quiet sob, clutching him tighter, pushing her forehead to his.

Then—A sharp inhale. David's chest rose.

Sybil's eyes flew open.

David's fluttered. Once. Twice. Then they opened fully, meeting hers.

Her heart nearly burst. "You're alive!" She kissed him, pressing her lips to his, desperate to feel him. "Thank the Gods."

The blonde woman reached a hand to Sybil. "Come. We must leave at once. We've created more damage than we can hide. We cannot be seen here."

Sybil stumbled to her feet, helping David up. "I—I don't understand. I saw him die."

The woman met her eyes. "I got here in time. I was able to heal him."

Sybil stared. "Who are you?"

The woman's expression remained unreadable. "I'm Ailith." She turned sharply, glancing down at the ruined street. "Now we move. There's no time to waste."

CHAPTER 25 ~ TRINITY

Trinity waited two days for Michael to return and bury his father and sisters.

He never came.

She stood by the front doors with Joseph. He was heading to York to broker a deal with a trusted food merchant, hoping to secure enough supplies for the next few months then get back before the funeral.

They had finished reviewing the ledger, leaving her drained. It was a disaster. The villagers and field hands were either sick, gone, or afraid to leave their homes. Goods hadn't been sold. Taxes hadn't been collected. And their stores wouldn't last much longer. With winter not far off.

Shaun rode into the courtyard, looking disheveled and weary. Dark circles shadowed his eyes.

For a fleeting moment, hope flared in her chest. Then he met her gaze. A slow blink. A slight shake of his head.

Hope shattered as pain spread through her heart.

"He's not coming." Shaun climbed the stairs, taking her hands. "I'm sorry, Trinity."

His anger and disappointment with Michael were evident, but more than that—he was worried.

"I've never seen him like this," Shaun said. "It's like looking at a stranger."

Trinity couldn't speak. She focused on breathing, willing the tears away.

"Every night, I try to convince him to come home, but the fool refuses."

A sob escaped her throat. She pressed a hand to her chest.

"What is his reasoning?" Joseph asked.

"He claims you don't need him." Shaun hesitated, glancing between them. "He drinks constantly, mutters to himself all day, saying things like, 'Dead and gone'. He keeps repeating that it was all lies."

"What are lies?" Trinity's voice came out broken.

Joseph tugged her close, steadying her.

"I don't know," Shaun admitted.

"Thank you for watching over him." Trinity tried to smile, but her lips wouldn't move. Instead, she pressed them together, eyes closing as a tear slipped free.

Shaun pulled her into his arms, and she let herself fall into his embrace. Sobs tore through her, shaking her against him. She let go, not caring who saw.

The nightmare she thought she'd escaped refused to release her. She wasn't meant for happiness.

As the grief consumed her, a tremor rippled through her body. And suddenly—She wasn't in Shaun's arms.

She was in a tavern. Michael sat hunched over his ale, gripping the mug with both hands, his head bowed.

Her breath caught. Then she was back.

She shoved Shaun away, gasping, but her body had already started shaking violently.

Joseph and Shaun grabbed her as her legs gave out. The world tilted. The sky blurred—Then blackness.

***

"Trinity? Come on, wake up." Sybil's voice was edged with concern, but Trinity didn't understand why.

She'd just had a terrible dream—Henry had died, the twins had died, and Michael had abandoned them.

Why was she being woken up?

"What's the matter?" she grumbled, sitting up and rubbing her eyes. They were swollen and sore.

Had I been crying?

"You had a fit. Shaun and Joseph were with you. Do you remember?"

Trinity frowned. "What? When?"

"This morning."

The confusion deepened—then everything came crashing back. A wave of nausea twisted her stomach, and she nearly gagged.

"I saw him."

Sybil leaned in. "Who?"

"Michael… He looked so broken." She squeezed her eyes shut, shaking her head. "What's happening to me?"

"It's the visions. For some reason, your body is rejecting your gifts. Causing the tremors."

"It. Is. Not. a gift, Sybil. Stop saying that." Trinity's voice sharpened. "If anyone heard you, they'd think I was a witch. I'd be imprisoned."

"I swear I'll never tell a soul. And I'm not saying you're a witch—just… gifted. Chosen." Sybil hesitated.

303

"Perhaps your Lord gave this to you for a reason, but I don't understand why the seizures?"

"I care not, Sybil. I only want it to stop."

"We need to tell Lenora."

"No!" Trinity swung her legs over the bed, trying to stand—instantly regretting it as the room swayed. She dropped back onto the mattress. "You swore you wouldn't tell her."

"Then you tell her," Sybil countered. "She can help with the fits, at least."

"I thought you could help me." Trinity's voice softened as she steadied her trembling hands. "You can help me."

Sybil sighed. "Not if it's a side effect of mag—" She halted. "If there's a reason, your visions are causing the seizures, then I won't be able to help. Lenora is the only one."

Trinity couldn't listen to another word. They weren't visions. They were hallucinations. Dreams. Symptoms of the fits.

She pushed herself up, but a knock at the door stopped Sybil from arguing further.

Thank God. "Yes?"

Joseph stepped inside. "Wonderful, you're up. Are you feeling better, m'lady?"

"Yes, thank you, Joseph. And thank you for helping me." She met his gaze. "I hope you'll respect my privacy and keep this to yourself?"

"Of course, m'lady," he said with a slight nod. "The priest is with Lady Susana, praying alone in her chambers. The rest are waiting in the main hall."

"Thank you, Joseph."

She studied his face, suddenly aware of the grief in his eyes. Henry had been like a son to him.

"I'm sorry," she murmured. "I forget how hard this must be for you, too."

Joseph's jaw tightened. "Henry was an exceptional man who will be sorely missed. And the girls… It'll never be the same without them."

"No, it won't," Trinity said softly.

And no matter how much she prayed, no vision—or dream—would change that.

***

The three of them entered the main hall.

Elizabeth sat beside Fleur at the long table; their hands interlocked in silent prayer. Their heads bowed; eyes closed. Both looked exhausted. No one cared about cauls, coiled hair or pristine gowns anymore.

At the far end of the room, Theodore spoke with David, his tone sharp and precise. "Make sure the carriage is ready the moment the funeral ends. I will not keep my wife and unborn child here for a moment longer."

David nodded, then left.

Theodore walked to Elizabeth's side, resting a protective hand on her shoulder.

Trinity understood his urgency. If she could spirit them away, she would too.

The door to Henry's parlor opened, and Shaun stepped out.

"Shaun!" Trinity hurried toward him. He took her hands and kissed both her cheeks.

"Thank God you're alright. I was returning to check on you." He lowered his voice, nodding toward Elizabeth. "She's driving me mad."

The teasing faded. His expression turned solemn.

"I'm sorry. I failed you." His eyes dropped.

305

"He's truly not coming?" Trinity had hoped it was part of the delusions.

Elizabeth's voice rang out, sharper than steel, as she shot to her feet. "Theodore, you must fetch my insolent brother immediately!"

Fleur was already there, placing a steadying arm around Elizabeth's shoulders.

Trinity's gaze locked onto Shaun's. "You didn't tell her yet?" she whispered.

Shaun exhaled. "He won't come. If I can't bring him back, no one will."

"What about me?" Trinity asked.

"You least of all." Shaun's grip on her hands tightened. "He refuses to see anyone. He won't leave his room at the inn except to order more wine." He hesitated, watching her tremble. "I'm so sorry. For all of it."

"This is outrageous!" Elizabeth stormed to the table, snatched her cup of wine, and hurled it to the floor. The cup shattered.

"Elizabeth!" Trinity moved toward her, but Fleur took Elizabeth's hand faster.

"Breathe," Fleur whispered.

Elizabeth ignored her. She turned on Trinity instead, voice raw with grief.

"I told you to go to him! You're his wife!" She collapsed into her chair, sobbing.

Trinity picked up the broken cup, setting it on the table with shaking hands.

The last two nights, Sybil's herbs had helped her sleep. But today, the funeral loomed. Henry. The twins. Her hands wouldn't stop trembling.

Elizabeth had demanded, over and over, that Trinity fetch Michael herself.

Perhaps she should have. But she was so tired. Scared. Alone. But mostly, she was just angry. Furious that he had abandoned them—abandoned her—when he had promised to protect her.

"I am his wife, and I'm sorry my husband has disappointed you." She had no strength to argue. No fight left in her. "I should have gone."

"There was nothing you could have done," Shaun said firmly. "I'm telling you; it would have made things worse. He's not in his right mind."

The door banged open as Sybil returned with linen, moving to clean the spilled wine.

"He's a fool," Elizabeth choked out, tears streaming down her face. "I will never forgive him."

A quiet cough interrupted them. The priest stood at the door, hands clasped, head bowed slightly. "It's time."

They followed him outside. The fresh spring air was warm, but dark clouds loomed in the distance, creeping closer.

Trinity scarcely noticed. She could swear even the birds had fallen silent.

Shaun walked beside her; her arm looped through his. She leaned into him for support.

"In London, they bury the bodies of plague victims in pits," she murmured.

He stiffened. "That's barbaric."

"I buried my aunt and uncle under a tree." Her voice was barely a whisper. "And now, I will bury another father. And my sisters."

Tears blurred her vision.

Lenora and Isabella stood beside Susana before the three freshly dug graves.

She looked like a hollow shell, empty of life, her eyes vacant as she stared at the dirt without seeing. Someone had braided her hair, but she had refused to wear a caul and veil. At least her dress was clean and new.

Fleur and Theodore flanked Elizabeth, who sobbed and moaned, her grief raw and unrestrained. Trinity was grateful for Fleur's presence but felt sorry for her. Fleur kept flinching under the weight of Elizabeth's wailing.

The priest stood beside them and began the sermon, but Trinity couldn't hear a word.

It was as if she was trapped in a bubble, the words muffled and distorted. Then something inside her cracked open. Her heart. Her soul. She didn't know which, only that the pain flooding through her was like a dam breaking.

Tears streamed down her face, and she sobbed even though she tried not to.

She would never hear the twins laughing and chasing one another again, never seeing Henry smoking his pipe, smiling at her with that familiar jolly warmth. She would miss them terribly—just as she missed her aunt, uncle, mother, and father.

She leaned into Shaun, and he held her up.

"Blessed are those who walk in the shadow of grief, for they have loved," the priest was saying…

But Trinity didn't feel blessed. She felt punished.

A storm cloud rolled overhead. Soft droplets of rain fell onto her face.

She whispered, "It always rains when someone I love dies."

The priest finished his sermon.

Susana dropped a handful of dirt into each grave. She wasn't sobbing anymore. She barely seemed to be breathing. Trinity was sure Lenora gave her something to keep calm.

"Come," Shaun said, taking her arm. "Let's go back inside before the sky decides to dump on us."

***

Later that afternoon, Elizabeth and her husband were leaving, and Trinity's heart cracked a little more.

Elizabeth hugged Fleur goodbye, then stepped toward Trinity.

"I'm sorry I was harsh."

"Don't worry. It's been a sad time for everyone. Look after yourself."

Trinity stepped back as Elizabeth and her husband climbed into the carriage. David had already loaded their belongings and stood by the horse, murmuring to the driver.

Lenora and Isabella had taken Susana to her chambers. Soon, they would return to York. Lenora had received a message—others in town were sick and showing signs of the plague.

The carriage rumbled through the gates, and Fleur walked back to the manor.

"Wait, Fleur!" Trinity called.

Fleur paused; her eyes glossy with unshed tears.

"I'm sorry…" Her voice broke, and she ran back inside.

Trinity couldn't blame her.

Fleur had confided in her, that her parents hadn't replied to any of her letters. She was worried. The last she'd known, they had been visiting family in France. Now, there was only silence.

Fleur was alone. And afraid.

"Well, it's just us now," Trinity said quietly to Sybil. "We need to help her. She's scared."

"We'll get through this together." Sybil took her hand, squeezing it gently.

Shaun draped an arm over Trinity's shoulder, holding her close. "I'm taking Lenora and my mother home." His gaze followed the carriage as it disappeared down the road. "If you need anything, let me know."

Trinity wiped her cheeks. "Bring him back to us, Shaun."

PART TWO

"When the shadow swallows the moon, the earth will weep with ash and blood. Darkness comes with a hunger that will devour the light."

The Oracle's Prophecy
Summer 1301

CHAPTER 26 ~ TRINITY
Ellsworth, July 1349

It was nearly three months since the wedding, since Henry and the twins died. Some days, Trinity wondered if it had all been a dream.

Michael came home occasionally, but always in the dead of night, muttering nonsense. He sounded mad. And she found herself afraid of him. Ashamed of him.

She'd pretend to be asleep when he collapsed onto their bed, too drunk to notice her. And by morning, he would be gone, along with more clothes and gold coins. She told no one. Not Sybil. Not even Susana.

It was a miracle he was still alive. Since his denouncement of God, she feared the plague would take him or worse, someone would finish him off. But he wasn't alone in his blasphemy. More people spoke out, rejecting God. Radicals filled the streets, flagellants came—some to atone, others to indulge. The days of carnival and celebration had vanished, replaced by despair and chaos. Death and grief.

She sat by her bedroom window as Sybil sat across from her, delivering the latest news about Michael. Nothing new. It was the same story—drunk and preaching blasphemy still.

She didn't bother dressing in delicate gowns anymore. No one was left to see them. Not even Susana, who locked herself away, leaving the household duties to Trinity and Sybil.

When Susana did go out, she'd pace the overgrown garden talking to herself, and wander the halls, whispering nonsense. At night, her moans carried through the manor, filling every corner like a despondent ghost refusing to find peace.

Sybil's voice pulled Trinity from her thoughts. "He's openly attacking the church and anyone who still believes in God. His drinking is getting worse. We need to do something."

Trinity put her hands over her face.

"I know. But what can I do? Tie him up and drag him home?"

"Not a bad idea," Sybil smirked. "David could knock him over the head."

Trinity had grown close to Sybil; without her, she might have lost her mind. She probably would have locked herself in her bedchambers like Susana, too. But she had something more to live for.

The words slipped out before she could stop them. "I'm pregnant."

Sybil's eyes widened. Then, to Trinity's shock, she grinned. "Me too!"

Trinity let out a breathless laugh and took Sybil's hand in hers. "Thank God, I won't be alone in this."

They laughed together, relief easing some of the weight on Trinity's chest.

"We need Lenora to examine you right away," Sybil said.

"I'm fine. I'm just a little sick in the mornings. Nothing to worry about."

"Peppermint tea with a sliver of ginger root will help."

"What's ginger root?"

"It's a strange root and very expensive. Lenora bought some for Lady Susana's pregnancies. One bag cost more than a sheep," Sybil said, shaking her head. "I've been trying to grow it, but it withers here."

"Then don't waste it. Peppermint will do."

"It's alright. I'll make some for you." She hesitated. "May I tell David?"

"Of course! And tell him how happy I am for you both."

Sybil beamed, and then her smile slipped to a grimace. "And the nightmares?"

Trinity shifted, uncomfortable. She told Sybil about every single one. Unless she drank tonic before bed, the nightmares came nearly every night. She had no idea what herbs Sybil used. It worked wonderfully at first but the last few nights the nightmares returned, regardless if she drank the tonic.

"They disappeared for a time but have returned," she admitted. "Is the tonic safe for the baby?"

"Perfectly. I'll lower the dose of valerian, but it's mostly chamomile and rose petals."

"Do you ever take it?"

"I did before I married David." Sybil sighed. "Now, he calms me at night." She immediately winced. "I'm sorry, Trinity."

"Why be sorry for something so natural and wonderful? I'm happy for you both."

But it was a lie. Some days, watching Sybil and David together made her stomach turn. It should have been her and Michael, but she'd never dampen their love.

She missed him so much it left her furious. She tried to keep busy, but it never worked. Every night, she cried herself to sleep.

Again, she had nowhere to run. No one to comfort her. Alone.

"What else is it?" Sybil asked, shaking her out of her thoughts. "I can see something's on your mind."

Trinity didn't want to hurt Sybil or insult her, but it still disturbed her, knowing she wasn't catholic, and a pagan at that. Trusting someone you were taught your entire life was evil was hard. Druids sacrificed humans. Drank their blood. Ate human hearts. They were animals, but Trinity couldn't imagine Sybil doing any of that.

She huffed, wincing a little. "An angel told me to find you."

"Yes, you've mentioned this," Sybil said cautiously.

Sybil hadn't broached the subject since Trinity confessed it all to her. There was too much death and chaos around them to deal with that nugget.

"I'm struggling to... to..."

"Trust me?"

"No. Yes..." Trinity huffed and chewed her bottom lip. "Oh, Sybil, I'm so sorry. I don't understand any of this." She gestured to the chest where the sword and shield were hidden.

"I understand, but I promise you, we have been grossly misunderstood, and the stories are not all true. I promise you, Trinity."

"So, you don't sacrifice people or drink their blood?"

315

Sybil barked out a laugh. "Gods, no!"

Trinity felt foolish, but she had to ask.

"Trinity, we are the guardians of this land. We protect it, including those who dwell upon it from… demons… from evil."

"In the vision of my aunt and druid. He said something similar. I think my aunt worked with druids, too."

"Perhaps."

They sat in silence as Trinity sorted through her thoughts. "Sybil, why was I told to find you?"

"I think we can help you access the sword's power."

"How?"

Sybil pinched her bottom lip, her eyes narrowing in thought. "We need to speak with my grandmother. She will know."

Trinity let out a deep, whooshing breath. Sybil knowing her secret was one thing, but Lenora, too. But the few times she picked up the sword, nothing had happened. She had no idea how even to wield it. The shield hadn't shown her anything more since she left London.

"Fine," she said, resigned.

Sybil stood. "Good. I'll make you the tonic now. Drink it every morning before you eat."

Trinity stood, too. "I'll come with you. I need to see Joseph."

They walked down the stairs. Dust covered the floor, and the manor smelled of stale air and neglect.

At the bottom of the steps, Sybil hesitated.

"I'd like to speak to Lenora about the nightmares and seizures, too. She has treated kings and queens. She understands discretion."

Trinity let out a frustrated sigh. "Fine."

316

"Good." Sybil squeezed her hand before heading to the kitchen.

Trinity watched her go. Sybil never judged her. Any other servant would have accused her of being cursed or possessed and reported her to the Church.

But Sybil never recoiled from her.

Trinity turned toward Henry's parlor and stepped inside.

Joseph was slumped at the desk, his head resting on his folded arms over an open ledger. Fast asleep.

His usually pressed attire was rumpled, and his silver hair was unkempt. He'd been working harder than any of them, travelling between York and the manor and keeping them supplied.

She hated to wake him, but they had to review the inventory. She couldn't do it alone.

Clearing her throat, she stepped closer.

Joseph sat up, rubbing his eyes.

Then she saw it.

A boil. Swollen. Oozing, right below his left ear.

Her breath caught. She pressed her hand over her mouth. His face was flushed with fever.

"What's wrong?"

"You're ill." She meant to ask, but the words came as a statement.

"No, I'm fine, m'lady. Just tired."

"Joseph, your neck."

His brow furrowed. "I'm fine." He tried to stand. His knees buckled and he collapsed back into the chair.

"Joseph!" Trinity's scream barely left her throat before Sybil ran in.

She stopped, covering her mouth. "No. Please, no," she whispered.

Joseph sagged against the desk. Eyes closed. A slow breath. "I'm sorry, m'lady."

Trinity didn't move. Couldn't speak.

What would they do without him? How could they manage the estate? He was their lifeline. In his absence, they would drown.

Joseph forced himself upright. He flipped to a page in the ledger.

"You know what to do," he said. "I've taught you enough these last months to manage. You understand the expenses—the purchases. David will have to travel to York for supplies. I'll write down my contacts."

No one moved.

"It will be fine." He braced himself against the desk, struggling to his feet. "I should retire to my chambers."

"Yes. I'll send for Lenora immediately."

"No." He shook his head weakly. "Send the priest. I want to confess before it's too late."

Trinity swallowed hard. "Of course. I'll fetch him."

Sybil rushed inside. "Joseph!" She wrapped an arm around his waist. "I'll help you to your room and make up the fire."

Joseph gave her a weary smile. "You are such a sweet girl. So much like your mother."

Sybil flinched then recovered quickly, helping him rise. "You knew my mother?" she asked softly.

"I did," he said softly.

Trinity stood rooted to the ground.

Sybil had confided in Trinity that she had no memories of her parents. They had died when she was a baby.

***

That night, Michael came home.

The bedroom door creaked open, and he stumbled inside, drunk again. He barely managed to stay upright as he wobbled to the bed. Clothes fell to the floor as he undressed carelessly.

He slid beneath the blankets, pressing his cold body against hers.

Trinity kept still, pretending to sleep, afraid—more than ever before.

It shattered her to know the man she had loved, the man she married, had become this—violent, godless man, drowning himself in drink.

His hand fumbled at her nightgown.

Her eyes flew open. "Stop, Michael," she whispered.

"You don't love me, do you?" His voice was rough and broken, but his hands didn't stop tugging.

"Michael, please. You're too drunk." She pushed his hands away, pulling the fabric back down.

He let out a bitter laugh. "You don't want me. You just used me."

The words stung. *Used him?* "What?"

"It doesn't matter." He sat up, dragging his hands through his hair and muttering.

"Please," she pleaded, tears spilling over. "Come home. We need you… I need you. I don't understand why you're saying these things." She sobbed. "I love you. I'm your wife."

He didn't look at her. He reached for his boots and clothes, yanked them on, and bolted for the door, slamming into the frame on his way out.

Trinity lay there in silence, staring at the ceiling. She forced her breathing to slow. Forced her tears to stop. But her heart felt like it was crumbling into dust.

She dragged herself out of the bed, not bothering herself with slippers or a robe. Her golden hair tumbled in tangled waves down her back.

Holding a single candle, she made her way down the cold dark hallway, down the stairs, and into the great hall. The shadows played tricks on her, and she flinched every time a shadow moved. No one was there. The manor was silent.

In the kitchen, she stacked wood in the fireplace and struck the flint until flames flickered to life. The warmth barely touched her. She moved methodically, numb, and as sank into Henry's chair at the head of the table, she breathed out a breath that held all her worries and fears.

A fat rat scurried across the floor. She should have gotten rid of it but didn't care. Her head bowed, arms wrapped around her stomach, and then the sobs came hard. All the thoughts, feelings, and memories—Michael's betrayal, Henry's death, the loss of the twins—ripped through her.

She gasped for breath between the waves of grief. Her gaze dropped to the floor beneath the table. Henry's pipe sat alone, forgotten.

Slowly, she reached down, fingers brushing over the worn wood and picked it up, turning it over in her hands. Fresh pain spread through her chest. She pressed it to her heart, rocking slightly, tears streaming down her face.

The staff door swung open, tearing a cry of surprise from Trinity.

Mrs. Bartlett stepped inside, pulling her shawl tighter around her frame. Her face was pale, dark circles pooling beneath her tired eyes.

She gasped. "M'lady! You frightened me." A rough cough rattled in her chest.

Trinity cringed. Mrs. Bartlett's eyes were red and swollen. "You're sick."

"I'm sorry, m'lady but it's in my lungs," Mrs. Bartlett said softly, with so much remorse it broke Trinity.

"I'll send for Lenora."

Joseph and Mrs. Bartlett—on the same day. Then Michael. It was too much.

Maybe the servants were right. They were cursed. She wiped her face and rose to leave.

Mrs. Bartlett stared at her. "Are you unwell, m'lady?"

"I'm fine." Trinity's voice was hoarse. "I'll have Sybil tell David to fetch Lenora. You should go back to bed. I've lit the fire—Sybil can manage today."

She turned and left, clutching Henry's pipe to her chest.

The entryway was cold, the darkness stretching ahead. The sun had yet to rise and already Trinity was forced to deal with another loss.

The front doors opened. A flickering glow filled the space, and Sybil stepped inside, candle lamp in hand.

CHAPTER 27 ~ SYBIL

Sybil entered through the front doors, clutching the candle lantern. Something had woken her—a gnawing unease in her gut. Shadows flickered across the walls as the flame trembled.

A figure moved into the light.

She gasped, stepping back. "Trinity?"

Trinity stood in the dim corridor, barefoot, bedraggled, her white nightgown ghostly in the candle's glow.

Sybil's heart pounded. "You frightened me."

Trinity lifted a hand, shielding her eyes. "Sybil?"

Sybil stepped forward, wrapping an arm around her. "You're freezing. Where's your robe? A cloak?"

Trinity ignored the question. "What are you doing up?"

"I couldn't sleep." Sybil searched her face. "Are you unwell?"

Trinity rubbed her eyes. "Mrs. Bartlett is ill. Can David fetch Lenora at once?" Her voice was flat, distant. "I'm fine. Just tired."

Sybil whispered. "When did you see her?"

"I was in the kitchen when she came in coughing. I told her to go back to bed." She exhaled, almost emotionless. "You'll manage things today, won't you?"

"Of course," Sybil said gently. "Come, let's get you back to your chambers and light a fire. I'll bring you warm milk with honey."

Trinity leaned into her for support as they climbed the stairs. "Michael was here," she whispered. Fresh tears welled in her eyes.

"I know. We heard him in the stable. David checked things out but was already gone."

Trinity's grip tightened on Sybil's arm. "Why is this happening to me?" Her voice cracked, barely audible.

Sybil wished she had an answer. "Come on, let's get you into bed," Sybil said, easing Trinity up the staircase.

She wished she could tell Trinity the truth—that demons were at play, poisoning Michael's mind, whispering darkness into his soul. But the poor girl struggled enough to accept that Sybil was a mage or witch as Trinity believed. Druid-kin. Evil pagan. Discovering Sybil's ability to perceive demons and receive visions would undoubtedly overwhelm Trinity completely.

But she had to try. "Trinity…" Sybil started, then stopped. "The angel Seriella showed you that demons exist. They are among us, and they pray on the vulnerable—the ones with a weakened soul due to grief, loss, and illness."

"Demons…" Trinity sighed. "Yes…"

"I'm certain they are influencing Michael. And others, too."

"How can you be sure? What if I imagined the angel? What if I am mad, like my mother?"

"You're not mad. They are real, and they're here."

They entered Trinity's bedchambers. Sybil helped Trinity to bed, pulling the covers over her. Then she tended the fire, stoking it higher.

"Are they inside my bedchambers?" Trinity's brows pinched together, her eyes darting across her room, lingering at the shadowed corners.

"No. Not here. We've warded the manor so they can't get inside."

"How do you know this, Sybil?"

Her ability to perceive demons, to sense them without incantations, had never failed her, and she'd kept it a closely guarded secret. But lately, it seemed it was faltering.

Sybil huffed out a frustrated breath, stoking the fire in the hearth back to life.

Three months. Three months searching for the demon hive, tracking shadows, sensing evil—but always one step behind. Always failing.

"Trinity, I can sense demons and see them."

Trinity sat up, her eyebrows scrunched, staring at Sybil. "You see them? Like how you said, I see them?"

"I do but not as you do."

"But you're a druid-kin. A pagan."

Sybil huffed out a laugh. "That again?"

Trinity blenched. "Sorry."

Sybil replaced the fire poker in the holder and sat next to Trinity. "It's alright. I get how hard this is for you."

"It's only... You've been such a dear friend. I'd be lost without you, but the Bible says..."

"I understand." Sybil gave Trinity a small smile. "I will do everything I can to help you get through this. I promise, and I don't hold any judgment. Very few grasp what we are."

"Thank you." Trinity gave her a weak smile and then lay down. "I'm so tired."

"Go to sleep. I'll take care of things today."

***

After, Sybil rushed to the stables.

She sank onto David's bed, covering her face with his pillow. He wasn't there. Exhaustion weighed on her, but there was no time for rest. Mrs. Bartlett needed tending. Joseph, too. Breakfast had to be prepared. But she only wanted to close her eyes and make the world disappear.

She looked up at David, who stood in the doorway, arms crossed, hay dusted across his sleeves. "What's happened?" he asked.

Her voice wavered. "Mrs. Bartlett should have been protected, but she's sick now. And Joseph—he wore the same charm as Trinity. I saw it on him every day." She released a loud sigh. "The tonics should have helped. The wards should have held."

"We've done everything we can, my love."

She stood abruptly, pacing the small space. "I feel them, David. Every time I step into York, the sickness, the filth, the demons' taint is everywhere." She pressed her hands to her face. "They're all over the city, but I can't find the hive!"

David crossed the room, resting his hands on her shoulders. Warmth spread through her, calming the storm inside her chest. She exhaled sharply, feeling him manipulating her energy, grounding her. He wasn't the strongest among them, but he always anchored her.

"This isn't your burden alone, Sybil." His voice was steady. "You're not expected to save everyone."

She clenched her jaw. "But I was supposed to protect them. Grandmother told me to be prepared. I felt something coming. I saw it, David. The visions weren't clear, but I sensed death was near. I failed Henry. I failed the twins. If I had warned them, insisted they wear their amulets every moment…"

David shook his head. "And they would've thought you mad. You said it yourself—your visions don't change fate. You would have been ignored, cast out, or worse."

Sybil pressed her forehead against his chest, fresh tears spilling over her cheeks.

"Perhaps only once… I could alter things."

David sighed, running a hand down her back.

"You see the truth as well as I do. The servants of darkness twist the minds of the weak. You didn't cause Michael to abandon his family. You weren't the one to bring the plague upon this house. But now, you must focus on protecting Trinity and Susana."

Sybil lifted her head, her face blotchy with tears and grief. "They don't believe," she whispered.

"They don't need to. You're their light. Let them trust in their God."

She swallowed hard, thinking of Trinity's nightmares. Of the sword and shield. Sybil had sworn not to tell anyone. Not even David. But Trinity was a traveler, perhaps a seer too. She needed help to control it and decipher what she saw.

David squeezed her hand. "Lenora said others arrived in York. More from London, too, ready to fight. They may have answers.

Sybil laced her fingers with his, pressing their hands against her chest. "Thank you, husband." She inhaled deeply, pushing back the exhaustion. "I have to check on Mrs. Bartlett and Joseph."

David nodded. "I'll fetch Lenora."

Sybil let out a slow, frustrated breath, then squared her shoulders. There was still so much left to do.

***

Sybil stepped out of the stables. The grounds were eerily still. The guards were gone, and the gates swung wide open after Michael's departure. Though it was summer, the birds had fallen silent.

"Death devours all things fair," Sybil quietly recited the verse from Aelfric of Eynsham, an Anglo Santon monk. David loved reading to her. No matter the religion and this passage stuck with her.

Evil abhors beauty. Love. The manor was a place of all those things and now stood as a tomb. Evil was winning.

She pushed open the manor doors, letting the morning light spill into the foyer. Dust hung in the air like a thin veil, and the rushes on the floor were flattened and stale.

Fleur hurried down the stairs, her blonde hair slipping from the messy bun atop her head.

"Sybil! Thank God you're here."

Sybil shut the door behind her. "What's wrong?" The question had become too familiar.

Fleur's hands trembled. "Mr. Dreyfuss—the gardener. I discovered him in the old woodshed. There wasn't any more wood in the shed next to the kitchen. I figured I'd check the other one. The older one. He's dead."

Sybil inhaled sharply. "How long has he been there?"

They hadn't used the old woodshed in years. They'd spoke about tearing it down after they built the new one closer to the manor, but they'd never gotten around to it.

"I don't know."

She let out a slow breath. "I'll tell David. But right now, I need to check on Joseph. He fell ill yesterday. Mrs. Bartlett, too."

Fleur's fingers curled near her mouth. "She's sick as well?"

"She was coughing last night."

"Could it be only a cough?"

"Perhaps," Sybil said, though doubt pressed against her ribs. She studied Fleur. "And you? How are you feeling?"

Fleur exhaled. "I'm well, but every morning I wake up afraid it'll be my last." A pause. Then, "I'm leaving, Sybil."

"What? Why? Where will you go?"

Fleur walked through the narrow hallway into the great hall, pausing in front of the hearth now aflame. Sybil followed. "I have documents and an escort from York to Bristol, then across to France. My parents finally sent word. I meant to tell Trinity, but she didn't answer when I knocked."

"She's exhausted. I sent her back to bed." Sybil hesitated. "Are you sure it's safe to travel?"

"My parents wouldn't have arranged it if they thought it was too dangerous. The man meeting me in York has guards as well."

Sybil stood beside her, warming her hands in front of the fire. "You've helped so much, Fleur. You'll always be welcome here, and I know Susana will miss you."

"I'll miss her too." Fleur's voice wavered. "Will you tell her I—" She faltered.

"I will."

Fleur nodded. "Thank you."

"When do you leave?"

"Today."

"So soon?"

"I need to see my parents. I know you understand."

"I do." Sybil sighed. "David will take you to York. With the guards gone, I won't send you alone."

"Thank you."

***

After checking on Joseph—who was still alive, though barely—Sybil stepped into the hall, dread curling in her stomach. Soon, only she and David would be left to care for Trinity and Susana.

She moved toward Mrs. Bartlett's chambers, bracing herself for another loss.

Mrs. Bartlett lay in bed, her breaths shallow. Sybil sat beside her, watching the rise and fall of her chest.

It didn't make sense. The illness had taken her too quickly. She had been given an amulet, protective herbs, everything meant to strengthen her body. This shouldn't have happened.

Sybil reached for her hand. The bracelet she gifted her was still there, but the amulet was missing. She turned it in her fingers, searching—gone.

Her heart clenched. "You lost it," she whispered.

A slight rasp came from the bed. "I searched everywhere," Mrs. Bartlett murmured. "I'm sorry."

329

Sybil swallowed hard. A tiny crystal. A small piece of jewelry. But to the sickness, it had been a shield.

Mrs. Bartlett's blanket was rough wool, her room reeking of stale hay. Along the corners, rat droppings dotted the floor. With no one left to clean, the vermin had begun their invasion.

"You're a good girl, Sybil," Mrs. Bartlett said weakly. "Like a granddaughter to me. I've always been proud of you."

Sybil squeezed her hand. "I've learned so much from you." Tears blurred her vision.

"Look after Lady Susana and Trinity." A faint wheeze. Then a final exhale.

Her grip became slack, and Sybil choked back a sob, but the tears came anyway.

David entered, his gaze falling on the lifeless form in the bed. He sank to his knees, wrapping his arms around Sybil and pulling her close.

"I'm sorry, my love," he whispered. "Lenora isn't coming. York is overwhelmed. Too many dead and sick."

Sybil wiped at her cheeks, nodding. "It wouldn't have mattered. It took her fast." Her breath hitched. "She lost her amulet days ago. I couldn't understand how she got sick. We've done everything to keep everyone safe."

David held her tighter.

"I'm trying," she said, her voice breaking. "But I'm failing."

Exhaustion settled over her, pressing her into him. "You need to prepare the carriage," she murmured.

David frowned. "For what?"

"Fleur is leaving today."

"What?" He pulled back, searching her face.

"She received word from her parents. She's departing as soon as possible."

David exhaled sharply. "I can't blame her."

"Neither can I."

He held her as she wept.

CHAPTER 28 ~ MICHAEL

The tavern was one of the last establishments still open. Most had shut their doors, fearing the unseen sickness that spread without warning. Killing hundreds within days.

Michael sat alone at a small round table, mumbling into his ale. The barkeep kept eyeing him, but he never refused to bring another drink.

"I know it's all lies," Michael slurred.

Across from him, Julian lifted his cup in a silent toast. To Michael, he was as real as the barkeep and the surrounding walls.

But to all others, he was a ghost. A delusion. That's what everyone said to him.

"They are lying."

Julian smirked. "True, my friend."

Michael gripped his cup tighter. "No benevolent God would forsake his flock. I see that now." He drained the ale and waved for another.

"You gave them everything," Julian murmured. "Your family. Their false God. You deserved more. Better."

Michael slammed his fist against the table. "I was an obedient son! I obeyed my father always!" His voice thundered through the near-empty room.

The barkeep stiffened, hesitating before stepping closer. "M'lord, we're closing."

"One more drink! For me and my friend!" Michael threw out his arm, knocking his cup, the remaining ale splattering onto the floor.

The barkeep hesitated, glancing at the seat across from Michael. His expression tensed.

"M'lord," he said carefully. "I need to close. My wife expects me home."

Michael shut his eyes, pressing his fingers to his temple. His cadence softened. "I had a wife once. For a short spell. She loved me."

Julian hissed, "It was a lie. She used you to secure her position. You said yourself—she rejected you after your father died."

Fog clouded Michael's thoughts. Trinity's face appeared wreathed in mist.

Her lips curled in scorn. "I could never love you," she hissed. "Look how pathetic you've become."

Michael shook his head. No. That wasn't real.

"Yes," Julian whispered. "She lied. Like all of them. Believing in this merciless God."

Michael's pulse pounded. "She never loved me."

He staggered to his feet, swaying. The barkeep, a broad-shouldered man, caught his elbow.

"I don't know about lies, m'lord," he said evenly. "But it's late. You should make your way home."

He guided Michael to the door.

"I have no home."

The cold night swallowed him as he stumbled outside. Rain drizzled, turning the road muddy.

He tipped his head back, staring at the sky. Spinning slowly, he let the cold rain hit his face, his arms limp at his sides.

Behind him, the tavern door shut. The last candlelight flickered out as darkness settled around him.

Michael continued to turn in circles, watching the sky swirl above him. His breath came in ragged bursts. "I curse you, God!" His voice cracked. "God of nothing!"

His foot caught on a stone, and he pitched forward, his skull cracking against the rocky street.

The world tilted. Then darkness swallowed him whole.

***

He awoke sprawled in the mud, freezing rain pouring down around him. He was drenched and reeking of piss and ale.

Hands grabbed his arms, hauling him upright. Shapes moved in the dim light—Shaun's familiar face and another man's, a stranger.

They slung Michael's arms over their shoulders, bearing his weight.

"What happened to you?" Shaun asked, his voice tight with frustration.

Michael blinked blearily. "Shaun?"

"Yeah, here to save your sorry hide again."

Michael's head lolled toward the other man. "Who're you?" he slurred.

"Nicholas," the man replied. "A friend."

Michael squinted. "Well, Nicholas-the-friend... Do you believe in God?"

A pause. Then, "No."

Michael barked out a laugh, his breath reeking of alcohol. "No! And yet your friends with this guy?" He gestured toward Shaun, who exhaled sharply.

"Yes," Nicholas said. "Any friend of Shaun's is a friend of mine."

Michael scoffed. "I don't need friends. They all lie. Betray you eventually. Right, Shaun Donaldson?"

Shaun sighed. "Nice to see you still remember my full name."

"Bah! I forget nothing. Least of all, you covet my wife. That's a mortal sin, isn't it?"

Shaun's jaw tensed. "Michael, enough. I do not covet her. We both loved her, but she chose you. And I respect that—because I love you too. You're my brother."

Michael's stomach twisted. Something in Shaun's voice rang with sincerity, making his chest ache.

Then Julian's voice slithered into his mind. *Remember how they looked at each other? Didn't she say he was beautiful?*

A memory surfaced like a misty fog. Trinity, standing by the river, gazing at Shaun with soft eyes. She blushed when he smiled.

Michael's head swam. "She only picked me because I could give her a better life."

"She isn't like that," Shaun said. "She loves only you."

Michael gritted his teeth. "Her beauty blinds you. Like a witch, she bends men to her will."

Shaun huffed an incredulous laugh, shifting Michael's weight on his shoulder.

Nicholas chuckled, "I'd like to meet this bewitcher."

"You can't have her! She's mine!" Michael hissed, spittle flying from his mouth.

"Easy, brother, I do not need another woman in my life," Nicholas chuckled again.

"Well, he wants her."

"No, I don't," Shaun countered.

Michael's balance wavered, the world tilting like a ship at sea. He wanted to shove Shaun away, wipe that patronizing smirk off his face—but his legs wouldn't hold him.

"I hate you," he muttered.

"No, you don't," Shaun replied.

Nicholas let out a low grunt. "Sounds like he does."

Shaun shook his head. "He's drunk and wallowing."

Michael blinked rapidly. "Am I... wallowing?" His voice slurred.

Shaun's patience thinned. "You have the right to grieve, Michael. To be angry. But you're not the only one who's lost someone. You don't get to abandon your family."

"You haven't lost anyone. You've never loved anyone in your piss poor life!"

"That's not true."

Michael barked out a laugh. "True!"

They reached Shaun's house. Nicholas disengaged himself from Michael's arm.

"You'll manage from here?" he asked.

"Yes," Shaun said. "Thanks."

Michael sneered. "Thank you, Nicholas-the-friend, for helping save the depraved lunatic."

"Good luck, mate," Nicholas's voice sounded further away, but Michael couldn't turn his head.

Shaun shook his head and shut the door behind them. "Come on. Upstairs."

Michael knocked into a chair, sending it clattering. Halfway up, he stumbled into a painting, sending it crashing to the floor.

"Jesus!" Shaun muttered.

A door flew open. Isabella stood in the hall, pulling on her robe. "What on earth is going on?"

Shaun grimaced. "Sorry, Mother. Go back to sleep. I'll handle him."

"Michael?"

Michael mumbled, "I'm sorry, mum," as Shaun dragged him to the bedroom.

Isabella sighed, pressing her hand to her mouth. "Sort yourselves out." She turned and disappeared down the hall.

Shaun tossed Michael onto the bed, fully clothed and caked in mud.

"You're awful, you know that?" Shaun muttered. "And you reek."

He lit a candle, its glow filling the room. Then, with a deep sigh, he set to work peeling off Michael's soaked clothes. Michael groaned but didn't fight him. He was too far gone.

Once finished, Shaun dumped the muddy garments outside the door. His mother would take care of them—she always did.

Michael squinted at the floor. "Where're you sleeping?"

Shaun bunched up a pile of clothes on the floor. "Right here. Go to sleep."

***

337

Morning light streamed through the window. Michael groaned, shielding his eyes. "It's too bright." His head pounded viciously. "I need a drink."

Shaun stretched stiffly from his makeshift bed on the floor. "At least you got a bed to sleep on."

Michael sat up sluggishly. "How did I get here?" He had the strangest sensation, like a trickle of water dripping down his spine. He felt clearer than he'd been in months.

"Nicholas and I carried your sorry ass after you passed out in the street."

Michael rubbed his temples. "Nicholas... Right." That sounded familiar. "How do you know him?"

"He's Lenora's relative. Visiting from Ireland."

Michael grunted. "Tell him thanks."

"Tell him yourself."

Shaun crossed the room, pulling back the curtains. A clear blue sky stretched beyond the rooftops.

"You need to return home," he said, voice firm. "Make things right with Trinity."

Michael's throat tightened. The words came out before he could stop them.

"I can't."

Shaun turned, face darkening. "What do you mean?"

Michael swallowed hard. "I can never go back."

A heavy silence settled between them. Shaun's brows furrowed. "Why?"

Michael shook his head. "I don't want to talk about it." His jaw clenched. "She's better off without me. Better with her God. The one she loves more than me."

Shaun's patience snapped. "You're a fool." His voice rose. "She loves you. She's hurting. And you're the one breaking her heart."

Michael sneered. "It's not true." But as he said the words, he wondered if he was wrong. What if Julian was wrong?

Strangely, his new friend had left him in the mud last night. And Shaun had found him and brought him home with him. Cared for him, as always.

Shaun's fists curled. "How can you believe that?"

Because she lied, but Michael knew Shaun wouldn't believe him. He had always worshipped Trinity and believed her incapable of any fault.

"I'm leaving," Michael said. An idea formed in his mind a few nights before. It gnawed on him, refusing to leave. It was the perfect solution.

Shaun's body went rigid. "To court? They are expecting us."

"No. I'm not going back to court."

The air between them thickened.

Shaun's anger flared. "Why would you do this? You've been knighted! You must return! You get that, right?"

"I do." He recoiled from the guilt flaring to life inside of him, replacing it with indignation. "I don't care."

Shaun's nostrils flared. "Well, thanks for that." He let out a harsh laugh, shaking his head. "It was your idea to drag me with you in the first place. I didn't want to go! And now you're abandoning that as well?"

Michael closed his eyes. His eyelids felt too heavy.

"Don't you look away from me, you spoiled brat!" Shaun bellowed.

The door flew open. Isabella stood with her hands on her hips, eyes flashing.

"I've had enough of the yelling in my home." Her voice cut through the tension. "For years, I've watched you two fight over one thing or another, and you always work it out. So, work it out! Now!"

She spun on her heel, slamming the door behind her. From down the hall, her voice rang back.

"I'm making breakfast."

Michael and Shaun stood in silence, anger cooling into exhaustion.

Shaun exhaled sharply. "Alright, idiot. What's your plan?"

"I'm joining a regiment and going to France."

Shaun barked out an incredulous laugh. "That's your plan?"

"Yes."

"Then please, I beg you to go and speak with Trinity first."

"No." Michael rubbed his pounding head. "I'm leaving today."

"Then I'm coming too."

Michael stood up to leave. There was no way he would allow Shaun to accompany him. "You're not coming."

"The hell I'm not."

CHAPTER 29 ~ TRINITY

Trinity woke up drenched in sweat. Sybil had stoked the fire so much it blazed, making the air sweltering.

The sun streamed in from the window; the blinds pulled open. It appeared to be late morning.

Trinity took a deep breath and sat up, running a hand through her tangled hair. "Oh, no…" she groaned. It was a mess—matted, full of knots. Brushing it out would be a nightmare.

Her body felt sluggish and weighed down, but she forced herself out of bed.

Mine and Michael's bed, she thought, swallowing against the ache in her chest.

She moved to the window, her gaze drifting outside. David rode into the yard alone.

He had gone to fetch Lenora but returned alone.

Panic gripped her. Mrs. Bartlett…

"Oh no. No. No."

She jumped up, fumbling with the ties on her corset before giving up and throwing on an old tunic dress. She wrestled with her hair but couldn't untangle it, so

341

she twisted it into a loose plait down her back. Not that it mattered.

She stopped. Michael's chest lay open and completely empty. The weapons on the wall and thrown over his desk, gone.

Her breath caught, a sharp, tearing pain slicing through her chest. She pressed a hand against it as if that could keep the pain at bay.

"Michael," she whispered his name. "What have you done?"

She turned away and caught her reflection in the mirror on her vanity. It halted her, stealing her breath. Gaunt, exhausted, aged beyond her years. She looked like someone who had survived something she wasn't meant to.

There wasn't time for vane worries. She had to take care of the people still here.

"Blast you, Michael!"

She stepped into the hallway, willing her tears to abate.

Not now. Keep moving.

Trinity focused on getting to the kitchen and Mrs. Bartlett. She pushed the thoughts of Michael aside and strode forward.

When she entered the kitchen, Sybil and David sat at the table. Sybil sipped a cup of warm milk, her face unreadable.

David stood the moment she walked in, reaching for another cup.

"Trinity! You're awake!" Sybil said.

"What time is it? How long have I slept? My head feels like it's filled with cotton." Trinity said.

"Late morning," Sybil said quietly. "I sedated you; you needed to sleep." There was no remorse in her admission, only resolution, and Trinity was speechless.

Finally, she pulled herself together. "I'm not sure I should fire you or be thankful, but don't do that again." Trinity rubbed her forehead.

"Mm," was Sybil's only reply, and then Trinity noticed Sybil's puffy, swollen red eyes.

"How is she?" Trinity asked, but the answer was clear.

"She's gone."

Trinity sat in Henry's chair with a thud. David brought the milk over to her. "Drink. It will settle your nerves and warm your stomach."

He sat back down next to Sybil. "I'll prepare a burial plot for her and bring the priest."

"We need to bury old Dreyfuss, too," Sybil mumbled.

"Dreyfuss? Trinity couldn't tolerate the smell of milk and pushed it away from her. "And Joseph?"

"Still alive, but not for long."

They sat in silence while battling their grief and tried to settle their thoughts. Too much had to be done, and they knew the responsibility lay with them alone.

"Put Mrs. Bartlett in the far plot next to the family and Dreyfuss, too."

"Should I prepare one for Joseph?" David asked.

"No. Not yet... It doesn't seem right."

David gave her a silent nod.

"I'm going to miss her," Sybil said, trying to hold in a sob that was released, anyway.

"Me too," Trinity whispered.

"Fleur left," Sybil said with no emotional weight to her words.

"I don't blame her."

"Her parents finally sent for her."

"That's good for her. I pray she will find safety with them." Trinity pulled the milk back to her and sipped it. "Have you checked on Susana?"

"Yes, she was doing needlework at the window in her bedchambers. The same, unresponsive. Won't speak." Sybil explained, shaking her head. "I'm uncertain about what more can be done for her."

"Pray," Trinity said, then flinched.

"Mm," again was Sybil's answer. "Trinity, you must realize that our food supplies are running low," Sybil said quietly.

More unwelcome news.

"The men in the fields are sick or dying," David explained. "The village is practically deserted. Already so many people have died, and the ones still alive fear leaving their homes, even for food," David finished with a deep sigh, weary. They all were.

Susana and Michael needed to come back to them.

"What are we going to do?" Trinity asked out loud.

Sybil took her hand. "I'll manage the kitchen and cleaning, and David can run the stables, the grounds, and what workers are left. Trinity, you'll have to manage the manor affairs and supplies from town.

No one said anything as they sat quietly, taking in the gravity of the situation.

"We will pull together until Susana snaps out of it and Michael comes home. We will keep things running as best as we can. Soldier on," Sybil said in her finest impression of Mrs. Bartlett.

They exchanged glances; then Trinity offered a nervous laugh.

***

Trinity left Henry's parlor with the heavy ledger when she heard Shaun's voice from the foyer.

"Hello!"

"Shaun?" She closed the parlor door behind her, gripping the book. "What are you doing here?"

"I must speak with you and Susana."

His gaze swept over her, assessing her. She tensed, feeling the weight of his scrutiny—her rumpled white dress, stained and creased, her uncombed hair falling in a loose braid. She knew she looked wretched.

Before she could respond, he stepped closer and took the ledger from her arms. "Are you well, Trinity? You look a mess."

"Thanks," she said dryly. "It's been a rough few months, Shaun. Mrs. Bartlett passed, and soon Joseph will be gone." She exhaled, the weight of it all pressing down on her. "Susana won't leave her room. We have no help, and my husband has abandoned us." She met his eyes. "Where's Michael?"

"I'm afraid I must tell you; he isn't coming home." Shaun stopped talking and held her gaze.

She saw pity there. Anguish. "I don't understand." Trinity was barely able to speak.

"He's left for France. He was drunk and said he would rather fight an enemy he could see. He left this morning." Shaun paused and brushed a single tear that escaped down her cheek. "I'm sorry. I tried to stop him, but he's gone mad."

"How come you never came to us, Shaun? How could you let us worry about him and not tell his wife where he was?" Trinity was angry.

"He made me swear not to."

"Oh well, that makes me feel so much better." She said, rolling her eyes and shaking her head like she was

345

trying to rid herself of a bad image. "You're such a good friend," she hissed. Eyes narrowed.

"Trinity, he told me you didn't want him here, that you rejected him and told him you didn't love him, that he was pathetic." He paused, raking his hand through his hair, frustrated. "I'm sorry, but I thought maybe it was what you wanted, and I didn't want him to hurt you."

"What?" Trinity's mouth dropped open as her eyes widened in surprise. "I'd never." She stopped talking and tilted her head, her eyes narrowing. "And you believed it?" She almost screamed the last words in his face.

"I'm sorry, Trinity."

She sat in Henry's chair on the dais, holding her stomach with one hand and her other over her mouth.

Shaun stood before her; shoulders slumped.

"I'm pregnant. I was waiting for him to come home to tell him. I hoped it would bring him back to me, but now, I see I've lost him for good." Trinity stared past Shaun. "I've lost him." Tears slid down her face.

"I figured I could keep an eye on him if I go with him, convince him to return." He paused, laid the ledger on the empty chair beside her, and took her hand. "I'm going to meet him in a few days. Do you want me to tell him?" Shaun asked.

Trinity pulled her hand away and put it over her chest. She didn't speak at first, eyes closed, trying to catch her breath, the pain radiating through her chest to her head.

She finally choked out in a whisper, "What does Michael expect us to do now? How can I cope with running this place with no one to help me? Susana is completely incapacitated, and only Sybil and David remain."

She kept talking, like in a trance. Panicking. She wasn't focused on Shaun standing in front of her.

"Am I the only one left to bring the family back to the light?" She closed her eyes and rubbed her fingers down her face.

"I'm sorry, Trinity."

"No," Trinity hissed softly, barely auditable to Shaun.

"What?" He asked.

"If he wants to abandon his family, let him go!" Trinity screamed; her tears falling unabashed.

She stood up and stepped towards Shaun, and he stepped back a few paces, probably thinking she would strike him. She raised her hand, wanting to.

Instead, she screamed, pointing to the door. "Go! Go with him!"

Shaun stepped toward her slowly. "I'll bring him home," he said, taking Trinity's hands. "I'm sorry. I'll do everything I can," he promised, then released her hands and left.

Trinity watched him walk out, then sat back in Henry's chair.

"Trinity?" Sybil approached her with a cup of hot herbal tea, which Sybil insisted they both take. It smelled like mint. "Here. It will soothe your stomach and help relax you and the baby."

Trinity thanked God she still had Sybil by her side. At least she wasn't completely alone.

She took the drink and breathed in the sweet, minty aroma. "Thank you, Sybil."

"You should rest. I'll prepare the day's meals for you and Lady Susana."

Trinity was tired and appreciated the gesture. At least someone wanted to help her. "Shaun just left."

Sybil gave a small, knowing smile. Of course, she heard them. "We'll get through this."

"I don't know; it's just... Lady Susana's in a bad way. I'm exhausted, and my heart hurts... It just hurts." Tears filled Trinity's eyes. "He's not coming home... he's gone to France to fight," she sobbed.

"Shush now. I understand how much you love him, and it's not fair what he's done to you or his mother." Sybil lifted the ledger and sat in Susana's chair next to Trinity. "But he loves you. He does. He'll come back."

Trinity sobbed as more tears fell. "He's abandoned us. He doesn't love me anymore," she said, taking a long breath with a whoosh at the end. Would she ever live without tears? "I want him to come home. What will I do if he doesn't come home?"

"You will raise your child. You will make this place a home for you both, and Susana will come around."

"What would I do without you?" Trinity sniffed and wiped at her eyes.

"Drink your tea."

Trinity took a sip. "I need to lie down for a bit."

"No problem, and I'll check on Susana. Go rest. I'll see you at supper."

"I'll visit her on my way to my room." Trinity walked out of the room carrying the hot drink.

***

Trinity arrived at Susana's bedchambers and found the door partially open. She walked in and dropped the cup of tea, the cup shattering on the floor.

Susana had hung herself from the bed frame, and her body was still in its death throes. Her arms and legs jerking about. Bulging red eyes stared up to the ceiling. Trinity jumped onto the bed and lifted Susana's body, screaming for help.

"Help! Susana! Why?" Trinity sobbed, struggling to hold Susana's weight and not fall off the bed. "Help!" She screamed again.

A few moments later, David and Sybil ran into the room.

"What on earth?" Sybil screamed as David quickly untied the noose from the awning post of the bed and Susana's neck, throwing it to the floor as if it was a snake.

Trinity fell to the bed, holding Susana in her arms. David checked Susana's heart and breathing. Trinity sat in shock, watching in horror as they worked over her mother-in-law.

"She's breathing," Sybil said, stepping back.

"Why would she do this?" Trinity asked, confused. "She knows she'd be damned to purgatory never to see her loved ones again. Why would she do this?"

Susana's lips were moving, but no sound came out at first. Trinity clutched her hand in her own.

"I'm here," Trinity said softly. "I'm here.

Susana's voice croaked as she whispered between ragged breaths, "He told me I needed to atone. It's my fault we're forsaken. The only way to atone."

"Who told you that?" Trinity asked.

David and Sybil stood staring at them, shocked.

"God."

Trinity dropped Susana's hand and put her fingers to her mouth. "He'd never…."

A voice echoed in her mind. There's a war coming. Demons. Find the others.

"My aunt warned me before she died," Trinity whispered. Susana would never have taken her own life. "Seriella…"

"Who's Seriella?" David asked, his eyes flashing between Sybil and Trinity.

"Trinity?" Sybil said softly, holding her stare.

Susana had quieted, her breathing slow but steady.

David lifted her gently, placing her beneath the covers. He checked her pulse, ran his fingers along her neck, and then exhaled, giving Trinity a nod. Susana would live.

Trinity gazed up at him. "I know you don't have faith in God as I do, but my aunt was the most pious woman I've ever known. She loved God with all her heart. Before she died, she warned me—a war was coming. That demons would…" Her voice wavered. "I told Sybil the story."

"You thought she was delusional," Sybil finished, "until…"

Trinity swallowed hard. "Yes. Until the seraph, Seriella, came to me."

David eyes grew wide. "An angel visited you?"

Both girls replied together, "Yes."

He turned to Sybil. "You knew?"

"Trinity swore me to secrecy, David. I wouldn't betray her trust."

"But the prophecy… Your vision!"

"David!" Sybil yelled as Trinity looked between them, confusion etched in the lines on her forehead.

"Visions? What prophecy?" Trinity asked.

Sybil sighed, sitting beside Trinity; she took her hand in hers. "I've been gifted to."

"By an angel?" Trinity asked.

That made Sybil laugh. "No, by the goddess Cailleach."

"Who?" Trinity had no idea what Sybil was speaking of—more pagan nonsense. But considering everything else, Trinity bit the condescending remark back. "Alright." She lifted her hands. "Tell me everything."

***

David sat beside Trinity as Sybil sat on the other side, finishing her story. It was a lot. But not any more far-fetched than anything that had happened to her already.

Perhaps this goddess was an angel the others have mistaken for a goddess? But Trinity decided to keep that idea to herself.

"Alright, so you can sense demons, see them, and you have visions." Trinity squeezed her lips together, furrowing her brow. "I'm trying, Sybil."

"Well, you have been gifted a prophesied sword and shield from an angel," Sybil said, raising her eyebrows.

"Yes, I have."

They sat quietly, letting the information sink in and allowing Trinity to digest it.

"So, you had a vision of me fighting a demon prince named Baal?"

Sybil held Trinity's gaze, unflinching. "Yes, I'm sure it was you now."

"And I had wings?" Trinity couldn't help the smile lifting the corners of her mouth or the cackle that had escaped.

David breathed out. Sybil closed her eyes but exhaled a breath, her shoulders dropping.

"We'll figure this out," David said.

351

"I suppose we better show David the sword and shield, but first…" Trinity looked back at Susana, still unconscious but alive. "Will she be alright?" She reached toward the red, swollen marks on Susana's throat, but stopped short.

"She's alright," David assured her. "She'll be sore, and the bruises will be awful, but she'll live."

Trinity stared ahead; her voice barely audible. "I must be dreaming. This can't be real."

David took a deep breath. "You're not alone. Sybil and I are here. We won't let anything happen to you or Lady Susana. Sybil will stay by your side, and I won't be far."

"If demons are what we must fight, then we shall fight them," Sybil said firmly.

"Thank you." Trinity squeezed Sybil's hand. "I don't know what I'd do without you both."

David hesitated. "Would you like to rest in your chambers?"

"I'll stay. I won't leave her alone."

Trinity moved to the other side of the bed, pulling the blankets back before curling up beside Susana. Sybil tucked the covers around them.

Trinity's eyes fluttered shut. Within moments, she was asleep.

A few hours later, Sybil returned to the bedroom.

Trinity was awake, but Susana remained sound asleep, her chest rising and falling in a peaceful rhythm.

Sybil moved closer, clasping a golden bracelet around Susana's wrist—a pendant with a small crystal set in the center.

Trinity sat up and laid a hand over Susana's chest, reassured by the steady rise and fall.

"It's nearly time for supper," Sybil said. "Would you like to come downstairs, or should I bring something up?"

Trinity glanced at Susana, then met Sybil's eyes. "Can you help me with my hair?"

"Of course," Sybil said with a smile.

CHAPTER 30 ~ SYBIL

A few weeks later, Lenora sent Sybil a message: Enzo heard whispers of demons in a secluded section of the city. They thought they might have found the hive but needed Sybil's help to verify it.

Riding through York always made Sybil sick now. This day was rife with demons. They had to stop often so she could empty her stomach.

She rode Moon Pie beside David, with Jacob, Enzo, and Luca trailing behind.

Midway through her pregnancy, she was already larger than most women at that stage. Hours on horseback left her aching. Her back and bottom throbbed.

Lenora had given her an incantation and a tonic to ease the sickness, but she refused them. It dulled her senses, and she needed to be sharp. The search for the hive dragged on, and the demons were winning.

Too many people were dead or missing. Baal was cunning, striking with small groups or alone, never in the open. She and Enzo had to find the hive and destroy the demon army before it grew any further.

Legionnaires attacked them during several missions, but David always made them flee from the demons. He wouldn't risk her or their unborn child in a life-or-death fight.

She argued that she should be allowed to continue scouting. No one else could do it. They were close—there was no doubt.

The summer sun bore down as they rode through abandoned streets. Not a soul in sight. The silence made her skin crawl. A dog barked in the distance, but no birds flew. Death lingered over York—churches burring the bodies of plague victims in large pits just as Trinity said, London had. Hell had arrived.

They entered a poor section near the city's southeast side. White crosses marked most doors. No one walked the streets. Buildings stood dilapidated and abandoned.

"I really don't want you scouting anymore. Today is the last time Sybil," David said as he rode next to her, glancing at her, then at her protruding belly. "It's not safe."

"It's never been, David."

"Where is Nicholas?" he asked rather than commenting. "He should be here, dammit!"

Enzo moved closer and answered. "Lenora ordered him to stay with the others. They need more training."

"Hey! I came," Jacob grumbled, holding his axe over his right shoulder and the reins with his other hand. His black hair was tied back in a ponytail, accentuating his square jaw and dark eyebrows. "I won't let anything happen to our girl," he said, giving David a pointed look.

David muttered under his breath.

Sybil nudged him with her horse. "In the last few weeks, we have lost too many mages from attacks or the plague. Some of them died even though they had amulets protecting them. We need to find the hive."

"Enzo can do it without you," David said as he reached for her hand.

She squeezed him. "No, he can't. It's strong blood magic hiding the nest."

"I don't like it. I have a bad feeling."

Sybil laughed, "You are not the one with visions, my love, and I haven't foreseen my death or yours."

"I still don't like it." He wanted to bring her home. She could see it written all over his face: pinched lips and brows, eyes flicking towards the west gates.

"I'm safe with you and perfectly healthy," she said as she gave him a fake smile and then stopped her horse. "We're close. The magic is stronger here." She turned in her saddle to Enzo, who rode behind them next to his brother Luca. "Can you hear anything?"

"No, nothing yet, but this is where I heard them before."

"They're here. I feel it," she mused, looking around at all the buildings they passed.

"I don't hear anything, Syb," Enzo said.

Her stomach cramped worse than ever. A sulfuric stench burned her nose. "You smell that?" She clenched her jaw, fighting the urge to vomit. She exhaled sharply.

They halted in the narrow street, buildings pressing in on both sides. Sybil twisted in her saddle and vomited. "David!" She straightened, pointing at a building. The front door swinging open and closed, half off its hinges. "They're there!"

David barely had time to react before two women stepped from the shadows.

Long black hair flowed past their waists. They were twins, wearing identical midnight dark tunics and linen pants, cloaks swaying behind them. Daggers were strapped across their chests, wrists, and hips. One reached for the broad sword on her back, drawing it with deadly ease. The steel rang in the air.

"Sybil, Run!" David bellowed, but she couldn't move. Her gaze was anchored to the one without the sword. Her black eyes, like orbs of obsidian, held her stare. *You are mine.*

Sybil had the sudden urge to dismount; her legs moved against her own will. "What are you doing to me?" She hissed as Moon Pie trotted in a circle, spooked by her sudden jerking movements.

"Sybil?" David grabbed the reins of her horse and steadied it, one eye on her and the other on the woman walking closer to them.

"I can't... She's controlling me," Sybil said, trying to catch her breath. "She's forcing me to dismount."

"Don't you dare," David growled, pointing his sword at the dark-haired woman. "Let her go!"

Enzo and Luca put themselves in front of Sybil.

"Jacob, get Sybil out of here! Now!" David ordered.

The big, burly man grabbed her and swung her onto his horse, locking an arm about her waist. As he turned to flee, the dark-haired woman flicked her hand. The horse reared violently, throwing them both to the ground. Sybil curled around her belly, landing hard on Jacob, who hoisted her up instantly.

Steel clashed behind them—Enzo already locked in battle with the other legionnaire. But Sybil's eyes stayed on David. Fury radiated from him as he moved his horse between her and the other twin, trying to control her. Her legs still pulled towards the woman, against her will.

"No, no, no." Sybil tried to stop moving.

Jacob wrapped his arms around her waist and hauled her backwards, further from them, and finally she regained control of her body the further away they got. He didn't stop dragging her down the street until they were completely out of sight of the twins.

"We can't leave them!" She cried. "They mustn't fight them alone!"

There was a high-pitched scream from one of the dark-haired women, and then hoofbeats sounded, and a few seconds later, David pulled her up into his saddle, and Enzo was helping Jacob onto his, with Luca and the two other horses racing past. They rode hard and fast back to Lenora's.

Sybil's heart didn't stop pounding the entire way, and she prayed to her mother Goddess Cailleach that her baby was unharmed. "David, the baby," she whispered.

"It'll be all right," he said, kissing her hair, then swung off the horse and lifted her into his arms, one arm under her knee and the other around her back. She leaned into his chest and closed her eyes.

"Lenora!" David called out as he followed Enzo and Luca inside the apothecary.

They hurried to the sitting room, where David placed her on a cushioned settee. The twins stood by the door, tense, as if guarding it or waiting for the dark-haired legionnaires to appear.

Jacob barged in. "I tethered the horses. Is everyone alright?"

"Keep an eye on her," David said, then walked out the door to find Lenora.

"David! No!" Sybil cried, but he was already out the front door.

Enzo came to her side and tried to comfort her. "He'll be fine. They won't attack here. There's too many of us in this neighborhood."

She noticed he had a deep gouge down the side of his face from his ear across his cheekbone. "Enzo, sit. Let me heal your cut."

"What cut?"

"On your face."

He reached up and touched the sticky blood dripping from the wound. "I didn't realize." He sat down next to Sybil.

"Luca, get me the healing poultice from the kitchen. Quick, and some water in a bowl and a clean cloth."

"Of course." Luca swiftly left, returning shortly with everything.

Sybil cleaned the cut, but it was deep and would need to be stitched. The blood kept flowing, no matter how much pressure she held onto it.

"How are you, Enzo?" she asked after several minutes, holding the cloth in place.

He went quiet, and his face had turned pale grey. "Not too well, I must admit."

"Enzo, you're losing a lot of blood. It won't stop bleeding. I think it hit an artery. I need Lenora here. I'm not sure...."

Luca came closer. "Is it bad?" he asked, watching his twin brother with concern.

"It shouldn't be...." Sybil looked at the ground at Enzo's feet. A pool of dark blood lay there, dripping from his side. "Enzo!" Sybil almost screamed, clutching at the wound, making him flinch. "You're hurt here too!"

"What? No, I didn't. I didn't feel anything...." He stopped speaking, slowly closed his eyes, and fell onto her.

"Enzo!" Sybil grabbed his upper body and laid him against the cushions. "Jacob, find David and Lenora now!"

Jacob ran out of the room, the front door slamming behind him.

Luca stood at the entry, staring at his brother, not blinking.

"Luca, come here," Sybil said, but he didn't move. "Luca!"

He walked over and then stumbled to his knees. She handed him a cloth, lifted Enzo's tunic and pushed it into the open wound. "Keep steady pressure on it."

Sybil leaned over Enzo's face and pressed her palm to his cheek. "Come on now. You aren't going anywhere," she whispered as she lifted the bloody tunic over his head and tugged his pants around his waist to get a better look.

"Luca, quickly move your hand away. I need to examine it."

Luca lifted his hand and sat back on his haunches.

It was deep, and the blood dark. She'd seen it before. A killing blow. Black blood was certain death unless Lenora got here fast.

"Luca put pressure on it."

Sybil stepped away, Luca taking her place, pressing down on the wound in silence, his eyes fixed on his brother's face.

"Is he going to…"

"No. He will live."

But Sybil wasn't as confident as she tried to convey. Internal injuries could only be healed by Lenora's magic. And if she didn't come soon. All was lost.

Minutes later, voices echoed in the hallway. Lenora rushed in, kneeling beside Enzo. Sybil and Luca moved aside.

She examined the deep cut, clicking her tongue. "Sybil, I need your help."

David and Jacob spoke in hushed whispers at the door as Sybil turned to her grandmother. "I've never used healing magic," she murmured.

"Just do as I say. You're my kin. You have it in you." She positioned her hands over the wound. "Put your palms on mine."

Sybil did as she was told, letting her grandmother's magic pour from her fingertips into Enzo.

"You'll need to concentrate. It's the same as when you call forth air, but this is energy straight from Mother Earth. Healing energy. It's unlike the chaotic flow of air. It's warm and soothing, but harder to find." Lenora took a deep breath. "Imagine white healing light flowing into you. Same as I taught you to do with air."

Sybil closed her eyes, searching for the right force, but only recognized air—her natural element.

"Focus, child."

She pushed deeper, ignoring the tug of her air magic. It was almost impossible, but then warmth bloomed inside her. "I think I have it."

"You better know, not think!" Lenora snapped.

The warmth slipped briefly before Sybil caught hold of it again, steadier this time. She let it grow, merging it with Lenora's, channeling it through their palms into Enzo's wound. Lenora whispered an incantation in a language Sybil didn't recognize. She made a mental note to ask about it later.

She wasn't sure how long they worked, but eventually, Lenora pulled away. "That's enough."

Sybil opened her eyes. The wound on Enzo's side was gone, and his face was fully healed. Only a faint scar remained. Color returned to his cheeks, breathing deep and steady, though his eyes stayed closed.

"He'll sleep for a while." Lenora straightened but gripped the armrest, wincing. "Ugh, my back."

Sybil stood, helping her grandmother into a cushioned chair. Sitting beside her, she pressed both hands to her rounded belly, aching from bending over so long.

"I'll check you now." Lenora exhaled, then motioned for her to stand. "Come here."

Sybil obeyed. Lenora placed her palms over Sybil's belly, eyes closed, shifting with a furrowed brow. Minutes stretched before she finally pulled back. "They are perfectly healthy. The healing energy would have mended them if they had been harmed."

"They?"

Lenora patted Sybil's belly gently. "Three. Two boys and a girl."

Sybil released a breath she hadn't realized she was holding. "Oh my Gods, are you certain?" She sank into her seat.

"Yes." Lenora sighed. "Now, tell me what happened. The men were squawking like old hens."

But her grandmother's words clanged around in her mind. Triplets? She was having triplets!

David had vanished with Jacob, Luca, and whoever else had been speaking in the hall. Sybil's mind reeled.

No wonder she was so much bigger than Trinity, though they were close in their pregnancy terms.

Sybil pinched her forehead. "We found the hive, but they were waiting for us. Two of the strongest legionnaires I've ever sensed stepped from the shadows—twin women."

She recounted everything, from the attack to the eerie control the woman had over her. But she hadn't seen Enzo's injury.

"They will move the hive now," said Lenora.

"I know what it feels like now and what it smells like. I can find them again, easier." Sybil placed her hand on Lenora's arm. "I can do this."

David and Luca walked in. David had a wooden tray with a strong-smelling tea brewing in a small pewter pot and two cups. "I made you something to help ease your nerves.

"It smells awful," Sybil complained.

"It's good for you, drink, child," Lenora said, taking the cup from David, and then he poured one for Sybil.

"Thank you."

Lucas sat beside his brother, who was still asleep but breathing normally.

David put the tray on a small table and sat across from them in another cushioned armchair, usually Isabella's seat.

"They know who we are," he said. "They were targeting Sybil."

"It doesn't matter." Lenora took another sip of her tea.

"I don't understand how she was able to control me. I'm wearing my amulet," said Sybil, pulling the necklace out and inspected the crystal teardrop. She could feel the power in it. "It's still charged."

"A powerful enough legionnaire can break through any amulet. These two are strong, and one seems to have mastered mind control.

"Yes, she spoke to me, in my mind," Sybil said and turned to David. "She said I was hers."

"I'll kill her if she comes near you again," he hissed.

"Most likely get your idiot self-killed instead, you foolish boy. You can't kill that one on your own." Lenora cackled a hoarse laugh.

"I won't let anyone hurt Sybil."

"I know," she said, resigned.

"Now, what do we do?" Luca asked.

Lenora's brows scrunched together. "We continue to train and make more weapons."

CHAPTER 31 ~ TRINITY

Trinity jolted awake, her body convulsing.

She had meant to only nap but slipped into a deep sleep. The nightmares and convulsions were constant now. On top of it all, morning sickness—or day sickness, as she called it—left her miserable from dawn to dusk.

The nightmare lingered, vividly in her mind. Her limbs quaking like a tempest storm lived inside her bones.

The dark-haired twins from Arthur Whiting's house haunted her dreams again. One had wielded a sword against Enzo, stabbing him in the side. She woke up right after. There was more, but the details faded as she surfaced from sleep.

Sweat beaded on her forehead. Her breath came in ragged gasps, not able to exhale fully before sucking in more air. She staggered from bed, barely making it to the privy before vomiting into the washbasin. She heaved until nothing remained but bile.

"I hate my life," she said to herself wiping her mouth with a small towel as the violent convulsions eased, but her hands continued to shake. "Why must women be cursed with sickness, lord?" She asked. Her face tilted upwards.

She stumbled back to bed, dragging herself under the thin cotton blanket. The summer heat was unbearable, but she couldn't summon the energy to go downstairs or check on Susana. Then she remembered...

Sybil and David are in town for supplies and to see Lenora.

"Dammit."

She swung her legs over the edge and forced herself up. The nightmare and convulsions had drained her.

She slipped a white cotton robe over her thin nightgown, not bothering to change, then shuffled to Susana's bedroom before making supper.

She hesitated at Susana's bedchambers. She was talking to someone inside. Since the attempted suicide, she often spoke to herself—her mind fractured, haunted.

Trinity pushed the door open. Susana sat at a small wooden table by the open window. But what stopped Trinity short was the fluffy, white-tawny owl perched on the sill.

Susana was deep in conversation with it.

The owl didn't startle when it noticed Trinity. Instead, it cocked its head, watching as she settled beside Susana.

Susana didn't turn to see who was beside her. "It's my new friend," she said.

"What's its name?" Trinity asked softly, noticing how calm Susana was.

"I call her Little One."

"Noctua, in Latin", Trinity said, remembering a story about the Goddess Athena and her owl, Athena Noctua. "A fine name."

"She is a rather good listener," Susana said, scratching the owl on its head. The owl made a hooting noise, flapped its wings, and bounced over the table to Trinity.

"You want me to pat you too?" Trinity said and laughed, amazed at how tame it was. She patted it and the tiny owl let out another hoot. "Hello, Little One, I am Trinity."

"She knows who you are," Susana said so casually that it took Trinity a few moments to understand what she said.

"Is that so?" Trinity scratched the owl again.

Given her current state, she avoided arguing with Susana. Any little thing could set her off. She turned her attention to Susana and was surprised that she had washed and dressed herself that day. It usually took Trinity and Sybil a considerable effort to dress her.

Trinity stood up. "I just wanted to say hello and ask if you would like anything to drink or snack on while I make supper?"

"That would be lovely, dear," Susan said wistfully, her mind drifting off somewhere else.

Trinity paused at the door, watching Susana murmur to the owl, gently scratching its head.

***

After bringing Susana a kettle of tea, she skimmed the ledger for the hundredth time, then moved to the kitchen to prepare a meagre supper—mutton stew. She glanced at the door, wondering when Sybil and David would return. Worry for Enzo gnawed at her. The dream wouldn't leave her.

What if I am this thing Sybil calls me... Traveler?

"He's fine," she whispered, trying to reassure herself.

She set a wicker basket of vegetables and herbs on the table and lit the fire. Moving like a ghost, she went through the motions—light the fire, take out the bread, retrieve the meat from cold storage. One step at a time. No thinking beyond the next task.

The mutton supply was low. How many meals before they survive on vegetables alone?

They were barely holding on. The kitchen hadn't been cleaned adequately in months. Rats scurried through the corners and maggots made their home in anything left uncovered, including rotted meat. The summer heat wasn't helping their plight.

The firewood dwindled. Soon, like at her aunt and uncle's, none would be left. Then what? Burn the furniture? David had promised to chop wood himself, but he was always gone. She didn't understand where he disappeared to, so often.

There was no time or space for self-pity. Just a deep, endless sadness. No bottom to it. No wonder Susana had lost her mind. Some days, Trinity wished she could too. Maybe insanity held some peace.

She cut the bread. On the second slice, the knife slipped, nicking her fingertip.

"Dammit!" She sucked the wound, dropped the knife, and grabbed a rag to wrap around it. "Dammit! Ugh!" The frustration burst out of her. She sank into Henry's old chair and broke down.

God, she missed them all. She hadn't known Sir Henry long, but it felt like she always had.

"Why?" She hunched over, sobbing, tears spilling freely. "God, I don't know if you're listening anymore. I'm sorry if I've failed you. Please forgive me. Give me the strength to survive this." Her voice dropped to a whisper; her face buried in her hands. "I promise to try harder. Even though our priest is gone, I'll go to the chapel and pray. I will keep going."

A hoot startled her. She sat upright, scanning the room.

Am I finally losing my mind?

Another hoot. Then, scratching at the back door.

She stood slowly, opened the door, and the tiny white owl flew in, wings flapping, before settling on a beam high on the kitchen ceiling.

Trinity tilted her head, staring up at it. "You little scoundrel. You scared me half to death." She slumped in the chair, releasing her breath.

The rag had fallen from her finger. Inspecting the wound, a sliver of flesh was missing. The bleeding had ceased, but now it throbbed. She exhaled a long sigh. "What next?"

Noise from the manor's entrance caused her to lift her head. David and Sybil's voices carried through the manor as they entered the kitchen. They both stopped short when they noticed her sitting alone.

She hadn't even realized it had gotten dark. Only fire in the hearth illuminated the room.

She held up her finger. "I cut myself."

Sybil ran to her and started fussing over her. "David, can you please get my bag from my room? The one with the ointments. I made some bandages, too."

"I'll be right back," he said and disappeared.

"We have a new pet, too," Trinity said, pointing to the beam where the owl was perched. "Susana says her name is Little One."

Sybil sighed, gazing upward at the owl, which hooted as if to say hello.

"I think it's tamed," Trinity continued. Her voice was monotone, lifeless. She lacked the energy to speak.

"It is."

Trinity watched Sybil tend the wound. "How do you know?"

"I just do," Sybil sighed again, throwing the owl a dirty look.

That was strange.

David brought a leather bag, and Sybil fished inside until she found the jar of ointment she wanted. "This will ease the pain and help it heal nicely but try not to get it wet for a couple of days." She applied it; at first, it stung, and Trinity sucked in a breath between her teeth. Sybil was efficient and quickly bandaged it up.

"I'll finish supper. Would you like a cup of warm milk with honey?" Sybil asked, lifting her eyes to David.

David walked to the back door. "I'll return soon. I need to check the stables and bring more firewood in."

Sybil smiled, then regarded Trinity. "Milk and honey?"

"That would be lovely, Sybil. Thank you. You are truly a godsend."

Sybil brought a milk container from the basement, poured some in a small kettle and put it on fire, then got stuck into making supper.

"How is Susana?" Sybil asked.

"Better than she's been for a long time. She bathed and dressed herself today. I walked in, and she sat there chatting to this owl as if it understood every word she said. The thing let her pat it, me too." Trinity tried to look up at it again, craning her neck.

"How are you today?" Sybil asked.

Trinity knew Sybil expected an honest answer, but Trinity didn't want to talk about her nightmares. She'd bring up all the mystic traveler nonsense and she just wanted to forget it.

"Trinity?" Sybil said after no reply.

Trinity sighed. "I had another nightmare, although I'd just laid down to take a short nap."

"Convulsions again?"

"Yes."

"Bad?"

"As usual."

"And…" Sybil prompted, trying to pull more info from her.

"And it was bad. I saw two dark-haired twin women I had dreamed about long ago when I was still in London. One of them stabbed Enzo, and I woke up."

Sybil dropped the cup of warm milk on the floor, and it splashed everywhere.

"Sybil! Did you burn yourself?" Trinity jumped to her feet.

The owl hooted again and flapped its wings.

"Trinity! That actually happened today!"

Trinity sat back down. "No, it was just a nightmare."

Sybil walked to her and sat down next to her. "Look at me, Trinity."

Trinity refused. She closed her eyes, shaking her head. "No, it was a nightmare."

"Trinity. You are a mystic traveler. A traveler sees things happening at the time it's happening. Unlike a seer who has glimpses of the future." Sybil sat next to

Trinity. "Sometimes they can even converse with others."

Trinity opened her eyes, and Sybil was staring at her. "There are stories of people long ago that could communicate with each other over large distances."

"Stories Sybil."

"You have the sword and shield of an angel."

"A Seraph, Sybil."

The owl hooted a couple of times and flew down, landing on the armrest of Trinity's chair.

"Well, hello, Little One." The owl hooted, cocking its head to the side. Trinity reached over and scratched it on the head.

Sybil sat straight back and stared at the owl as if it would attack her. Trinity laughed. "It won't hurt you."

"Trinity, that owl…."

"It's truly tame, I promise."

Sybil cradled her fingers in front of her. "Cauilleach-Oidhche," Sybil whispered, closing her eyes and lowering her head. The owl flapped its wings and hooted at Sybil.

"Caul, what?" Trinity asked.

"It's her name." Sybil huffed. "Trinity, in the old religions of these lands, there are stories of… You see, owls are the guides between life and death. They come to deliver one from death to the after. But some accounts say that the owl protects one from evil. Some are messengers."

Trinity laughed so loud that Little One flapped his wings and gave a sharp hoot. She scratched the top of its head again. "Please, Sybil. Sorry, little one."

"The owl is the companion of our mother goddess, Cailleach."

"I don't know who that is, Sybil."

Sybil scratched the owl's head. "The owl is called Cauilleach-Oidhche, which means White Lady of the Night." Sybil sighed and smiled at Trinity, whose eyes were narrowing, and her mouth set in a tight line. "The old Gods, Trinity."

"I am only aware of one God, Sybil, and I've said nothing or admonished you over your lack of faith because you've protected me and my secrets, but please do not speak to me about this. It's blasphemy."

"But you believe demons are..."

"Yes, I do, but even in the bible, it speaks of demons. Fighting demons is a holy mission, but I will not be tempted to question my faith, and I don't know how to fight anything but the never-ending responsibilities we carry now."

Trinity let out a deep sigh. "Please understand."

"I do, and I'm sorry if I made you uncomfortable. Tis only stories."

Trinity took Sybil's hand in hers and squeezed it. "You are my family now, and I will not turn my back on you because you don't share my faith. I know you and David are good people."

Sybil was about to speak when David entered carrying firewood. The owl soared back to the beam.

"Was that an owl?" He asked, surprised as he walked to the firewood box, unloaded the wood, and wiped his arms off.

"Yes, its name is Athena Noctua or, as Trinity has named it, Little One," Sybil said, still staring at Trinity.

"I didn't name it. Susana did."

"Susana?" David was looking at each of the women like they'd gone mad.

"Long story," Sybil said and waved him off.

373

"There's spilled milk all over the floor," he pointed out.

"Oh yes, the milk. I'll clean it right away. David, be a love and make Trinity and me new warm milk with honey while I clean this up and finish supper."

David just huffed a laugh and lit the candelabra on the table.

"Of course."

CHAPTER 32 ~ SYBIL

Sybil doused the kitchen's fire while David snuffed out the candelabra candles on the table.

He flipped open his hand, palm up, and a soft orange flame danced above it, lighting the room in its gentle embrace.

Sybil loved his fire. It wasn't as potent and bright as Luca's or as chaotic and restless as her air. She had no ability with fire as most elemental mages preferred a single element, and as they aged, it strengthened.

"Did you recognize the owl?" Sybil asked.

"Who?" David said, walking from the kitchen to the main hall, and Sybil followed.

"The owl, the one they named Little One...." Her voice echoed through the empty room.

"You think it's Cailleach's owl sent to protect Susana and Trinity?"

"Or it Cailleach is summoning me again," Sybil said cringing.

She'd expected Little One to guide her to the grove. And recognizing its pull all day. "I can feel... I don't know." She huffed. "I've sensed a pull to the grove all day but usually her owl will bother me until I stop what I'm doing and go. It's just sitting in the kitchen, sleeping. Strange really."

"Hmm."

"That's all you can say?" Sybil asked as David opened the front doors of the manor and let Sybil pass. "I should have gone."

"It didn't fly away, and it would have insisted you follow it had she summoned you."

"Yes."

It was pitch black, and the moon was hidden behind dark clouds pregnant with moisture. The air smelled wet, and the scent of sulphur was gone for once. She sighed in relief.

"What?" David asked as they walked down the steps into the yard towards the stables.

"I can't smell anything, only the rain."

"That's good."

"Yes." Sybil wrapped both arms around her protruding belly.

They were halfway across the yard when Little One hooted, flew down, and landed on David's shoulder.

Sybil jumped back, startled and looked at David, then froze.

A black mist rose from the ground.

David turned slowly then pushed Sybil behind him. She pulled magic into her, but it quickly dissipated into the earth before she could touch it.

"What the…?" Sybil asked, looking at her hands, confused.

The dark mist grew until it hovered above them, and a shape began to grow within it—nothing solid or recognizable but human-shaped.

"You do not need to fear me," a familiar voice echoed from the mist. Female that reminded Sybil of crumbling old parchment crackling. A slight ringing accompanied it, like tiny bells chiming in the distance. "You are both so brave."

"Who are you?" David asked, but Sybil already knew.

"The Goddess Cailleach," Sybil answered, closing her eyes.

"You are clever too," the Goddess said as her form became more corporeal. Her long white hair hung past her waist and floated in the mist as if underwater, and her eyes were the exact silver-blue with the black ring around them as Sybil's.

"Your eyes...," David whispered.

He'd never seen their mother goddess.

"Are you here to take one of us to the underworld?" David asked, his voice trembling.

"Soon, my child, but not tonight."

Her reply was a dagger through Sybil's heart, and a vision of David's lifeless eyes flashed in her mind.

"When? Who?" Sybil asked, stepping in front of David and pushing him back.

"It is unimportant." Cailleach glowered at Sybil, making her teeth snap together.

Sybil huffed out an irritated breath "Why have you come then?" she asked as David grasped her hand. "Am I to endure another vision?"

"No. But I don't have much time."

Sybil exhaled. "I have found the girl in the vision, but she refuses to do anything with the sword or her magic." Sybil glanced to David then back at Cailleach. "She's a traveler and wields the sword of a seraph named Seriella."

377

"Yes. I have seen. You must ready her or else the vision will not come to be, and all will be lost."

"But she doesn't want to hear anything I say."

"Then you must show her."

Sybil huffed out another annoyed breath, shaking her head and worrying her bottom lip.

Little One ruffled his feathers and settled again, not moving from David's shoulder.

Cailleach continued, "We fight a great war, but what you see here is only one small battle. Nonetheless, it is an important one. Sacrifices will be made and loved ones lost, but hear me now... You are running out of time, and the darkness is on the cusp of consuming everything." The Goddess reached out and petted Little One on the head. "My friend, you've done well."

Sybil caught a scent of frankincense and pine as Cailleach pulled her hand away.

The Goddess smiled fondly at the tiny owl, then folded her hands. "She helped guide me here to you and will stay to protect the ones you love." She looked at David, and the smile faded. "But I come for you, David."

"Why me?" he asked, stepping beside Sybil. A shiver ran down her spine, and tears welled in her eyes.

The news wouldn't be welcome. It never was.

"You must protect your wife at all costs, even if it is with your life. Do not fail in this, or you'll deal with me in the after. Am I clear, child?"

"What do you mean? With his life? No!" Sybil said, pushing in front of David. "No, I cannot live without him! He won't sacrifice himself for me."

"He will not sacrifice it for you..." The Goddess reached down, her hand hovering over Sybil's stomach and looked into Sybil's eyes. Her gaze sent a ripple of cold fear through Sybil's body, and she couldn't help but tremble. "Would you not sacrifice your life for your children?"

Her head tilted, mirroring her owl.

"Of course," Sybil breathed out.

"I'll always protect my family," David said, interrupting. "I do not need to be threatened to do so."

"Indeed, you don't... So strong... So loyal to your last breath... Yes, you will do." The Goddess turned to Sybil. "Fate has guided you, and you must listen to me closely now; I will not return until it is time... You and your children must survive what's coming, no matter what you or he...." She nodded at David. "Must do. You understand the ways. The time has come... Remember. You and your children...."

Sybil blinked, and Cailleach was gone, swallowed by the mist.

Little One flew into the sky with a shriek, leaving them blanketed in darkness.

David threw his arms around Sybil and pulled her into his embrace.

"You can't die," Sybil said, her voice muffled against his chest.

David stroked the back of her head. "Shh. I'm right here, and I'm not leaving you."

"Please, David. I will not lose you."

***

Grey clouds lingered in the morning air, drifting from York to Ellsworth Manor, carrying the stench of death. The rain began to fall, soft and steady, yet the day remained unexpectedly warm.

Sybil paused outside the stables. Grounding herself to the earth. It would be another grueling day, and she was already beyond tired.

A carriage rattled through the gate and came to a hard stop before the manor.

Sybil pressed her hand to her rounded belly. Waiting to see who it was.

The door swung open, and Elizabeth stepped out, her belly heavy with child. Her blue dress hanging in wrinkled tatters, its hem torn and dirty. She looked as though she hadn't changed in days. Her braided hair, once neatly coiled, was loosened into a haphazard mess. Dark circles rimmed her red, swollen eyes.

"For God's sake, girl, don't just stand there! Fetch my things at once—and tell Mother I'm home." She swept past Sybil without waiting for a response.

"Yes, m'lady." Sybil turned to leave but halted as David approached, his stride quick.

"Go with her, love," he murmured, then moved toward the driver.

Sybil fell into step behind Elizabeth as she strode into the main hall. Trinity sat slumped in Henry's chair, resting. With effort, Trinity rose and stepped forward.

"Elizabeth?" she said, a sob catching in her throat.

Elizabeth ran to Trinity and hugged her. Tears fell down her face. She sobbed uncontrollably. "My husband is dead. I'm a widow. They're all dead!"

Trinity held Elizabeth tight, stroking her back, looking at Sybil over Elizabeth's shoulder. "I'm so sorry," she whispered.

Elizabeth sniffed, pulled away and tried to compose herself. "My child will never see his father." She paused, peering wide-eyed at Trinity's newly round belly. "Oh, my lord! Trinity, you're pregnant too! Where is Michael?"

"He's gone. Fighting the French with Shaun," Trinity said.

"What?" Elizabeth exclaimed; her eyes widened even more. "How could he leave now? Is he completely mad?"

"He's unaware." Trinity's lips pinched as she lifted her chin higher.

Sybil's heart broke for them. Raising children without their husbands would be a hard life, far from the fairy tale they had dreamed of.

"M'lady, would you like to dine in the hall tonight?" Sybil interrupted them.

"Yes, thank you, Sybil. That would be lovely." Trinity smiled at her.

"Very well." Sybil turned to Elizabeth. "David is putting your belongings in your old room and making sure the bedding is made and the fire lit, m'lady," Sybil said to Elizabeth.

"Why is David tending to my room?" Elizabeth asked, but before Sybil could answer, Elizabeth looked down at Sybil's belly. "You're pregnant too?"

"To answer both questions, no one else is here to help us. All the servants are gone, and yes, I am pregnant, probably due around the same as you, I'd guess."

"Huh." Elizabeth turned back to Trinity. "Where's Mother?" Elizabeth asked, still wiping her cheeks and shaking her head.

"She's in her room," Trinity answered. "She refuses to come out."

"What?" Elizabeth narrowed her eyes in disbelief. "That's ridiculous. Why would she do that?"

Trinity's gaze fell on Sybil, pleading.

Sybil stepped forward to explain. "After you and Michael left, Lady Susana didn't fare well. The servants, kitchen help, and field hands all abandoned us. They feared her. She screamed and carried on like she was possessed." Sybil hated saying it. Susana had been strong once. Seeing her reduced to this—mind shattered crippled woman—was heartbreaking.

"Does she know Michael is gone?" Elizabeth asked.

Trinity wiped her eyes. "No. But we found Mother in her bedchamber, Elizabeth… She tried to hang herself. Thank God, I found her in time."

"Oh God." Elizabeth sank onto the edge of her father's seat.

Trinity sat beside her. "She said our Lord told her to do it—to atone for her failures. She blames herself for everything. She keeps saying it, even now. She's gone quite mad."

Sybil stepped closer, wanting to ease their pain—the image of Susana with the rope around her throat burned in her mind. "I'm so sorry, Elizabeth. For your loss, for what's happened to Lady Susana. It's a lot to bear."

Elizabeth shook her head. "No. No. That makes no sense. She was the perfect wife and a good mother. No one was as pious. How? How could she think such a thing?"

"I believe demons tried to possess her," Trinity said, glancing at Sybil.

"Don't be ridiculous! Demons, Trinity?" Elizabeth huffed.

"Something was inside her, whispering these things. Even poor Olivia thought Mother was possessed. I didn't believe it at first either, but… maybe it's true."

"Is anyone watching her now?"

"No, but we take turns checking on her. She doesn't seem aware of anyone. She stumbles around, mumbling. We've been giving her poppy milk to keep her calm and removed anything she could harm herself with."

"I can't believe this is happening." Elizabeth's broken gaze shattered Sybil's heart.

"I understand. I feel the same."

"Trinity, who's been managing the estate?" Elizabeth asked.

"I have, with the help of Sybil and David." Trinity nodded and smiled at Sybil. "They've helped me tremendously."

"Your assistance is very appreciated, Sybil," Elizabeth said, giving Sybil a small, tight-lipped smile.

"Thank you, m'lady. Your family has always been kind to me." Sybil nodded.

Elizabeth rubbed her stomach in small circles. "What happened to Joseph, to Mrs. Bartlett?" She asked.

Trinity sat back in the chair and let out a deep breath... "The plague got them. I'm sorry. I know how fond you were of them and how long they've been here for all of you."

"They were family." Tears rolled down Elizabeth's cheek. "Everyone is gone?"

"We have each other, and Mother will come around in time," Trinity said.

Sybil knew the winter would be brutal, but she also knew spring would return. A fresh start. She would not lose hope.

"We are not forsaken, sister," Elizabeth said, taking Trinity's hand. "Let's pray now."

Just as Sybil was about to leave and give them privacy, Elizabeth cleared her voice.

"Won't you pray with us?"

Sybil stopped and turned around, glancing at Trinity, who watched her with one eyebrow raised.

"Of course, I thought you'd want privacy."

Elizabeth lifted her chin. "Don't be ridiculous, come."

Sybil walked to them, and the three women held hands, closed their eyes and prayed for their salvation, protection and strength.

CHAPTER 33 ~ MICHAEL
France, December 1349

Michael spread his fingers before the fire. The flames flickered, licking at the cold air. He rubbed his hands together, trying to shake the numbness from his bones.

The wind howled through the frozen trees, rattling the brittle branches like dead men's bones—the camp stank of unwashed bodies, damp wool, and the acrid tang of old wine and vomit.

He pulled his cloak tighter, but it did little against the bitter wind. His body ached from exhaustion, his muscles stiff from the cold.

For the hundredth time, he tried to remember how he got here. His mind was fractured, with pieces missing.

Perhaps I'm going mad. He stared into the flames as he tried again to remember.

Scattered memories surfaced.

A black warhorse beneath him, galloping through a ripe wheat field. The sky stretched clear and blue, a late summer breeze in the air.

"Where are we?" he asked Julian.

"Almost to Bristol." Shaun's voice cut in, distant.

"I wasn't asking you," Michael snarled.

He wished that Shaun stayed in York. He didn't need him. Didn't want him. Shaun followed anyway, always trying to convince him to turn back. And, right on cue…

"We can go back. It's not too late."

"Shut up, Shaun." Michael spurred his horse ahead.

Another memory…

The same warhorse, mud-caked and weary. They reached an army base in Gascony just before autumn winds made sailing impossible. Shaun made sure they were stationed together. He wouldn't leave Michael alone.

"I write to mother," Shaun said. "Do you want to write anything to Trinity? Your mother?"

Michael sneered; eyes narrowed. "Go away!" But he wouldn't.

The memory shattered.

Now, the same warhorse stood tethered to a tree nearby and snorted in protest against winter's cruel bite. Its ribs jutting beneath its mud-slicked coat. Starving. Just like all of them.

The sky was no longer golden. It was a slate of endless grey, pressing down like a shroud.

Michael crouched, moving his hands closer to the fire. The snow melted, where the flames licked the ground.

Their unit camped on the outskirts of Poitiers, near a frozen brook and a dense forest. By midday, the snow had turned to icy mud. Supplies were meagre. Fire pits burned throughout the camp, soldiers huddling around them for warmth.

Three hundred men, starving, waiting for orders. Too weak to train, too cold to move. The only mercy: no plague. No deaths from the wretched illness since arriving in France. That, and the wine—cheap and tasteless but endless. Food was scarce, but wine flowed like the river La Boivre.

Michael stared into the fire, empty inside as if his soul had frozen within his body. Maybe he had no soul—only habits drilled into him from birth—expectations and lies. He trusted nothing and no one.

Shaun approached, pulling off his gloves. His armor was tarnished, his cotehardie torn and mud caked. He set his helmet beside Michael's in the dirt, rubbing his hands over the fire.

Michael sensed Shaun's stare. They barely spoke, and Michael avoided him. When forced to reply, his words dripped with venom—the banter, the friendship — gone.

Two other soldiers joined them.

"It's too cold. I'm sick of it," muttered a blonde soldier with a long, straight nose.

"I'm starving," grumbled the other—a boy. Too young to be wearing that uniform.

"Weak as a woman's piss," Julian sneered, and Michael laughed.

The blonde's head snapped up. "What's funny?"

Michael met his gaze, eyes gleaming with menace. "My friend said you're weak as a woman's piss."

Shaun raised his hands. "Hey, hey now. I didn't say anything. Just relax, Michael."

But he didn't. Relax. They could all go to hell.

"Do you have a problem?" the bigger man asked, standing up and stepping to Michael.

Julian laughed. "Beat him to a pulp, would you, Michael?"

Michael saw red.

He didn't remember stepping forward—only the sensation of his fist colliding with bone, the sickening crunch beneath his knuckles.

The soldier yelped, reeling back, but Michael was on him before he could react. Another blow. Then another.

Blood spattered the snow, a sharp contrast against the white. The soldier groaned, but Michael didn't stop. He couldn't.

Everything burned. He wanted to experience something. Anything.

A distant voice—Shaun? —shouted his name. Hands wrenched at his shoulders, dragging him backward.

Michael snarled like a feral dog, twisting violently, nearly breaking Shaun's grip.

"Enough!" Shaun's voice cut through the madness.

Michael blinked, chest heaving.

The soldier lay motionless in the icy mud.

He didn't even remember what started the fight.

***

They threw Michael in the brigade again—for nearly beating the soldier to death.

Sitting in his makeshift cell, he barely recalled the fight.

Packed mud and hay lined the walls. The roof sagged with damp beams. It stank of dung. He didn't care.

They fought several skirmishes with the French. Michael charged into battle, unhinged and fearless, with a death wish. He cut men down without hesitation, which earned him some respect, but his comrades mostly feared him.

He preferred it that way. Fear kept them away.

But now, the walls closed in on him. The darkness pressed against him, seeping into his skin like rot. How long had he been in here? Hours? Days?

Somewhere, a rat scratched at the dirt. He imagined its beady eyes watching him, waiting for him to die.

Something whispered his name.

Michael turned sharply, but there was nothing.

Somewhere in the dark, something was watching him.

Footsteps sounded outside, then Shaun's voice, "Michael?"

He ignored him.

Shaun sat outside the makeshift brigade on the other side of the wall.

"I just want to go home, Michael," he murmured through the thick material. "They've called a halt to the war. We're freezing to death for nothing." He sighed. "I just want to go home."

Their orders were clear: secure the area around Poitiers. Hold the position. But more perished from exposure than battle.

"I thought getting you out of York would help," Shaun said. "What's happened to you?"

Silence. There was nothing Michael wanted to say.

"My mother is well, and so is yours, but it's been a few weeks since I've received anything more... I'm worried about our families, Michael."

Shaun shuffled to his feet, and Michael breathed a sigh of relief. He couldn't take much more of his insidious lamenting.

"You could write one damn sentence." Shaun's voice was tired, quieter than usual. "Just let them know you're alive."

Michael ignored him. Alive? He wasn't sure he was anymore.

Shaun sighed. "She still prays for you, you know."

Michael's jaw clenched. He didn't ask who Shaun meant. His mother? Trinity? It didn't matter.

"I feel guilty leaving them to fend for themselves," Shaun said. "But I couldn't leave you. I can't leave you, Michael."

Silence. Then a sharp exhale of frustration. "I'm going to bed."

His footsteps faded into the night. Only the voices of a few soldiers, still awake, drifted to him.

***

His superior finally released him after he swore to stop fighting among the men. Michael scoffed but agreed. They were all useless, weak.

Now he stood over another fire pit, clenching his jaw. It took every ounce of will power not to punch the man next to Shaun. Or Shaun for that matter.

"It's bloody freezing," the soldier grumbled for the hundredth time.

Michael forced himself not to respond. The man was weak, pathetic—not worth his breath. And he held no desire to sleep in the brigade again.

Shaun laughed. "Yeah, my balls might freeze off, I reckon." A joke meant to draw Michael in. He knew Shaun's tricks, his manipulations.

No response. Michael wouldn't indulge him.

A week in confinement left him hollow. He loomed over the fire, more a ghost than a man. Broken—and he didn't care.

Moments passed. Michael blinked and straightened. A fleeting image of his mother in her garden crossed his mind.

"Do you think Mother is freezing?" He spoke so softly that he doubted Shaun had heard.

"What's that?" Shaun asked.

Julian appeared beside him. "It doesn't matter, friend."

"It does, doesn't it?" Michael whispered, eyes narrowing.

"Who are you talking to, Michael?" Shaun frowned.

Again, the game. Shaun ignored Julian as if he weren't there. Jealous, as always, of anything that pulled Michael's attention from him. It was pathetic. Michael wouldn't dignify it with a response.

Michael frowned because something about Julian was... off.

His copper hair gleamed unnaturally in the firelight, and his green eyes caught the glow too sharply. His movements were smooth—too smooth.

Michael blinked, trying to focus. Julian had been with him since York. Hadn't he?

He should have been comforted by his presence. Instead, unease prickled at his spine.

"False gods, lies, manipulation," Michael muttered. "That's all any of them know."

Julian smiled, slow and knowing.

"I'll help you," he murmured. "And I won't lie to you."

Michael grunted, pulling on his gloves, then bent to pick up his helmet. "I will not be their slave!" He yelled, then stomped away, throwing his helmet on his head. Men scattered out of his way, throwing him weary glances.

I need to crush something. Someone. Rage burned in his chest.

He once trusted them all. And for what? Deceit in Trinity's eyes. Manipulation in Shaun's. His mother was smug and satisfied when he obeyed. His father, the worst of them—treating him like an animal. A stud to breed.

He hated them all. He hated everyone.

"That's right, my friend." Julian's voice was soft, steady.

Michael exhaled. The words soothed him and gave him peace. In his drunken haze, he smiled—a crooked sneer, the left side of his mouth ticking up.

A sharp whistle cut through the air. Shouts echoed from the forest—the sounds of battle.

Without thinking, he ran toward the sound of swords and men screaming. He pulled his long sword free and growled as he entered the forest.

***

The skirmish was larger than usual, the French taking them by surprise. Better supplied, well-fed, they knew the terrain, and they fought fiercely for their land.

The woods were thick, and with his helmet on, it was easy for him to lose track of friend and foe.

The forest exploded with chaos, but Michael didn't run. He wanted this. Needed this as he sliced and chopped. Felling men in waves, one after another.

Their bodies tumbling to the ground in a haze of red blood.

Michael stopped and bellowed at the top of his lungs. Blood slicked his hands, his sword an extension of his rage.

A French soldier lunged but Michael sidestepped, blade flashing. The last thing he heard was a gurgling scream and blood spraying his cheek.

And then another. And another.

There was no exhaustion. Only fire. He laughed—a sharp, broken sound—as he carved through them like animals.

Somewhere, a horn sounded the retreat.

Michael ignored it. He had one purpose. One hunger. Kill them all.

Hundreds of soldiers clashed in the forest.

Movement was nearly impossible. Bodies littered the ground—some ran through, others missing limbs, throats slashed, blood pooling everywhere.

The tangy smell of fresh blood and piss spurred him on. The sound of screams and grunts a song.

More French soldiers rushed in when another horn sounded.

"Retreat!" His comrades screamed. "RUN!"

But he refused.

A French soldier came at him. He parried and sliced the man's arm. Another attack—he dodged and charged toward the enemy, not away.

The coppery stench of blood filled his lungs, fueling his adrenaline. He swung at every man in his path, cutting them down. Carnage was all he wanted—to punish the world for its failures and lies.

He was invincible. Alive! His blood surged. He roared, more beast than man. Time no longer existed.

The faces he cut down were nothing. Only this moment mattered—this freedom, this ecstasy.

A group of soldiers fled. He ran after them—then stopped.

Archers surrounded him.

He was alone.

The whizz of arrows filled his ears. A thumping sensation threw him back a step, then another, and another. He looked down. His chest bristled with them like a pincushion.

He roared again and raised his sword—then cold steel struck his back. A French soldier ran him through.

His body hit the earth.

This was the end.

He closed his eyes, waiting to die and roared.

Trinity's face appeared.

Her green eyes were filled with fear and sorrow. "Michael, please come back," she whispered. "I love you."

Then Julian was there, shaking him. "Open your eyes, Michael." He locked eyes with him. "Do you want to live?"

Michael couldn't answer. But he knew. He nodded. He must get back to Trinity.

Pain flooded his body, but then it suddenly stopped. He was floating. Weightless.

The battlefield melted into shadows—moving, writhing.

Julian crouched over him, his face a blur now, his eyes gleaming like polished jade. "Do you want to live?" His voice boomed inside his skull.

Michael's lips parted, but no sound came.

Julian's voice echoed smoothly inside his mind. "Say yes."

A pause. A heartbeat. Michael nodded. One whispered word, "Yes."

Then darkness swallowed him whole.

CHAPTER 34 ~ TRINITY

Trinity woke with Michael's roar ringing in her ears. Sweat soaked her shift, her body trembling uncontrollably. She gasped, embracing her belly, her fingers splayed protectively over the swell. Inside, the baby stirred, a gentle flutter beneath her palm.

The fire had gone out, leaving the room deathly cold. A few dying embers glowed red in the hearth, pulsing like a heartbeat fading into silence. Her legs, unsteady and stiff, dangled over the edge of the bed as she forced herself upright.

"Please…" The whisper barely left her lips.

Her shoulders curled inward, every muscle tense, as though bracing for another strike. Her chest burned, air catching in her throat. She pressed her fingers to her temples, willing the images away, but they clung to her mind like a shroud.

Michael—trapped in a forest, swinging his sword wildly at ghosts, roaring like a wounded beast. Then he fell. His blue eyes, so familiar, locked onto hers. For a moment, she saw him—the man she loved. But his gaze darkened, swallowed by blackness. He bared his teeth and roared again, fury consuming what was left of his soul.

Trinity pressed a hand over her mouth to smother the rising cry. The absence of him was like a physical wound for her, raw and unhealed. Had she imagined the man he once was? Had grief, loneliness, and love twisted her memories into something softer than the truth?

"He's alive," she whispered. "He has to be."

Outside, the wind howled, rattling the windows. Rain lashed against the glass in relentless waves. Sleep was impossible. She grabbed her robe and slippers, wrapping herself tightly before entering the darkened hall.

***

The manor lay in silence. Only the storm outside stirred. Her candle cast flickering shadows along the stone walls as she padded toward the kitchen.

Trinity passed Susana's door and hesitated, peeking inside. She lay curled beneath her blankets, unmoving. A faint moan escaped her lips as the candlelight brushed against her face. Trinity let the door close softly.

Susana had barely spoken in weeks. She ate only when forced. Sitting for hours at the window, staring at the road, waiting for her family. Waiting for ghosts.

Trinity's chest ached at the sight.

She hurried on, pushing open the kitchen door. The scent of lavender and dried hay lingered, but the room was just as cold as her bedchamber.

She set her candle on the table, searching for the flint to light the fire. It was never where she left it.

"Dammit, girl, where did you put it?"

"Trinity?"

She spun at the sound of Sybil's voice. Her friend stood in the doorway, hair loose over her shoulders, rubbing her eyelids sleepily.

"I was looking for the flint," Trinity admitted, sagging in relief. "I wanted warm milk with honey. Couldn't sleep."

Sybil crossed to another cupboard and produced the missing flint.

Trinity glared at her. "I never would've found it there."

Sybil smirked, kneeling to light the fire. The flames licked hungrily at the logs, casting warmth into the room.

Trinity sighed. "Why are you sleeping in your old room? Everything alright with you and David?"

"I was reading," Sybil shrugged. "Didn't want to wake him." She disappeared into the pantry and returned with a pitcher of milk.

Trinity took down two cups, setting them on the table. "I had a nightmare," she admitted, watching Sybil stir honey into the milk.

Sybil handed her a cup. "About Michael?"

Trinity nodded; fingers wrapped around the warm cup. "He was dying. He was fighting ghosts—then he fell. His eyes turned black. He roared at me like he hated me."

Sybil's expression darkened. "If he's fallen in battle... you'll receive news soon enough."

Trinity swallowed. "I don't believe I'm a traveler, Sybil."

"How do you explain those awful twin women and Enzo?"

"It was just a nightmare. A coincidence." Trinity wrapped her arms around herself, ignoring the question. "Michael must come home." Her voice cracked.

Sybil hesitated before reaching across the table, squeezing Trinity's hand.

"Michael wasn't always this way," she said softly. "You didn't imagine his kindness." She took a sip of her milk before continuing. "David told me a story once. About when Michael was thirteen."

Trinity glanced up, blinking through the haze of grief.

"There was a man who worked for his father. Poor, struggling. His children were starving. Michael had caught him stealing food from the storage. He could've told his father. Had every right to. But he didn't." Sybil gave Trinity a small smile. "Michael waited for him the next day," she laughed then continued. "He had two full baskets of food waiting for the man and walked him home. Made him promise to stop stealing, and in exchange, Michael swore to bring them food every week."

Trinity sighed heavily.

"He was a good man," Sybil murmured. "Whatever has happened to him isn't because he is inherently evil. Grief breaks people. And when a soul is broken, evil finds a way in."

"Of course." Trinity had tears running down her face. She had always known this. "But I still failed him."

"No, no. How could you say such a thing?" Sybil's head moving in a slow refusal. "You loved him so much. We could all see it."

"I rejected him many times in those first few weeks. I've experienced so much death, that anguish was a

399

familiar friend to me, so I couldn't understand why he was reacting the way he was." A sobbed wracked through her, and her lids shut, her throat tightening. "I turned my back on him, looked down at him with disappointment, in his most dire time of need."

Her chest felt like it would burst, and then so many memories of those first few weeks swirled in her mind.

Michael trying to hold her in bed at night and her turning her back, pretending to be asleep.

Of her admonishing him for speaking blasphemy and walking away instead of listening to him and holding him, reassuring him.

Her fear and disappointment showed on her face every time he looked at her. He needed her, and she turned away.

The realization hit her so hard that tears streamed down her face, sobs racking her body.

Sybil was beside her in an instant, arm around her, cooing gently. "Shush, shush now. It's not your fault. We can all take the blame for something, but every one of us is responsible for our actions. No one forced him to leave Trinity."

"He wouldn't have left if I had been there for him."

"You don't know that. Sometimes, no matter what we do, a person's path is already destined."

"Do you truly believe that?" Trinity asked, sniffling and wiping her tears.

"No use wallowing in regret either; you can't change the past; we can only learn from it. That is what my grandmother says." Sybil pushed Trinity's milk closer to her. "Drink more."

"Your grandmother is very wise." Trinity sniffed again, then took a sip of her milk.

***

A few weeks later, York's market hummed with quiet unease. Trinity insisted they go for more supplies. Plus, she needed a change of scenery, and it had been month's since she'd left Ellsworth. She was beginning to feel like a prisoner in her own home.

"Thank you for coming with me," Trinity said, pulling her black hooded cloak tighter around her as the winter rain fell relentlessly.

The plague seemed to have dissipated, but no one was becoming too hopeful. The city remained a tomb. Everyone moved in shadows, heads down, avoiding eye contact.

"I needed to get out of the manor for a spell too." Sybil clutched Trinity closer.

They walked arm in arm; Trinity's fingers curled protectively around her coin purse. She watched everyone closely. The environment created an opportunity for those who would feed on the weak. Many derelict men and women turned to thievery and even murder. People weren't safe from the plague or from each other any longer.

Several soldiers in rag-tag uniforms pushed people apart and kept telling everyone to move along. They gave some people a sense of security, but Trinity knew not to count on it.

She glanced up at the tower of the cathedral looming above the city. She hadn't been to see the archbishop in a while and intended to go that day. Volunteer maybe. The church's archbishop remained, but most of his flock had fled. His grand manor stood empty of staff, and she was told he spent most of his days praying over the sick and dying. The cathedral was full of orphans and widows who couldn't feed themselves.

"I think the church could use some help," she said to Sybil.

"So do we," Sybil grumbled in response, throwing a dark look at the church towers.

Sybil..." Trinity wanted to help. To feel useful. Not just survive. "The body collectors are bringing poor souls dying of the plague to the back of the church and just leaving them curled on the floor with little more than a blanket to stave off the cold."

"And why is this our problem now?" Sybil guided them towards the vegetables and herbs.

"Some die of the cold before the illness even takes them. Perhaps a blessing for some, I guess. But perhaps we could bring more blankets to town on out next visit?"

The sense of doom was genuine to everyone. The pain of their loss was a collective sadness that permeated the entire community. Soul-crushing pain and grief so poignant its presence was palpable like the wind and visible in the eyes of every person Trinity passed. No one was spared. She had to do something.

"You must be a damn saint, Trinity Ellsworth," Sybil said, chuckling and shaking her head. "I will personally deliver the blankets if you promise not to drag me there today."

"Fine. We have an accord."

Sybil laughed and pulled Trinity gently through the mob to the stall where the herbs were sold. She spoke fluent French, her voice clipped and urgent. The woman scowled, crossing her arms. The exchange was tense.

When Sybil finally took the bundle of herbs, she turned on her heel, muttering, "Stupid old hag."

"I didn't know you spoke French," Trinity remarked.

Sybil snorted. "My family were French."

Trinity's brows lifted. "Lenora?"

"Yes. But don't remind her—she'll deny it to her last breath."

The rain pounded harder, and Trinity huffed.

A shadow shifted in the crowd, just past the sea of cloaked figures. A flicker of movement—then blue eyes, burning through the misty rain.

Michael.

Trinity's lungs seized, her pulse surging. Was it truly him? She blinked. The crowd pressed forward, a crush of bodies between them. When she looked again—he was gone.

Her pulse thundered. No. He was here. She saw him. She turned desperately, scanning the mass of cloaks and faces.

Sybil seized her wrist. Her face was pale as death. "Trinity," she whispered. "We must leave. Now."

Trinity yanked her arm free. "No! I saw him! Michael is here!"

"Trinity—Michael is gone."

The words struck like a blade, and Trinity took a staggering step back. "No," she whispered, shaking her head, her brows pinched. "That's not true.… I saw him!"

Sybil's hands trembled. "We are not safe." Something dark flashed in Sybil's stare, and Trinity stopped.

"Please," Sybil begged. "We have to run."

Trinity hesitated. The rain drummed against the dirt street, soaking her cloak. Her breathing came in ragged bursts, her pulse hammering in her throat. She turned back toward the market, desperate to find him. "I know I saw him," she choked out. "I know it was him."

Sybil seized both of her arms, her grip bruising. "It was his body. But his soul is gone."

Trinity jerked away, violently. "What are you talking about!"

Sybil swallowed hard, her attention darting around the thinning market. She clutched her stomach, bending slightly, her face contorting in pain.

"Sybil!" Trinity moved toward her, but Sybil held up a hand. She squeezed her eyes shut, exhaling through clenched teeth.

Then she wrenched her gaze back to Trinity. "We're being watched."

Trinity turned instinctively. The market seemed wrong. Some people moved strangely—too fast or too slow. A handful of cloaked figures lingered under the eaves of a butcher's shop, shadows shifting unnaturally around them. A man in ragged clothes leaned against a cart, his head tilting at an unnatural angle—watching her.

The hairs on the back of her neck rose.

Sybil grabbed her hand.

"We have to go."

Trinity hesitated, casting one last frantic look through the market to find Michael. The moment she turned her head, the cloaked figures moved.

Sybil yanked Trinity forward. "RUN!"

They bolted through the market, dodging merchants and carts. Mud and filth splattered their skirts. The crowd seemed to shift. Some people backed away; others moved closer.

Trinity's heart thundered. Sybil shoved her toward the carriage at the edge of the square.

"MOVE!"

The stable boy stood frozen under the awning, wide-eyed at the sight of the women barreling toward him.

"Get the damn carriage!" Sybil barked.

The boy leapt into action, scrambling for the horses.

Trinity gasped; her chest squeezed around her heart like a vice. She risked a glance back. The cloaked figures had picked up their pace. Her blood ran cold.

The boy barely had the carriage pulled forward before Sybil threw Trinity inside, scrambling in after her.

"GO! NOW!" Sybil shouted.

The driver cracked the reins.

The carriage lurched forward violently, sending them both tumbling into the wooden seats.

Sybil clutched at the curtains, peering through the slit. "They're following us."

Trinity's chest heaved. "Who are they?"

Sybil turned to her, face pale as death. "They're Legionnaires."

Trinity shook her head. "What's a Legionnaire?"

"You don't understand." Sybil's voice trembled. "Michael… is one of them. They're demons, Trinity!"

Trinity recoiled. "No."

"I saw him, Trinity. I felt it. He's been claimed."

Trinity jerked her head in dismissal, tears blurring her vision. "No, you're wrong."

"Damn it, listen to me!" Sybil gripped her wrist so hard it hurt. "I had visions of this for months. That's why I stayed—to protect you."

Trinity wrenched away from her grasp. Michael. Her Michael. It couldn't be true.

The carriage tore down the road, wheels rattling over the uneven dirt path. The horses ran hard, hooves pounding.

Sybil sat rigid, gripping an amulet on a necklace around her throat. It pulsed with soft, golden light.

"What is that?" Trinity screeched.

"Keep your eyes shut," she murmured.

Trinity frowned. "Why?"

Sybil closed hers. "Just do it."

Something shifted in the air, and Trinity obeyed.

The world outside went silent. The wind stopped. The pounding hooves vanished. For a moment, there was nothing. Then—a whisper.

Not in her ears but in her mind.

Trinity…

A sharp inhale burned through her lungs.

My love… my light…

Her body trembled.

I'm coming… Michael's voice.

A choked sob escaped her lips, and she almost opened her eyes.

But Sybil's grip tightened. "No."

The warmth of her cross at her neck flared, sending a pulse through Trinity and she clutched it in her hand.

Then the whispers in her head turned to screams.

She dropped her cross and pressed her hands over her ears, but the sound wasn't coming from outside but inside her skull.

Then, as suddenly as it started—Silence.

The wind rushed back, and the carriage jerked, nearly throwing them from their seats.

She choked, gripping her chest. Her heart slammed against her ribs.

Sybil exhaled sharply. The glow of the amulet at her neck faded.

The air returned to normal.

Trinity swallowed hard, voice barely a whisper. "What was that?"

Sybil looked at Trinity with something like pity. "They're trying to get inside your mind to make you stop the carriage. They would have killed us."

Trinity pressed her fingers to her temples. The ache was still there.

Michael's voice still echoed in the depths of her memory.

I'm coming...

She shuddered. "It was Michael. He would never hurt either of us."

Sybil reached for her hand again, this time gently. "Please, Trinity," she murmured. "You have to believe me."

Trinity stared at Sybil; her throat tight. She couldn't speak because she was starting to believe. And it terrified her.

CHAPTER 35 ~ MICHAEL

Michael stood beneath the awning, his cloak drawn tight, a hood hiding his face. He clung to the shadows, wary of familiar faces.

His fingers twitched, hungry for violence. The hunger gnawed at him—not mere thirst or hunger, but something primal. A need to rend, to consume. He pressed his palms against the cold wall. Forcing control over the wraith inside of him.

Not yet. Not here. He wouldn't lose himself. Not while he still remembered what it meant to be human.

He came through the East Gate—farthest from home and not by choice. He belonged to someone now—a master who demanded obedience. Something he'd always been good at.

Others like him lurked near the market stalls, cloaked in shadows. He sensed them—sometimes even hearing fragments of their thoughts. A new ability. Useful. They were here on assignment.

Hunting a witch.

A specific one.

Sybil.

He searched the crowd, but every hooded figure blurred together. The press of bodies grew. He moved swiftly beneath another awning.

Since waking, everything changed. The fog that dulled his mind for months lifted. Memories returned in a crashing wave. They whispered at the edges of his mind, fleeting as candle smoke.

His father's voice calling him home.

The scent of fresh bread in the kitchen.

Trinity's laughter.

He clenched his jaw, rounding another corner, shouldering others out of his way.

A brown mare. A woman picking wildflowers by the roadside. Her smile.

Her lips pressed against his. Her veil, white as snow. A priest speaking Latin. His wife.

"No, no, no," he whispered, gripping a barrel until the wood cracked beneath his fingers.

The memories clawed at him, but he forced them down, pushing rage to the surface instead.

His father on his knees—blood pooling.

The twins, lifeless in their beds.

Trinity in their bed, tear-streaked, horrified by him.

A gust of wind cut through the alleyway, snapping him out of the memory. His fingers curled into a fist.

He thought the French killed him, but Julian pulled him through.

Julian—the man he'd once trusted. Now revealed to be a monster. A demon who tricked him into becoming a legionnaire. A soul damned and bound to the devil and Baal—a prince among demons.

The oath's sealing revealed the truth.

The others embraced their darkness without hesitation, but something in Michael resisted. A flicker of defiance within him.

Why did he believe such vile things about his family? Am I so weak?

Julian was like him—but older. Their "new family" was made up of the dead, brought back through blood magic and something far worse. Some were ancient. Terrifying. Most, like Michael, were freshly turned. Wraiths lived inside them now, whispering violence, granting strength and immortality.

Before sending him back to England, Julian warned him: never reveal himself to those who loved him. Never go home.

But Baal had plans for York.

But the pull toward Trinity was stronger than ever. Raw. Visceral, simultaneously revolting.

A weakness, Julian said. One that would pass.

Surrender and welcome the dark.

But he didn't want to.

He turned a corner and froze.

Trinity stood only a few feet away. Her hood was drawn, but he knew her face. Her eyes.

He stared, paralyzed.

She turned. Their gazes locked.

Sybil seized her, urgency in her movements, whispering that they needed to go. The moment her attention shifted, Michael ducked into the crowd and disappeared.

Did she see me?

His chest tightened, pulsing with something almost forgotten. A whisper of love. Of devotion shattered. His head swam as he pushed forward through the crowd.

A vision of warmth. Sunlight on golden fields. Laughter.

A sharp shove knocked him sideways.

"Watch where you're going!" an older man barked.

A merchant stumbled in front of him, and Michael's body reacted before his mind could stop it—his hand shooting out to grab the man's throat. His fingers curled, tightening, the pulse beneath his grip fluttering like a trapped bird.

No. He released him, shoving him aside instead. The merchant gasped, clutching his throat, but Michael was already gone. Shame curdling in his stomach. The others wouldn't have hesitated.

I am not like them.

But Baal owned him now. And the faces of those he'd killed in France haunted him, too.

Their last gasps. Their terror.

The other legionnaires reveled in it. He should, too. But the more he killed, the less of himself remained. So, he fought it.

Shame twisted in his gut, swallowed quickly by fury. He let out a scream—an inhuman, primal sound. Then ran.

The rain pounded down, soaking his cloak. Thunder rumbled in the distance.

Michael moved faster than any mortal. Cold and heat no longer touched him. Even walking felt unnatural—each step covered more ground than it should. He was stronger too.

But at what cost?

What was he now? Not living. Not truly dead. A thing—half-shadow, half-man. And what had he given up becoming this thing?

Frustration simmered beneath his skin, clawing for release. His fists clenched as he quickened his pace, heading for where his "new family" resided.

He wouldn't wait any longer and risk Trinity searching for him.

The location was temporary. The witches of York were powerful and hunted them, but so far, the hive remained hidden. Baal's magic and a dozen blood mages masked their presence.

Michael was shocked to discover the witches' identities. He'd grown up under their watchful eyes.

How many times had Lenora mended his bones? Eased his fevers?

The boys had called her the hag, but his mother had trusted her completely.

They'd never questioned their presence. Now he saw the truth.

I must kill Lenora should we meet. The thought made him stop cold. I can't kill Lenora.

The realization hit like a blow.

His rage burned hotter, but now it wasn't directed at her. Not at anyone. It was directed at everything.

Michael scanned the area and moved toward the next building. Wooden homes and businesses stretched two or three stories high, pressed together in narrow alleyways.

He stopped in front of a darkened, two-story building. Abandoned after, the family inside succumbed to the plague. It stood beside one of the larger warehouses.

Baal didn't reside here. Only the soldiers did.

Michael stilled, listening.

Footsteps echoed from a distance, carried on the damp air. His sharpened senses picked them up long before the figures appeared. He pressed against the wall, sinking into the darkness, becoming part of it.

Three figures rounded the corner, cloaks drawn tight. Two men. One woman. Their hushed voices betrayed frustration. Something hadn't gone as planned, and they were late.

Michael caught snippets of conversation as they entered the same building he was about to.

Julian's voice snapped at them to be quiet.

Recruits. Amateurs.

Michael waited a moment, ensuring no one else approached—something the others failed to do. He inhaled, catching a trace of their scent. Julian was growing sloppy.

Michael stepped inside, letting the door shut with a loud thud behind him.

Low voices murmured all around him. Shadows shifted, some like him, lurking, uncertain, adjusting to their newfound existence. More than a hundred filled the space of the warehouse, blending into the gloom.

Michael passed through the dim corridors, silent as a wraith, toward the back room.

Inside, Baal stood, speaking with two others. A man and a woman. Their backs were to Michael.

Julian's recruits.

Baal was unnaturally tall, his frame thin and stretched. Skin pale as bleached bone clung tightly to sharp features. His eyes—black, endless voids— reflected no light. Ageless. Ancient.

He wore the latest fashion—black knee-length breeches, white stockings, polished high-heeled shoes—and a fur-lined cloak draped over his shoulders, flowing like a king's robe.

The Prince of Demons lacked only a crown.

Hello, Michael. I'm so glad you finally joined us. The voice slithered into his mind.

Michael's body stiffened then moved forward against his will. He fought it, but his limbs obeyed Baal's summons, drawn like a marionette.

He halted before the trio, and they turned.

Michael's breath caught. Shock. Then horror.

"Well, well, look who's here." Fleur smiled. It was the first smile he'd ever seen one grace her statuesque face.

"What are you doing here, Fleur?" he growled, the sound feral, like a predator ready to strike.

"Easy now," she purred, placing a delicate hand on his chest. "Remember, we're old friends."

Her complexion was ghastly, and her skin was thin and almost translucent, making her look like something caught between a demon and a human. Whatever beauty she once possessed was now a faded echo.

"I must say, I'm as surprised to see you as you are to see me. I stopped by the old manor on my way here to check if you were still there. Funny thing—I only found the little wifey, belly full of child, and those two witches still playing nursemaid. I should've killed them both when I had the chance. Pity my mortal sentimentality got in the way." She glanced at Baal. "Thankfully, that's no longer a problem."

"You will leave my family alone," Michael said through clenched teeth. He was seconds from ripping her arm off if she didn't back away.

Then her words sank in. Trinity is pregnant.

Shock crossed Fleur's face, and her arms dropped to her side, as she turned to Baal.

Baal's smile vanished. "I do hope no one saw you."

414

Before Fleur could respond, he groaned, eyes narrowing as he delved into her thoughts, rifling through her mind.

"You stupid girl! And you, Robert! You were instructed to watch her, help instruct—not let her kill in broad daylight. You fool. And then you left witnesses alive?"

"Who'd you kill?" Michael shouted, his voice echoing across the room. Fleur didn't even flinch.

He reached into her mind, catching a glimpse of a woman's lifeless body in a narrow alley. Not Trinity. No one from Ellsworth. Relief washed through him as he pulled away.

He knew the thirst could overwhelm newborns after the blood oath. That's why they were confined to the manor until they learned control. He'd experienced it himself, but the hunger never dominated him.

The man beside Fleur, Robert, collapsed to his knees. Before he could utter a word, his neck twisted with a sickening crack. He dropped—motionless but not truly dead. The boy, probably in his early twenties with a full head of black curly hair, lay crumpled on the floor.

Baal must've summoned help because two others stepped forward, lifting the boy by his arms.

"Throw him in a box and bury him for a few days," Baal said coolly. "Let that serve as a reminder."

They carried him off without a word.

Fleur stood frozen, clutching her neck and sucking in shallow breaths—Baal was strangling her with his mind.

"You will not be allowed to create chaos unless I command it."

"Baal, release my daughter," said a voice from the shadows.

Fleur's mother, Jacqueline emerged at his side, her golden ringlets piled high and wreathed by a diamond-studded tiara. Her wine-red gown swept behind her like a train of blood. A black mask covering the top half of her face.

"This is your only warning," Baal said coldly. "You'll spend a decade entombed if you lose control again. I don't care who your mother is—you will not fail me."

The weight of his anger was palpable. The entire room fell silent.

He released her. Fleur gasped falling to her knees, gulping air.

"Yes, m'lord," she rasped. "I understand. It wasn't intentional, m'lord. I couldn't stop."

"Ensure it never happens again."

"It won't," Jacqueline answered for her and crossed to her daughter's side, pulling her up.

Michael met Jacqueline once as a boy. Fleur's father often visited Henry, sometimes bringing Fleur along. The resemblance was unmistakable.

He steeled his mind, locking every thought of Trinity in the deepest recesses of his consciousness, focusing instead on the rage that surged within him.

"Michael. I have a task for you," Baal said. "Julian will accompany you."

At the mention of his name, Julian stepped forward. His russet-colored hair oily, pulled into a limp ponytail. His clothes were filthy and tattered—ripped trousers, scuffed leather shoes, and a threadbare black wool coat with a hood over his shoulders.

"I'm here to serve, m'lord," Julian said, voice low, submissive.

416

Michael's revulsion rose instantly. The mask of friendship shattered. He knew what Julian truly was. Born into darkness like himself—but there was something more twisted beneath Julian's surface. Something venomous.

They were all different from Michael. Or perhaps he was the aberration.

The chaos in his chest churned, the pull of power tempting him, but he didn't crave blood like the others.

Baal's voice slid through his mind.

"You will live long, my son, because of this. It is not a weakness—it is your greatest strength. Many moons will rise and fall. Our armies will perish, undone by reckless hunger. But not you. There is greatness in you. Now go."

Michael and Julian turned, leaving Fleur before Baal and her mother.

He couldn't fathom Fleur's presence here—how she became a legionnaire while her mother remained something else.

Not human. Not like them. More akin to the witches of York—only far more powerful.

Did Baal place Fleur in his home? Or Julian?

Was she the one who orchestrated the ruin of his family?

The murder of his father?

The death of his sisters?

He didn't believe she possessed the power to do it alone. But maybe she hadn't been.

Julian moved beside him with ease, matching his pace. He spoke mind-to-mind without effort— something Michael still couldn't manage. Others could reach him, and he could reply, but he hadn't yet learned how to push his thoughts outward.

Julian turned his head slightly, eyes gleaming with smug amusement.

We're to watch a pair of witches. Sisters. We need to locate their dwelling. Julian's voice sounded in his head. Our Lord wants us to uncover as many of their sanctuaries as possible—so we can strike them all in a single night.

"How do you do that?" Michael asked.

Julian laughed. "I see you're speaking to me again."

"Just answer the question."

Julian huffed a laugh. "It takes time unless you have a talent for it. Can you read someone else's mind?" he asked.

"Yes," Michael answered. "Easily."

"Then it's a simple thing; you push your will into their minds. It just takes practice."

They walked in silence for several minutes, Julian leading them. Michael tried several times to project his thoughts onto Julian, but he was unsuccessful.

His mind kept drifting to Trinity.

She's pregnant with my child. Could it be true? Maybe she wasn't lying about her feelings for me.

His eyes flicked to Julian.

"You need to learn to shield your thoughts better," Julian said suddenly, as if plucking the suspicion straight from Michael's mind. "Could make things... complicated. For you—or for those you once cared about."

Michael stopped. "I don't care about anyone. I feel nothing, Julian."

Julian raised both hands, palms up. "I can help. I'll teach you. My purpose is to show you how to use your new gifts. How to survive."

Michael's stance eased slightly, but distrust didn't leave his eyes.

Julian was an unlikely ally, but at the moment, Michael had no other choice.

And the skill was one he needed—urgently.

CHAPTER 36 ~ SYBIL

Trinity jumped out of the carriage and ran into the manor, leaving Sybil alone.

David walked out of the stables, and she threw herself into his arms.

"She saw Michael. I must go."

David pulled away, studying her face. "How?"

"He's a legionnaire!"

He tugged her back into a gentle embrace. "It will be alright. We can deal with this."

"No! I must convince Trinity she has magic like us..." Sybil turned and headed for the manor; David closed behind her.

"You what?" He raised his voice in surprise. "She has magic?"

"Yes. I know she does. And it's time she learns to use it! This was my only job, and I have failed!"

David grabbed her hand, and she whipped around. "The demons surrounded us, David! They were waiting for us! I dragged her away from them... From him."

"But she won't even touch the sword. Much less admit she has magic." His eyes said it all. Trinity would never accept her fate. Not without a monumental push. Or shove.

"We need to make her. Time is running out."

Entering the manor, Chailleach's owl flew from a rafter to her. It hooted and flapped its wings as it landed on her shoulder, careful not to dig in its claws.

Sybil stopped and gasped. "Is everything all right?"

The owl hooted and flew to the audience hall, frantically flapping its wings at the closed door. Sybil looked at David. "Something's wrong."

As soon as she opened the door, she heard Elizabeth moaning and Trinity speaking gently.

"Sybil!" Trinity screamed.

Elizabeth sat in Henry's chair, panting, crying and clutching the arm of the chair in pain. The baby was coming.

Little One rested beside Elizabeth on the arm of the chair.

"Let's get you to bed," Sybil said softly. "Trinity, help me lift her. David, boil some water!"

They escorted Elizabeth to her bedchambers while David rushed to the kitchen. Little One followed behind them, hooting. Elizabeth breathed heavily and moaned quietly with each contraction. Her head drooped and tangled brown hair fell loose around her face—wild and unkempt.

They had just reached the top of the staircase when Susana appeared from nowhere. Her long, dark hair, untamed and streaked with grey, spilled freely down her back. She wore only a nightgown, barefoot and ghostlike in the dim light.

All three stopped in front of her.

421

Susana's voice was startlingly clear. "I started the fire in her room, but I couldn't carry her alone, and David was nowhere to be found. Bloody useless man!" Susana cursed loudly. "Come now, girls. The baby's coming!" She seemed to be herself again, taking control and helping her daughter.

After settling Elizabeth into bed, Sybil disappeared to bring up more water and linen.

As Sybil ran down the stairs and into the kitchen, breathing hard, her hands shook violently.

"Whoa!" David called out before she almost barreled into him. "Breath, love." He clutched her arms.

She pushed past him and gripped the table, trying to catch her breath.

"I need you to bring the water up once it starts to boil. I'll grab some linen. The baby is coming." Sybil looked up at David, her eyes wide. "The baby, David!"

"It's just a baby. You'll do fine."

"Can you please fetch Lenora?"

He touched her cheek gently. "You can do this. There's no need."

David's faith was touching, but fear coursed through her veins. She'd never delivered a baby before and knew many women died from childbirth.

"Could you please?" She pleaded, hoping he'd go.

"Yes, I will. As soon as I deliver the water."

Sybil threw her arms around him, laying her head against his chest. She closed her eyes and breathed out. "Thank you."

He lifted her chin to look up at him. "I love you, and you will be great. Don't worry. Trust yourself."

***

Trinity sat beside Elizabeth, gently holding her hand as Sybil entered the room. David followed close behind, setting a heavy pot of water beside the table while Sybil placed a bundle of linens on top.

The fire kept the space warm as rain poured steadily outside, the sky already swallowed by darkness. Susana lit several candelabras, their soft orange glow flickering across the walls.

Elizabeth moaned in pain, sweat dripping from her brow. "Mother!" She yelled. "Mother, it hurts!" The last word stretched out as tears streamed down her face, and she choked out a sob.

Susana went to her side and kissed her forehead. "It's normal and shall pass, my dear. Try to relax. You're bringing life into this dark world." Susana sounded hopeful.

Sybil stopped and stared at Susana, surprised. Not fully understanding the transformation, but thankful, it happened.

Will Susana be the one to bring hope to everyone? Would the child's cries and laughter replace the terror, loss, and pain of the past?

Sybil's apprehension peaked as Elizabeth screamed again in agony, clutching the blanket, knees bent.

Sybil laid her hand protectively over her own belly. "Please, if any gods are listening, give me the strength to bear it," she prayed.

Trinity knelt next to the bed, clasped her hands together, and closed her eyes. "Heavenly Father, forgive my trespasses..." She grew quiet in silent prayer for several moments. Then she glanced at Sybil, brows furrowed, before continuing. "Please, watch over Elizabeth and her baby. With your divine love, my lord, I beg the child be born healthy."

423

Trinity briefly met Sybil's gaze again.
"Amen."

***

Hours passed; exhausted, Elizabeth held her baby girl, Mary, close. The baby nursing peacefully.

Little One curled up at the foot of the bed; chin tucked in; eyes closed in sleep.

Lenora told David to assure Sybil she could manage alone. And in the end, Sybil handled everything with Susana's help. Both mother and child pulled through beautifully.

Trinity and Sybil gathered the soiled blankets and stepped out just as Susana entered, balancing a tray with three steaming bowls of broth.

"You girls drop those right now and eat."

"Mother, you must eat first." Trinity insisted. "I'll return in a moment."

"I already ate in the kitchen. Now take this, and I'll bring the linen down. Then sit with your sister. You too, Sybil."

They swapped loads, and Sybil took the tray. Susana took the linen, then left. Sybil placed the tray on the table by the window and brought Elizabeth her bowl, setting it next to her bed.

"When you're ready, I'll hold the babe while you eat," Sybil offered.

The baby continued to nurse as Elizabeth gently ran a finger over the chubby cheek. "As soon as she's finished. Thank you, Sybil. Please eat. Both of you look exhausted."

Elizabeth appeared different, transformed from a young lady to a mother within hours. It was miraculous.

There was no time to think about what occurred in York. Everything had happened so fast, but now, as Trinity and Sybil sat across from each other at the small round table, eating their broth, Sybil knew they needed to talk.

"I'm sorry, Sybil," Trinity whispered first, so Elizabeth couldn't hear. She put her spoon down. "I was scared, but I shouldn't have screamed at you. You have been my loyal and loving friend. I can't judge you, no matter how much this frightens me. You have always been there for all of us, and without you, we would have been lost."

Sybil was speechless. "Wasn't expecting that." She laughed. "Thank you. I know this is hard for you, but I promise nothing I do is evil. I fight evil. Like your prayers, I have my way of keeping the darkness at bay."

"I think I understand," Trinity breathed. "I will not turn my back on you and repeat the disastrous mistake I made with Michael."

Sybil reached across the table and patted Trinity's hand. "That wasn't your fault. He made his choices."

"Yes, I know, but..." Trinity looked out the window and saw David riding a horse through the open gate. They'd even forgotten to close it. "David is home. Where was he?" she asked.

"Helping the other field hands and workers secure their homes with protective wards. He's been going out every night, helping everyone he can." Sybil watched her husband lovingly as he walked his horse into the stables. "We are fighting a war, Trinity. A war you are fated to be a part of. Whether you desire this or not."

"I don't know how to fight this..." Trinity closed her eyes and shook her head. "You don't understand. I don't have power. I have a legacy of lunacy and a stolen sword. And my delusional aunty with her mad ravings." Trinity huffed out a laugh, then whispered, "What if I'm mad and the vision of the seraph was all in my head and never truly happened?" She glanced at Elizabeth, who'd fallen asleep. "I have touched the shield, and it shows me nothing. The sword is just a sword. There's nothing magical about either of them."

"What if it's not a stolen sword but gifted by your god? And you're not mad? What if you just need help to access its…" Sybil paused. She didn't want to say magic. "Accessing its power?"

Trinity raised an eyebrow. "Are you saying you now believe in my god?"

"I'm saying that perhaps your aunt wasn't delusional. And that you are not mad."

"And what if you're wrong?" Trinity countered, taking a sip of her broth.

"What of your dreams?"

"You mean my nightmares?"

"They are not nightmares or dreams." Sybil held Trinity's stare.

Trinity stood up, closed her eyes and shook her head. "I can't do this right now," she said, walking out and leaving Sybil alone.

Sybil sighed and walked over to the bed, where Elizabeth and the baby had fallen asleep. Sybil gently lifted the swaddled infant out of Elizabeth's arms and carried her to the window. The child already had bright red hair and a creamy, soft complexion.

"I promise, sweet girl, I'll do everything I can to protect you."

***

Sybil didn't knock at Trinity's bedchambers. As expected, Trinity stood before her fireplace, arms wrapped around her belly. She lifted her head and scowled at Sybil.

"What is it now?"

"We need to speak about this."

"I don't want to, and I don't want these!" Trinity gestured to the chest that lay open. The sword and shield atop, glimmering in the firelight. "Take them and use them yourself if you truly believe them magical!"

"It is not my destiny but yours." Sybil lifted the sword as thunder rolled across the sky. She shivered as warm heat flowed from the sword into her.

It did have magic. Powerful magic. "Oh Trinity, it is powerful."

"I can't do this," Trinity sobbed.

The sword pulsed. Sybil held it out to Trinity. "You must wield the sword. You are the chosen one. Not me."

"I said I don't want it!"

The force of her words made Sybil stagger back a step. "Trinity."

"Haven't I done enough?" Trinity paced to the window. Lightning flashed as rain pebbled against the glass. "I pray three times a day! Not just for myself but for you too! For everyone!"

"Prayers aren't enough." Sybil held the sword out again. "Wield it."

"Please… I tried. I felt nothing!"

"Trinity, you have magic inside of you. You must only believe."

Trinity screamed, throwing her hands in the air and then grabbing the sword.

Sybil stepped further away.

"I feel nothing..." she stopped speaking, froze, only her eyes darting from the sword to Sybil and back. "Sybil?"

"It's alright. Let it flow through you."

"How..." Trinity pushed the sword back at Sybil. "Take it! Now!"

She sighed and reached for the sword, but before she could take it, a small blue flame licked up the blade, causing Trinity to scream and then drop it.

The sword clattered to the floor, the flame dying.

"It... It..."

"It's magic, Trinity, and you are not mad! This is your fate."

Trinity's breaths came in giant gulps, her body quaking. "Get out!"

"Trinity, please!"

"Get out!"

Sybil huffed and left the room, with Trinity staring at the sword as if it were going to attack her personally.

***

Sybil entered the stable, shutting the doors behind her. Moon Pie whinnied, and she stroked its neck, speaking quietly to calm it.

Like a drowned rat, the rain soaked through Sybil's cloak, her hair matted to her face.

David laughed when he walked in from his room and handed her a small towel.

"Thank you, my love." She wiped her face and dried off as much as possible. "Elizabeth delivered a baby girl early this morning. It was a long labor through the entire night."

He took the towel from her and unpinned her coiled braid, letting it fall free. "Is the babe and mother healthy?" He asked quietly as he dried her hair.

"Both are perfect. She's named Mary." Sybil smiled. "The owl warned us, then refused to leave Elizabeth's side."

"Cauilleach-Oidhche," David murmured.

"Or as Trinity believes: Athena Noctua," Sybil said, rubbing her forehead. "I don't know how to get through to her."

"Did you give Elizabeth the bracelet for the baby?" He asked. It matched the one she'd given Elizabeth when she arrived home months before.

Sybil removed the towel and hung it on the stable door. "Yes, and I've made one for Trinity's babe when it's born, too." She began to peel off her clothes and hang the heavy petticoat over the gate.

"Can we go to bed, please?" she asked.

"Who's watching Elizabeth?" David asked.

"Susana is back to herself and is staying with them tonight," she explained.

"Her daughter going into labor must have shaken her enough to wake her up," David added, then sighed, smiling. "This is a good day."

He took her hand, and they walked to his room. Sybil told him about the confrontation with Trinity afterwards and the sword.

"We still have to deal with Michael, too," she said sadly.

"We will, but not now. Now you sleep."

He led her into bed.

CHAPTER 37 ~ TRINITY

Susana's renewed zest for life ignited an urgent desire to restore their home. Within weeks, the manor began to appear clean again—almost normal. On borrowed funds from a friend in York, Susana hired a cook, another scullery maid, two cleaners, and a steward from Scotland, expected to arrive in a few days.

They had struggled for months without help, but Trinity held her tongue, not wanting to upset Susana. The bitterness of being abandoned by Michael and Susana tasted like acid.

The manor now buzzed with voices and laughter. It was alive again. Still, the work remained demanding and rations tight. Ellsworth villagers gradually resumed normal life despite many farmers' absence from the fields.

Trinity stayed close to Susana, trailing her like a shadow. She worried constantly about her state of mind. Susana wasn't entirely herself yet, but she seemed stronger each day. Trinity clung to that progress, focusing on that and ensuring their family had food.

Trinity's eyes constantly lingered on the front gate— waiting for Michael. Deep down, Trinity knew he was alive, in York. But he didn't come home. And she couldn't go back to town to search for him. Susana and Elizabeth needed her.

She followed Susana into the garden, a large wicker basket in her arms, as Susana filled it with herbs and vegetables. Just like old times. When she arrived almost a year before. Bittersweet memories filled her with sadness, so she shoved them deep inside, buried.

The sky hadn't opened yet, but the air felt heavy— like something was coming.

Trinity glanced over her shoulder. Expecting someone to be there.

"Is Friar Brook coming today?" Trinity asked. He'd come every day to pray with her and Susana since he'd returned from the highlands. The friar stayed with family after the plague struck and stayed away until Susana wrote to him. Begging him to come home.

"He is not," Susana said but didn't elaborate. Instead, she bent down and pulled some weeds from around a rosebush. Before she stood up, a soft sob escaped her, and Trinity knelt next to her.

"What's wrong?"

Susana looked up at Trinity, tears in her eyes. "I miss Dreyfuss and Joseph." She quickly added, "I miss Henry too… I hadn't realized how much I depended on them all."

Trinity wrapped her arms around Susana and pulled her into a tight embrace. "I know. So do I."

"No one cooks like Mrs. Bartlett either." Susana sobbed.

"Cookie is quite impressive," Trinity defended the new cook.

She was younger and less experienced than Mrs. Bartlett but was passionate about her dishes and could whip something out of nothing. The eccentric woman, who called herself Cookie, was a godsend.

Susana sobbed again into Trinity's shoulder. "They were my family."

Trinity understood replacing them and restoring Susana's high standards would take considerable effort, yet believed Ellsworth offered a prosperous future, particularly for their children.

"Do you want to see Mary for a visit before supper?" Trinity suggested, hoping that the infant would lighten Susana's mood.

When Susana wasn't in the garden, she was in the nursery with Mary, holding her, singing to her, and telling her stories. It was the one thing that made Susana smile. Despite a mighty scream, the baby charmed them all.

"Yes, that would be nice."

***

"Trinity, stop looking at me like that. You must not worry about me so much. I'm perfectly alright." Susana sighed and shook her head. She hadn't gone back to wearing her cauls and veils. Preferring a single braid down her back. Claiming she was a widow and old. She could very well dress as she liked from then on. Even her gowns were simpler, more modest but without the wimple. But everything black. No color. No extravagance.

They sat across from each other at the kitchen table, sharing an early supper while reviewing the day's

432

business. Susana had insisted on the routine the day after Mary was born. It kept them focused—and everything on track.

The account books were more complicated than either Trinity or David had expected. Neither managed to make sense of it. It was a relief when Susana took over, explaining that the system was hers—not Sir Henry's—a surprise to everyone. She had things under control, but the estate was in rough shape. For nearly eight months, they'd earned nothing—no taxes, rent, wheat, or crops sold in town.

They were broke.

Elizabeth still didn't join them for meals. Her recovery was slower than expected. Trinity suspected she was mourning her husband and a different life. So, Susana, Trinity, and even Sybil took turns visiting her and baby Mary—holding the newborn and spending quiet moments in the nursery.

It offered a rare solace.

Trinity huffed. "You must eat more. You're all bones." She watched Susana fiddle with the food on her plate but barely touched it.

"I promise you I am. You must stop this worrying." Susana tried to put Trinity's mind at ease. "Your fussing will drive me mad." Susana's lips curled up into a mischievous smile.

"That's not amusing," Trinity said, trying to hold back a chuckle. How long had it been since she'd laughed?

"Too soon?" Susana asked then laughed.

Trinity shook her head smiling. "I'm only happy you are better."

Sybil came through the back door carrying bread, vegetables, and eggs. "I've collected all that we have left, m'lady, as you've asked."

"That's all?" Susana said, shocked at how little supplies they had. "So, little it can be carried in one basket? It won't be enough."

She stood to inspect the basket's contents while Sybil glanced at Trinity, disheartened. They had survived on bare rations for months, but now Susana was determined to restore the manor without restriction. It wasn't realistic.

"I think I can help with that!"

All three women turned as Shaun stepped into the kitchen, his soldier's uniform streaked with dirt. He looked as though he'd come straight from the road.

Susana dropped everything and ran to him, clutching his hands.

"Shaun, my dear boy, welcome home. Is Michael with you? Did he come back?" she asked, guiding him to the table beside Trinity. She had prayed—morning and night—for their safe return.

Neither Trinity nor Sybil had the heart to tell her the truth. Trinity still refused to believe he was truly gone.

"Trinity, how are you?" Shaun asked, ignoring Susana's question.

"I'm well, thank you," she replied with a calm that held none of their old warmth. "Tired. My feet ache, but I'm managing. What news do you bring of Michael?"

Her chest tightened. She prayed Sybil had been wrong.

But Shaun's eyes spoke volumes.

"Susana, will you sit with me, please?" He asked, pulling a chair out for her.

She obediently sat next to him, silent, waiting.

"Michael won't be returning. I'm sorry he fell during battle."

Susana put her hands to her mouth and sobbed, "No, no, he was better than most men with a sword. He can't…."

"I tried to stay by his side, but we got separated. I'm so sorry."

Susana stood up and ran from the room, muttering."

Trinity sat still, looking at the table, unsure of what to believe. Shaun's words, or Michael at the market and Sybil's words of demons and death filled her head until she felt dizzy.

"Shaun, we need supplies." Trinity stood up and walked to the basket at the table.

Sybil had discreetly left the room.

Shaun went to her side, taking her hands in his. "I will have my mother send everything you need. You will want for nothing. I promise."

"Shaun, he isn't dead. I saw him. I saw him at the market a few weeks ago."

"Trinity."

"Did you recover his body?" she asked.

"No, he was behind enemy lines. There were too many French and so many fallen men. The priests came to the field to give them their last rites. I'm sorry. I know it's a shock, but I'm here. I will help you."

Trinity put her hand over her mouth and her other over her belly. She stared into nothing, pictures in her mind flittering in and out.

Michael falling in the forest. His eyes turning black.

Then other memories came…

The day she arrived, seeing Michael for the first time in years.

"No, I cannot accept this." She knew she had seen him in town. If they didn't retrieve the body, perhaps Shaun was wrong and Sybil.

Shaun took her by the shoulders. "Look at me, Trinity. There is no way he survived."

She lifted her glazed eyes to him but barely saw his face. She just wanted Michael. Her husband. She didn't want to live without him and wouldn't accept Shaun's words.

"Trinity, marry me. I will take care of you. You are all my family already, anyhow. Let me help you."

That shocked her back to reality. The glazed memories were gone, replaced with outrage.

"I will not!" she yelled. "I will always be Michael's wife, in life or death. I am his wife, Shaun Donaldson! How dare you say this to me?" Ignoring him, she left. "Leave me alone, Shaun. Just go."

Not understanding her anger, he walked after her. "Please, Trinity, I'm only trying to help. Don't be angry with me."

"Just Go! Go!" Trinity turned on him, tears streaming down her face. She couldn't bear to look at him a second longer. "I can't talk about this. I won't! He's not gone!"

"I apologize. I'll leave and return with supplies in the morning but hear me now. I will not stop protecting you or this family. I'm not your enemy, Trinity!"

Trinity spun around to face him and screamed, "You left us, too!" She released a frustrated scream between clenched teeth.

"I thought I'd be able to bring him home!" Shaun yelled back, his face turning red.

Shaun's anger finally bested him as he stormed out of the manor, leaving Trinity alone in the hall sobbing.

She crumbled to the floor and cried for the thousandth time.

David walked in straight after. "M'lady?" He helped lift her, righting her onto her feet.

Trinity couldn't speak at first, then blurted out, "He asked me to marry him!" She laughed through her tears. "Can you imagine the nerve?"

"Come, let me help you back to the kitchen. A cup of warm milk with honey will help. I'm sure he had good intentions. Shaun's a decent man. You must know this."

They walked back to the kitchen. When they entered, David helped Trinity to the table while Sybil packed away supper.

"Love, will you warm the milk for Trinity?" David said and sat Trinity in Henry's old chair.

Sybil poured two cups and took a seat beside Trinity. They hadn't spoken since baby Mary's birth—both too busy helping Elizabeth and Susana restore the manor.

"I'm sorry, Trinity," Sybil said softly.

Trinity sipped her warm milk. She was so confused that her emotions swirled like a whirlpool, ready to drown her.

"David, please get Elizabeth to check on Lady Susana," Trinity asked.

He wasn't the Stewart of the manor; it wasn't his job, and at any other time, it would have been wildly inappropriate for Trinity to ask him to go anywhere near their private chambers. Those days were gone, though; David was the only one left.

"Of course. What should I tell her?" He asked.

"Tell her Shaun arrived to tell us Michael was killed in battle, and Lady Susana didn't take it well."

"I'm so sorry, Trinity," David said. "I didn't know." He stood up, nodded at Sybil lovingly, and left them alone.

"I know what you're going to say... Save it." Trinity cut off Sybil as she started to speak first. "I don't think we need to rehash what we believe or do not." Trinity's anger had returned.

"No, but we must discuss this. Shaun is your closest friend. He loved you as much as he loved Michael. He's only trying to do right by you. By his best friend, who he believes is dead."

"Please, Sybil. I can't."

"Well, we need his help. At least accept his help, or we will starve before the end of winter."

"I'll consider it."

"And Michael?" Sybil said tentatively.

"He's alive and not a demon," Trinity hissed.

"If that's true, why hasn't he come home, Trinity? Why?"

CHAPTER 38 ~ MICHAEL

Michael stood at the edge of the woods, which gave him a vantage point over the entire Ellsworth manor and surrounding area.

He'd gotten into the habit of watching them all from afar. It tortured him but also gave him a twisted sort of relief. His behavior defied logic. He was largely emotionally numb, harboring mostly resentment and fury—more than remorse. But there was this pull towards his home he couldn't resist.

He tilted his head, listening to the newborn baby crying from where he stood. Elizabeth's new baby girl.

Under cover of darkness, he discovered his sister in her old room, a newborn in her arms.

It had been almost a year since he'd seen her, but it seemed like a lifetime ago.

How did I lose so much time?

He stayed for hours, watching Elizabeth and the newborn, until the pull to Trinity became painful.

Her voice moved him between past and present. He followed the sound, his heart aching.

439

Do I have a heart? He touched his chest, the rhythmic beating still there.

It wasn't hard to find her. She spent all her time in his father's parlor, poring over the financial ledgers and speaking with Sybil or David.

He'd peered through the window, where she and David discussed the finances—something Michael should have been doing. Guilt churned like spoiled milk in his stomach.

But watching her brought him a warmth he didn't deserve.

Memories looped in his mind…

Walking with Shaun to her old home. Their first kiss. The second. The kiss in the parlor after they were married was full of promise. Their first night together as husband and wife. Hope filled him then—so much happiness and longing. His wife. The woman he knew he'd love forever.

Michael recognized a connection from the moment they met as children. He could still recall the sting of jealousy over Shaun, the possessiveness, and the heartbreak when his father sent her away.

Her return years later was a miracle. A second chance. And he let her go. He relinquished his love. Blinded by grief and drowning in self-pity, he forgot the one thing that mattered. Her.

Now, he stood in the rain, far enough away Sybil wouldn't sense him. The rain fell heavier, and the wind picked up, but yelling echoed through the yard, dragging Michael from his reverie.

He couldn't mistake the sound of Trinity's voice. Anger, sadness, pain. He knew she suffered.

The manor yard was overgrown, the fields untended. The tell-tale signs of neglect everywhere.

He should have felt something about his responsibility for his home's degraded state, but he didn't.

The screaming grew louder. Michael narrowed his eyes, listening and reached out to pick up their thoughts.

Shaun's mind was easy to penetrate, but he recoiled as soon as he did. Tremendous pain, grief and red-hot anger.

"Please, Trinity, I'm only trying to help. Don't be angry with me."

"Just Go! Go!" Trinity screamed.

Michael hesitated before piercing her mind... A blanket of sadness so heavy, he fell to his knees... But there was more... Determination. Anger. Confusion.

"I can't talk about this. I won't! He's not gone!"

Michael's head snapped up. She'd seen him.

"I apologize. I'll leave and return with supplies in the morning but hear me now. I will not stop protecting you or this family. I'm not your enemy, Trinity!"

"You left us, too!" She screamed so loud; Michael grimaced.

"I thought I'd be able to bring him home!" Shaun yelled back.

A minute later, Shaun threw open the manor's front door and stormed out. "I'm such an idiot!"

He marched into the stables, and a few moments later, he was saddled and rode out of the gates towards York at full gallop.

Michael couldn't comfort or go to Shaun, but desperation clung to his friend.

Michael needed to know what happened. What caused this upset?

He entered Shaun's thoughts again. It was surprisingly more straightforward with humans, and as Shaun rode hard out the manor walls, cursing and swearing, his injured pride and his grief peaking, Michael followed him and let his friend's emotions wash over him like the rain that fell harder around them by the second.

Sadness at losing his best friend and his overwhelming desire to make things right with Trinity.

Shaun's thoughts swirled around like a tornado.

Caring for Michael over the last few months proved a nightmare.

Relief at not having to watch him anymore but missing him so much his heart broke.

The brother he never had. The constant companion. Gone.

His love for Trinity since they were children. The jealousy when she favored Michael... but he loved them both so much, he forced himself to put his feelings aside and support their decision to marry each other.

Michael closed his eyes momentarily as Shaun's thoughts and pain ripped through him.

Rain poured over Shaun like a shroud, masking the tears on his face. His horse galloped through the mud-slicked trail, slipping more than once. Shaun barely noticed. He was lost in memory, drowning in grief.

The leather reins were soaked and slick in his hands, making them difficult to grip.

Michael ran faster, struggling to keep up.

Shaun's mind drifted to simpler days.

Laughter by the stream, all three of them.

"Isn't it strange how everything's changed but still feels the same?" Trinity's voice echoed in his thoughts.

442

Her smile. Her light, musical laughter that rose a little too high when she let go.

Shaun made her laugh like that. For this, Shaun would willingly give his life.

Michael never knew how deeply Shaun loved her. He'd always respected her choice and never stepped between her and Michael.

For so long, Michael doubted and accused him. He believed Shaun wanted more.

I was such a fool.

He was about to pull away when another memory surged forward.

Michael gripping Shaun's hand and pulling him into a firm embrace—beaming with excitement. Michael telling him they were going to court together.

Shaun never aspired to anything beyond his place, but Michael challenged him. That day, Shaun was so proud of his friend and proud to stand beside him.

So many memories. So much joy. They lived a blessed life, never imagining how death would be. Even in battle, the fear wasn't real—until it came for them. When it did, it was a nightmare.

They'd been inseparable all their lives. And no matter what happened, Shaun's love for Michael and Trinity would never fade.

A crack of thunder split the air.

Shaun's horse reared, throwing him violently. He crashed at the base of an old tree. His head hit the trunk; his shoulder popped.

Michael was beside him in an instant.

"Shaun?" He asked, not knowing what to do at first.

The horse bolted out of sight as thunder and lightning lit up the sky.

He bent down to check if Shaun was still breathing and found him alive, but his shoulder appeared twisted and broken. Blood flowed heavily down his neck from his head.

He couldn't bring himself to walk away and let his friend die, despite knowing he should. Like his morbid fascination with Trinity, he lifted Shaun into his arms.

***

Shaun woke with a start. He blinked several times and rubbed them in the dark bedroom. Then he tried to push himself up.

"Easy, go slow, you've broken..."

"Michael?" Shaun asked, looking into the dark. "I can't see you."

"I'm here, Shaun," Michael said but stayed inside the room's shadow.

"Why are you over there?" Shaun asked incredibly, shaking his head. "Everyone thinks you're dead! Your mother, Trinity." He let out a deep breath, closing his eyes. "Oh, Michael." He shook his head. "You need to go there now. Trinity is grieving, but refuses to give up hope, even after I told her you were killed in battle. She told me she saw you, and I didn't believe her."

"I can never return. I'm going away soon." Michael turned to leave. "I only wanted to make sure you were alright. Goodbye, Shaun."

"Wait!" Shaun threw himself out of his bed, but as soon as his feet hit the floor, he collapsed, and in a second, Michael was lifting him back to bed as if he were a baby.

Shaun searched Michael's face. It was Michael's face but changed, and Michael cringed at his friend's thoughts.

Is he dying?

"Are you unwell? You don't look so good."

"I'm fine, Shaun." Michael stood back a step.

"Please don't go. What happened to you?"

"I can't talk about it." Michael crossed his arms and stepped further into the shadows.

Shaun started to light the candle on the table next to him.

"Please don't," Michael asked.

"What happened? How did you know where I was?" Shaun asked, trying desperately to keep Michael from leaving.

"I visited Ellsworth to… anyways, I saw you riding out like a demon. You didn't seem in control of your horse, so I followed you."

Michael ran both hands through his hair. "I had to push hard to catch up to you. You were flying. Then, the thunder and lightning. Your horse reared up, and you flew off. By the time I reached you, you were unconscious, bleeding."

"You saved me," Shaun laughed.

"For the last time, my friend." Michael sighed, making to leave. "I owe you one for carrying me home so many nights."

"Please sit with me, just a while longer. What's the rush? You said I broke something. I don't feel like anything is broken. I'm sore all over, but other than that, I'm only lightheaded. How is that possible?"

Michael moved Shaun's chair from the desk to bed, clearing some clothes. "You're still a slob." He sat down. "I healed you."

"How? Are you sure it was broken?"

"I healed the bone and tissue around it. I healed your head concussion and stopped the bleeding. You

445

would have died if I hadn't been there. I couldn't just leave you, and I didn't want the others to turn you like they did to me, or worse."

"What others? Turn you? I don't understand," Shaun said, confused.

"I'm sorry, Shaun, I can't tell you, and I don't want too either. I need you to stay alive and take care of my family. I know you love her. Please, keep loving her, don't leave them."

"Michael, I proposed to Trinity. In her moment of grief, I offered to marry her like a fool straight after I told her you were dead. She practically threw me out of there. She screamed at me that she would always be your wife in life and even death. She will never give up hope that you'll return."

Michael huffed out a small laugh. "You are so impulsive, but honestly, I thought you possessed all the charm with the ladies. How could you screw this up?" Michael sighed.

"Yeah, rub it in," Shaun said. "But you need to go back to them, brother. She won't love anyone but you."

A picture flashed in his mind… The sun on her face, her smile, and the love in her eyes when she looked at him. Was it all lies?

"I was a fool, Shaun. I'm sorry. But I can't go back. If I do, you'll all die—she will die. And if anyone finds out I've been here, they'll kill you. I'm sorry, brother. Just coming here has put you in danger again. Maybe I am the monster they made me."

"You can never be evil, Michael. I know your heart. We were raised together. I know you."

Shaun closed his eyes for a minute and rubbed his left ear again, and Michael was gone when he opened his eyes again.

"Goodbye," Shaun whispered.

CHAPTER 39 ~ SYBIL

"It's madness! You can't go out in this storm!" Sybil shouted.

After Shaun left, Trinity remained at the kitchen table, locked in a fruitless, hour-long argument with Sybil.

But Trinity, gripped by obsession, had made up her mind—she would ride to town and find Michael and Shaun, convinced Michael wasn't dead nor a demon.

David had returned to the stables, suggesting a sedative before leaving again. Then, without warning, Trinity stood and stormed to the great hall.

"Think of the baby! Please, Trinity, you can't go! It's nightfall. The road is treacherous, and you know what's out there! For God's sake!" Sybil screamed.

"I'll have David accompany me if you are so worried."

"I don't want him out there either! Please, Trinity, be reasonable."

"I'm tired of your orders, Sybil! You are not my mother—you're a scullery maid!"

Sybil reeled as if slapped. "Yes, I am the scullery maid," she said sharply, "but I'm also your friend. I care about you."

Trinity had never used their stations against her before. The sting of it made Sybil pause—but she refused to be bullied into silence.

"This is brought about because of your sinfulness!" Trinity's voice echoed throughout the room.

Thunder cracked overhead as Sybil stepped forward. Lightning lit Trinity's face, twisted in frustration. The wind screamed down the chimney, a cry of warning.

The candlelight flickered violently, casting strange shapes across the stall walls. Something brushed past her mind—cold, ancient, malevolent. Her breath caught in her throat.

Sybil reached up, grasping her throat gently; her voice cracked as she shook her head. "You've never spoken to me like that." Her eyes were wide, pleading. "Don't do this, Trinity. Don't let grief make you cruel."

Trinity threw up her hands, her energy frantic. "I will prove to you and Shaun that I am not mad. I know what... who I saw, and he is very much alive!"

She pushed her fingertips into her forehead. "I need to find Shaun and apologize. I should never have spoken to him so harshly. I can't lose him too."

"That would never happen. He loves you," Sybil said, folding her hands over her heart, which felt like it would burst at any moment.

Trinity's grief was massive. Sybil was sure some deep magic kept her standing—no ordinary soul could survive such sorrow.

"There could be demons on the road," Sybil said.

"I can outride them."

"No, you can't."

Trinity pursed her lips, throwing back her shoulders. "I'll have David accompany me. He has magic, too. He can protect me."

"Trinity, please."

"NO!" Trinity shoved Sybil.

Sybil pulled her air magic into her and was a moment away from using it to contain Trinity, but... she stopped. She closed her eyes briefly, her lips pressed together so tight they hurt.

She could use her air magic. Just one push and Trinity would be grounded and safe. But what then? Trinity would never forgive her. Would Shaun? Would she even forgive herself? And what if it didn't work—what if it only pushed her further away?

Sybil's breath trembled in her throat. The storm outside wasn't nearly as wild as the storm within her.

She breathed deeply through her nose and let out a long, frustrated sigh. Resigned. "Fine! If I can't stop you, I'm going to!"

"Fine!"

"Go get your warm riding cloak, and I'll have David saddle the horses."

With that, Trinity left Sybil alone and walked upstairs.

Sybil flung open the doors and ran towards the stables. The rain struck her like needles, soaking her within seconds. Mud clung to her skirts, and her braid slapped against her back with every step. She nearly slipped as she rounded the corner, but her urgency propelled her forward. The thunder cracked again, so loud it rattled her teeth.

She slammed the stable doors closed behind her. The interior was dim, shadows stretching from a single candle burning in David's back room.

"What is it?" David asked, stepping into the stables from his room.

"She insists we ride to town. Now!"

He pulled her into his arms, and she clung to him, drawing the comfort she always found in his embrace. He was her anchor—her strength.

"You couldn't stop her?" he asked, kissing her forehead.

"I tried. We have no choice. We either tie her up or accompany her!"

"If we stick to the main road and ride hard, we should be fine. You can sense demons. If we're ambushed, I'll fight while you get Trinity out."

"You can't hold off a pack of ghouls alone—and I won't leave you."

"Then we pray the gods carry us safely to York."

Thunder cracked overhead, rattling the stables. The horses stamped and whinnied in their stalls.

Sybil looked up. "They're already spooked. This is a terrible idea."

Little One swooped down, crying out as she landed on a saddle. She flapped her wings, cried again, then darted toward the doors.

A sharp cramp struck Sybil's stomach. Her knees buckled as she gripped her belly with one hand and steadied herself on David's shoulder. "Oh no."

"What's wrong, love? Is it the babies?" David caught her in his arms and steadied her.

She pointed towards Little One, flapping her wings and scratching at the doors. "They're here, David. I can feel them."

He rushed into his room, returning moments later with a warded sword and a knife strapped to his hip.

He handed her a gold-hilted dagger, its curved silver and obsidian blade gleaming.

It had been her mother's blade. A mother she only heard stories about.

"How many?" He asked.

"I'm only sensing two, maybe three. I'm not sure, but no more."

"We can fight two." David kissed her hard and whispered against her lips, "I love you, Sybil. I will always love you."

They stood at the threshold, just inside the stables. The wind howled beyond the wooden doors. Sybil's heart beat loud in her ears. David gripped her hand tighter, and she felt the buzz of energy between them like a silent vow.

They would not fall tonight. They couldn't.

David flung open the doors, and the wind blasted Sybil back a step. She called to it gently, forming a barrier. The air popped, and calm settled around them. Together, they stepped out to face the demons.

The dark-haired twins who'd tried to kill them in York stood across the yard near the manor's doors, waiting. Their long black hair whipped in the wind.

"David, they were waiting for us to come out. Be careful. They are stronger than the others," Sybil said.

She grabbed his hand and began chanting, drawing power from air and earth. It flowed between them, strengthening their bond. This time, they wouldn't run. They had trained for this. They would protect their family—and destroy whatever came for them.

Sybil squared her shoulders, focusing on every ounce of energy. Anger fueled her barrier, but she dared not draw too much—for the babies' sake.

Nicole Moore

Power surged through her like never before. She felt her full potential for the first time—and it thrilled her. The storm only making it stronger. The wind was her ally.

She looked at David, his eyes glowing almost white with the amount of energy he was channeling. He looked at her.

"I love you," she said.

He squeezed her hand tight. "I love you, my darling."

The twin women with black hair walked closer brandishing long silver blades.

We killed him once. We will kill him again. The women's voices rang in Sybil's head.

"Get out of my head!" she screamed, flinging her hands upward. Power surged through her. Electricity danced at her fingertips. She thrust her hand forward—lightning cracked, striking the ground before the women.

They split apart like a river divided. One vanished into shadow. The other, closest to David, clenched her fists—but the barrier held firm this time.

David raised his hands and hurled a blast of orange fire. It hit the woman in the chest, slamming her into the stone wall with a crunch. Slowly, she rose, tossing her hair from her face as if unfazed, the flames doused a moment later.

He's a strong one, she purred into Sybil's mind. Too bad I'll have to kill him.

Then she charged—faster than any human should move, a blur racing toward David.

Sybil didn't think. Instinct took over. She hurled her hands forward—lightning erupted, not once, but

453

repeatedly. Lightning bolts slammed into the woman until her body collapsed, burned to ash and bone.

Sybil dropped to her knees and vomited. She wiped her mouth with a shaking hand. The ash smoldering smelled acrid, electric. She'd never used that much power at once. The storm hadn't just enhanced her magic—it had nearly consumed her. She looked at her hands, still tingling, half-expecting to see them scorched. But the barrier she'd put up was gone. Drained.

Little One swooped down, landing on her shoulder and nuzzling her neck.

"I'm okay," she whispered. "I'm okay."

David stared at her, then the burning remains, then back to Sybil—stunned.

A raw guttural scream, more chilling than the lightning—pierced the yard. The second twin burst from the shadows.

What have you done? Her voice banging in Sybil's mind like a hammer.

Sybil clutched her skull and screamed. Pain blazed through her, sharp and unbearable.

Little One took flight towards the manor.

David ran to Sybil. "What's happening?"

She couldn't open her eyes or speak. The pain blinding.

"Leave her alone!" David bellowed.

The demon lunged before Sybil could react—and she didn't dare strike with magic, not with David in the way. He blasted the demon back with a fire ball giving him enough time to draw his sword.

He fought like he'd always fought—brave, relentlessly. He slashed at her neck, but she was too fast.

Sybil knelt in the mud, frozen.

Then she heard it before seeing the sickening rip of flesh. And David's eyes met hers one last time.

In a blur, the demon tore out his throat and flung it to the ground. His body collapsed after it.

Sybil's scream caught in her throat, strangled by the shock as she crumpled to the ground.

The demon screamed, her hand bloody, standing towering over David's dead body.

Sybil couldn't summon her magic—she'd drained too much. The babies writhed inside her. She knew she was next but couldn't look away from David.

His head lay in the mud, hair soaked, blue eyes lifeless staring wide and empty. A trickle of blood snaked from the corner of his mouth, washed clean by the rain. Sybil's lungs refused to fill. She reached for him with trembling fingers, but her body no longer obeyed.

Memories hit her like falling glass.

His laugh, the way he hummed off-key when brushing her hair from her face, the strength of his arms when holding her through nightmares. His love.

"I'll be with you soon, my love."

The demon turned to her, voice low and venomous. "I will kill you. You filthy witch. You will watch as I pull out your insides."

The demon stalked closer, a predator savoring its kill. Sybil tasted iron on her tongue. Her babies kicked, restless, frightened. She pressed a hand to her stomach and whispered goodbye.

She couldn't win. Not now. But she could die with dignity. Sybil closed her eyes. "Come then, demon."

CHAPTER 40 ~ TRINITY

A scream tore through the night—bone shattering, inhuman.

Trinity burst into her room, her heart thundering. She skidded to the window, flinging open the wooden shutters with shaking hands.

Rain lashed the yard in sheets. A woman stood in the downpour, her long black hair plastered to her pale, twisted face. Rage warped her features as she screamed. Her eyes black—empty, bottomless pits.

Sybil knelt in the mud, clutching her head, her mouth wide in a silent scream. David crouched beside her, his lips moving—saying something. Then he screamed at the demon woman, "Leave her alone!" And sprang to his feet just as the dark-haired woman charged him, swinging a massive sword that looked too heavy for her slim frame. An orange ball of fire flew from David's hand, a moment before he was able to draw his own sword.

"What on earth?" Trinity whispered, closing her eyes and making the sign of her lord over her chest.

Steel clanged against steel. The clash rang out, louder than the thunder cracking above. They moved as twin tempests, blades flashing like lightning, each strike a resounding clap.

She stood frozen.

Then time slowed. She could see every droplet of water falling from the sky. Just for a moment—until the woman lunged forward in a move so fast you would have missed it if you blinked. In a single vicious motion with outstretched clawed fingers, she tore David's throat open.

Trinity screamed. "NO!"

She stumbled back from the window, hands flying to her face. Her breath came in sharp bursts, chest heaving. The scream echoed in her ears, but she forced herself forward again, gripping the windowsill.

David lay motionless in the mud, blood soaking the collar of his shirt. The storm pelted his body with rain. Sybil knelt farther away, frozen, her dress soaked and clinging to her. Mud streaked her arms and hands, which hung uselessly at her sides.

She didn't seem to notice the dark-haired woman standing over David's dead body, letting lose a feral scream of victory.

Little One hooted flew into the window, causing Trinity to stumble back. "What on earth?"

The owl flew to the chest screeching. Trinity covered her ears. "What?"

Agitated, Little One flapped her wings, letting lose another urgent sharp cry.

The sword. A soft female voice sounded inside Trinity's mind.

Little One flapped her wings again, cried once more, then flew out the window.

457

Trinity knew what she needed to do. She wouldn't let her friend die. She snatched the sword from its resting place and bolted from her room.

She thundered down the hallway, breath ragged, heart slamming against her ribs. At the front doors, she halted for half a second—just long enough to draw a deep breath—then flung them open.

Rain slapped her face like a wall. Little One attacked the demon, slashing the woman's eyes with tiny claws. The woman shrieked in fury, flailing wildly, but the owl was too quick, darting and weaving with impossible speed. Protecting Sybil.

"No!" Trinity shouted, racing across the muddy yard, standing in front of Sybil.

Sybil knelt in the mud, head bowed, eyes shut, unmoving. Just beyond them, David's body lay still, his throat a torn ruin. Blood soaked the surrounding earth.

The demon turned.

She froze mid-motion. Their eyes locked, and her face momentarily contorted, not in anger but in confusion—recognition. Her head tilted to the side, and she studied Trinity and the blade she carried. "You."

That hesitation was all Trinity needed. She screamed—a sound torn from her soul—and charged. Grief and fury burst from her in one violent cry as she swung the sword with both hands.

There was a brief moment of utter surprise on the demon woman's face before the blade sliced cleanly through her neck.

A dull thump followed as the body hit the ground. The head rolled into the grass, dark hair slick with rain. For a heartbeat, Trinity stood motionless, staring at what she'd done. It was effortless, like cutting through butter.

The sword slipped from her hands and landed in the mud with a hollow clank.

Thunder cracked overhead, and lightning flared across the sky, bathing the scene in stark white light.

David's body lay sprawled in the mud, his throat nothing but blood and torn flesh. Another body smoldered nearby—reduced to ash and bone. And the last... the one she'd struck down... headless.

She'd done that.

The weight of it was a punch to the chest.

The storm raged on, and for the first time, she felt the cold and relentless rain pouring over her.

Sybil stirred. Her face tilted upward, rain streaming down her cheeks. Her wide, unblinking eyes looked almost black in the shadows, filled with shock and something deeper—surrender.

Trinity didn't hesitate. She crossed the distance and dropped to her knees, pulling Sybil into her arms.

"I'm here. I've got you. I. I. I killed her."

Sybil glanced down at the decapitated body. "She killed David," she mumbled, not as a question but as a statement. A deceleration of disbelief.

Trinity's gaze drifted to where Little One landed—perched silently on David's lifeless arm.

The owl let out a soft hoot.

Sybil staggered to her feet as if pulled by an invisible thread and stumbled to him, arms wrapped around her bulging belly. Trinity couldn't tell if it was rain or tears streaming down her face—maybe both.

Sybil collapsed beside him. She rolled his body gently onto its back, then buried her face in his chest.

Her scream tore through the night—raw and agonizing. It didn't echo; it resonated, vibrating through the rain, mud, and Trinity's bones.

Pain lanced through Trinity's chest as she watched her friend lose the love of her life.

David—the steady one, the anchor—was gone.

Tears welled in Trinity's eyes, blurring her vision. But she would not fall apart. Not now.

The scream would draw attention. Someone would come—perhaps the new servants or, worse, the ones who sent the demons. She had to move. Quickly.

She turned to the manor, then to the stables. Options flashed through her mind—none good, but the delay meant disaster.

"Sybil, we need to get David into the stables."

Sybil didn't move but continued to cradle David in her arms and kiss his face, sobbing, "No, no, no. Please take me instead. Please. Please. Please," she moaned, looking up at the tiny owl. "Bring him back. I know you can. Please," she begged, sobbing.

Little One hooted and flew into the stables, its lower body and claws covered in blood.

Trinity knelt next to Sybil and pulled her arms away from David. "Love, you need to let go."

Sybil stiffened, dropped her arms, and turned her head so fast it almost made Trinity fall backwards. She peered into Trinity's eyes with such raw pain and desperation that it took Trinity's breath away.

"We need to get him inside the stables before anyone comes out here," Trinity whispered. "Come on. I need you to be stronger than you've ever been before."

Trinity rose and extended her hand.

460

Sybil stared at it, dazed as if unsure what it meant. Then, slowly, she reached out. The moment their fingers touched; magic surged between them—wild, overwhelming. The wave of power rushed through her so fast that her vision went dark around the edges.

Trinity gasped and her knees buckled slightly, but she held firm, gripping Sybil's hand as she pulled her upright.

They clung to each other, soaked to the bone, rain pouring down like heaven itself wept.

For one breathless second, Trinity felt something otherworldly—warmth, light, grace. A force that felt... divine.

The touch of an angel. Or God.

***

The night settled around them like ash, heavy and silent in the wake of blood and smoke.

After hiding David in the stables, Trinity moved silently as the shadows—wounded, weary, and without words. Sybil collapsed onto David's bed, trembling, her face pale beneath streaks of grime. Trinity stayed beside her, holding her hand as the girl's body shook from the aftershock of battle and grief. But even as she comforted Sybil, a strange warmth clung to Trinity's skin as if a celestial touch still lingered on her flesh.

The rain stopped, and the stars above blinked softly, veiled by spermatic clouds. Yet something in their distant shimmer called to her soul.

That was the last thing she remembered after slipping into her own bed, tilting her head toward the heavens. Then, darkness folded around her—not the familiar darkness, but a more primal and intense force. The world slipped away.

461

Trinity opened her eyes to the black fog surrounding her. She wore a long, flowing white gown and held her aunt's sword. She pointed it downwards, dragging it behind her. The tip scratched along the stone ground, echoing all around her.

"I see you, princess."

"I'm not a princess."

"You wield the Guardian of Light."

"Who are you?" Trinity turned in a circle. "How come I can't see you? Show yourself."

"You don't want to see me, child. I am one of nightmares and monsters."

"Leave me alone then!" Trinity hefted the sword and ran into the darkness.

"I'm dreaming," she said to herself. "Wake up!" But she couldn't.

"Wake up!" She screamed and clenched her eyes closed.

Trinity's eyelids snapped open. Her entire body thrashed against the bed, seized by violent convulsions that arched her spine until she thought it might snap. Pain shot through her head like lightning. The shaking continued.

She forced herself to breathe. Gaze locked on the wooden mantel above the fireplace. The flames still burned—steady.

Another breath.

The spasms eased gradually. Her limbs settled, and she pressed her palms over her stomach.

Her baby.

Her womb clenched, cramping into a tight, aching knot. For a terrifying moment, she thought the child was coming—but then the pain loosened, and her body began to calm.

"Thank you, God," she whispered.

She sat up slowly, her hands trembling. Her nightgown clung to her like a wet parchment, soaked in cold sweat. Her skin was clammy, and her breath was still shallow.

Firelight glinted off something on the clothes chest beside the bed—the sword. Her aunt's sword. She'd left it there after cleaning the blood from the blade.

It gleamed silver, sparkling in the firelight.

"Seriella," she breathed. "Help me."

She rose, changed into a dry nightgown, and slipped into the adjoining washroom. Her movements were stiff and mechanical, every step dragging through exhaustion.

The night before still haunted her as if a ghost were on her shoulder.

After getting Sybil into David's room—tucked in, quiet if not truly asleep—Trinity ran back into the storm and dragged David's body into the stable. Her arms ached just remembering it. She prayed the entire time no one would come outside. Most of the new servants slept behind the kitchen. Hopefully, they'd stay asleep. But after the screaming... she wouldn't blame them if they woke.

She had to hide the bodies until she found Lenora or Shaun. But touching the dead nearly broke her.

She'd braced herself, expecting David's eyes to snap open or for the charred corpse to reach for her. The scorched bones—what little remained—were easy enough to move. But the decapitated woman...

The moment her hands touched the cold skin, nausea rolled through her so hard she doubled over and vomited. She'd emptied her stomach three times before she dragged the body inside the stables.

She buried the head, the burned remains, and the torso beneath piles of hay in an unused stall. It was all she managed to do.

Then she stood in the stable doorway, staring at David's body.

She could lie. Blame it on wolves. Something brutal and believable. But nothing would erase the truth from her mind.

Tears stung her eyes. A crushing weight settled on her chest. She pulled David's body to the side and covered him with a horse blanket, whispering a prayer through chattering teeth.

Now, she slipped on a cloak and padded swiftly down the stairs and into the courtyard. It reminded a ruined, muddy mess, but there was no sign of blood or the battle.

The sun barely lifted above the horizon, making the grey sky appear blue with pink hues. A blackbird sang from the wall, its song too tender for the silence it broke, each note a cruel reminder that the world had already moved on. The sun would rise and set without David.

She opened the door to the stables, trying not to look at David's covered body, quickly making her way to David's room, expecting Sybil to be asleep.

Instead, she found her sitting on the floor before the small hearth. A blanket cocooned her thin frame, and her eyes stared into the fire as if it held all the answers she no longer knew how to ask.

Trinity sat beside her, pulling her robe tight around her shoulders. The wood crackled, the flames casting warm orange light across their faces. For a moment, neither spoke.

"He's gone," Sybil whispered so softly that it sounded more like a sob. Her eyes were swollen and red, cheeks pink, with wet tear stains.

"I'm so sorry," Trinity said, staring into the fire, but she noticed Sybil clutching her belly. "Are the babies alright?"

"I think so. They've quieted down." Sybil looked up at Trinity. "I can't do this without him." Tears fell in a river, silent. Her eyes pleading.

Trinity knew that pain too well. She wished she could make it better for her, but there was no easy way.

"I couldn't help him," Sybil sobbed. "I used too much of my power too soon. I was weakened. The babies... I felt I was hurting them."

"The lightning?" Trinity asked. She heard the strikes from inside the manor. And the charred corpse lay outside. "That was you?"

"Yes."

"So, you are a powerful witch," Trinity said, more to herself than a question.

"I prefer mage," Sybil let out a sigh. "It doesn't matter."

"I'm sorry I didn't listen to you."

Sybil broke down again, her sobs wracking her entire body. She folded forward; arms wound protectively around her stomach as if trying to shield the babies from her grief.

"This isn't happening. This isn't happening," she whispered over and over, her voice shaking and cracked.

Trinity pulled Sybil into her arms, holding tight and rubbing slow circles on Sybil's back.

"I'm here, love," she murmured. "I'll always be here—for you and the children. I swear it. I'll do

465

everything I can to protect you and the babies. You're not alone."

The words came quickly, but each hit a deeper place inside her, striking truths she hadn't known she carried.

They were bound by loss and something unspoken. Their lives woven together like threads in the same tapestry.

She would do anything for Sybil.

Sybil gave everything to defend the people she loved, even when it shattered her. Trinity would do the same.

Trinity tensed, jaw locking. Her eyes slid shut, but the sound of the demon's voice in her head caused her eyes to snap open.

I'm one of nightmares and monsters.

Not now. She wouldn't let herself unravel. Not when her friend needed her. Not when the world still felt like it might fall apart around them.

She pushed it all away, stuffed it deep, and kept holding on.

"Did you take care of him?" Sybil asked, her eyelids squeezed tightly closed.

"Yes. I'll ride to York and fetch Lenora. She'll know what to do, right?"

"Yes."

"Is she a witch? … I mean a…"

"Yes."

"Shaun?"

"No, he doesn't know, but I've long suspected Isabella does."

Trinity sighed.

Sybil glanced at Trinity. "You are truly blessed, Trinity. I had a vision of you when you first arrived,"

Sybil said, barely a whisper, tears rolling down her face. "You saved me."

"Little One helped."

"Thank you, Trinity."

Trinity hugged Sybil tightly and held her for a long time. "I'll always be here for you."

CHAPTER 41 ~ TRINITY

Trinity secured her horse to the post outside Lenora's apothecary. She hesitated, glancing at the neighboring shop—Shaun's place. The windows were dark, and the door shut. She'd go to him next.

The morning air was thick with the tang of blood and brine drifting from the butchers up the lane, where mud covered the streets and stray dogs nosed through refuse. A fishmonger shouted over the din, hawking salted haddock while a boy scurried past with a basket of bread nearly spilling from his arms.

Shaun and his mother lived above their store, just like Lenora. His family had owned the shop for generations, and now he carried the torch. Trinity admired what he'd built—steady and dependable, even with his teasing smiles and foolish charm. He was a successful merchant.

He and Isabella had kept the shop running through the worst of the plague. By some miracle, his mother had remained untouched.

Trinity's body urged her to rush next door, to throw herself into his arms and tell him everything—but Lenora came first.

Her hands quivered. Her heart thundered like a war drum.

She approached the carved wooden door and knocked. No response. She knocked again—harder.

"I'm coming!" Lenora's voice called from within, gravelly but firm.

A moment later, the door creaked open.

Lenora blinked at her in surprise. A thick robe was cinched tightly around her; a long grey braid hung over her shoulder. "Lady Trinity. What brings you out in this weather? Come in before the sky opens up."

Trinity stepped inside.

"I bring grim news," she said softly. "Evelyn must hear it too."

Lenora's expression tightened as she led Trinity into a sitting room with a fire already crackling to life. She moved slowly toward a cushioned armchair and gestured to the one beside it. "Sit, child."

Trinity adjusting the folds of her black cloak. Her hair was a rough braid, her appearance disheveled—she didn't care. She lowered herself into the seat, the worn cushions sighing under her weight. The scent of dried sage and musty parchment hung in the air—familiar and oddly comforting. The fire popped in the hearth, but she felt no warmth, only the cold dread coiled in her gut.

"David died last night," she said, tearing the bandage off quickly.

Lenora stilled. Her silence stretched too long.

Trinity leaned forward, reaching out to touch her knee. "I'm so sorry."

469

The spell broke. Lenora inhaled sharply and gave a stiff nod. "Tell me everything."

And Trinity did. The demons. The clash. The sword. The rain. The blood. The final scream.

When she finished, Lenora leaned back, unreadable.

"You carry the sword of a seraph," she said at last.

"I suppose I do."

"And you're a traveler."

"I'm not sure what that means." Trinity stiffened, but Lenora raised a hand.

"You are."

A beat passed between them.

"What does it mean?" Trinity asked, voice tight. "What about David? That's why I came. I need help... before someone finds him."

"My daughter's boys will be here soon. They'll fetch Evelyn and assist you."

Trinity pressed her palms to her eyes. Weariness clawed at her.

"How's Sybil?" Lenora asked.

"Shattered. I gave her poppy tea before I left. She didn't sleep, but it calmed her a little."

Lenora exhaled and shook her head. Then her eyes narrowed. "So. You understand who we are."

Trinity met her gaze. "I'm beginning to. It's a lot to take in."

"And do you understand your fate?"

"My fate?" The sword flashed in her mind. Her aunt's final words echoed: A war is coming. Find the others.

"A war is coming," she repeated aloud. "My aunt told me to find the others. I suppose... she meant you?"

Lenora's voice dropped. "The war is already here. We've been fighting it for months. But the last battle—that has yet to come. The Prince of Demons tightens his grip."

Trinity stared.

Lenora waved her hand. "I knew your aunt," she said with a wistful smile. "She was a fierce warrior in her youth. Faithful. We fought side by side until love found her—and peace was her reward."

Trinity shook her head slowly. "She wasn't a witch. She was a devout Catholic. She loved God."

"She did. And she served Him well. She was pious but never judgmental. She always saw the light in others—even when the Church could not."

The words settled on Trinity like wet mud. Ashamed, she looked down at her hands, calloused and still faintly stained with blood. She had judged Sybil and Michael. Harshly.

Trinity's thoughts reeled. Her gentle aunt—a fighter? The woman who could barely carry a basket of herbs? But… the tales she'd told—the one about the saint with the flaming sword.

Guardian of Light.

They hadn't been other's stories. But her own.

"The twins will come this afternoon," Lenora said. "I'll see to David's burial. You're not safe, dear, so take Shaun and return to Ellsworth."

"He doesn't know about any of this," Trinity murmured.

"His mother does. And now, he must. He has a part to play in this war as well."

***

471

Trinity stood outside Shaun's shop, heart racing, stomach clenched. Her hand hovered over the door, uncertain.

The rain had eased, but thick clouds still loomed—low and brooding, ready to burst.

Shame twisted in her chest. She regretted how she'd treated Shaun the last time they spoke. And now, he'd know everything—about Sybil, David, the sword, the war she wasn't ready to face.

He deserved more than an apology. He deserved the truth. And she silently prayed that it wouldn't cost her his friendship.

She squared her shoulders and stepped inside.

Warmth enveloped her like a soft shawl. The scent of leather, beeswax polish, and fig jam clung to the air—cozy and oddly nostalgic. It reminded her of simpler times, before swords, demons, and death.

Shaun stood by the counter, unfurling a bolt of dark green fabric for a young mother, her child clinging shyly to her skirts. He wore a clean frock coat and pressed linen trousers, and his red hair was tied neatly at his neck with a black ribbon.

Still devastatingly handsome—but older now. Sharper. More composed.

He smiled with effortless charm, his presence calming. Trinity understood why women fell for him. His confidence was disarming, his warmth effortless.

She didn't understand why he was unmarried. He'd make a good husband. Then again, she remembered their last conversation—the hurt in his eyes.

Shaun caught sight of her and lifted a hand. "Excuse me," he murmured to the woman, then turned with a courteous bow. "I'll be right with you, m'lady."

Trinity pretending to study the shelves.

472

It had been too long since she shopped for the house. They needed everything—flour, lamp oil, salt, thread—but the coin purse was nearly empty. Owning a grand manor meant little when the pantry echoed, and the hearth ran cold.

She was tired. Bone-deep tired. Tired of scraping by, of tears that never thoroughly dried, of trying to make it one more day.

Her hand rested over her belly. There was still something worth fighting for. She only wished Michael could be there when their child arrived.

Shaun appeared beside her without a sound, startling her. She nearly dropped the small jewelry box she wasn't even looking at.

"Must you move like that?" she snapped; her voice frayed.

He chuckled. "Still jumpy, I see."

Then his face sobered. He reached for her hands, holding them gently, eyes scanning hers. "Are you alright? I'm sorry—for how things ended. I was an idiot."

Trinity pulled away, smoothing her wrinkled gown. Her braid was uneven, her dress tight across her belly, and she felt like a shadow of herself.

"I'm the one who should apologize," she murmured. "I was harsh. You didn't deserve it."

"You don't owe me anything."

"I do. I mean it. You've always been loyal, kind... better than I gave you credit for."

He smiled faintly. "You give me too much credit— but I'll take it."

He pulled a chair from against the wall and offered it to her. "How are you?"

She sank into it with a quiet sigh. "I'm exhausted. The baby's fine... but that's not why I came."

He grabbed another chair and sat beside her. "Listen, I'm sorry. I shouldn't have asked you...I always loved you, Trinity. But I loved Michael, too. I would never have stood between you. I shouldn't have proposed."

"It's alright. I know," she said, giving him a weak smile.

He retook her hand. This time, she didn't pull away—but she went still.

"There were days I wished I could hate him—make it easier on myself. But Michael was impossible not to admire. He was the kind of man who made you feel seen, who believed the best of everyone. Including me. I envied him but I loved him. And when he chose you, I understood. I was just grateful you let me stay close. That was enough."

He let go gently. "Want some warm milk? With honey? You always liked it that way."

"No, thank you. I can't stay long." She drew a breath. "I need you to tell you something. What I'm about to say is... will sound... impossible."

His shoulders stiffened, but he nodded. "Alright."

So, she told him.

All of it.

Seriella. The blade. Her visions. The demons. David's final moments. Sybil's sorrow. Michael—maybe alive, maybe something else entirely.

Shaun didn't speak. He just listened, still and silent, absorbing it all.

When she finished, he leaned back and closed his eyes.

She braced herself—for disbelief, for anger. Neither came.

"I saw Michael too," he said at last.

"What?" Trinity blinked. "He was here?"

The words struck her like a blow. Michael—alive? Her mind reeled. The image of his pale face, still in death, flashed before her eyes. He had died. She had felt it. But then she'd seen him at the market. It was him.

"After I left your house. My horse spooked and threw me. I hit a tree and dislocated my shoulder. Blacked out."

He rubbed the back of his neck. "I thought I was dreaming. But Michael found me. Got me home. When I woke up, I was in bed. No bruises. No pain. My shoulder—completely healed."

"That's not possible."

"He said… it's something he can do now. He's not alive, not really. He said he felt nothing. No warmth. No pain. But I don't believe that. If he truly felt nothing, why save me?"

"Then why not come to me?" Trinity whispered, voice cracking.

"I don't know. He was shaken. Confused. He said anyone who knew he'd returned would be in danger. Even me. He begged me not to tell you."

Shaun looked away, a hand covering his mouth. "I'm sorry, Trinity. I didn't know what to do."

They sat in silence, the truth settled like dust in the space between them. Outside, the rain began again—light at first, then steady. Footsteps passed, muffled by the storm.

Shaun rose, still holding her hand. "It's going to pour again. You should go back to the manor."

"Lenora asked for you to accompany me, as it's not safe," Trinity said. "Lenora's arranging David's funeral."

He nodded. "Of course. Mother can ride with Lenora and Evelyn. And I'll send supplies to Ellsworth," he added. "Let me speak with mother then we'll depart."

He met her gaze, steady and sure. "Whatever's coming—I'm with you. Always."

CHAPTER 42 ~ SYBIL

Sybil moved as if through water—slow, heavy, numb.

Trinity and Elizabeth held her upright, one on either side, arms hooked gently through hers. But Sybil barely noticed. Her legs carried her forward on instinct alone, and her feet may as well have belonged to someone else. Each step echoed in her bones like a hollow drumbeat. Her arms hung at her sides, limp and brittle as dead branches.

Beside her, Trinity kept a steady rhythm, jaw tight, shoulders tense with the effort of holding her friend together. On the other side, Elizabeth offered quiet strength, her touch gentle but grounding.

Behind them, Lenora walked slowly, keeping Evelyn close, her arm around her waist. Jacob on her other side, an arm around her shoulders. Enzo, Luca, and Nicholas followed in solemn silence; their boots muffled on the damp ground. Shaun and his mother, Isabella, trailed close behind.

Sybil tried to lift her gaze, to take in the mourners gathering around them, but her neck resisted, and her head felt weighted down by stones. The faces blurred in her periphery—figures more than people, shadows moving in the fog.

It seemed as if all of York had come to say goodbye.

Members of the coven had gathered, too. For one brief moment, Sybil caught sight of Ailith standing to the side, her eyes wet, though no tears fell. Everyone bowed their heads as she passed, a gesture of reverence that hit her harder than words ever could.

"Wolf attack," she'd heard people whisper.

It rolled through the crowd like a breeze through wheat.

But the truth was louder in her mind—words spoken not long ago by a hag with a voice like wind through brittle bones. *You must protect your wife at all costs—even if it is with your life.*

David had listened. And he had obeyed.

The weight of that vow pressed into her chest. A slow, burning ache climbed up her throat, and nausea twisted her insides.

She clenched her lips together, trying to hold it back. In through her nose, out through her mouth—each breath more difficult than the last. Her limbs trembled as if her bones themselves mourned him.

Trinity's voice brushed her ear. "It's alright. We can stop if you need to."

Sybil couldn't speak. She couldn't even nod. Her muscles locked; her body froze mid-breath. The procession halted behind her in quiet solidarity.

Rain, once relentless, had eased into a gentle mist. It drifted down like a veil, softening the edges of the stone path and the gravestones ahead.

Sybil exhaled, eyes screwed shut, as a low, fractured moan broke from her lips. It wasn't a sob—it was deeper, fractured. It ripped from the depths of her being, from the place where David had lived inside her. Her twin flame had been snuffed out, and she only wanted to follow him into the dark.

Memories rose unbidden.

David's arms around her, pulling her close at night. The sound of his heartbeat beneath her ear. The faint scent of hay and cloves lingered on his skin. Their wedding in the meadow—moonlight spilling through green leaves, friends and family laughing all around them.

They were supposed to grow old together.

"Why?" she whispered through gritted teeth. "Why did you take him? We were happy."

A soft hoot pierced the silence.

Her eyes flew open. She scanned the sky, frantic. Her gaze landed on the gate tower. There, perched on the stone ledge, sat Little One. Silent. Still. Watching.

"Why?" Sybil cried. "He was mine!" Her knees gave out, and she crumpled to the ground. Her voice broke into a sob. "He was supposed to be a father…" Strong arms lifted her, one under her legs, the other around her back. She didn't resist.

"I've got you," said a deep, gravelly, and kind voice. Jacob.

She rested her head against his broad shoulder, letting his warmth soak her frozen skin. "She. took. him. from. me," the words came out fractured in between sobs. Tears ran freely now. She stopped trying to hold them back. Her body went slack in Jacob's embrace.

She didn't know where they were going. She didn't care. All she knew was that Little One had failed. The owl sent to protect them had watched David die.

It had all been for nothing.

Another distant hoot.

Then something shifted inside her. A cold wind swept through her chest, and a voice—no louder than a thought—echoed in her mind.

Your hate is misdirected, my child. I mourn with you. Had I intervened, you would have died in his place. And the gods have chosen your children. Do not resent the price David paid. He understood.

The message sent a chill through her spine. Every part of her went rigid. For a moment, she couldn't breathe.

Jacob's hand rubbed her arm, grounding her. His warmth slowly returned her to the present.

"Leave me alone," she whispered under her breath, barely able to form the words. "I want nothing to do with you or your gods.

"What's that, love?" Jacob asked, gently shifting her in his arms.

She pressed her forehead into his collarbone. "Thank you," she murmured.

"You're welcome, child."

When he stopped walking, she didn't want to move. His arms reminded her of David's—solid, safe, steady. She could almost pretend she hadn't lost everything.

But pretending wouldn't bring him back.

"We're here," Jacob said softly. "I'm going to set you down now."

She gave a faint nod.

He lowered her carefully to the ground. Her feet met the earth like anchors, too heavy to lift again. As Jacob released her, two more sets of arms wrapped around her.

"I'm here," Trinity whispered. "I'm not going anywhere."

Elizabeth stepped in on the other side. "You're not alone, Sybil. Not ever."

Still, Sybil kept her eyes shut. The world beyond her lashes felt too cruel, too real. But she had to face it.

She took a trembling breath and forced her eyes open. The scene sharpened slowly, the mist parting to reveal the waiting priest and the simple wooden coffin beside a freshly dug grave.

David's final resting place.

Trinity had told her Susana chose the plot herself—secluded, near the edge of the family burial grounds. A quiet, thoughtful place. She had insisted on a priest, even though Sybil had no care for prayers anymore. The goddess had taken her husband. What comfort could holy words offer now?

The priest began to speak, voice low and rhythmic. The words floated over her, almost surreal beneath the soft rainfall. A shaft of sunlight broke through the clouds, casting golden beams across the droplets. For one strange, painful moment—it looked like heaven was weeping.

Then the men stepped forward to lower the casket. And something inside her snapped.

Sybil fell to her knees, her cry breaking the solemn quiet like a crack of thunder. The air thickened around her, crackling with the strain of her grief. She clawed at the wet earth as if she could stop the coffin from descending.

"No. No, no, please—don't take him!"

She bent forward, gasping through sobs. Her chest burned. "How do I live without you?"

Strong hands pulled her back.

She squeezed her eyes shut and saw him—*his lopsided grin, those brilliant blue eyes, the crook in his nose.* Every inch of him carved into her memory.

"Take me with you," she whispered.

Then, in the silence of her mind, she heard him.

Sybil, I'm not in that box.

She froze.

Listen to me, love. I'm still with you. You must be strong—for our children. Love them enough for both of us.

It sounded like him. Too much like him. Her chest heaved; her heart tore open again.

"I can't," she sobbed. "I can't do this without you."

The scream that followed tore through her like lightning, cleaving out anything left in her lungs or her heart. She collapsed, lungs burning, heart breaking and hands grasping at the soil, trembling.

Time blurred.

She wasn't sure how long she knelt there, but the grave was nearly filled when she opened her eyes. Dirt covered the wood.

Covered him.

Forever.

She stayed where she was, mud soaking into her dress, tears carving clean tracks down her cheeks. Trinity and Elizabeth knelt beside her, arms still wrapped around her shoulders, their faces wet with sorrow.

A gust of wind rushed through the cemetery, sending leaves tumbling across the ground. The mist swirled, cloaking the mourners in a grey veil.

Some coven stood with heads bowed, eyes closed, whispering silent blessings or prayers to the goddess. Others kept their eyes fixed on Sybil, hearts breaking as they watched her fall apart piece by piece.

Jacob shifted on his feet, uneasy. He exchanged a glance with Lenora, whose lined face looked etched in stone, her usual fire dimmed by sorrow. Even Evelyn, who had cried quietly the whole way there, now clung to Lenora's cloak and stared wide-eyed at Sybil.

They didn't speak. They didn't need to.

Three women. Three widows. And children who would grow up never knowing their fathers.

Sybil's belly tightened suddenly, a sharp squeeze that made her flinch. Then came warmth. Wetness.

She gasped and clutched her stomach, eyes wide with panic. "Trinity…"

Trinity turned to her instantly, face pale. "What is it?"

Sybil looked down, breath shallow. "I think—I think it's time."

"We have to get you inside."

Sybil's breath came fast and shallow. "It's too soon," she whispered, though she wasn't sure if she meant the baby or David's death.

Elizabeth touched her shoulder, worry tightening her expression. "We need to go, Sybil. Come on. Lean on us."

"I can't," she murmured.

"You can," Trinity said more firmly. "For the babes, you will."

Sybil nodded faintly, and they helped her to her feet, one on each side. The group began to move, urgency pushing against grief. Shaun had already broken from the crowd and pulled a cart towards them. He waved to

483

Enzo and Luca, who sprinted to help. They reached the cart just as the sky finally opened up again. Rain fell hard and steady, soaking cloaks and hair within moments. Shaun and Luca lifted Sybil into the cart, wrapping her in their cloaks while Elizabeth and Trinity climbed in beside her.

The ride back to the manor was muddy and uneven. Each jolt sent pain through Sybil's body, her hands clutching her swollen belly. It contracted again, pain spearing through her. She screamed and clutched Trinity and Elizabeth's hands.

As they passed the gate, Sybil's eyes lifted again to Little One, still perched above. This time, the owl did not look away. It simply blinked, solemn and still, as if standing vigil.

I have a gift for you, a female voice said in Sybil's head.

"Little One?" She mumbled, confused.

And then, amid the haze of pain and exhaustion, another memory returned.

It was late summer a few years before. She and David snuck away to the orchard after supper, escaping the noise of the house. The sunset bathed the sky in gold and lavender. They lay on the grass with their fingers entwined, watching the clouds shift overhead.

"What do you think heaven looks like?" she asked.

David chuckled. "Exactly like this. Only warmer. And quieter. With better food."

She laughed, teasing him. But then he turned serious. "Wherever it is, I'll wait for you there. You know that, right?"

"I know," she whispered, nestling closer.

That memory returned now with such force that it took her breath away. Tears rolled down her cheeks, mixing with the rain.

484

Little One opened her wings and flew towards the manor.

The cart pulled through the gates of Ellsworth Manor just as thunder rumbled overhead. Enzo ran ahead to open the doors, and Jacob lifted Sybil from the cart.

Every few minutes, a contraction halting any progress. Bent inwards, pain and more pain drowning her. Something was terribly wrong.

They finally got her to Trinity's old bedchambers, stripped off the wet garments, and wrapped her warmly under a heavy wool blanket.

Elizabeth brewed tea laced with calming herbs. Lenora appeared moments later, pulling vials from her satchel, her face set with grim determination.

The labor had begun, and everyone knew what she'd already determined. It wasn't going as planned.

Trinity sat by her side, gripping her hand, whispering prayers.

Sybil gritted her teeth against the pain, every contraction pulling something deeper from her. She felt as though she were being split in two—not just by the baby's arrival, but by grief and life colliding in the same breath.

Outside, the storm howled.

Inside, Sybil fought to hold on.

"David," she whispered. "Help me."

And in that moment, she swore she felt him. A warmth surrounded her belly, and her next breath came easier. Not painless, but bearable. She clutched Trinity's hand and pushed forward into the night—into the birth of something new. Into the world, he had died to protect.

485

CHAPTER 43 ~ TRINITY

Sybil screamed, her back arching off the bed, hand clamped around Trinity's hand in a crushing grip. Trinity winced but didn't let go.

"I'm here. It's going to be alright," she whispered, though the words felt empty. The air hung heavily in the room, thick with sweat, blood, and fear. Each breath tasted like desperation.

Too much blood was pooling beneath Sybil's bottom. Something was terribly wrong.

She turned to Lenora, who'd finished examining Sybil and wiped her bloody hands on her apron. The older woman's face was palled grey. Her lips were pressed into a hard line, and her brow furrowed with more than concentration.

"What is it?" Trinity asked, a voice barely above a whisper.

"One of the babes is breech," Lenora said flatly. "If I don't cut them out now, Sybil will die. And so will they."

Trinity staggered back, hand flying to her mouth. "Dear God, no…" Her voice cracked. Cut them out. It was a death sentence.

"All shall survive if I have any say in the matter," Lenora snapped, reaching for her satchel.

The conviction in her voice should have reassured Trinity—but it didn't.

She stared, unmoving her feet planted like stone.

"Do you understand, child?" Lenora barked.

Trinity jolted out of her daze. "Yes," she gasped, sitting at Sybil's side and clutching her hand.

Her pulse roared in her ears. She had never heard of a woman surviving that. It always ended the same—both mother and child died before the doctor could even close the wound.

A sense of urgency replaced the earlier grief. The silence that had once honored David's memory was now filled with commands, movement, the rustle of fabric, and Sybil's cries.

Lenora spun around to Elizabeth, "I know you want to be here for her…"

"I am not leaving!" Elizabeth lifted her chin and squared her shoulders, but no one ever won a battle of wills with Lenora.

"I need you to help me."

"Oh."

"You need to boil as many pots of water as you can and gather as much linen as possible."

"Yes, of course," Elizabeth consented, turning to leave at once.

Lenora huffed a breath and worked quickly, assisted by Evelyn, who looked pale but steady.

"Ailith shut the door and lock it. Jacob. Shaun. Hold Sybil down," Lenora said sharply.

Trinity hadn't realized they were there. Everyone moved at once.

Both men braced Sybil's shoulders and legs. She writhed beneath them, incoherent with pain.

Lenora poured a dark liquid into a chipped wooden cup and brought it to Sybil's lips. "Drink. It'll take the pain away and make you sleep."

Sybil took a shallow sip. The bitter herbal concoction twisted her face in disgust.

Lenora pressed a thick piece of wood between Sybil's teeth. "Bite down. Even with the drought, this will hurt. We can't wait."

Lenora leaned close, clutching Sybil's hand in one of hers, the other holding a gleaming knife.

"You listen to me," she said, voice low, steady, and merciless. "I won't apologize for what I'm about to do. But you and your babies shall live. Do you understand?"

Sybil locked eyes with her grandmother and gave a faint nod. She squeezed her eyelids closed and bit down hard on the wood.

Trinity focused on Shaun standing next to her. "Trinity, don't watch, keep your eyes on me," he said softly staring into her eyes, holding her gaze. Steady.

Lenora didn't wait a moment longer. With surgical precision, she made the first incision, slicing into the taut, swollen skin of Sybil's belly.

A fresh scream tore from Sybil's throat, muffled only by the wood between her teeth. Her body twitched and convulsed once, then went still, her consciousness slipping under from the pain.

Lenora's hands worked fast and steadily despite the sweat trailing down her temples. Evelyn handed her clean towels, a bowl of hot water, and another blade.

Trinity kept her gaze locked onto the faces of those around her. Not Sybil's belly. She couldn't look.

Shaun whispered prayers under his breath, eyes wet, jaw clenched.

The room pulsed with dread.

But still—Lenora worked. Steady. Unyielding.

She would not lose them. Not after everything they'd survived.

Not being able to resist, she dared a glance at Sybil's belly—and the sight hit her like a blow. A wave of dizziness surged through her, bile rising hot and bitter in her throat. As she staggered backward, desperate to escape the grotesque tangle of innards and bloody flesh, the room spun around her. Her knees buckled. Darkness closed in. Trinity collapsed in a graceless heap, swallowed by the void before she hit the floor.

***

Trinity could still hear the echo of Sybil's scream even as the darkness swallowed her.

When she came to, everything was blurry. Warm hands cradled her, and the sensation of movement grounded her back in the present. Shaun carried her across the room, holding her like she weighed nothing. His eyes—so painfully blue—looked down at her with a tenderness that hurt more than comforted.

Guilt twisted in her chest. She cared for him, loved him even—but not in the way he longed for. Not the way he deserved.

The sound of voices broke through the haze. Lenora and Evelyn whispered nearby, low and urgent. A baby was crying, and another sound—a faint melody, soft as breath—drifted through the air.

A song?

489

"Put me down," Trinity murmured. "I'm fine. I can stand."

Shaun obeyed, sitting her gently in a chair near the window. She stood on shaking legs, willing her strength to return, and walked slowly back to the bed.

What she saw next froze her in place.

Jacob remained a statue beside Sybil's still form, his expression unreadable, his jaw clenched, and his eyes rimmed with red.

On the bed, two newborns—bundled in thin blankets, squirming, crying. Lenora and Evelyn placed them side by side, their cries sharp and alive.

Lenora reached into Sybil's open abdomen. Her arm disappeared deeper, and when it came back out, she held a third child. Smaller. Half the size of the others. Limp.

No breath. No cry.

Trinity gasped. Her hands locked over her chest like she could hold her heart together.

Sybil lay unconscious, her face pale and waxen, lips tinged blue. Blood soaked the bed beneath her—far too much.

Evelyn took the tiny baby and placed her gently on her back. Tilting the head, she covered the baby's mouth with her own and breathed for her.

"Come on," Evelyn whispered between breaths. "Come on, little one."

Lenora bent beside her. "Enough. Let me."

"I can get her to breathe," Evelyn insisted, voice cracking as tears spilled down her cheeks.

"She needs more than breath," Lenora said gently. "Step aside."

Evelyn hesitated before moving.

Lenora laid both hands over the infant's chest, closed her eyes, and began to sing. It was unlike anything Trinity had ever heard. Low and reverent, it shimmered through the room like ripples on still water.

A chill rolled across Trinity's skin. "What are you doing?" she whispered.

She still wrestled with fear—fear of what they were and of what this power meant.

"She's opening the baby's lungs," Evelyn replied quietly. "Helping her breathe."

"But… she isn't alive."

"The soul hasn't left," Evelyn said. "The body only needs a little more time to awaken."

Shaun stepped beside them, his face pale. "Is it safe?"

"Completely. If it works, she'll live," Evelyn said, watching Lenora closely.

Silence fell.

Trinity held her breath, every heartbeat a drumbeat of dread.

Lenora didn't stop singing.

After several long moments, she leaned forward and breathed into the baby's mouth again.

And this time, the child's chest lifted on its own.

A pink hue slowly replaced the mottled purple of her skin. Then came a sound—slight at first, then stronger—a cry.

A loud wail filled the room.

Relief broke through Trinity's chest like a tidal wave. "Thank God," she exhaled, sobs shaking her chest.

Little One swooped in from the open window and landed on her shoulder, hooting softly into her ear. She reached up, stroking the tiny owl's feathers, her heart racing.

491

Lenora carefully wrapped the baby and placed her between her two siblings on the bed. Turning to Shaun, she said, "Fetch Ailith. We need her now."

He didn't ask questions. He turned and sprinted out of the room.

Lenora and Evelyn returned to Sybil. Her chest barely moved. The blood still flowed.

Trinity stood helpless; eyes locked on the gaping wound in her friend's abdomen. Logic told her Sybil couldn't survive such damage. The blood loss alone should have killed her.

But Lenora was already threading a needle, her hands covered in crimson as she began stitching the wound shut. Evelyn pressed fresh towels against the bleeding, her face pale but focused.

The sound of the babies' cries pulled Trinity back. She rushed to the bedside and scooped the smallest one into her arms. A girl. The child's cry softened as she held her close, rocking gently.

"Shhh… it's alright now," she murmured, voice trembling.

Jacob picked up one of the others and cradled it against his chest. He smiled at Trinity through the tears in his eyes.

"I have a grandchild," he said, wonder in his voice.

Moments later, the door opened. Ailith entered, Shaun on her heels. She locked the door behind her.

Lenora looked up from her work. "We need your help to finish this."

Ailith moved swiftly to Sybil's side. Evelyn and Lenora placed their hands over the stitched wound. Ailith joined them, fingers steady as she closed her eyes.

The three of them sang. A song more profound and enchanting than anything Trinity ever heard before.

She inched closer, holding the baby, mesmerized by what she saw.

A barely perceptible glow pulsed from beneath their palms. The wound, still leaking blood moments ago, began to seal. The skin grew firm and pink, the edges knitting together beneath the stitches. The bleeding slowed and stopped completely.

Sybil's color returned. Her breaths, once shallow and faltering, became steadier.

Trinity's mouth parted in disbelief. Her gaze moved between the women and the miracle they had wrought. "How...?"

The three women opened their eyes and looked at one another, faces drawn but serene. Their bond was unmistakable—an unspoken language of trust, love, and years of sacred work together.

"Will she live?" Trinity asked, stepping closer.

Lenora nodded. "She'll recover. She's stronger than she looks—but she'll need rest. The inner tissue still needs healing. No standing. No lifting. At least two weeks."

She gently opened each blanket to examine the infants—two boys and one girl. They were all healthy, pink, and breathing strongly.

Shaun, standing nearby, dipped a cloth into a bowl of cool water and wiped Sybil's forehead.

"She looks peaceful," he said softly.

"The herbs I gave her will keep her asleep for several hours," Evelyn explained, wiping her hands clean. "It's best this way. The pain would be unbearable."

She turned to Trinity. "Please inform the others that the babies are safe. And fetch Elizabeth. We'll need her help here now. The children must be fed."

Trinity nodded and handed the little girl to Shaun. He cradled her awkwardly, arms unsure what to do with such a fragile thing.

"Am I doing this right?" he asked, his expression a mix of panic and humor.

Trinity managed to smile. "You're doing fine."

She turned to leave as Little One fluttered from her shoulder to the window, perching silently on the sill.

***

Trinity pulled a chair beside Sybil's bed. Full-bellied and asleep, the babies finally lay quiet in their wooden bassinets, nestled near the fire for warmth. Sybil insisted they remain close to her. She turned her head and reached out a trembling hand. Trinity took it, their fingers interlacing.

"Shaun is adorable with them," Sybil whispered with a faint smile.

"He'll make a wonderful father one day." Trinity smiled.

Sybil arched a brow. "He'd make a fine father to your child."

Trinity winced and looked away. "Please don't. I care for him deeply, but I won't marry him."

"Well," Sybil said, "he and Isabella leave for town with Lenora in the morning. Speak with him before he goes. You're still friends, Trinity. You both need each other."

"I have," she said, gently squeezing Sybil's hand before leaving. "We spoke in town. All is forgiven."

"I can't fight this war with you anymore," Sybil said quietly.

Trinity paused. "Perhaps it's over." Her words came out more like hope than certainty.

Sybil's voice cracked. "It's not. The Prince of Demons is in York. He won't stop until we're all gone."

Something cold twisted in Trinity's chest. She shut her eyes and inhaled deeply, releasing it slowly, forcing herself to remain calm.

"I wish I'd told you sooner. Prepared you better," Sybil whispered, the regret heavy in her tone.

Trinity hesitated and reached for her again. "I don't have magic, Sybil. I have the sword but no power. Not like you."

"You do," Sybil said, firm now. "There's no more time for you to deny it. Trust me. Trust Lenora."

She did. Trinity knew Sybil would die to protect her, as David had. Her trust ran deeper than doubt.

"I'll do whatever I can," she vowed.

"Good. Listen closely. Under the floorboard beneath my bed, you'll find my grandmother's grimoire. Please bring it to Lenora. She'll guide you."

***

The grimoire lay open on Lenora's lap, its pages aged, and ink faded but legible. Trinity sat beside her on the stable bench, the sword resting across her knees like a slumbering beast. The stable doors were barred from the inside. She didn't want anyone to stumble upon what they were doing.

Little One perched high above a beam, hooted softly. Her head tilted left and right like she was listening.

"Your aunt had power," Lenora said. "But it was channeled through the sword."

"I didn't feel anything when I used it."

"Because you haven't summoned it properly. The spirit of the seraph resides in that blade. Only the chosen can call it forth."

"Seriella?"

"Yes."

"And you're sure I'm the one?"

"Only you can be sure," Lenora said plainly.

Trinity groaned. "Wonderful."

Lenora patted her knee. "Pick up the sword."

She stood; her cloak heavy on her shoulders. Grasping the hilt, she lifted the weapon and held it out in front of her, its weight far lighter than it looked.

"I don't even know how to hold it," she muttered.

"You don't have to. Seriella will show you."

"I'm not ready."

Lenora snapped, "If you'd come to me earlier, you would be."

Trinity's guilt burned hotter than the fire. "I'm sorry."

The sword wobbled awkwardly in her grip.

Lenora bent over the book, reading with a furrowed brow. She flipped a page and traced a line with her finger. "Here. This is where you begin. Repeat after me."

Trinity blinked at the strange symbols. "Is that French?"

Lenora scoffed. "Of course not. Follow my lead. Sound it out exactly."

They tried once. Twice. Three times. Nothing happened.

"No, not like that! Roll the Rs, lengthen the vowels!" Lenora demanded.

Minutes turned to an hour. Trinity's arms burned. Her feet ached. Her voice grew hoarse.

"It's not 'Uh.' It's 'Oh!'" Lenora barked.

Trinity's patience shattered. "I've had enough! It's not working! Perhaps I'm not meant to do this." Part of her wanted that to be true.

"Stop being a coward," Lenora snapped. "Your aunt was never this soft."

"Soft?" Trinity's voice cracked as she blinked several times. She threw the sword down with a clatter and screamed. "I've survived more than you'll ever understand! I am not a coward!"

"Prove it. Pick it up. Summon the fire."

"You do it!"

Lenora calmly closed the book. "It's not mine to wield. You are chosen. And chosen ones suffer, Trinity. We survive because we must. Pain makes us stronger—unbreakable. That's the bond we share with the divine. Do you think that angels do not feel our pain? Or grief? Do you not believe that they take all of it from us in times of need and carry it themselves so that we may survive?"

"Of course."

"Your aunt understood this. She was a warrior of God."

Trinity's anger broke into tears. "My aunt wasn't a warrior. She was kind. Gentle."

"She was both. And far stronger than you ever realized. She would want you to stand. To fight."

"I miss her," Trinity whispered. A single tear tracked down her cheek.

"Then honor her. Pick up the sword."

Trinity knelt. Her fingers curled around the cool hilt. The handle pulsed in her grip.

"Close your eyes this time."

She obeyed.

"Now… breathe. Let the blade become familiar—like an extension of your arm. Let go of doubt. Of grief. Loss. And allow the words to come."

Trinity spoke the chant once. Then again. A third time.

Nothing happened.

She squeezed her eyes closed, tears welling, frustration eating her from within. "I can't."

"Try again," Lenora's voice caused her to jump.

She lifted the sword, blew out a breath and concentrated harder than ever before. Emptying her mind completely.

The chant fell from her lips easily now. Over and over again, until Trinity was sure it wasn't working.

Then, finally her palms tingled. The hilt warmed. Heat spread through her arms. A strange pressure kissed her cheeks.

She opened her eyes.

Blue flames danced across the blade, swirling and bright. The fire didn't burn. It welcomed her.

"I did it," she whispered, stunned.

"You are the chosen one," Lenora said, her voice reverent. "And now you fight."

CHAPTER 44 ~ MICHAEL

Michael stood motionless among hundreds—men and women, legionnaires like him, inside a vast, empty warehouse stinking of mildew. Shadows stretched across every wall. The eclipse offered no light, and thick clouds swallowed any hint of starlight. Rain peppered the roof, rhythmic and constant, masking the presence of so many in the dark.

No torch flickered. No breath stirred the silence.

They didn't need light. Or warmth. Or food. Legionnaires no longer suffered from mortal discomfort. Hunger, exhaustion, pain—all gone. Their altered bodies endured everything. And so, they waited—silent and still—for hours.

Tonight, they would strike. The darkest night. The night of an eclipse.

Michael shifted slightly, his gaze sweeping across the line of soldiers near him. His eyes landed on Julian—his companion and unwilling confidant. Next to Julian stood Fleur, now a permanent member of their trio.

499

Her mother determined to follow through on her wish that him and Fleur would be together.

A knot coiled in Michael's gut.

Fleur barely resembled the woman she once was. Whatever beauty she once possessed had twisted into something predatory—her features sharpened, her expression hollow and cruel.

There was a time he wished she'd smile. Before...

Now, that mocking smile never left her face, stretched thin with hunger and malice. Her eyes shimmered with venomous delight, always watching him and waiting like a snake coiled to strike—or inviting him to do it first.

And he would. Soon.

They hadn't exchanged a word in days. He had nothing to say for now.

The silence between them was razor thin, a fragile truce ordered by Baal and sustained only by mutual necessity. But Michael was done playing by rules, not his own. Before she died, he would extract the truth—whatever foul secrets she kept buried under that smug expression.

Since arriving in York, they'd lived in shadow, stalking the witches with tireless precision. Every alley, every rooftop, every sanctuary had been charted and reported. Baal knew their sanctuaries, their hiding places, beds, even their most sacred groves.

They thought themselves safe.

They were wrong.

No one would survive the night.

A whisper brushed the edges of his mind— slithering, oily. Familiar.

I sense your restlessness, Michael. Do you long for this to be finished? Do you yearn to abandon this place?

Baal's voice threaded into his thoughts like smoke through a keyhole.

Michael stiffened but didn't respond immediately. He focused on silence—on emptiness.

Too slow.

Ah… Lady Trinity. And the child she carries.

Michael clenched his jaw, but his face remained a mask. He had to do better. Julian had shown him mental shields, but they were fragile, like glass under pressure. Not enough to keep Baal out.

She will die before dawn. You will be free of her.

The words hit like a blade to the chest. Still, Michael exhaled slowly, offering no visible reaction.

Thank you, m'lord, he replied silently, bowing his head as all the others did.

Baal stepped forward, facing his army. He lifted his arms. No sound passed between his lips. Instead, his presence surged into every mind at once—a crushing weight, a shared invasion. His message was simple and soaked in blood.

Burn them out. Rip them apart if they flee. Let none live.

The warehouse doors groaned as they swung open.

A gust of cold air swept through the ranks.

Go now, my warriors. Claim your victory.

Michael turned with the others, stepping into the rain, and the storm swallowed them.

***

When Michael arrived in front of Lenora's Apothecary and Shaun's home, flanked by Julian and Fleur, the alley was bedlam—smoke, fire, and steel clashing among screams and grunts.

Julian had brought him here on purpose. Michael knew it. It was a test—a cruel, deliberate one. Baal wanted to see if he could kill Lenora—the woman who helped raise him like a grandson.

Michael's memories pressed at the edges of his mind: the scent of sage in Lenora's shop, her hands rough from years of brewing tinctures, the way she'd once tucked a blanket around his shoulders during a fever.

And now, he was supposed to kill her. Betrayal curdled in his gut like poison.

She stood at the center of the chaos, surrounded by half a dozen witches. Her grey braid caught flashes of firelight, her blade steady in one hand. Beside her was a blonde woman who looked hauntingly like Sybil. She had no weapon—just both palms open, raised in quiet defiance. Around them, cloaked legionnaires crept closer, black hoods shadowing what little humanity remained in their faces.

Then the door to Shaun's building blew open. Smoke poured out in a choking column. Shaun emerged, supporting his mother, Isabella, as she wheezed and choked in his arms. Her body sagged, and he lowered her to the ground, shielding her with his frame.

"Get back!" Lenora shouted. "Nicholas—protect Isabella!"

A tall young man stepped forward from the shadows—Nicholas. Michael didn't know him, but there was something familiar about him. He drew twin curved swords and handed one to Shaun.

"You know how to use it?" he asked.

Shaun nodded without looking away from the encroaching legionnaires. "Well enough."

502

"They're not human," Nicholas said calmly.

The air snapped with movement. Two legionnaires launched forward, blades flashing like dark fire. But as they met the witches' swords, they erupted in shrieks— cut down in a burst of holy light.

"What in the name of Lucifer?" Fleur hissed, recoiling.

"Don't move!" Julian barked. "They're wielding warded black obsidian. It can kill us."

Michael's blood ran cold. "Obsidian?"

Julian nodded, glancing side long. "Consecrated by the old gods."

The blonde woman radiated with a blinding glow. It wasn't gentle but searing, divine, as if the sun had descended to earth in feminine form. Her radiance stripped the shadows from the alley, exposing every demon's twisted face.

Michael flinched.

The legionnaires in front of her screamed as their skin blackened and cracked, their bodies curling inward like burning leaves.

Her light continued to pulse, humming with an ancient rhythm that made Michael's ears ring. It scorched the legionnaires, peeling the skin away like wax. The scent of burning skin, hair and sulphur filled the air. Yet she stood untouched.

More demons poured into the alley. A siege unfolding—but the witches stood their ground.

Lenora raised her voice in chant, joined by several others, their voices building into something primal. A wave of power surged, unseen but tangible, slamming into the attackers and driving them back. The blonde woman lifted her arms again, and light burst from her, wrapping the witches in a brilliant dome. Every demon who neared it hissed and burned.

Swords gleamed like fire. Smoke rolled through the alley, thick and choking. One by one, the legionnaires fell back—screaming, clawing at their heads as if something inside them ruptured.

"Return to hell!" Lenora cried; her obsidian blade raised high.

Some demons turned to flee. Others clutched their skulls and dropped, writhing in agony before their heads burst like overripe fruit. Lenora and the others struck quickly, severing limbs and heads with grim efficiency.

Julian melted into the shadows. "We're outmatched."

"Baal will know we fled!" Fleur shouted, grabbing his arm. "He'll kill us!"

"Then keep him out of your mind!" Julian snarled. "Or stay behind and die. I'm not wasting myself on this folly."

He vanished into the smoke. Fleur followed a second, leaving Michael behind.

Michael lingered. Shaun was lifting Isabella, aided by the blonde woman. Behind them, the fires climbed higher, eating through wood and stone. Lenora and her companion raised their arms and began to chant again.

A watery mist rose like a ghost, coiling around their ankles before lifting into the air. Millions of large droplets condensed mid-air, forming orbs of water that hovered for a heartbeat before smashing into the flames. Smoke curled, hissing in protest. One building groaned, its roof sagging. Still, the witches stood firm, soaked with sweat but unmoved, their voices unwavering.

They chanted again—more assertive this time—and more water smashed into the flames until the inferno finally gave way to smoke.

Michael backed into the shadows. He had seen enough. They'd survive. Lenora. Shaun. Even Isabella.

But Trinity—she was vulnerable. Baal had promised her death, and Michael knew too well what that meant. He turned sharply, heading for Ellsworth. She couldn't die.

He moved fast, slipping through the back alleys. Legionnaires hunted across the city. Witches fled or fought. York was ablaze. He was halfway to Micklegate when a house exploded beside him, the blast throwing shards of glass across the street.

Pain sliced through his face. Heat scorched his skin.

Hands steadied him from behind.

He spun around.

Fleur.

"Where's Julian?" he demanded.

"He ran! He left us to die!" she shrieked; eyes gleaming with rage. "This is madness—they're slaughtering us!"

A group of legionnaires circled the burning house, flames crackling around them. One turned to Fleur and Michael.

"They're inside," the man said calmly.

They waited, still as statues. The witches would have to come out. And when they did, they'd be slaughtered.

Michael's wraith roared to life. Bloodlust swelled in his chest. His vision tunneled. Doubt vanished. Fear is erased.

He embraced the fury.

The building groaned as the fire ate through its walls. Windows shattered. Glass sliced his skin again, but he didn't flinch. Blood trickled to his lips. He licked it. Tasted nothing but rage.

Next to him, Fleur crouched low, grinning through gritted teeth.

The front door blew open.

Three young women, an older woman, and several young men ran out, coughing, clutching rags to their mouths. One dropped to his knees, gasping.

The chanting began instantly.

Before he could move, pain erupted in Michael's skull. His vision went white as an invisible force slammed into him. Around him, legionnaires screamed. Some fell. Some turned and fled.

But he pushed through it.

He roared, charging forward. A young man stood in his way—The boy couldn't have been more than seventeen. His sword trembled in his hand; mouth open as if to plead. Michael hesitated—just for a breath. Then rage swallowed the doubt. Bone cracked beneath his grip, and the light in the boy's eyes flickered out.

He tossed the boy onto the muddy street—the sword landing with a thud beside him.

The other men pulled back, raising spears and swords. One lunged, screaming.

The spear drove through Michael's side. He staggered.

Pain. Real pain. Hot, consuming.

He howled, staggering. The fire inside him blazed through every limb. The wound burned like molten iron poured into his side. His vision blurred as it surged through every nerve. For a moment, the world tilted— and then steadied.

Gripping the spear's shaft, he ripped it free. The man stumbled forward. Michael caught him by the neck and slammed his fist into the man's skull. It cracked like an eggshell.

A woman screamed. Her sword arced toward him.

Michael leapt back just in time, recognizing the obsidian blade.

He looked around. The alley was empty of demons. Even Fleur had fled.

More humans closed in. The woman's blade missed him by inches. He saw her eyes—furious, tear-filled, determined. She chanted in a tongue older than English, her voice rising like a war drum.

Blood poured from his side, making his grip slippery. Around him, humans shouted, emboldened now. He was no longer the hunter—they were.

He wasn't afraid—but he wasn't stupid. He turned and ran, the blood dripping from his side, painting a trail behind him.

CHAPTER 45 ~ TRINITY

Little One landed beside Trinity and hooted sharply into her ear, jolting her upright in bed. For a moment, she thought it was a dream—until the owl beat its wings, took off toward the window, and cried out again, louder this time. A sharp, acrid scent hit her nose. Smoke.

She leapt from the bed, threw open the window, and gasped. Flames devoured the stables. Firelight cast eerie shadows as the horses screamed in terror, galloping through the doors into the yard, their bodies slick with sweat and rain. The doors hung open, swinging in the wind, while billows of smoke poured into the sky.

Luca and Enzo sprinted out after the fleeing horses. Luca wielded a short sword, face grim with focus. Enzo had two knives glinting in his hands, but he paused near the blaze. With a sweeping motion, he bent low as though lifting an invisible weight, then flung his arms upward. A burst of wind spiraled forward. The fire sputtered. He did it again. The flames hissed and shrank, leaving only thick smoke curling upward into the rain.

Cloaked figures emerged from the shadows—legionnaires—a dozen or more.

Luca's face twisted in determination as he squared his shoulders, gripping his knives.

Trinity had never seen him look like that before—a true warrior—cold, lethal, unflinching.

Enzo shouted something in a language she didn't understand, eyes shut tight, summoning power. Wind burst from him in a mighty wave, forcing the enemy back. At the exact moment, Luca gave a piercing whistle that made Trinity wince and cover her ears. Moving his hands around each other, a ball of white flames encircled them.

Heart hammering, she spun, grabbed her aunt's shield, wrapped her arm through the leather loop, and snatched the sword before bolting from the room.

She tore through the manor barefoot, her nightgown clinging to her skin, blonde hair loose around her shoulders. She burst through the front doors and raced down the stone steps into the rain.

Jacob stood at the ready, his massive axe swinging in his hand. Three more witches who'd stayed after David's funeral, joined the fight, blades and spears raised. Lightning flashed above them, casting momentary halos around their weapons.

Trinity didn't hesitate. She thrust the sword forward and chanted the sacred words of the seraph. Heat bloomed in her chest, then her arms, racing down to the blade. The blue flames ignited along the edge, roaring to life in a brilliant blaze.

For a heartbeat, the world paused.

Every head turned.

Luca and Enzo froze in mid-motion. Luca's white flames sputtering out. Jacob halted; his axe still lifted. Witches and demons alike stared as Trinity stepped forward, shield firmly in front of her and flaming sword held high.

The legionnaires regrouped, shaken but not deterred. Snarls echoed as they surged toward her.

"You will not desecrate my home!" she shouted.

One demon lunged—and she struck. The sword sliced through him like paper, severing him in two. The top half dropped first, then the legs, his body disintegrating into flames on the ground.

The others hesitated, stunned by her power—but it wouldn't last.

More rushed the twins. Enzo and Luca raised their voices in unison, chanting. Half the legionnaires collapsed, clutching their skulls, howling. Luca dashed into their midst, his blades flashing like silver lightning. Heads rolled; bodies crumpled.

Enzo flanked him, hurling a knife that sank into a demon's chest. But two others closed in, grabbed him, and flung him across the yard like a discarded rag doll.

Trinity heard Luca scream.

Two female demons advanced toward her, younger than most but no less deadly. Trinity backed toward Enzo's motionless form; sword raised. Panic crept into her lungs. Her flame faltered.

Not now. Not yet.

She tried to steady her breath, but dread tightened around her like a noose. The flame dimmed. Her power slipped like sand through her fingers.

No! She couldn't lose it.

The red-haired demon raised her blade—but a gust of wind blew the woman off her feet, sending her flying back- cracking against the curtain wall.

A man bellowed, "You will die now, witch!" his thick Irish accent cutting through the chaos.

Enzo groaned and then grabbed her hand. "Trinity."

She didn't answer. She would not fail them. Gripping the sword, she pointed it toward the legionnaires and roared the sacred words again.

The flame surged back to life.

The man who threatened to kill her, spread his arms wide. "Our lord will have your soul!" he shouted.

Enzo and Luca rejoined her, bloodied but unbroken. She didn't look away from the enemy. As the other three witches and Jacob circled behind them.

"Are you hurt?" Luca asked. White flames flickering around his hands.

"No," she whispered, fire crackling from her blade. "I'm ready."

The demons charged.

Trinity swung wide, her sword carving a blazing arc through the night, incinerating two legionnaires in a single blow. Luca sent arcs of flames hurtling across the battlefield. Enzo weaved and sliced, his blade slashing with surgical precision.

The Irishman slowly approached her, sword slashing, grunting curses as he fended off the witches in his way.

Trinity stepped forward, unwavering. "You will not defile my home," she said, her voice calm and powerful. "I cast you out—all of you. Back to hell!"

Then something she didn't know would happen, or could, blazed through her. Light erupted around her. A sphere of blinding white radiance pulsed outward.

There was no heat, no wind, just stillness and a sensation like being wrapped in the arms of the Devine.

The demons screamed in unison. One by one, they dropped to their knees. Even the copper-haired man fell silent. A pregnant pause. Sound stretched. Screams muffled.

Then, all at once, their heads burst—like eggs thrown against stone, gore splattering in every direction.

Complete silence followed.

Trinity dropped to her knees. The light receded. The shield shimmered, and her lifeless sword fell beside her as rain poured down harder than before, smothering the battlefield in a hush.

She exhaled shakily and pressed a trembling hand to her chest. It was over.

"It's done," Trinity breathed, her voice trembling with exhaustion and disbelief.

But a figure stepped from the shadows—tall, broad, clad in wet black velvet. His dark hair clung to his face, and his voice dripped with mockery.

Something of nightmares and monsters.

"Oh, princess… it is not."

Behind him, hundreds poured out of the darkness. Some walked, others slithered, their forms inhuman. Ghouls, legionnaires, creatures she hadn't seen before—grotesque, rotting things with hollow eyes and snarling mouths. They filled the yard like a plague, surrounding her.

"I should've known better than to send anyone else to kill you," the man sneered, spreading his arms as if this were some grand homecoming.

Trinity's stomach dropped. *We can't fight them all.*

Jacob, Luca and Enzo stepped protectively in front of her. Another witch who'd survived, pressed behind her. Enzo's left arm hung at his side, useless, and he gripped a sword with his good hand. Blood-soaked Luca's tunic from a jagged gash across his chest, but he still stood tall, knife ready. Jacob was covered head to toe in blood and gore, a snarl on his lips, swinging his giant axe.

The demon tilted his head. "Come now, men, no need to die tonight." Then, with a flick of his wrist, both twins, the man behind her, and Jacob dropped their weapons and clutched their throats, gasping.

Trinity surged to her feet, sword clenched, the cold biting her skin through the drenched nightgown. "Stop it!" she shouted, raising the blade toward him. "Let them go!"

"I will," he said smoothly, "if you hand over that pretty shield and sword and come with me. There's someone who would dearly love to see you." He cocked his head. "Or die. Matters not to me."

Her arms ached. Her legs shook. But she raised her chin. "Stop hurting them, and I'll do what you want."

The demons behind him growled and shrieked, clawing the air with gnarled fingers. "They're impatient," the man said, glancing back. "I might not be able to hold them much longer."

"I'll come!"

She stepped forward, hefting the shield and dragging the blade behind her. The ground was littered with limbs and broken bodies. Mud and blood clung to her feet. Rain poured in steady sheets, running down her arms, soaking her to the bone.

This is how I die.

Tears welled and spilled freely. She didn't try to stop them as she kept her gaze riveted on the demon in front of her. The monster of nightmares.

My child, your time is not now. Close your eyes, Seriella's voice rang in Trinity's mind.

It wasn't the future that Trinity saw, though. It was a tapestry of memory—threads of gold and crimson woven with light—unfurling behind her eyes. Each glimmering strand revealed a moment: her mother's laughter, the brush of a Michael's hand, the warmth of his love, the ache of longing. Not a vision, but a soul's remembrance, painted not in time, but in truth. Love. She'd known real love. Her life had been more than grief—it had been joy, warmth, and family. Love was her shield and sword.

Halfway across the yard, she stopped. Her voice barely carried, but it didn't need to be loud. "I pity you," she whispered. Meaning it fully to the depths of her soul.

The demon recoiled as if she'd struck him.

"You'll never know, love," she continued. "You'll never know what it's like to be held or chosen. You are hollow. Nothing."

"You know nothing!" He bellowed.

"I know, you are the ones rejected by God because of your betrayal and sinfulness. Forever to suffer, alone, unloved for eternity. Darkness with no light."

His composure cracked. "Enough!"

Trinity laughed, a soft, trembling sound. "Love is our weapon. That's why you wish to destroy us."

A flurry of hooves tore through the silence.

She looked up to see Shaun leaping off a horse, sword drawn. Lenora, Nicholas, and a blonde woman Trinity recognized from the funeral followed. The demon turned as the new arrivals formed a wall before Trinity.

"Well," Lenora said with a dry chuckle. "Didn't think I'd see your ugly face again, Baal."

"Lenora," Baal hissed. "Still clinging to your illusions of power?"

He turned his gaze to Nicholas and narrowed his eyes. "Oh, now this is a surprise. The exiled nephew returned to the fold."

Lenora didn't blink. "Release the men."

Baal raised a brow. "Make me."

Lenora extended his hand, and a gust of wind slammed into Baal, knocking him back into his horde. The man behind Trinity, the twins and Jacob dropped to the ground, gasping. They scrambled to Trinity's side, retrieving their weapons.

"You think this handful of mortals can defeat me?" Baal sneered, dusting himself off.

"We've done it before," Lenora said with a smirk.

A new voice cut through the rain. "Not this time."

A tall regal looking woman with golden blonde hair, wrapped in a black cloak and hood stepped into the yard. A black shining mask covering the upper half of her face. This woman was evil, cruel and the power radiating off her hit Trinity like a blast.

She looked far too pleased with herself and wielded a red flaming sword. "She's mine," she said, eyes locked on Trinity.

"You'll have to get through me first witch!" Lenora hissed.

The woman scoffed, "As you wish." And hurled fire with one hand at Lenora then raised the flaming sword.

Lenora blocked the fire ball then swung her short sword. The blonde woman blocked, the steel screaming against each other.

"You will never defeat me!" the woman bellowed.

Suddenly, the manor doors slammed open.

Trinity turned—and froze.

Sybil stood dressed in only a white tunic, that barely fell past her knees, lightning crackling at her fingertips. Her presence alone made the air hum.

She was chanting softly, but Trinity didn't need to hear the words to understand and joined the chant. The sword in her hand reignited, blue flames racing along the blade.

Power surged into Trinity. Her spine straightened; her limbs flooded with strength. She and Sybil locked eyes.

"No demon scum," Sybil said, voice like thunder, "but she will defeat you."

She raised her arms, and lightning ripped across the sky, striking the nearest ranks of legionnaires. "Trinity, only the sword can kill Baal!"

The battle descended into chaos. Screams filled the yard; steel rang out. Lenora fought the blonde woman, their duel a blur of blades and sparks. Nicholas stood firm beside his aunt, defending against wave after wave of legionnaires using a strange black mist almost as a whip emerging from his palm, wrapping around necks and popping off heads, as if it was nothing.

A scream tore through Trinity as searing pain ripped from her tail bone to her neck. She clutched the shield & sword tighter, dropping to her knees as fire licked along her spine, her shoulders.

It's time, my child, Seriella's voice echoed. Accept me.

Agony exploded through Trinity's body, then transformed into pressure. She released an earth-shattering scream that cut through the battle.

"What's happening to me?" She panted and looked down at the shield.

Shock rippled through the pain.

Great white wings unfurled from her back, stretching wide. White-hot pain shifted into a rushing torrent of power.

Her feet left the ground as she clutched the shield against her chest and wielded the sword. She hovered above the chaos, eyes glowing, wings beating like thunder.

Baal looked up at her, his expression caught between wonder and fury.

"Come then Demon," Trinity said, her voice layered with something divine. Vibrating. Echoing around them. "Let's end this."

He roared and leapt, swinging dual blades wreathed in shadows.

She countered effortlessly. One swipe she disarmed a sword, it hurled through the air and stuck into the ground. Baal's magic tried to push her back, but she absorbed it like air.

"I am Seriella, and you demon are no match for me." The words came from Trinity's mouth, but they were not her own.

His face twisted, his body swelling and reshaping into something monstrous horned, hunched, and... massive.

The demon prince's true form emerged, and sickening nausea swept through Trinity. He was a beast.

His words from her vision swept into her mind. *I am one of nightmares and monsters.* It was true.

He swung again, the shield blocking it with a loud clang, but he didn't stop or slow. His last blade drove her backwards. Seriella's power flooded through the Trinity, but Baal was powerful.

She dodged again, but it nicked her wing, wincing but held steady. Swinging the blue flamed sword, she drove him back into the mob of ghouls.

The sound of the others fighting around her disappeared. But there were hundreds, thousands of monsters and overwhelming fear and hopelessness settled in Trinity's gut.

Let go of your fear, Trinity; I will end this now, Seriella said. Trust in me, child.

It took every ounce of strength to let go and trust. But she'd always been devout, pious, loyal to her god. She had complete faith in Seriella.

Trinity released a deep breath and let go.

She dove towards Baal, sword blazing, and it struck true—piercing straight through Baal's chest.

The scream that followed wasn't Baal's alone. It came from the other demons as each one fell to the ground or ran. The depths of hell itself raged. The ground shook as everyone stumbled to stand upright.

Black mist poured from his body as it collapsed and morphed into the shape of a man.

Trinity's feet touched the ground as her wings slowly disappeared.

You have done well, my child.

She watched Baal's black mist twist and writhe around her. A monstrous face pushed out from the smoke, snarling.

The light within her flared. The mist recoiled, burned, and then disintegrated.

518

She dropped the shield and sword. Her knees hit the ground.

"My baby," she whispered.

Then darkness swallowed her whole.

CHAPTER 46 ~ SYBIL

Sybil watched in stunned silence as Trinity's wings slowly folded into her back. They vanished as though they had never existed. Where Trinity's arm was cut, blood soaked through her nightgown. She swayed.

Shaun rushed forward, catching her just before she collapsed. He lifted her, cradled his arms and shouted, "The baby!" as he ran past Sybil, his voice frayed with panic.

Sybil already sensed it before the words reached her ears. A ripple of energy moved through her body, the same way the tide shifts when a storm is nearby. The child was coming—and fast.

It would be born on the darkest night, during an eclipse, in the wake of one of the bloodiest battles ever fought.

Sybil tried to move, but exhaustion clung to her limbs like iron shackles. Her body protested each step, the stitches in her abdomen pulling tighter with every movement. She forced herself to walk down the stairs.

Something compelled her. Urged her forward as she looked out into the yard.

It was a graveyard of twisted corpses. Smoke rose in tendrils from burnt patches of earth. The corpses of demons—vile, half-rotted, or decapitated—lay still. And when the demon prince fell, so did every last one of his legionnaires and ghouls. Swallowed by the earth.

Beyond the carnage, Ailith, Nicholas, Luca, and Enzo surrounded a still figure sprawled in the mud.

Lenora.

Sybil's breath caught.

The woman who had raised, loved and protected her. The matriarch of their family and the most powerful druidess she had ever known—lay crumpled like a broken doll.

Sybil dropped beside the twins, tears already blurring her vision. Lenora's chest was torn open, her lifeblood soaked into the earth. Her mouth was slightly ajar, as if she had tried to speak one last word.

"She fought so hard," Enzo whispered hoarsely. "We were overrun. That woman—she tore out her heart seconds before Trinity struck Baal down."

He was crying. So was Luca. Even Nicholas looked shattered.

"Where is she?" Sybil asked, her eyes searching the wreckage for the demon woman responsible.

"She ran." Jacob stepped beside them. "I chased after her, but she disappeared into the shadows."

"Thank you, Jacob," Sybil said quietly, reaching for Lenora's lifeless hand.

"She was a powerful blood mage and necromancer. One of the most powerful I've ever seen." Enzo whispered.

Luca sobbed, hunched over their grandmother.

Sybil couldn't speak. She just wept. For Lenora. For David. For everyone they had lost.

***

A knock came before Shaun stepped into the quiet bedroom. Ailith and Jacob lingered near the door like silent sentries. The candlelight flickered against the walls, casting golden shadows on the wall. Sybil sat in a cushioned chair beside Trinity's bed. Her legs propped up onto a cushioned stool. A blanket covering her.

Trinity lay against several pillows, her face deathly pale. A sling supported her wounded arm, and her eyes were sunken with fatigue.

On her other side, Elizabeth sat cradling the newborn—wrapped snugly in a wool blanket, his tiny pink face peeking out with a mass of brunette straight hair.

"Trinity," Shaun murmured, approaching gently. "How are you? Your arm?"

"I'll heal," she replied, voice soft, weary but steady.

"And the baby?"

"It's a boy," she said, offering a small, tired smile. "I've named him Eric... after my father."

Shaun walked to Elizabeth, who shifted the baby to show him the infant's face. "Hello there, Eric," Shaun said with a grin. "I'm your uncle Shaun."

"I was just going to lay him down with Mary and the triplets. Trinity needs her rest," Elizabeth said warmly. She looked peaceful. Happier than Sybil had ever seen her. Motherhood suited her.

Once Elizabeth left with the baby, Shaun took Elizabeth's seat.

"Does Elizabeth know what happened?" he asked, leaning forward on his elbows, fists under his chin.

"We told the servants it was wolves," Sybil replied. "And the twins fought them off."

Jacob cleared his throat. "I had the servants' doors and Elizabeth's and Susana's doors barred and told them it wasn't safe outside."

Ailith chuckled. "Perfect."

Shaun huffed. "They'll love that story." He glanced at the floor. "I still can't believe you're all witches. I never suspected."

Sybil smirked. "Call me that again and I might hex you."

"I'm not sure what to call you." His voice was softer now. "I've been thinking about Lenora. She was the oldest person in my life—and so strong. Always Healthy. Never sick a day, I can recall." He snorted. "I understand now. She was a... different."

Sybil lifted a brow and smirked. "She was extraordinary," she whispered. "But others like us have existed for thousands of years. Most of us are healers. Protectors. We protect the earth. And most important the veil between our world and hell."

"But those others, they are w..." Shaun cleared his throat. "They're evil."

"Like priests and men, some can be corrupted."

Shaun sat back, his hands clutching his knees nervously. This was a lot for him to take in. Sybil understood.

"So, you're not evil?"

She shook her head. "Magic itself isn't evil. It's how it's used that can be evil or not. It's supposed to be a tool for good."

"And you don't sacrifice humans to your gods?" Shaun cringed after he said it.

Sybil and Ailith chuckled. The sound so similar it cut her short. She eyed Ailith suspiciously. "No, we don't, but my grandmother taught me that sacrifice of self in service for a higher purpose is the truest form of devotion. She believed we were stewards of balance between the light of darkness."

Shaun nodded, thoughtful. "Do you believe in God?"

Sybil hummed. "That's a heavy question, Shaun. Ask me when I'm less exhausted."

He turned to Trinity. "And you? I don't have a right to ask, but... what are you?"

"They call me a traveler or the chosen one," she said after a long sigh. "I don't have my own magic. Not like Sybil. But with the sword... I channel power from a seraph into it."

"An angel?" Shaun's brow furrowed. "The wings."

Trinity nodded. "Yes. An archangel. The light and wings you saw... it wasn't me. It was Seriella. She was inside of me, using my body as a vessel."

Shaun looked at Sybil, then back. "So, you were both chosen?"

"We are blessed," Sybil said.

"But no one can ever know," Trinity added, her voice hardening. "Only those in this room."

"I swear it," Shaun said, squeezing her hand. "I'd never betray you."

"I'm sure you'd never do anything to hurt us, Shaun." Sybil stood slowly, glancing at Ailith. "I'll say my goodnight now. Ailith, would you mind helping me?"

Ailith wrapped her arm around Sybil's waist and the warmth gave her a comfort she didn't realize she needed. Like a warm bowl of soup on a cold winter day or the sun blanketing your body in warmth.

Sybil breathed out as she steadied herself for the painful walk to her temporary bedchambers. "Thank you."

She glanced back to see Shaun clasping Trinity's hand in his own.

She let out a deep sigh... So much love.

***

Ailith helped Sybil back to her chambers, neither spoke until they were alone inside. As Sybil settled into bed, she turned her eyes on the woman beside her. The resemblance was undeniable now. Her face, though drawn from battle, carried echoes of Sybil's own. The cheekbones. The mouth. Even the curve of her eyes.

"You let me believe you were dead," Sybil said quietly. "Why?"

Ailith sat down heavily in a chair, her movements slow. "Because I was broken. When your father died, I lost more than a husband—I lost myself. Our love... it was more than human. It was a bond of the spirit. And when it was severed, I thought I would die too."

Sybil tried to keep her mother's words from sinking too deep—but they hit like stones dropped in still water. No matter how she tried to rationalize it, to understand the pain Ailith had endured, there was still a part of her—a child's voice buried deep, that cried out in betrayal.

"So, you left me. You didn't love me enough to stay," said Sybil sharply.

Sybil's love for her own children burned so fiercely that the idea of parting from them, even for a day, was like imagining life without air. Even now, stitched and

The Light of Darkness

sore, barely able to stand, her instincts screamed to protect them. To leave them behind would be worse than death. She could never do it. Not for grief. Not for anyone.

So, what did that say about her mother?

"I loved you more than anything," Ailith whispered.

Sybil's breath hitched. Her chest tightened, and her voice cracked as she asked, "Then why? I could never leave my children behind."

Tears brimmed in her eyes, threatening to spill, her heart hammering against a wall of old hurt.

Ailith drew in a slow breath, steadying herself before answering. "Kendra had a vision. She said that if I stayed, I would go mad... take my own life. I didn't believe it of course—not at first. I refused to. But the grief..." Her voice trembled. "The grief devoured me from the inside. I stopped eating. Stopped sleeping." She let out a small huff. "It felt like someone had torn me apart, and I couldn't find the pieces to put myself back together."

She pressed her fingers to her eyes, wiping away her own tears before continuing. "One night, Lenora made the decision for me. She sent two of my dearest friends. They drugged me and carried me away to Ireland, to my father's land. I hated her for it... until I began to heal."

Sybil remained silent; her emotions caught between betrayal but also... understanding.

"There were others there, others like us. Healers. Mages. Druids who remembered the old ways. My father taught me how to live again. Slowly, painfully. I trained. I studied. I remembered what it meant to be strong."

Ailith paused, eyes turning distant. "But Lenora made it clear—I was not to return until a sign came. Kendra's vision had named it: when the crow carries the snake across the water. It sounded like nonsense then. But one day, while training with my sword on the lakeshore, I saw it—a black crow swooped from the trees, a serpent dangling from its beak, gliding across the lake like a shadow cast by fate itself."

Sybil swallowed hard. "And that's when you came back."

"I had to. I'd waited long enough." Ailith looked down at her hands. "Not a single day passed that I didn't miss you. That I didn't mourn the life we were meant to share. I watched your growth through messages and letters. I felt in my soul; you were safe with my mother. I trusted her. I had to."

She gave Sybil's hand a gentle squeeze. "I'm so sorry. I never wanted to leave you. Will you… can you forgive me?"

Sybil didn't answer right away. Her eyes remained on the quilt across her lap, tracing the stitching absently. "I grew up believing you died of an illness. Both of you."

"I understand," Ailith said, softly. "I hated that lie… but at the time, it felt like mercy."

Sybil's brows furrowed as she wrestled with the weight of everything. Her mother hadn't abandoned her from selfishness—but from heartbreak. And Sybil, of all people, understood that kind of sorrow now. The wound of David's absence ran deep.

"It's hard," Sybil admitted. "To reconcile the mother, I lost, with the woman before me now."

"I understand," Ailith said gently. "But I'm here now. And I want to be part of your life—of your children's lives—if you'll let me."

Silence settled between them, not cold but contemplative. Then Sybil broke it with a question that had been quietly burning in her thoughts.

"The light you used—the way you healed me, and brought me back after the birth... and David that night in York... was that something you were born with? Or something you've learned?"

Ailith smiled, a touch of pride flickering across her face. "Some of it was instinct. I was born with the ability to heal and tether the soul to the body. But wielding light, drawing power from water and flame— that I learned. My father was one of the last Druids in our line. He taught me to channel ancient energies, to master what was already within me."

She hesitated, her gaze warm and unwavering. "I can teach you. If you want."

Hope rose in Sybil's chest like the first blooms through winter snow.

"I do," she whispered. "I want to learn."

She reached out, this time taking her mother's hand of her own accord. It was a small gesture, but one laced with promise.

In the quiet, with the scent of firewood and herbs lingering in the air, Sybil realized something she hadn't dared believe since David's death—she wasn't alone. Not anymore.

She had her mother. She had Trinity. Elizabeth. Her children.

And a new beginning, if she chose it.

CHAPTER 47 ~ MICHAEL

"Michael? Did you hear me?" Fleur asked again, standing over him with her arms crossed and shoulders rigid.

He didn't answer. The night's horrors clung to him like smoke—thick, choking, inescapable. They had fought until dawn crept over the city like a ghost; still, it hadn't been enough. The witches had fought back with the power they never expected—blades warded with ancient symbols, obsidian-tipped spears, and shields of light and force. They had bled the legionnaires dry and forced demons to scatter like rats from fire.

Julian had vanished sometime during the battle. Fleur, surprisingly, stayed. She fought beside him, held her ground, and didn't try to kill him—even when she had the chance. Still, trust was beyond reach.

"Michael, we must return," she said for the third time, her voice strained.

He sat beneath the gnarled limbs of an ash tree, sheltered slightly from the drizzle that still fell over the scorched earth. Mud clung to his boots, blood to his shirt and face. His hands were caked in soot; his nails blackened from gripping broken blades and torn limbs.

Fleur didn't look much better. Her once-elegant dress now hung in tatters, crusted with blood. Her long golden hair, tangled and wild, stuck to her cheeks. A jagged rip ran down her sleeve, revealing bruises already forming on her shoulder.

They were shadows of who they once were— warriors in name, wreckage in truth.

"If you want to go back," he muttered, "then go. I don't care what you do."

"I'm not leaving you here," she snapped. "We need to stay together. We can find Julian—perhaps regroup."

Michael exhaled a slow, deliberate breath. Her desperation clung to her like damp wool. He could almost taste it in the air—like iron and ash.

"I don't care about Julian," he said. "Or you."

That should've made her flinch, but she stood her ground. And that, more than anything, irritated him.

"Did you kill my father?" he asked, lifting his gaze to hers.

She blinked. A flicker of something crossed her face—a twitch in her cheek, a brief narrowing of her eyes. She didn't answer.

"You did," he said coldly. "And the twins?"

"I didn't kill the twins," she said too quickly. A beat passed. "That wasn't me."

He didn't believe her. Not entirely. But the regret in her eyes seemed real—if fleeting.

"How could you kill him? He adored you." His voice cracked with more anger than sorrow. "You weren't even a legionnaire then."

Fleur turned her back to him, perhaps foolishly or as a provocation. A test. He would be able to crush her before she drew another breath.

"You've met my mother," she said over her shoulder. "She's a blood mage. I was trained from birth to obey without question. I didn't have immortality, but I had power. Enough to kill."

Michael scoffed. "I always knew there was something wrong with you."

"Everyone did," she said flatly, then turned to show him the ring on her finger. "This hides my power. Sybil couldn't sense me. But you did. Even before you turned."

He didn't respond.

"You always did," she said. "Something about you... I couldn't mask it from you."

"Perhaps I was always a monster," he said, tone devoid of emotion.

Fleur didn't argue. Instead, she looked at him, eyes soft for a moment. "I loved your parents, Michael. I didn't want to hurt them. I tried to stop it, but Baal sent Julian to remind me what loyalty meant. He said if I didn't obey, Baal would kill me and my father."

A silence fell between them, heavy with the weight of too many betrayals.

"He has your father?"

"Yes."

"And you're mother?"

"Always served Baal." She cringed, shaking her head. "I believed him, Michael," she whispered softly. "Maybe he still will kill me and my father."

Michael rubbed a hand across his jaw, smudging blood into soot. "What about the others? Did you help Julian kill them, too?"

531

"I was told only to deal with your parents," she said, voice shaking.

He looked out across the field toward the manor. His mind churned with images of Trinity—her face, voice, and laugh. For hours, he had forgotten her entirely. The battle had consumed everything. But now, it was as if a dam had broken inside him.

"Trinity," he murmured. "I have to see if she's alive."

"You will do no such thing!" Fleur's voice exploded in rage. "If she breathes, I'll fix that myself! Would you betray everything we've become over that…?"

Michael was on his feet in a heartbeat; his hand wrapped around her throat before she finished the sentence. He slammed her back into the tree.

"If I rip off your head," he growled, his voice low and dark, "do you think it will grow back?"

Fleur clawed at his wrist, her nails drawing blood, but it was no use. His strength far surpassed hers.

"I'm sorry," she gasped.

He released her, and she crumpled to the ground, coughing and wheezing, her voice hoarse. "I'm sorry."

He stood over her, his black eyes slowly shifting back to a deep blue. Rain dripped from his lashes. "You will never go near her. Do you understand me?"

She climbed to her feet slowly, brushing mud off her arms. "If you stay with me, I'll never touch her. I swear it. We need each other now, Michael."

"I don't need you," he snapped. "But I will say this once: if you harm her or my child, I will kill you with my bare hands. I will tear you apart while you're still alive to feel it."

Fleur didn't answer right away. Her chest rose and fell; her pride bruised more than her body. Finally, she asked, "Then what will you do?"

"I'll make sure she lives," he said. "Then I'm leaving this godforsaken place behind."

A bitter smile twisted her lips. "You think they'll let you walk away?"

"They can try to stop me," Michael said. He looked to the east towards Ellsworth. "But I'll carve my path if I have to."

A distant scream echoed across the hills, carried by the wind. Michael's jaw tensed.

Fleur stepped beside him. "Then let's get this over with."

They walked through the forest, side by side but not together, toward the manor. Toward the woman who would break him. Toward the child, who was the last piece of his soul.

And behind them, the shadows watched.

***

Michael sat in silence beside Trinity's bed, barely breathing, afraid any movement might shatter the fragile peace of the moment. The faint flicker of candlelight cast soft shadows across her face, illuminating the dried tear tracks on her cheeks. She looked pale, even more delicate than he remembered, and yet more radiant too—made luminous by motherhood, by grief, by the weight of all she had endured.

He watched her and the others all day. Just watched. The witches he once called friends helped clean up the yard, while some travelled back to York.

Now he watched her sleep. Her chest was rising and falling. Her brow twitched with dreams he was unable to enter or shield her from.

He didn't deserve to.

But when she whimpered in her sleep—when the soft sound of her sobs broke the stillness—he couldn't bear it. His hand reached out instinctively, hovering just above hers before brushing her fingers. The warmth of her skin stunned him. He hadn't touched something so soft or real in what felt like forever.

"Shh… it's alright," he whispered. "You're safe now."

She flinched at his voice.

Her eyes fluttered open, disoriented, then widened in panic as the candle's light revealed him. She scrambled upright, pulling the blanket to her chin as if it would protect her from him.

"Michael?" Her voice cracked. Her entire body trembled. Whether from fear or shock, he wasn't sure.

He lit another candle to soften the room's shadows, showing her, he meant no harm. "I had to see for myself that you were unharmed."

She stared at him, haunted. "I killed him."

He blinked. "Who?"

"Baal. The Prince of Demons. I killed him." Her voice shook as its weight crashed down again. "But Lenora died. And David…" Her breath hitched. "David is gone."

The words hung in the air like a noose tightening around both their throats.

Michael barely processed what she said. He had believed Baal was eternal. That death didn't apply to creatures like him. That Baal would go on forever, orchestrating destruction like a symphony of damnation. But Trinity—his Trinity—had slain him.

"Are you certain?" he asked quietly.

"I watched him fall." Her voice was soft and shattered. "I felt it. The world shifted. His darkness... left."

She buried her face in her hands, weeping. A deep, aching sorrow that had no end.

He leaned forward and brushed her hands aside gently. "Don't hide from me."

She lifted her eyes, and he saw everything: the devastation, the pain he had caused, the ache of lost time, and the love that still burned despite it all.

"I've missed you so much. Every day has hurt. Every night, I looked for you in my dreams." Her voice cracked. "Please... come home. I don't care what you are. You're still you."

"I can't," he said, voice thick. "Not now. Not ever. Not because I don't want to. But because of what I've become."

"You're a father, Michael." She reached for his hand, her fingers trembling. "We have a son."

"I know." His voice softened. "I've seen him. He's perfect." A faint smile tugged at his lips. "What's his name?"

"Eric. After my father."

His chest tightened. "That's a strong name. Fitting. He would be proud of you. I know I am."

"You don't have to go," she pleaded. "Or we will leave York together. Find somewhere quiet. Somewhere, no one knows us. Safe."

He looked away, eyes on the window where the night pressed in. "You and Eric deserve better than exile. He deserves a childhood filled with sunshine and laughter. Not hiding in shadows with a father who isn't truly alive."

"I don't care," she said, her voice growing desperate. "He needs you. I need you."

"You are so strong. You don't need me." He turned back to her, brushing her cheek. "You've kept everyone together. You held my family in your arms and gave them hope. You have a fire, Trinity. You are the light in this world filled with darkness."

"I'm so tired," she sobbed, pressing her forehead to his. "So tired of being strong. I don't want to be the light. I want to be Trinity Ellsworth, wife to Michael Ellsworth."

He gathered her into his arms. She collapsed against him like a broken thing as he held her tight, tighter than he ever had before. Her sobs were muffled against his chest, his hand stroking her back in long, steady lines.

"I love you," she said between sobbing gasps. "God help me, I still love you."

His lips pressed to her temple. "I've never stopped. Not for one moment."

"Then don't leave."

"I must." His voice was breaking now. "The world isn't ready to see what I am. And I won't put you or our child in danger. I could lose control and hurt you. Hurt Eric."

"I don't care, I know you'd never hurt us," she whispered. "Let the world burn if I have to live in it without you."

He pulled back, looking into her eyes for the last time and smiled at her fierceness. God, he loved her. "That is not who you are, and you know it."

"I don't."

"He's going to change everything, Trinity—our son. I can feel it. The blood that runs in him... it's different... ancient... The power of angels and witches."

"You speak like you won't see him grow up."

"I probably won't," he said quietly. "But he'll know me in other ways. In the stories you tell him. In the things we share—my laugh, my stubbornness. He'll carry pieces of me, even if he doesn't realize it."

Trinity shook her head violently. "No. Don't say goodbye. I can't survive another goodbye."

"I'm already gone," he whispered, voice hoarse. "This... this moment, this night... That's all I can give to you. I'm sorry, Trinity. For everything. I failed you."

He kissed her then. Desperate. She clung to him, trying to draw him back to her. Into her arms. Into their story. But the moment it ended; he was slipping away again.

He stepped toward the window. The wind had picked up, and rain traced the edges of the glass like tears.

"Please, Michael," she whispered.

He turned one last time. Memorizing her face. The curve of her shoulders in the moonlight. The way her lips trembled, her beautiful green hazel eyes. Then she smiled—a genuine, aching, devastating smile.

"I love you. Always," he said, a painful ache so profound he felt it in his bones and to the depth of his black and tarnished soul.

And before she could reach for him again, he leapt through the open window and vanished into the night.

CHAPTER 48 ~ TRINITY

Trinity watched Michael vanish into the night. For a heartbeat, the world stopped spinning. Her breath caught in her throat, suspended in disbelief. Had he truly been there, or was it a dream? But his words still pulsed through her mind, burning through every wall she had tried to build. She had heard the cadence of his voice, seen the sorrow in his eyes, and—most vividly— his lips against hers. It was real.

She touched her lips. He's alive.

Still, he had left her. Again.

A sob broke free, rattling her entire frame as she folded inward, her arms clutching her midsection. The pain radiated from somewhere beyond the physical, deeper than anything her body could contain. Trembling, she stumbled toward her bed and collapsed beneath the blankets. She curled herself around the aching hollow inside her chest and shut her eyes tight, willing the world to disappear.

Everyone she had ever loved had died or walked away. Her parents. Her aunt. David. Lenora. And now

Michael. Again. Her body heaved as the sobs continued, relentless and painful. She pressed her forehead into the pillow and cried until her throat burned.

***

Three days passed.

Sunlight streamed through the window of Trinity's chamber, but it failed to touch her. She lay buried beneath thick covers, her golden hair tangled across her pillow, her nightgown damp from sweat and tears. The tray of untouched food beside her bed had gone cold and stale hours ago.

"Trinity." Shaun's voice broke through the silence. He stood beside her, sitting on the edge of the mattress. "You must get up."

She didn't respond. Her back turned to him. Only the subtle rise and fall of her breath betrayed that she was awake. Or alive.

Shaun walked around the dim room, picking up the untouched meals and huffing.

"Elizabeth is doing her best, but the baby cries for his mother every night."

"I can't," Trinity murmured into the pillow, barely loud enough to hear.

"Yes, you can." His voice sharpened. "You just won't."

"Go away," she said hoarsely, voice cracked from disuse.

Shaun's patience thinned. "Michael is gone. He left us all. You're not the only one mourning him, Trinity, but hiding in this room like a ghost won't change that. Eric needs his mother."

Her jaw clenched, but she didn't move.

"Stop this," Shaun snapped. "You're acting like a child."

That pierced her and she flinched beneath the blanket.

Shaun abruptly grabbed the bedding and yanked it off her. Trinity gasped, stunned, and sat up instinctively, arms crossing over herself.

"What are you—?" she cried.

He didn't give her time to protest. He scooped her up—blanket and all—and carried her from the room. She beat her fists against his chest, but weakly, as if her limbs belonged to someone else.

"Shaun! Stop this right now! Put me down!"

But he didn't. He descended the stairs, past startled servants, past Elizabeth rocking the baby in the kitchen, and pushed through the back door into the garden.

Sunlight spilled across the lawn, golden and blinding. The warmth hit Trinity like a slap. She cried out, hiding her face in the blanket.

"I told you I didn't want to go outside!"

"And I told you to live." He dropped her—unceremoniously onto the soft grass beneath an old apple tree.

Trinity pushed herself upright, her hair tangled and her face pale and blotchy. "You're mad."

"No, Trinity. You are if you think I'm going to allow you to bury yourself another day!"

He dropped to his knees in front of her, eyes fierce. "You're not the only one who lost him. I did, too. We all did."

"I didn't just lose him. I lost everything," she whispered. "He left… knowing I would never stop loving him."

Shaun's expression softened, pain flickering through his eyes. "You're not the only one who loved him. I've loved you both my whole life."

Trinity stared at him, breathing hard. Her shoulders slumped. "I can't live without him."

"Yes, you can. You must. For your son, for everyone who looks to you. You're the flame that still burns in this place."

"I don't want to be," she said, voice cracking, remembering the similar words Michael spoke to her before he left.

Shaun grasped her arms. "Do you want Eric to grow up motherless as well as fatherless? To feel the way, you felt when you were orphaned?"

That struck a nerve.

Trinity's eyes widened. She looked away, blinking furiously. A memory flashed—*her mother, broken, sitting on the hearth in their old cottage, staring into the fire until it consumed her.* Her father's death had hollowed her out. Within a year, she was gone, too.

"I'm becoming her," she whispered. "I'm doing the same thing."

Shaun exhaled and pulled her into his arms. She didn't resist. "You are not your mother. You're stronger than her."

"I've failed, Shaun."

"No," he said fiercely. "You survived. And you're still alive. That means there's still time to keep living."

Silence fell between them, broken only by the birds and the distant cries of a baby.

"I need a bath," she muttered.

Shaun laughed. "Yes. Yes, you do."

She pulled back, wiping her face with the edge of her sleeve. "Tell one of the girls. And send Elizabeth. I want to feed him."

He smiled. "Of course."

As he turned to go, she stopped him. "Shaun…"

He paused.

"I love you too. But not the way you deserve. I can't."

"I know," he said, turning back to her. "I've always known. And I've loved you, anyway."

Trinity's eyes filled again, but this time, they weren't only tears of grief. There was something else there, too. Gratitude. A flicker of hope.

As Shaun walked away, Trinity turned her face to the sun and let it warm her skin. She sat in the grass, letting the wind thread through her tangled hair. Her soul was still shredded. But the breath in her lungs, the baby's cries drifting on the wind, and Shaun's stubborn loyalty reminded her that she wasn't alone.

Not entirely.

The pain remained; an ache she knew would never entirely leave her. But in time, maybe she would learn to carry it.

Michael was gone—but her son was not.

Her friends were not.

And she was not dead yet.

She stood slowly, lifting her eyes to the manor. Her limbs trembled as she walked toward the house. Each step felt like climbing a mountain, but she didn't stop.

Because Shaun had been right.

She had no choice but to live.

And maybe—just maybe—one day, she would remember how.

EPILOGUE ~ TRINITY
A Year Later, Spring 1351-Ellsworth

"Elizabeth! Look at the children!" Trinity laughed, hands on her hips, watching Mary and Eric on the grass. They stuffed wildflowers into each other's mouths with the solemn determination of toddlers discovering the world.

Nearby, Susana knelt, skirts fanned out like a rippling lake of blue. No more black mourning gowns. She smiled with unfiltered joy, clapping her hands in delight and laughing.

Sunlight spilled across the garden, warming Trinity's rose-hued gown, making it shimmer with golden undertones. The fabric hugged her figure beneath the bust and flowed over her collarbone. She'd filled out since childbirth, her body reshaped by strength, softness, and sorrow. Her blonde hair—loose except for the pinned sides—flowed behind her like a silken banner.

Elizabeth swooped in, green skirts swirling as she snatched the daisies from the children's chubby fists. "No, no, no," she chided, bouncing Sybil's daughter, Sarah, on her hip. "Darling, we do not eat flowers. That's not for little mouths."

"They're only playing," Susana called, unbothered. "Let them taste a petal or two. It won't hurt them."

"You'll say that until someone's sick," Elizabeth retorted, shifting Sarah into a more secure position.

Braided hair crowned Elizabeth's head like a coronet. Her sleeves were pushed above her elbows, revealing strong arms used to carrying children and burdens alike. Despite her practical tone, she kissed Sarah's temple with tenderness and glanced toward the others with a quiet smile.

Trinity scooped Eric up, pressing a kiss to his cheek as he squealed and flailed. Dark hair stuck to his forehead, and his blue eyes sparkled with mischief—just as Michael's once did. She let him wriggle out of her grasp and toddle after a bee.

Mary, a month older and at least a pound heavier, sat squarely in a flurry of dandelions, picking them with glee, her fingers and lips yellow. Her crimson hair gleamed like fire in the sun. Trinity shook her head, laughing under her breath. "That girl's going to be a force to be reckoned with."

"She already is," Elizabeth muttered, handing Sarah off to Trinity and retrieving Mary, trying not to smirk.

Every warm morning, they came out into the garden. Bees buzzed around the lavender bushes. Swallows dove through the air, wings slicing the sky. The war, the plague, and the battle seemed distant under the canopy of blooming apple trees.

But the city beyond Ellsworth Manor still bore scars. Faith fractured under the weight of unanswered prayers. Priests scrambled to hold services with half-empty pews. People whispered their doubts more boldly now.

But Trinity clung to her belief. She wore it like armor, no longer pleading with God but thanking Him—for survival, for Eric, for another day. She never asked Sybil to join her at church. Their faith diverged, yet somehow coexisted.

Only Elizabeth and Susana joined Trinity each Sunday.

They never spoke of that night—of the sword that burned like heaven's fire, or the demon prince turned to ash. But the memory dissipated a little when they held hands in silent prayer.

Michael hadn't returned. His voice dimmed in her mind, tucked in the quiet corners of her memory. But the love stayed rooted deep. Shaun's devotion remained quiet but unshakable. He no longer proposed. Instead, he stayed for dinner, held Eric when Trinity needed sleep, and walked the grounds each night, a sword strapped to his back.

A rumor surfaced—whispers of a widow, once stricken by the plague who'd survived, now seen often at Shaun's side. Trinity never asked. She saw the softer look in his eyes and felt only gratitude. He deserved someone to hold.

Months earlier, she met with Arthur, now the new chancellor of the king. He helped her sell the family estate in London. The wealth from the sale allowed her to restore Ellsworth Manor. Stone by stone, she rebuilt a home from the wreckage. New roof tiles. A repaired hearth. The fields were replanted. The village restored.

545

Elizabeth stayed with them; her inheritance lost to her late husband's family debts. Though pride kept her chin high, Trinity saw the shadow of what-ifs in her sister's gaze. They stood side by side—partners in motherhood and survival.

Trinity caught Eric in her other arm. He squealed in delight as she kissed him and then set him back down. He took off toward a patch of thyme, giggling. She sat in the grass, setting Sarah in her lap, breathing in the scent of crushed herbs and sun-warmed grass.

A hoot, then wingbeats from Little One as she settled onto the roof, near the back door to the kitchen. She ruffled her feathers and hooted again, to get Trinity's attention. Trinity laughed. The owl was always hungry.

Footsteps approached—Sybil, Ailith, and Evelyn, laughed. Ailith carried Lucien, the child, wrapped around her like a second cloak. Sybil cradled Gabriel, his legs hugging her waist, his arms gripping tightly. His dark curls and solemn eyes mirrored David so exactly that Trinity's throat tightened. Sarah and Lucien were the image of their mother.

Gabriel glanced up at her. His stare—sharp and searching—stilled her. Then he buried his face in his mother's shoulder.

"Eric's already hunting bees?" Sybil teased.

"He thinks they're his pets," Trinity replied, lifting her chin in mock exasperation. "Stubborn like his father."

"He'll outgrow that," Ailith added, grinning. "When he's stung a time or two."

The women gathered beneath the blooming apple trees. Pink petals drifted down, sticking to their hair and gowns like blessings.

After the battle, secrets dissolved. Susana learned the truth about demons and angels, witches and warriors. Elizabeth and Isabella joined the conversation. Arguments turned to tears and finally to unity. None of them left. No one walked away. That mattered more than anything: staying together.

Elizabeth and Sybil grew close in the quiet aftermath. They shared wine at night, whispered by candlelight, and sometimes just sat silently. Trinity let them have that. Healing from shared grief bloomed best in small, private places.

Susana never turned from Sybil. Her God remained, but she welcomed Sybil's magic with open arms. No threats. No ultimatums. Just love threaded through faith.

Trinity ruffled Sarah's curls and leaned over and planted a kiss on Mary's forehead. "A cherub and a tempest," she said, laughing.

"She's no tempest," Elizabeth huffed, though pride shimmered in her eyes. "She's, my Mary."

Sybil cleared her throat. "I've made a decision." Her voice steadied. "I want you both to be the children's godmothers. It's what your faith calls it, yes?"

Trinity blinked. "Godmothers?"

Sybil nodded. "From what I understand, it's usually one godmother and one godfather. But…" She didn't finish. She didn't need to.

Emotion surged through Trinity like a wave. "I would be honored," she whispered.

"So would I," Elizabeth added quickly. "Truly."

"Good," Sybil smiled, soft and warm. "Evelyn's already planning something small. Just us."

"I do love a party," Evelyn piped up, smiling.

They stood in the garden like the roots of something ancient—three mothers, three grandmothers, a circle of children orbiting their love. The wind stirred petals. Laughter rippled through the trees.

Trinity tilted her face to the sun and whispered a quiet prayer—not for a miracle or peace. Just the strength to keep choosing love.

Even when it hurt.

Even when it meant letting go.

Even when it returned in a child's smile and reminded her that nothing was ever truly lost.

EXTENDED EPILOGUE
MICHAEL
20 years later

Michael pressed deeper into the cave, ducking under a jagged stone where massive stalactites loomed like the fangs of sleeping beasts. The air thinned with each step. Damp moss clung to the walls, slick beneath his fingertips. A steady trickle echoed through the tunnel, water running somewhere out of sight—the scent of sulphur and something ancient coiled through the darkness.

He moved as a shadow, silent and deadly. His boots brushed over rock and bone, disturbing the dust that hadn't shifted in centuries. Something about this place hummed in his blood. A current. A pull. As if he were not walking but being drawn.

Years had passed since the voices began. At first, whispers during sleep—one rough, masculine, echoing like thunder in a cathedral. The other was soft and sultry, wrapping around him like silk in the dark.

Neither voice gave answers, only beckoned. Always further. Always deeper.

He resisted in the beginning. He buried himself beneath ruined tombs and sealed himself inside crypts to shut them out. At one point, he'd lain underground for days, motionless among insects, letting rot fester over his skin. He'd wanted silence. He'd wished for death. But death never came.

Eventually, the pull became too strong. The voices grew louder when he starved. Curiosity outweighed the fear. He abandoned the last remnants of humanity and followed them across oceans, through snow-capped mountains and desert ruins, from crumbling cities to forgotten jungles.

They never gave directions, only fragments. Visions. Dreams. The outline of a map he followed by instinct alone.

Eventually, he came to a land untouched by modern hands. Tribes moved as ghosts through the hills, covered in animal skins and mud paint. Spears in hand, fire in their eyes. He kept his distance. These people didn't take kindly to strangers, especially ones such as him. They spoke in hisses and guttural growls. Superstition coated their every movement. They believed this cave sacred. A forbidden place. Cursed.

He stepped inside anyway.

Down and down, winding through stone corridors like veins leading to the earth's heart. Weeks passed. His face grew leaner, eyes sharper, and his skin pale as dried bone.

He dreamt of Trinity more often. Her laughter echoed in caverns, and her scent lingered in shadows. Sometimes, he imagined Eric walking beside him, no more than a boy. Once, he even reached for his hand in a dream and wept when it vanished.

He had missed everything—his son's first words, his first steps, birthdays, milestones, moments. Time hadn't touched Michael, but it had stolen everything else. Now he needed to reclaim it.

A low ceiling forced him into a crouch. The stone underfoot grew smoother. Cooler. Water dripped steadily, the rhythm hypnotic. And then, suddenly, the tunnel opened.

A vast chamber yawned before him, domed like a cathedral of earth and stone. The air shimmered with energy. A well of water sat at its center—so deep it swallowed the light whole.

He stepped closer.

"You finally come," said the man's voice, low and knowing.

A woman's voice followed, velvet and smug. "He is more beautiful than I imagined."

"Welcome."

THE END

ABOUT THE AUTHOR

Nicole Moore's love for storytelling began at 13 when she discovered her grandmother's stash of Harlequin romance novels. One dramatic love story later, she was hooked. From then on, she devoured every romance novel she could find—especially historical ones, because everything is better with pirates or lost love.

Her passion for history made writing a natural path. Whether watching documentaries or sitting in class, she couldn't help but imagine untold stories behind every historical event. She started writing short stories in the 6th grade, and wrote her first novel at 21, her second at 25. She spent time on the college newspaper as a reporter and editor and graduated with honors with a double degree in Graphic Design and Business Management, but motherhood put her dreams and publishing on pause. Instead, she spent years crafting bedtime stories on demand, spinning tales from her children's wild prompts until they drifted off to sleep and developing logo designs for different sign companies to make ends meet.

When she returned to writing, she embraced indie publishing, learning marketing, social media, and publishing on her own—thankfully with the help of many different marketing gurus and capacious amounts of coffee.

A meticulous researcher, taught as a college newspaper reporter and editor, she dives deep into history to ensure accuracy, often spending more time fact-checking than writing (because, of course, medieval pirates *must* have had opinions on socks).

Born in California and raised on the West Coast, Nicole moved to Australia many years ago, now splitting her time between Melbourne and Cairns with her husband, six kids, and two cats—one fat cat, one tiny assassin. When she's not writing or reading (which is rare), she's planning her next book or travel adventure, always with a novel and her laptop in hand.

DULY NOTED

Want updates, giveaways, and sneak peeks?
Or interested in joining her ARC team? Join Nicole's
newsletter Duly Noted at:
www.NicoleMooreAuthor.com/Duly-Noted

Subscribe Today!

www.ingramcontent.com/pod-product-compliance
Lightning Source LLC
Chambersburg PA
CBHW021131090426
42740CB00008B/744